Not a
Catholic Nation

Not a Catholic Nation

THE KU KLUX KLAN CONFRONTS
NEW ENGLAND IN THE 1920S

Mark Paul Richard

University of Massachusetts Press

Amherst & Boston

ISBN 978-1-62534-189-1 (paper); 188-4 (hardcover)

Designed by Jack Harrison
Set in Adobe Garamond Pro
Printed and bound by The Maple-Vail Book Manufacturing Group

Library of Congress Cataloging-in-Publication Data
Names: Richard, Mark Paul, 1960–
Title: Not a Catholic nation : the Ku Klux Klan confronts New England in the 1920s /
Mark Paul Richard.
Description: Amherst : University of Massachusetts Press, 2015. |
Includes bibliographical references and index.
Identifiers: LCCN 2015030472 | ISBN 9781625341884 (hbk.: alk. paper) |
ISBN 9781625341891 (pbk. : alk. paper)
Subjects: LCSH: Ku Klux Klan (1915–)—New England—History—20th century. |
Anti-Catholicism—New England—History—20th century. |
French-Canadians—New England—History—20th century. |
Borderlands—United States—History—20th century. |
Borderlands—Canada—History—20th century.
Classification: LCC HS2330.K63 .R54 2015 | DDC 322.4/2097409042—dc23
LC record available at http://lccn.loc.gov/2015030472

British Library Cataloguing-in-Publication Data
A catalogue record for this book is available from the British Library.

CONTENTS

ILLUSTRATIONS FOLLOW PAGE 120

ACKNOWLEDGMENTS

The origins of this book date back more than two decades when, while researching another topic at the Chancery Archives of the Roman Catholic Diocese of Portland, Maine, I came across material evidence of the Ku Klux Klan's presence in the state during the 1920s. Bishop Louis S. Walsh had penned entries in his diary about the KKK, had received correspondence concerning its activities, and had in his files rare copies of the organization's newspaper, the *Maine Klansman.* From the late C. Stewart Doty, my M.A. thesis supervisor at the University of Maine, I learned that French-Canadian immigrants and their Franco-American descendants had constituted the Klan's major target. A few years later, while conducting research for my first monograph, I discovered considerable documentation of the activities of the 1920s Klan in central Maine in the French-language newspaper, *Le Messager,* of Lewiston, Maine. After Doty retired, moved to New Mexico, and decided not to do any further work on the KKK, I decided to expand my research on the Klan to the rest of Maine and to each of the New England states. For over ten years I combed through all of the French-language newspapers of New England from the twenties and traveled to each New England state to examine the small existing repositories of Klan materials from the region. This book is the product of those efforts.

Along the way, I received generous financial support from sources that I hereby gratefully acknowledge. A grant from *Le Club français* of Maine's Saint John Valley provided some of the seed money for research conducted in Maine. Grants from the Center for the Study of Canada at the State University of New York, College at Plattsburgh, and administered by the Plattsburgh College Foundation, allowed me to expand my research to the other New England states, as did individual research travel grants over five consecutive years from the State of New York United University Professions Joint Labor-Management Committee. The SUNY Plattsburgh Office of the Dean of Arts and Science contributed funds that allowed me to complete my research. No less important, SUNY Plattsburgh provided me a year's sabbatical leave, allowing me time away from my teaching and administrative responsibilities so that I could finish drafting my manuscript. I am grateful for all of this support.

In addition to institutional support, I benefited from the help of numerous individuals. They include the archivists at each of the repositories listed in my citations and the conference participants who offered thoughtful feedback on the papers I presented at meetings of the American Council for Québec Studies, the Association for Canadian Studies in the United States, and the American Historical Association. I also wish to thank Nicholas Clifford, Emeritus Professor of History at Middlebury College, for reading and commenting on chapter 5.

Family members provided moral support on the long journey, offering encouragement when the process of producing a book seemed interminable. My parents (to whom I dedicated my first book) and my three sisters listened to numerous tales of my findings over the years. Now those stories are finally gathered in one place, and I dedicate this book to Jeanne, Judy, and Lisa.

Not a
Catholic Nation

Introduction

ALARMED BY the resurgence of the Ku Klux Klan in the United States after the Great War and concerned that it had begun organizing in his state, Rep. Peter F. Tague, a Democrat from Massachusetts, sponsored a resolution in 1921 calling on Congress to conduct an investigation into the group's activities. During the investigation, the Imperial Wizard of the Klan, William J. Simmons of Atlanta, Georgia, testified before the U.S. House of Representatives Committee on Rules: "It has been charged that the klan is organized for the purpose of intimidating the Negroes in the South. It may surprise this committee to learn that the growth of the klan in the North and East has been much larger than in the South." Few individuals, including Tague, likely believed Simmons's statement. Fewer still would have anticipated the KKK's astounding rise in New England in the years to follow. According to the *Washington Post,* from the Klan's formation in each individual state until it peaked in 1925, it admitted 21,321 members in Rhode Island, 65,590 in Connecticut, 75,000 in New Hampshire, 80,301 in Vermont, 130,780 in Massachusetts, and 150,141 in Maine.[1] KKK membership remains difficult to determine with precision, but even if the actual numbers in the New England states were a fraction—say, one-tenth—of the *Washington Post's* reported figures, they would nonetheless be phenomenal for the region. Each of the six New England states had witnessed significant Catholic immigration in the late nineteenth and early twentieth centuries, much of it consisting of French Canadians from Québec, and the Ku Klux Klan took notice.

As immigrants supplied the labor to help the United States evolve from a rural agrarian to an urban industrial nation in the late 1800s and early 1900s, their religious and ethnic origins often served as grounds for division within the nation-state. Prior to the Civil War most immigrants came from northern and western Europe and, like native-born U.S. residents, were largely white, Anglo-Saxon, and Protestant. Catholic immigrants seeking to escape the famine in Ireland in the 1840s and 1850s were a notable exception. In the late nineteenth century and early twentieth, massive immigration from southern and eastern Europe, predominantly of Catholics and Jews, provided the country with a large supply of labor for its industries; during the same era, French-Canadian Catholics migrated south to work in the textile mills of New England, where, at the turn of the last century (1900), they constituted 10 percent of the region's population. Between 1890 and 1925 nine million Catholics immigrated into the United States, making the Roman Catholic Church the largest religious denomination in the country. While the native-born turned against immigrants, particularly the Catholics during the economic crisis of the 1880s, nativism became even more intense in the 1890s. That decade was noted for its nationalism and jingoist sentiments, the historian John Higham points out, and anti-Catholicism was a particularly strong and central concern of nativists who pushed for immigration restrictions. In the early twentieth century the continued religious xenophobia directed against Catholics stemmed largely from the Ku Klux Klan. Because Jews were fewer in number than Catholics in the 1920s, they constituted a smaller threat to the Klan.[2]

During the twenties, several conditions fueled anti-immigrant sentiment. An agricultural depression began in the United States in 1920, and some felt that continued immigration was undermining the country's economic system. Immigrants who consumed alcohol during the prohibition era were viewed as lawbreakers who were challenging American mores.[3] Additionally, immigrants who retained the languages and lifeways of their homelands were perceived as resistant to American ways of living. The Ku Klux Klan sought to confront these issues.

Unlike its earlier incarnation in the post–Civil War era, the Ku Klux Klan in the 1920s expanded far beyond the southern United States, extending its reach into the northern states and into Canada. The Klan became a mass movement during the decade, attaining a membership of between three and six million women and men, thus becoming one of the largest social movements in U.S. history. The 1920s Klan generated appeal beyond the South because it had evolved into an organization that, besides promoting white supremacy, embraced such themes as Americanism, nativism, prohibitionism, and traditional moral and family values. According to the historian Leonard Moore, white Protestants used the Klan organization in an attempt to reassert control over their communities.[4]

The same was true in Canada. The KKK migrated north to Montréal in 1921 and allegedly burned Catholic buildings in the Province of Québec in 1922, but it did not develop into a strong organization in that province, where Catholics made up about 85 percent of the population. Besides Catholics, the Klan's Canadian targets included Jews, blacks, Asians, and central and eastern Europeans. The Klan spread to the Maritime provinces and to Ontario, but it drew its strength in western Canada where white Protestant majorities existed. In Alberta and Saskatchewan, for example, the Klan directed its energy against Catholic immigrants from Europe as well as French Canadians, in order to assert a Protestant and British character over the western provinces. In this task, the KKK was assisted by the Orange Order, an anti-Catholic, Protestant organization. As the journalist J. B. McGeachy explained of the Saskatchewan Klan in 1929, "Like the American Klan, it is nativist and Protestant. While it is by no means officially allied with the Conservative party, the Klan has drawn support from those who fear Catholic ascendancy, oppose unrestricted immigration and resent the separate school privileges allowed to the religious minority in the Province."[5] Anglo-Canadian immigrants in the United States drew upon these homeland experiences to support the KKK movement in their adopted country. One of the unique features of this study, then, is its exploration of the history of the Canada–U.S. borderlands and particularly its consideration of the role of Canadian immigrants as both proponents and victims of the Klan's activities in the United States.

This book contributes to the history of Catholicism in the United States, which has largely excluded French-Canadian Catholics, and to American religious history, in which Catholics have largely been viewed as outsiders. It argues for the centrality of Catholics to New England and U.S. history. What the historian R. Laurence Moore wrote of nineteenth-century Mormons, that "they aroused opposition precisely because they were so profoundly a part of the American scene," can also be said of the New England Catholics whom the Ku Klux Klan confronted during the 1920s. Rather than being viewed as "evidence of Catholic powerlessness," historical attacks on Catholics should instead be interpreted, Moore asserts, "as evidence of Catholic power."[6] This work will demonstrate the agency of New England Catholics of that era and provide evidence of their power in repelling the Klan.

Although various scholars have examined the resurgence of the Ku Klux Klan during the twenties, they have all but ignored the group's presence in New England.[7] Even Rory McVeigh's recent study of the Klan as a national movement implicitly suggests that the organization was insignificant in the region. McVeigh's content analysis of the group's activities as reported in its national weekly newspaper, the *Imperial Night-Hawk*, reveals that 40 Klan events took place in the six New England states in 1923 and 1924, peak years for the organization nationally, representing a mere 1.5 percent of the 2,669 events reported throughout the country.[8] As this study will demonstrate, the Ku Klux Klan was far more active in the northeastern reaches of the United States than previous and contemporary scholars have thought.

A comparison of the estimates of Klan membership to U.S. census figures implies that the KKK had considerable strength in New England during the 1920s. Comparing the *Washington Post*'s reported Klan numbers with state population figures from the 1920 federal census, one finds that Klan members may have constituted as much as 19.5 percent of the total population of Maine, 16.9 percent of New Hampshire's, 22.8 percent of Vermont's, 3.4 percent of Massachusetts's, 3.5 percent of Rhode Island's, and 4.8 percent of Connecticut's. The proportions are astoundingly larger if one weighs the *Washington Post*'s Klan numbers against the 1920 U.S. census figures of the "native white" population of "native parentage" (that is, cases where neither parent was foreign-born.) By this measure the Ku Klux Klan made up approximately one-third of the native-born white population of the northern New England states of Maine (30.3 percent), New Hampshire (33.3 percent), and Vermont (35.2 percent); and from one-sixth to one-tenth of the native white population of the southern New England states of Massachusetts (10.6 percent), Rhode Island (12.3 percent), and Connecticut (14.6 percent.) Because so many native-born whites who were not members of the KKK were sympathetic with its aims, even if the above representations of the group's strength are high, they help one to gauge the probable extent of Klan influence in the Northeast, an influence that far exceeded that of its dues-paying membership.[9] Given the large Catholic population of New England in the 1920s, this book will challenge notions that the KKK was active in the country predominantly where white Protestant majorities existed.

This work will also challenge the historiography of the Klan in the 1920s as framed over the past several decades. Traditional interpretations have tended to emphasize the secret society's nativism and extremism.[10] Monographs published in the late twentieth century, however, have largely downplayed the Protestant Klan's expressions of hostility toward minority groups and focused instead on the organization's normative behavior. According to Leonard Moore, "These studies demonstrate that the Klan served different purposes in different communities, but that in general, it represented mainstream social and political concerns, not those of a disaffected fringe group." The Klan grew dramatically during the decade, these works argue, because it offered social and fraternal outlets to ordinary citizens. These analyses also contend that the KKK provided citizens a vehicle through which to promote constructive change in their communities, particularly to deal with problems that existing governments did not resolve.[11]

The Ku Klux Klan's confrontations with Catholics in New England do not support this "populist" revision in our historical understanding of the 1920s Klan. To be sure, the organization did sponsor social events for its members. The headquarters in Portland, Maine, for example, sponsored masquerade balls, card games, Valentine's Day parties, dances, circuses, and concerts by the group's own band. In fact, the Klan of this period viewed itself as a fraternal order. A commercial fisherman from Maine named Charlie York told his biographer that the Klan's fraternal activities were what had attracted him to the organization in 1924: "I never enjoyed any Lodge so much as I did the Klan at first," he noted. "It had the principle of brotherly love for feller members and they [*sic*] was a high moral tone to it."[12] Evidence of the Klan's community activities in New England does exist, and at least some individuals did join the Klan to assist their communities. But the politics of ethnicity and labor played out differently in the northeastern borderlands than in other regions of the United States. In New England, nativism, religious prejudice, and class differences account for the Klan's remarkable growth during the twenties much more convincingly than do its functions as a social, fraternal, or civic organization.

The New England Klan differed in another respect. During the 1920s, the Ku Klux Klan in the South and in most of the Southwest drew its membership from the Democratic Party. In New England, however, as in other northern states and in the West, it allied itself with the Republican Party.[13] This regional difference in political party affiliation points to the chameleonic nature of the secret society.

The Ku Klux Klan as it existed elsewhere in the United States did not translate to the Northeast, and its organizers made adaptations in order to confront the supposed "enemy" of New England's large Catholic population. One result of that confrontation was to propel more of the region's ethnic Catholics into the ranks of the Democratic Party, a shift further facilitated by the 1928 presidential candidacy of the Catholic governor of New York, Alfred E. Smith, a prohibition antagonist whom the Klan vehemently opposed. This political realignment made possible the New Deal coalition that President Franklin D. Roosevelt forged during the 1930s, a coalition that helped Democrats to become the leading national party for several decades.

The New England experience during the 1920s serves as a reminder that the Ku Klux Klan's prejudice and violence did not respect state lines and were not confined to specific regions of the country. Similarly, the same forces that caused the Klan to collapse in the rest of the country led to its demise in New England. Rank-and-file Klan members in New England, as elsewhere, witnessed the hypocrisy and financial improprieties of KKK leaders and came to realize that the its law-and-order rhetoric was a facade of morality that often gave way to extralegal violence.

In short, the interactions of the Ku Klux Klan and its sympathizers with the residents of New England offer a rich, multilayered look at American society in the 1920s. In examining the conflicts between the Yankee Protestant Klan and the Catholics of French-Canadian and other ancestries, this book sheds light on religious, ethnic, and class differences that existed in the United States during the early twentieth century, differences that have shaped the history of this nation and that resonate still in contemporary society. One of the defining characteristics of modern U. S. history can be found in the nation-state's identification of and focus on internal and external crises and enemies, such as the Great Depression of the 1930s, Fascism during the Second World War, Communism during the Cold War, and terrorism in the present day. The central theme of this work is that, during the 1920s, many white Protestant Americans in New England joined the Ku Klux Klan to confront the "enemy" of ethnic Catholics who supplied much of the labor for the industrializing northeastern states. This book presents the most comprehensive analysis to date of the organization's antagonism toward Catholics in the United States. Chapters 1 through 10 explore how ordinary citizens acted in extreme ways to deal with a perceived internal enemy and how the Klan's Catholic targets fought back in the twenties to preserve the constitutional freedoms of their country of adoption, thus helping to rid the Northeast of right-wing extremism. Chapter 11 examines the Ku Klux Klan's return to New England more than half a century later and reveals how the metamorphosed organization pursued its primarily racist agenda by incorporating individuals and groups who had earlier been the objects of the hooded empire's fear and hatred; the chapter illustrates the mutability and the persistence of prejudice in American society over historical time. This book is a regional story of national phenomena.

1

Arrival in New England

In 1865 six former Confederate soldiers formed a club in Pulaski, Tennessee, that they named after the Greek word *kuklos,* or "circle." The men at some point modified the name to *kuklux* and, reflecting their Scottish-Irish ancestry, added the word *klan.* Draping their bodies with sheets, the club's members traveled by night around their community, frightening African Americans with their pranks. The concept of the Ku Klux Klan spread to other communities after the Civil War and before long became diffused throughout the southern United States.[1]

During the Reconstruction of the South after the war, the Ku Klux Klan promoted the interests of the Democratic Party, which centered on white supremacy. The KKK functioned as a vigilante movement to prevent blacks from exercising their newly acquired rights, including the right of black men to vote, and they also worked against the northern "carpetbaggers" who had migrated to southern communities to challenge the authority and power that whites had held prior to the Civil War. As Nathan Bedford Forrest, a former Confederate lieutenant general and the first Grand Wizard of the KKK, put it, "There was a great deal of insecurity felt by the southern people. There were a great many northern men coming down there, forming Leagues all over the country. The negroes were holding night meetings; were going about; were becoming very insolent; and the southern people . . . were very much alarmed."[2] Consequently, southern Caucasians utilized the Ku Klux Klan as a means of regaining racial supremacy during Reconstruction. Through the KKK they unleashed a lethal wave of violence against both black and white Republicans, effectively destroying Republican organizations so that the Democratic Party could regain power in the South.

In 1869, as a result of declining membership, negative public opinion, and unspecified concerns that some of the local Klan organizations were out

of control, Forrest disbanded the society, but it continued to survive. After
Congress investigated the group in 1870–1871, it passed anti-Klan legislation,
and the resulting arrest and conviction of over one thousand Klansmen, as
well as the imposition of martial law, effectively brought the Ku Klux Klan to
an end in 1871, just six years after its founding.[3]

Within a few decades, however, the United States witnessed a resurgence
of the Klan. In 1905 Thomas Dixon Jr. published a novel titled *The Clansman: An Historical Romance of the Ku Klux Klan.* The film director D. W.
Griffith adapted the content of this publication to produce a motion picture
called *The Clansman,* which premiered in Los Angeles in 1915 and received
an enthusiastic reception. Renamed *The Birth of a Nation,* it was shown
twice daily in Boston from April to September 1915, and nearly one hundred
thousand people watched it. Viewed by millions across the United States,
The Birth of a Nation extolled the Ku Klux Klan and played a central role in
reviving the organization.[4]

William J. Simmons, an itinerant preacher and fraternal organizer whose
father had been a member of the post–Civil War Klan, capitalized on the
success of *The Birth of a Nation* to reestablish the KKK. Simmons gathered
a group of thirty-four friends, several of whom had been members of the
Reconstruction Klan, to file a petition in October 1915 for a Ku Klux Klan
charter in Georgia. The next month, on Thanksgiving evening, fifteen of
them pledged atop Stone Mountain their oath of allegiance to the Invisible
Empire, Knights of the Ku Klux Klan. Individuals who joined the KKK
purchased their memberships as well as life insurance from Simmons, who
viewed the organization as a moneymaking venture. By June 1920 the secret
society numbered from four thousand to five thousand men.[5]

Not until Simmons hired Edward Young Clarke and Elizabeth Tyler of
the Southern Publicity Association in June 1920 did the Klan's membership
begin to increase dramatically. So did the Klan's profits. As the owners of an
early public relations firm, Clarke and Tyler developed a marketing scheme
that expanded the KKK from a southern organization to a national one, a
development that enlarged scope of the 1920s Klan and distinguished it from
the Reconstruction-era society. The pair split the country into regions called
domains that were headed by Grand Goblins and then divided the domains
into state realms, each headed by a King Kleagle during the realms' provisional stage and then by a Grand Dragon after they became chartered. Clarke
and Tyler also had Klan organizers, called Kleagles, working at the local level
to draw members into the national organization. Recruitment was a money-
making venture for everyone involved in the Klan hierarchy. Of the $10.00
initiation fee every new member paid out, $4.00 went to the Kleagle, $1.00 to
the King Kleagle, $0.50 to the Grand Goblin, $2.50 to Clarke and Tyler, and

the remaining $2.00 to Simmons. In part as a result of this scheme, the Klan expanded to about one hundred thousand members nationwide by October 1921. Besides membership fees, the national organization earned revenue from the sale of robes at $6.50 apiece and from the imposition of an imperial tax of $1.80 on each member after their local branch reached one hundred members and received a charter. William Peirce Randel contends that the Ku Klux Klan became a big business during the 1920s, with up to six million people paying $10.00 each to join the organization and many of them purchasing Klan regalia, possibly bringing up to $75 million to the Klan's coffers. Edgar Fuller, who served as Clarke's executive secretary and later left the Klan because he no longer supported its goals and methods, wrote that "money, easily and quickly to be had, is the sole objective" of the organization. Fuller noted that people from all stations in life joined the KKK, and he lamented that "great numbers of wage-earners denied themselves and deprived their families of necessities in order to pay the initiation fee."[6]

Publicity generated by newspaper accounts, together with a congressional investigation in 1921, helped the Ku Klux Klan attract members. The *New York World* wrote a series of articles denouncing the group in 1921, and they were syndicated across the country in eighteen newspapers. "It wasn't until the newspapers began to attack the Klan that it really grew," Simmons once stated, going on to boast that "certain newspapers also aided us by inducing Congress to investigate us. The result was that Congress gave us the best advertising we ever got. Congress made us." Simmons had skillfully defended the KKK before Congress, where he portrayed the organization as "a standard fraternal order" and argued that it had the right to restrict membership in the same way as other fraternal societies, including the Knights of Columbus. Simmons collapsed dramatically—undoubtedly for effect—at the conclusion of his testimony. Congress did not continue the investigation, "and its failure to do so was like a government stamp of approval on the Invisible Empire," writes Wyn Craig Wade. Unlike the action it took after the investigation of 1870–71, Congress did not follow up with legislation to quash the organization in the early twenties. Wade indicates that Klan membership increased by 20 percent after the hearings and that within a year membership figures had increased from one hundred thousand to over one million. Despite an internal struggle and publicly fought court battles that took place from 1922 to 1924, during which period Hiram W. Evans, a dentist, wrested control of the national leadership of the Ku Klux Klan from Simmons, the KKK's numbers grew into the millions before peaking in the mid-1920s.[7] Unlike the post–Civil War society, the Klan of the twenties became a mass movement, one that included women as well as men.

Like the earlier Klan, the new incarnation adopted garments, language, and rituals that cast an air of mystery and intrigue about the organization and lured unsuspecting citizens to become part of a select group. A sociology professor at Dartmouth College, John Moffatt Mecklin, observed in 1924, "The Klan has learned, as its inveterate enemy, the Roman Catholic Church, learned long ago, the power of the appeal to the spectacular and the mysterious." Wade has similarly noted that the KKK's practices resembled those of its Catholic targets: "The unity, secrecy and exclusiveness of Klansmen rivaled that of the 'Romanists' they detested." Even their robes were similar to those of Catholic priests, Wade contends, although the Klan's white, pointed hoods with small eyelets distinguished their garments from those of priests and certainly gave the members a sinister appearance. The outfits also transformed some: "There seems to be a quality of metamorphosis in the hood and the robe of the Ku Klux Klan," stated A. J. Padon Jr., a Grand Goblin of New England in the early 1920s. "It frequently changes sober business men as the secret chemic potion changed the character of Dr. Jekyl to the sinister Mr. Hyde. While all members are not affected in that manner, only too many are."[8]

The Klan's language and nomenclature were also sinister. Local organizations, for example, were expected to have thirteen officers: an Exalted Cyclops (president) "and his twelve Terrors." Most of the "Terrors" had enigmatic titles beginning with the letter *K*: Klokard (lecturer), Kludd (chaplain), Kligrapp (secretary), Klabee (treasurer), Kladd (conductor), Klarogo (inner guard), Klexter (outer guard), Night Hawk (supervisor of candidates for admission into the organization), Klokan (investigator and auditor), and the Klokann (three individuals who made up the board of investigators.) The Klan Kalendar was equally enigmatic. It renamed the days of the week using austere, mood-setting adjectives that all began with the letter *D*: Desperate, Dreadful, Desolate, Doleful, Dismal, Deadly, and Dark. In similar fashion, the Klan's weeks all began with the letter *W*: Weird, Wonderful, Wailing, Weeping, and Woeful. While the names of the months utilized more letters of the alphabet, they were no less evocative and grim: Appalling, Frightful, Sorrowful, Mournful, Horrible, Terrible, Alarming, Furious, Fearful, Hideous, Gloomy, and Bloody. To take one example, when the national KKK chartered the Androscoggin Klan no. 46 of the Realm of Maine on October 24, 1925, it represented that date on the charter as "the Desperate day of the Wonderful week of the Alarming Month of the Year of the Klan, LIX." Beyond their arcane titles and calendar, Klansmen developed secret codes to identify other members of their society, codes that encrypted the first letters of a phrase. For example, "Ayak" posed the question "Are you a klansman?" and the response, "Akia," acknowledged "A klansman I am."[9] This peculiar language added to the mystique of the white-robed organization.

The Klan also had mysterious rituals, some of which were reported in the press. A. J. Gordon, a reporter for the *Boston Herald,* recorded his observations of the Maine Klan in 1923. Referred to as "aliens," candidates for membership underwent a "naturalization" ceremony during which they might walk to different stations and take various oaths of obligation, including obedience to the Imperial Wizard and a pledge of secrecy about the society's inner workings. Candidates had to stand before an altar bearing an open Bible that was placed on top of the U.S. flag. A dagger also lay on the altar, and Gordon reported that candidates learned it signified that they would meet their death if they violated their oaths. Behind the altar were burning candles and a wooden cross. During the naturalization ceremony, each candidate had to answer a series of questions, pledging, for example, that he was "a native born, white, gentile [*sic*] American citizen" who was "absolutely opposed to and free of any allegiance of any nature to any cause, government, people, sect or ruler that is foreign to the United States of America" and who would "faithfully strive for the eternal maintenance of white supremacy." After the Klan chaplain, or Kludd, offered a prayer, the candidates became members of the KKK. Such rituals attracted public attention and served to entice people to join the organization. As Padon put it, "One of the greatest selling points of the Ku Klux Klan is the atmosphere of secrecy which surrounds it, and the highly weird and dramatic effect of all its ceremonies."[10]

One of the most notorious Klan rituals in the 1920s, cross burning, had no connection to the Reconstruction Klan. The idea of Klansmen burning crosses came from Dixon's novel, in which fictional Klan members of Scottish ancestry ignited crosses to signal other Klans, a practice reminiscent of pagan fire festivals celebrated in medieval Europe. During the twenties, the KKK often burned crosses as a publicity stunt to make its presence felt in local communities. A Klansman from Iowa explained the practice of cross burning in a statement that the *Maine Klansman* shared with its readers: "The Fiery Cross symbolizes to the Klansmen the final triumph of truth over falsehood, of liberty over slavery, of life over death, and of good over evil."[11] Surely the New England targets of the KKK interpreted the blazing crosses differently.

The Ku Klux Klan arrived in New England in 1921. Citing army intelligence officials as its source, the *New York Times* suggested that year that the group was trying to establish itself in Boston and in Portland, Maine. Evidence of the Ku Klux Klan's origins in New England comes in part from the interviews Grand Goblin Padon gave the *Boston Daily Advertiser* after he had left the society. Padon informed the newspaper that Imperial Wizard Simmons had sent him to Boston to assess the potential for establishing a Klan organization there. Originally from Memphis, Tennessee, Padon had

served as a Klan recruiter and Grand Goblin in Colorado—a Klan stronghold among western states in the 1920s—before relocating to New England.
Padon initially worked through Protestant fraternal societies like the Masons
and the Knights of Malta in Boston, but he was Catholic and eventually
decided to leave the KKK, he stated, "when I could no longer condone its
bitter battle against my religious faith." The Ku Klux Klan, this southern
transplant learned, was not focused on white supremacy in New England
but had different aims in the region. "No one knew I was a Catholic," Padon
acknowledged, "but they wondered sometimes why I wouldn't let them air
their anti-Catholic views in the meetings." Padon tried to refocus the energies of the KKK: "I used to tell them: 'The business of this order is to establish white supremacy: why spend your time knocking white men?' And they
didn't like that much."[12]

Padon's self-acknowledged goal of promoting white supremacy did not
fit well in New England. While African Americans made up 9.9 percent of
the total population of the United States in 1920, the 79,051 blacks in New
England were a mere 1.1 percent of the region's population. Whereas the Klan
of the post–Civil War era had targeted African Americans in the southern
states in order to reestablish white rule, the later configuration broadened its
practice of bigotry to include Catholics, Jews, the foreign-born, criminals,
and bootleggers.[13] Each of these groups existed in New England in the 1920s,
and undoubtedly the membership of some of them overlapped, but as we
will see, Catholics of foreign descent became the Klan's primary New England target in the twenties.

By 1926, the Roman Catholic Church had the largest membership of any
religious denomination in thirty-three states in the country. In each of the
six New England states, Roman Catholics outnumbered the followers of the
next two largest denominations combined (table 1). A comparison of the
numbers of Catholics to the total population of each state, as represented in
the 1920 federal census, reveals that Catholics constituted from more than
one-fifth to over one-half of the population of each state: in Maine, 22.6
percent, New Hampshire, 33.1, Vermont, 25.4, Massachusetts, 42.3, Rhode
Island, 53.8, and Connecticut, 40.4.[14]

This demographic transition, brought about by the huge influx of immigrants from Canada and Europe, affected public school enrollments. In
1920 Maine, New Hampshire, Vermont, Massachusetts, and Rhode Island
had fewer children registered in public schools than in 1900, a decline Rory
McVeigh attributes to the growth of Catholic parochial schools in the region.
According to figures McVeigh compiled, fourteen of the forty-eight states
in the country showed a drop in public school enrollments during the first

two decades of the twentieth century. Proportionally, the greatest declines nationwide took place in four New England states: Massachusetts (-4.9 percent), Maine (-5.1 percent), Vermont (-8.8 percent), and New Hampshire (-9.7 percent.)[15] Each had a sizable Catholic population.

That so many Catholics resided in the traditionally Protestant states of New England was the result of continental and transoceanic migrations. By 1920 New England had a higher proportion of foreign-born residents than any other region in the country. In fact, New England's foreign-born population (25.5 percent) was nearly double that of the national average (13.2 percent.) While the proportion of foreign-born residents in Maine (14.0

TABLE 1. Membership of the Top Three Religious Denominations in New England, 1926

Maine
Roman Catholic Church....................................173,893
Northern Baptist Convention 32,031
Methodist Episcopal Church 22,938

New Hampshire
Roman Catholic Church....................................146,646
Congregational Churches 20,346
Methodist Episcopal Church 14,018

Vermont
Roman Catholic Church.................................. 89,424
Congregational Churches 20,915
Methodist Episcopal Church 16,950

Massachusetts
Roman Catholic Church.............................. 1,629,424
Jewish Congregations..213,085
Congregational Churches 159,252

Rhode Island
Roman Catholic Church....................................325,375
Protestant Episcopal Church...........................36,197
Jewish Congregations.. 24,034

Connecticut
Roman Catholic Church....................................557,747
Jewish Congregations..90,165
Protestant Episcopal Church...........................89,434

Source: U.S. Department of Commerce, Bureau of the Census, *Religious Bodies, 1926,* vol. 2 (Washington, D.C.: Government Printing Office, 1929), 44.

percent) and Vermont (12.6 percent) approximated the national average in 1920, that in New Hampshire (20.6 percent) and in the southern New England states of Massachusetts (28.3 percent), Rhode Island (29.0 percent), and Connecticut (27.4 percent) far exceeded it. According to the *U.S. Census, 1920,* the top three countries of origin of New England's foreign-born population were Canada (25.3 percent), Ireland (14.2 percent), and Italy (12.6 percent), nation-states from which large numbers of Catholics emigrated.[16]

Of the Canadian immigrants in New England, approximately half were French-speaking Catholics, a group that made up 12.7 percent of the region's foreign-born population in 1920. In the northern New England states that border Québec, French Canadians naturally made up a substantial proportion of those born abroad. Specifically, French Canadians made up 33.1 percent of Maine's foreign-born population, 42.0 percent of New Hampshire's, and 31.8 percent of Vermont's. French Canadians also constituted a significant percentage of the foreign-born residents of Massachusetts (10.1 percent) and Rhode Island (16.6 percent) and a small proportion (3.9 percent) of those in Connecticut.[17]

Nearly one million French Canadians emigrated to the northeastern United States during the century preceding the Great Depression. During the second half of the nineteenth century, Québec experienced such demographic and economic challenges as a growing rural population that lacked sufficient access to arable land, indebtedness incurred through the specialization and mechanization of agriculture, and an urban industrial development that did not proceed at a pace rapid enough to absorb the province's surplus rural population. These conditions produced unemployment, prevented advancement, created distress, and precipitated emigration. Although emigration slowed during the first two decades of the twentieth century as Québec's economy improved, during the 1920s an additional 130,000 French Canadians crossed the border to take up residence in the United States, particularly when a recession hit Québec between 1920 and 1922.[18] The immigration restrictions the United States imposed during the twenties to stem the tide of immigrants from southern and eastern Europe did not apply to Canadians until 1930. Most French Canadians settled relatively close to home in such New England industrial centers as Lewiston and Biddeford, Maine; Manchester, New Hampshire; Central Falls and Woonsocket, Rhode Island; Lowell, Worcester, and Fall River, Massachusetts; and the mill towns of the Quinebaug River Valley in Connecticut. In these urban centers, French Canadians succeeded the Irish after the Civil War as the predominant source of unskilled labor, and they and their offspring made up a substantial proportion of the population of New England's industrial cities. In Lewiston, for example, people of French-Canadian birth and background constituted approximately half of the city's residents by 1920.[19] The French language, the Roman Catholic faith, and the formation of ethnic enclaves distinguished the descendants of French-Canadians in Protestant Yankee New England.

Commenting on New England's changing demography, the journalist John E. Pember wrote in 1925 about the distinctiveness of the New Englander of years past: "The 'Yankee' speech and physique, the sturdy democracy, the intense religious and political convictions, the mental capacity due to the Nordic heritage of the first settlers, produced a type that for two centuries maintained itself apart from its neighbors of other and different lines of descent." Continuing his description of prototypical New Englanders, Pember highlighted the themes that preoccupied nativists of his era: "The New Englanders of that early generation were racially homogeneous. They were even nationally akin. They spoke the same language, had the same religion, entertained the same beliefs. They held the land of their origin in affectionate remembrance, but with the crossing of the Atlantic had completely identified themselves with the new country they had set upon these shores." One can imagine Pember sighing while he typed the next sentence: "But that was a century ago." Pember was acutely aware of New England's changing ethnic composition, and he went on to note that the typical New Englander of the 1920s was either of foreign birth or foreign descent. What struck him most about the immigrants was that "to a large extent they retain their national characteristics and 'stick together,' generation after generation, forming peoples within a people, as it were." Pember's observations paralleled the concerns of those who worried that unrestrained immigration would dilute the national culture of the United States. Pember specifically cited Italians and French Canadians as examples of groups that retained their distinctiveness in their adopted country, and he further complained that French Canadians were less likely than Italians to Americanize.[20]

Pember was not the only one to write about the perceived reluctance of French-Canadian immigrants to assimilate into American society. In an article from 1924 titled "Fifty-Fifty Americans," Robert Cloutman Dexter (who was himself of Anglo-Canadian and American descent) wrote, "The French-Canadian desires to be an American and at the same time to remain a French-Canadian. He is unwilling to assimilate his culture to that of the prevailing group, and does not hesitate to rationalize his position by maintaining that his own culture is superior—indeed, is sacred." When Dexter published his essay, French-Canadian immigration in the United States was slowing, but he expressed his misgivings about the group's expanding numbers as a result of natural increase. He worried that this ethnic population would eventually dominate the entire eastern half of the country, from the Mississippi River to the Atlantic Ocean. The Catholic faith of French Canadians especially worried Dexter, for he felt it harkened back to medieval times and allowed their clergy to exercise control over all aspects of their lives, including their politics.[21] As we will see, the Ku Klux Klan in Maine shared similar concerns about the state's French-Canadian descendants.

2

Invasion of the Pine Tree State

IN FEBRUARY 1923 the Ku Klux Klan organizer F. Eugene Farnsworth stumped in Portland, Maine, to express the Klan's desire "to keep Protestant Americans in the lead, not only in numbers, but in fact." Farnsworth urged the thousand men who had gathered at the Pythian Temple to hear him: "Let us get together and fill up our Protestant churches. We can do it, and we can control Maine." By 1921, when the KKK began organizing in the state, the Roman Catholic population exceeded 150,000, a figure constituting about one-fifth of Maine's total population. Irish and French-Canadian descendants made up Maine's largest Catholic groups, but the state's Catholics also included Italian, Polish, Lithuanian, Lebanese, and Slovak immigrants as well. By the mid-1920s, only several years later, the number of Catholics in the state was approaching 175,000, a figure that far eclipsed the membership of Maine's top two Protestant denominations—the Northern Baptist Convention and the Methodist Episcopal Church—which together had not quite 55,000 members (see table 1).[1] This chapter examines the Ku Klux Klan's organizational and political activities in Maine during the early 1920s, as it worked to counterbalance the influence of the state's growing Catholic population. As the Klan pursued its anti-Catholic activities in the Pine Tree State, it undercut its nativist agenda by incorporating foreign-born Protestants into the movement.

Anti-Catholicism in the United States dates back to the colonial period, but its best-organized and strongest manifestations took place in three waves that corresponded with periods of large immigration in the country: the 1850s, 1880s–1890s, and 1920s. The Know-Nothing movement constituted the first wave. Organized in 1852 as a secret society called the Order of the Star Spangled Banner, Know-Nothings gained their name by responding, "I know nothing," to the queries of nonmembers about the organization. Members had to be native-born and have no personal or family ties to

Catholics. After the society became public in 1853, it organized the American Party to preserve U.S. institutions and values from immigrants, particularly Catholics, who might change them through their political participation. This anti-Catholic movement spread throughout the United States, attracting one million members nationwide by 1854, a year in which the movement scored impressive political victories in northeastern states like Massachusetts, which had a large Irish Catholic population. That same year the Know-Nothing national political movement also took root in Maine's coastal and river towns, where much of the state's Irish population had settled. Anti-Catholic sentiment fomented by the Know-Nothings led to the burning of Catholic churches not only in the coastal communities of Bath and Ellsworth but also in the industrial city of Lewiston and to the tarring and feathering of Ellsworth's Catholic priest. The state's Protestant ministers helped spread the Know-Nothing movement, which reached the height of its popularity with approximately 27,000 members in 1855, the year Maine received its first Catholic bishop. Internal conflicts, increasing public opposition, and the rise of the Republican Party precipitated the collapse of the Know-Nothings in Maine in 1856 and, paralleling a national trend, they thereafter became absorbed into the Republican Party.[2]

The American Protective Association (APA) served as a second wave of anti-Catholic sentiment. A national political movement that attracted up to half a million members, the APA worked to reduce the influence of Catholics in labor and politics throughout the United States during the 1880s and 1890s. Members swore an oath not to strike along with Catholic workers, not to hire them when Protestants were available, and not to vote for Catholic candidates. While the sources do not shed much light on the size of the Maine APA, we know that the society had established a branch in Auburn, Lewiston's twin city, by 1896. One of the association's tactics was to spread anti-Catholic propaganda, usually sensational and fabricated stories about the actions of men and women religious. The APA in San Francisco alleged, for instance, that the Dominican priests who served Lewiston's French-Canadian population were torturing Catholics who refused to submit to their authority in the basement of their new monastery, which the APA claimed was a medieval-like castle. So compelling were the APA's stories that one compassionate woman in California wrote to Lewiston's mayor asking him to intervene on behalf of the Dominicans' hapless victims.[3]

The Ku Klux Klan represented the third wave of anti-Catholicism that the United States had witnessed since the 1850s. Like the Reconstruction Klan, the 1920s Klan advocated white supremacy, but it also broadened its appeal beyond the South by defining itself as a reform movement. Concerned about such issues as urbanization and the resultant loss of rural values, rising crime, and the growth of radicalism and Communism, white, native-born Anglo-Saxon women and men joined the Second Klan to fend off what they saw as the undesirable changes taking place in their communities. In its resistance to modernity, the KKK sought to rid society of criminals, radicals, and those who trafficked in illegal alcohol as well as those who appeared to threaten the values of a white, Anglo-Saxon, Protestant nation. Consequently, mirroring the Know-Nothing movement and the American Protective Association, the Ku Klux Klan in Maine, in New England as a whole, and in other parts of the country portrayed itself during the 1920s as a Protestant backlash to the surging Catholic immigration. Some of the group's oldest members had been Know-Nothings and quite likely members of the APA as well. A ninety-year-old Klansman from Bath, Maine, acknowledged: "I belonged to the Know-Nothings, whose principles were in some respects quite the same as [the KKK of] the present."[4]

The Ku Klux Klan's activities in Maine in 1921–22 remain fairly obscure, but they did not escape the notice of political leaders such as the Republican governor Percival P. Baxter. Baxter initially spoke out forcefully against the Klan, in September 1921 sending a telegram to the *New York World* in which he stated, "Anarchy results the moment an individual, or group of private citizens, take the law unto themselves and I consider the present situation in the Ku Klux Klan movement a menace to Law and Order." Moreover, in November 1922, after receiving some Klan literature, Baxter issued a press release criticizing the organization's secrecy and characterizing the movement as "unwholesome and un-American." Baxter, conceding that the KKK had established branches in Maine, asserted that it "must not, and never will, get a foothold in this State." In a letter to a constituent that the press published in January 1923, he reiterated his opposition to the society even more directly: "I earnestly hope that the citizens of Maine will not join the Klan or have anything to do with it. You can count me as absolutely opposed to it."[5]

But Baxter underestimated the Klan's attractiveness and its potential to become a strong political force in the state and soon modified his negative remarks about the organization. When asked to comment on the KKK in September 1923, Baxter stated that he had not heard that Maine's secret orders had committed any crimes, engaged in violence, or broken any laws. Baxter's reversal did not go unnoticed by the press. A. J. Gordon, a *Boston Herald* reporter, pointed out that when Baxter had previously made his strong anti-Klan comments the KKK had not yet demonstrated its political muscle. There appear to have been other political reasons for Baxter's change of course. According to Edward Bonner Whitney, Baxter actually shared some of the Klan's views, including its opposition to the provision of state aid to sectarian institutions. In fact, Baxter argued in his inaugural address of January 1923 that "public money should be used exclusively for public institutions," a position he repeated in his farewell address in 1925. In addition to these reasons for his about-face, Robert H. Boone suggests, Baxter changed his attitude toward the Klan because its activities in Maine were far more moderate than in other states, most of its supporters were Republicans just as he was, and because he did not want to hamper the political efforts of Ralph Brewster, a Republican lawmaker who had assisted him with his legislative agenda. (As we will see, Brewster won the governorship of Maine with the Klan's support in 1924.) In northern states like Maine, the Ku Klux Klan allied itself with the Republican Party, which dominated politics there, unlike in the South, where the organization backed the ruling Democrats. Baxter appears to have been worried that the Klan would divide Republicans in the state, and this led him to temper his critical remarks about the organization.[6]

As Baxter retreated, the Maine KKK became more conspicuous during 1923 as press reports illumined the secret society's activities and rhetoric, especially those of its organizer, Farnsworth. Farnsworth had a colorful past, and he captured the imagination of the press and of willing followers. He was born in the eastern Maine town of Columbia Falls in 1868 but moved at a young age to New Brunswick, Canada, where he spent the early years of his life before migrating to Fitchburg, Massachusetts, in 1892. An opportunist, Farnsworth jumped from one occupation to another during the course of his working life, sometimes changing direction after getting himself into trouble. He trained to become a barber, worked for the Salvation Army, and even practiced hypnosis until someone died during a 1901 demonstration in Woonsocket, Rhode Island. During that demonstration, Farnsworth hypnotized Thomas Bolton, a resident of Fitchburg, Massachusetts, but when a viewer questioned whether Bolton was merely pretending to be asleep while positioned with his head on one chair and his feet on another, Farnsworth attempted to disabuse the audience of that idea. The incident reveals Farnsworth's proclivity for audacity. In a 1923 article introducing *Boston Herald* readers to Farnsworth, Gordon described what happened: "A large flat stone was found and placed on the patient's chest. Clifton Trask, a Woonsocket blacksmith, secured a sledge hammer and hit the stone a terrific blow. The patient never came out of the trance, passing on quietly into the next world." Farnsworth was arraigned for manslaughter, but the case was discontinued with the approval of both the Providence city solicitor and the police chief after payment of court costs. He subsequently worked as a newspaper photographer in Boston for eight years and then, by 1911, had become a traveling lecturer, giving talks on distant lands to which he had traveled, an occupation that was not especially remunerative but that perhaps prepared him for his later role as a Klan lecturer in Maine and New England. Farnsworth thereafter opened a motion picture studio in Medford, Massachusetts, but that venture failed. In another ill-fated scheme, he became president of the Society Players Film Company, an outfit with a studio in Medford that lasted from 1916 to 1919, when it dissolved and left its investors shortchanged.[7]

Perhaps Farnsworth's best preparation for his eventual role as a Ku Klux Klan leader was his presidency of the Boston Loyal Coalition, a position he assumed in 1922. A nativist organization, the Loyal Coalition worked to discourage immigrants from maintaining loyalties to homeland causes, such as the republican movement in Ireland. The Loyal Coalition argued in an advertisement that appeared in the *Boston Herald* in 1921 that the United States should not become involved in the domestic affairs of Ireland or any other nations, and it further implored the reader to remit a financial contribution "*if you are a good American, desire good government and propose to keep the hyphenates from controlling America.*" During and after the First World War, U.S. immigrants were subjected to great pressure to abandon identities from their native lands and to adopt an exclusively American identity—one without such hyphenation as German-American or Italian-American. The Loyal Coalition contributed to this push for Americanization. What it advocated, however, was Anglo-Saxon superiority, favoring, for example, Great Britain in its conflicts with Ireland. The Loyal Coalition undoubtedly opposed the American Association for the Recognition of the Irish Republic, which held its first statewide convention in Boston in 1921 and called for Britain to repay its entire war debt to the United States. Speaking out against such examples of "Irish politics" at home, the Loyal Coalition asked readers of the *Herald* to support the organization in its opposition to "the sinister current that is moving beneath the national life of America." As we will see, the KKK in New England promoted anti-immigrant and pro-Anglo-Saxon themes similar to those of the coalition both in its attacks on Catholics and in its recruitment of members. As president of the Boston Loyal Coalition, Farnsworth developed contacts with the Ku Klux Klan and became its principal organizer in Maine, later assuming the title of King Kleagle.[8]

In January 1923 Farnsworth visited Portland with Telphair Minton, the secretary of the Boston Loyal Coalition, and they spoke at the Pythian Temple to a group of about five hundred men in an attempt to recruit them to the Ku Klux Klan. Minton told the audience about the coalition and indicated that it opposed Sinn Feinism, which sought the political and cultural independence of Ireland from Britain. For his part, Farnsworth attacked the Roman Catholic Church and the Knights of Columbus, calling the Catholic fraternal order "the political machine of the Church of Rome in the United States." Farnsworth argued that "native born Protestant Americans have never taken issue with the Catholic religion. We do take issue with Rome's political machine." The problem, he emphasized, was that the Roman Catholic Church did not allow its members to exercise independent political judgment. When individuals joined the Ku Klux Klan, they had to assert that they "hold no allegiance to any foreign government, emperor, king, pope or any other foreign, political or religious power."[9]

In Maine the KKK focused its organizing efforts on Portland, the episcopal seat of the state's Roman Catholic Church and Maine's largest city. When the Klan requested a permit to hold a meeting at Portland City Hall, Mayor Carroll S. Chaplin gave his consent on condition that members not wear masks or disguise themselves. During this gathering in February 1923, four thousand men and women filled the hall to capacity to listen to Farnsworth and a national Klan lecturer, Dr. William J. Mahoney of Atlanta, while another one thousand people had to be turned away for lack of space. The next month, at a meeting attended by six hundred persons at the Pythian Temple, Farnsworth complained about the frequent appearances of Bishop Louis Walsh before the state legislature in Augusta. "Bishop Walsh has said that his Church is not playing politics and has no political machine," Farnsworth observed. "Did you ever see anything introduced at Augusta but what he was there with his gang?" At the same meeting Farnsworth protested that the "Knights of Columbus[,] and others who owe allegiance to the Pope in Rome, have no business or right even to be naturalized citizens of the United States." Another Klan meeting at the Portland City Hall in March again attracted four thousand women and men. Although Mayor Chaplin had stipulated that the Klan not attack the Catholic Church, the speakers, Farnsworth and Dr. George S. Robinson, the pastor of the Lewiston Trinity Episcopal Church, made remarks against the "Roman political machine" and parochial schools. As Farnsworth put it to the one thousand women who gathered to hear him at another meeting in Portland that same month, "These aliens came here and said our schools were not fit to educate their Catholic youth. They were not forced to come here but in the near future they are going to be forced to go to our public schools because we want to make American citizens of them."[10]

In lashing out against parochial schools, Farnsworth took up a theme that would energize the Klan at the national level for some time. In 1925, for example, Imperial Wizard Hiram W. Evans told an interviewer that Catholics "are aliens, and that the Church not only makes no effort to help them become assimilated to Americanism, but actually works to prevent this and to keep the Catholics as a group apart [in parochial schools.]" The KKK felt so strongly about this issue that it became part of the creed members had to recite: "I believe that our Free Public School is the corner-stone of good government and that those who are seeking to destroy it are enemies of our Republic and are unworthy of citizenship."[11]

On the stump King Kleagle Farnsworth often contended, explicitly or implicitly, that Catholics and ethnics made undesirable citizens. In March 1923 Farnsworth spoke at the Odd Fellows Hall in Lewiston against Roman Catholics and hyphenated Americans. In April he continued his attacks against ethnic groups that had brought to the United States religious traditions other than Protestantism. In Auburn, Farnsworth asserted: "This is not an Italian nation, this is not an Irish nation, and this is not a Catholic nation, it always has been and always will be a Protestant nation." Voicing a major concern of the national as well as the local Klan, Farnsworth alleged yet again that the Knights of Columbus functioned as part of "the Pope's political machine," and therefore insofar as Catholics were involved in U.S. politics, they would be tainted with foreign influence. At another meeting in Lewiston Farnsworth argued that as immigrants were gaining political power in the United States, Protestants were losing control of the country. "I believe in the limitation of foreign immigration," Klan members would proclaim in reciting the creed, and they would relegate immigrants to an inferior status in American society in their affirmation "I am a native-born American citizen and I believe my rights in this country are superior to those of foreigners."[12]

Although King Kleagle Farnsworth was himself a transnational migrant, he alleged that individuals of foreign birth were "hostile to our government, our traditions and ideals," and he insisted that "a house-cleaning is needed in every state of our Union and this is the Klan [*sic*] job." Farnsworth wrote some sheet music, titled "It's Your Land and My Land," which he sold for fifty cents a copy at Klan gatherings; sometimes members would sing the song during intermissions at rallies. The chorus of Farnsworth's song highlights the theme of patriotism as well as the need for vigilance:

> *It's your land, and my land, to own, to rule, to love.*
> *It's bled for, and died for, and blessed by God above.*
> *It's your land, and my land, and while the world shall be,*
> *We'll fight to keep it our land, America the free.*[13]

Implicit in Farnsworth's song is the determination of Klansmen like himself to protect the country from foreign-born Catholics.

Catholics were not the only targets of the Klan in Maine. In contrast to the state's Roman Catholic population, which in 1926 numbered 173,893 individuals (about 23 percent of the state's population in 1920), Jewish congregations had only 7,582 members that year (about 1 percent of the 1920 population); for their part, blacks numbered 1,310 individuals in 1920 (a mere 0.2 percent of the state's population then.) Thus Jews and blacks represented smaller adversaries of the KKK. Yet, as elsewhere in the country, the Klan exhibited racism and anti-Semitism in the Pine Tree State, and blacks and Jews occasionally received hate mail attributed to the secret society. The *Sunday Press Herald* reported in January 1923, for instance, that "the colored woman on Fore Street" had received a handwritten note, allegedly from a Klan member, addressing her as "Nigger" and accusing her of distributing alcohol and drugs as well as consorting with white men; the letter writer threatened her with unspecified harm if she did not leave the community. To take another example, in February 1923, the *Boston Daily Advertiser* reported that five Jewish men—two attorneys and three merchants—had received letters signed by the KKK telling them to leave Portland. Most often, however, the Klan's central target in Maine was its Catholic population.[14]

As the Ku Klux Klan gained numerical and financial strength in Maine, it purchased in April 1923 an eight-acre estate in Portland, secured through the efforts of Dr. W. H. Witham. According to the *Maine Klansman,* Witham was the state's first Klan member, and he became a leader of the Portland branch. With three other men Witham formed the Loyal Realty Company in order to purchase the private estate for the Klan and to secure a forty-two-thousand-dollar mortgage from Maine Savings Bank.[15] By November 1923 the company had obtained a permit to build a four-thousand-seat auditorium with a basement banquet hall at an estimated cost of fifteen thousand dollars. Over three thousand KKK members from Maine, other New England states, and the national headquarters in Atlanta gathered in Portland to celebrate the opening of the structure in February 1924.[16] On its estate the Ku Klux Klan of Maine established its headquarters—as well as a visible presence in the Pine Tree State.

The Maine Klan used the Portland headquarters as a base from which to confront Catholics in the city and beyond. Among other measures, the KKK wanted to challenge the appropriation of Columbus Day by Catholics. One member complained in the *Maine Klansman* that "Protestants are profoundly weary of all this 'Columbus a Catholic' propaganda that is being disseminated." Focusing on the religion of European explorers, the writer maintained that the celebration of Columbus Day served "to outweigh in importance and priority the landing and colonizing of the English Pilgrims in 1620" in order to give "a big boost to the Latin church in this country." He further pointed out that Norsemen had actually discovered North America hundreds of years before Columbus, and he suggested creating a "Norseman Day" in place of Columbus Day to highlight the non-Catholic background of the Viking explorers.[17]

To challenge Catholics, the Maine KKK sought a permit to march in Portland on Columbus Day in 1923. The mayor turned down the request, expressing his concern that a Klan parade "on Columbus Day will inevitably result in disorder and riot." The editor of the *Portland Press Herald* supported the mayor's decision, noting that Catholics traditionally marched in the city on that day and suggesting that the KKK be allowed to parade on other days if its members did not wear their masks. When Columbus Day arrived, the Knights of Columbus marched from their hall to the Cathedral of the Immaculate Conception, where they heard Bishop Walsh extol the deeds of Columbus and heap praise on the non-Catholic Grand Master of the Grand Masonic Lodge of Maine, Albert M. Spear, who had voiced his opposition to the Ku Klux Klan. They also listened to Walsh question why other leaders, such as the mayor and the governor, did not similarly speak out against the Klan. While the Knights of Columbus enjoyed their parade and Mass, the KKK held a bean supper and an initiation ceremony on its estate, an event that added approximately one thousand men and up to five hundred women to the organization. An estimated six thousand non-Klan members observed the ceremonies from outside of the walled estate, which the KKK reportedly guarded with clubs, revolvers, and shotguns. The Klan concluded its Columbus Day activities by lighting a fifty-foot electric cross.[18]

Columbus Day festivities were not the only activity that separated Maine's Catholic and Protestant populations. The issue of Bible reading in the schools likewise provoked divisions between the two religious groups. During the 1920s the Ku Klux Klan worked to integrate the reading of the King James Bible into the curriculum of the public schools of communities across the country. In Maine the hooded knights and those sympathetic with them similarly supported such efforts. King Kleagle Farnsworth, for example, occasionally voiced support for Bible reading during his speeches. The reading of scripture was customary in nineteenth-century public schools, and in 1854 the Maine Supreme Court had affirmed the practice of public school officials of having children read the King James Bible, something to which Catholics objected. In December 1920 the Lewiston school board voted to allow a period of silent prayer to replace the scripture reading and the recitation of the Lord's Prayer. The Protestant ministers of Lewiston, including the school board member Archdeacon Robinson of Trinity Episcopal Church, who was absent when the vote was taken, opposed the change. When Robinson sought to overturn the board's decision at its meeting in February 1921, two Franco-Americans and the pastors of Lewiston's two Irish Catholic churches (who also served on the school board) opposed his efforts, and Robinson's motion was defeated. The state legislature subsequently took up the Bible reading bill, an action Bishop Walsh interpreted as "a direct attack on the Catholic Church," but ultimately tabled it.[19]

The legislature brought up the bill again in 1923. In March, when Robinson spoke alongside Farnsworth at a KKK gathering at Portland City Hall, he grumbled that "in our city (Lewiston), all was going peacefully until a man was elected a member of the school board who was high in the Knights of Columbus. In their pusseyfoot [sic] way, he took the Bible from the public schools." Robinson further stated, "I fought this in the Legislature, and I'll fight it as long as I have a breath of life until it is put back." Probably because most of Maine's Catholic children attended parochial schools, Bishop Walsh chose not to speak against the Bible-reading bill at a legislative hearing, recording in his diary his sentiment to "let the Devils do their own dirty work and put whatever they like into their schools" and noting, "It will not affect us, and may drive many out of the schools." With the support of Governor Baxter, both bodies of the Maine legislature passed a bill in 1923 to require the state's public schools to hold scripture readings on a daily basis but without "denominational or sectarian comment or teaching."[20] On the issue of Bible reading in the public schools, the Klan merely jumped on the bandwagon by encouraging the efforts of Klan supporters like Robinson to influence the political process in Maine.

The Ku Klux Klan similarly supported prohibition efforts in Maine and did not itself initiate a change in public policy. Maine had a long history as a dry state. With the exception of a brief interlude under a Democratic governor in the mid-1850s, Maine had been a dry state since 1851, and prohibition became incorporated into the state's constitution in 1884. In December 1923, a federal grand jury indicted the sheriff of Aroostook County and an attorney for violating the Volstead Act, legislation that enforced federal prohibition against the manufacture, sale, and transportation of alcohol. Having allegedly received from $200 to $625 a month to protect smugglers who were running rum from New Brunswick, Canada, into Maine, they were found guilty and sentenced to federal prison. "No more important case than this has been tried in this State in many years," claimed the *Maine Klansman*. "It will have a far-reaching influence, affecting not only the State of Maine but all the rest of the country." The newspaper further contended that the antiprohibition sentiment that existed in various parts of Maine did not constitute an excuse for the lack of enforcement. The case did not have the effect the Klan had hoped for, however. As late as July 1926, for instance, the branch in the coastal community of Rockland placed ads in the local newspaper asserting, "The man who buys the booze is as much a criminal as the Rum-runner who delivers it."[21] On the prohibition issue, as in the case of Bible reading, the Klan backed existing efforts rather than initiating a new course for the state.

In a similar fashion the Ku Klux Klan supported ongoing efforts to create a new municipal charter for Portland rather than initiating policies of its own. Through its involvement in the city elections of September and December 1923 the Klan established a conspicuous political presence in Maine. In 1921 Portland voters had narrowly defeated a new city charter that would have led to the adoption of a council-manager form of government in which five council members would be elected at large rather than by individual wards and running under a political party. Instead, voters retained the mayor and bicameral city council government in which the mayor shared power with nine aldermen and twenty-seven members of a common council elected annually in wards. In 1923 the charter issue again went before the voters, with the press reporting Klan support for the council-manager system framework and a city manager chosen by the council. The new charter would also change the structure of the school board from twelve members serving two-year terms to a board of seven members all elected at large for three-year terms. Religious divisions appeared to motivate the Klan's interest in securing the new city charter. The *New York Times* reported that the Klan wanted to change the composition of the school board because two Catholics and one Jew served on it, and Farnsworth himself stated in Portland prior to the election, "We will not permit Catholics on the school board any more."[22]

Although the *Portland Press Herald* and local businessmen supported the new city charter because they believed it would lead to more efficient and less costly local government, the KKK's unofficial backing of it received significant attention after Portland's citizens approved it with 56.4 percent of the votes cast. When Bishop Walsh learned of the election results, he noted in his diary that "a real 'Social & Political Revolution'" had taken place, and he further commented, "The Anti-Catholic feeling is now on top." The election results attracted wide media attention. The *New York Times* wrote of the election as "the Klan's first venture in the political field of New England." The *New Republic* stated, "What may prove to be the most important political development of the week is the victory of the Ku Klux Klan in the municipal election at Portland, Maine." The journal saw the election results as an "exhibition of the power of the Klan." The *Boston Herald* reported, "This election marks the first entrance of the Ku Klux Klan into local politics, and it is conceded that without the klan support the change of government would not have taken place." *L'Etoile,* the French-language newspaper of Lowell, Massachusetts, highlighted the Klan's role with front-page headlines: "Le Klan triomphe à Portland" (The Klan triumphs in Portland).[23]

Following the election, however, various newspapers downplayed the role of the Klan in the Portland municipal election. An editorial in the *New York Times* indicated that the KKK had simply sided with the majority: "Indeed,

. . . public disgust with the Klan didn't go so far as to defeat an excellent plan of city government simply because a lot of hooded noodles gave it their unwanted help." The *Times* went on to state, "The Kludd of the Klavern [Klan meeting place] should let that unpleasant fact temper the ardor of his thanksgiving prayer." *L'Opinion Publique,* the French-language newspaper of Worcester, Massachusetts, also felt that the Klan should not claim the Portland election results as a victory because the city had narrowly defeated the proposed city charter two years earlier, and it viewed the later result as a chance occurrence. Even the *Boston Herald* tempered its comments from the previous day, when its editor wrote, "To say that the klan won the Portland election is to overstate the case." The *Lewiston Evening Journal* offered its opinion that the *Portland Press Herald* and "thousands of citizens who are neither 'crooked' [n]or 'secret'" deserved credit for the election results.[24]

The Ku Klux Klan nonetheless felt smug about the matter. The *Fiery Cross,* the Klan newspaper based in Indianapolis, Indiana, boasted one week after the election, "Cold shivers are today chasing up and down the spines of politicians throughout the state when they think of the Portland election." The newspaper went on to suggest that the KKK was civic-minded and was poised to clean up Maine's government: "With the growth of the Klan in this state a sentiment has been created for better civic government and the result last week shows that the people of Maine are ready for a new deal from the politicians, who before the advent of the Klan, which organization has crystallized sentiment in favor of better things, ran things pretty much to suit themselves."[25]

King Kleagle Farnsworth expressed similar thoughts. At a rally of three thousand people gathered at Portland City Hall just prior to the elections in December 1923 to select the school board and city council under the new municipal charter, Farnsworth stated candidly, "All we are interested in is a clean, wholesome, wholly American schoolboard. We are interested, too, in wholly American management of the City of Portland." Farnsworth continued, "We who are klansmen have got nerve enough to believe that this Country belongs to us and that we belong to the Country. We are native-born Protestant men, and we stand for the old-fashioned Protestant principles of our fathers." On December 4, 1923, Bishop Walsh remarked in his diary that the three Catholic candidates for the school board and city council had each been narrowly defeated. But the Klan got its wish, and it gloated in the election results. "Portland citizens are, for the first time in decades, represented by a Protestant city government," the *Maine Klansman* rejoiced. In an undated, typed note sent from Klan headquarters, G. S. Mertell (who likely was a Klan official) taunted Bishop Walsh: "Perhaps you noticed that no Cathlics [*sic*] got elected in the recent election in Portland. It is the 18th place in New England that the Klan has kept Catholics from holding office. Hereafter no niggers [*sic*] catholics [*sic*] nor Jews will ever hold office in Portland." Threatening further KKK political action in Maine, Mertell informed the bishop, "We begin a big drive in Saco this week."[26]

As the Maine Klan gained notoriety beyond its borders as a result of the Portland municipal elections, King Kleagle Farnsworth ventured to other New England states and into Canada to promote the group's ideas. He stumped in Toronto to encourage Protestant Canadians to join the movement. According to the *Toronto Star,* Farnsworth proclaimed, "We propose not to punish with tar and feathers, but to avenge wrongs. We propose not to indulge in law breaking, but in distributing retribution. We call upon all good, native-born Protestants to join us in our work."[27] In Canada, as in the United States, Farnsworth underscored the necessity of being a native-born Protestant to join the society.

Among the native-born Protestants Farnsworth recruited to the Maine KKK were women, whom he organized into an auxiliary of the men's Klan. In March 1923 one thousand women attended a meeting Farnsworth planned at Portland's Pythian Temple to form a Klan auxiliary, and approximately the same number of women attended a meeting at Portland City Hall in September for the same purpose. In January 1924 Farnsworth and Gertrude Witham, the Major Kleagle of the Maine Women of the Ku Klux Klan and the wife of the Portland Klan leader W. H. Witham, spoke together at a gathering of over two hundred women in Bath, where they organized another women's auxiliary. They told the women that, just as they cleaned their homes, they could clean up politics, thus extending the domestic sphere to the public. To this end, one goal of the women's Klan was to elect women to the state assembly, while another was to promote civic education among women. Farnsworth's intention was that the women's organization would help promote Americanism and work against the influence of Catholics in public education. An additional purpose of the auxiliary was to raise funds for charitable institutions such as orphanages, and they did so by hosting suppers and bazaars for KKK members.[28]

In organizing the Maine women's Klan auxiliary, Farnsworth and Gertrude Witham apparently did not screen applicants closely enough because some foreign-born women ended up joining the group. One of them was Mrs. Jean McNair, a Protestant born in Scotland. According to McNair, during her initiation "Mrs. Witham read a piece out of the Bible and asked me before everyone if I was a Protestant. I said I was. She asked me if I was willing to swear on the Bible that Mrs. Kimball's statements that I was a Catholic were untrue, and I swore that they were false." But McNair did not meet the citizenship requirement of the Women of the Ku Klux Klan (WKKK).

When Farnsworth learned during the initiation ceremony that McNair had been born abroad, he reportedly stated matter of factly, "She's holding up the whole line; we'll take her in and if there's any trouble, we'll put her out tomorrow. Cut the ceremony short and don't give her any of the secret signs." Apparently the women's Klan did dismiss McNair the next day along with another woman who had not been born in the United States, for the two women subsequently sued the organizers to recover their initiation fees and dues.[29]

Despite this episode, the reality was that Farnsworth recruited both native- and foreign-born female Protestants to the Klan cause in Maine. "Women of Maine came to me in groups following perfection of the men's organization and requested that a branch for women be started," he explained in April 1924. "In working out plans for such an auxiliary we discovered that wives of many Maine klansmen were born in Canada or in other foreign countries, which fact automatically barred them from membership in the women's organization officially recognized by the National Klan."[30]

Incorporated in June 1923, the Women of the Ku Klux Klan, based in Little Rock, Arkansas, constituted a legal entity separate from the men's organization. But the WKKK was supervised by the Imperial Wizard as well as by the Grand Dragon of Arkansas, James Comer (who became the husband of Robbie Gill, Imperial Commander of the WKKK.) In practice, then, as was the case in Maine, the national WKKK functioned as an auxiliary of the men's Klan society, and its principles were identical to those of the Ku Klux Klan, as the following examples illustrate. The WKKK Kloran expressed the importance of public school education to ensure that "the oncoming generation may have every chance to develop into pure, honest and upright American citizens." The candidate application form underscored the importance of "White Supremacy and the principles of 'pure Americanism.'" A pamphlet titled "Ideals of the Women of the Ku Klux Klan" complained that immigrants arrive "here to serve the interests of the land from which they came, regardless of the interests of this land in which they make their homes and seek their fortunes." Further, the WKKK insisted that "a divided allegiance means no allegiance. There can be no half American, and any sort of hyphen absolutely makes impossible any kind of loyalty to the American government, its ideals and institutions." Moreover, the WKKK supported English-language use in public and private institutions "as the best means of inculcating a definite knowledge of American ideals, and as an impartial test of the good intentions of all prospective citizens." In these ways, the views and objectives of the WKKK paralleled those of the men's division. Like the men's society, the WKKK promoted the reading of the Bible in public schools as well as immigration restrictions to "prevent the landing upon our shores of all undesirable aliens who are unable to demonstrate their ability and willingness to speak the English language, absorb the Anglo-Saxon ideals upon which our government is founded, and live according to the standards of the White race."[31]

While the opportunity to promote white supremacy attracted women to the Klan in the 1920s, its appeal to them, writes the sociologist Kathleen Blee, "also lay outside the realm of traditional nativism and racism: in its purported quest for women's rights and in its offer of collective support, friendship, and sociability among like-minded women." The WKKK, which formed chapters in every state and attracted probably half a million members nationally during the 1920s, was an exclusive society. "No woman of foreign birth is eligible to citizenship in the Invisible Empire," stated a WKKK pamphlet likely produced in 1923. When national Klan membership subsequently declined from the mid-1920s on, the WKKK did not modify its position, for its constitution of 1927 stipulated that each "applicant must be a white female Gentile person, a native-born citizen of the United States of America."[32]

Farnsworth's work to recruit foreign-born women to the women's Klan in Maine therefore violated both national KKK and WKKK principles. His organizational efforts also brought him into conflict with Maine Klanswomen and ultimately led to his ouster as King Kleagle. Farnsworth saw the potential to make money from the women's Klan, and he charged the women ten dollars each to join the Klan rather than the five-dollar "donation" permitted by the national women's organization. This naturally caused friction between him and the women. Such disputes, often over money issues, also arose between the women's and men's societies in other states, including Arkansas, Pennsylvania, and Oregon. Blee points out that while the conflicts in those states revealed that the women's Klans were not independent of the men's, the women demonstrated their willingness to protest if the men tried to dominate rather than support their organizations. In Maine, tensions with the women's Klan, along with Farnsworth's organizing efforts outside of the national Klan, led to an internal revolt that forced his resignation as King Kleagle in April 1924. Newspaper accounts suggest that W. H. Witham engineered the coup against Farnsworth.[33] Possibly he did so at his wife's behest.

The month after his demission, Farnsworth again went on the stump, but this time to promote a new organization called the Christian Crusaders. He formed the society to promote Klan principles among Canadian immigrants and other foreign-born Protestants. Speaking to an audience of three hundred in Portland, Farnsworth stated, "This country was not built by native born Americans, but by Anglo-Saxon races and blood." Contradicting the pronouncements he had made against foreigners when he was King Kleagle,

Farnsworth questioned, "Why, for God's sake, should we have anything against another Protestant because he happened to be born in England, Canada, or Ireland?" He also voiced his support for the Klan and its anti-Catholic principles: "Let's make it a point to help the Klan. And let's put Brewster in the chair, and then we [will] have excluded Romanism from the schools." Farnsworth also promoted his new organization in other New England states.[34] Despite Farnsworth's earlier rhetoric against the foreign-born, it is clear that, in his mind, religion trumped nationality. Protestants originally from Canada and Europe, like native-born Protestants in the United States, could help him work against papist influence in his country of birth.

Some expatriate Anglo-Canadians were quite overt about their support for the Ku Klux Klan. A biographical sketch of Aroostook County sheriff George H. Knox published in 1928 reveals, for example, that this former New Brunswicker "is inclined toward the Republican party and he is fraternally affiliated with the Ku Klux Klan." Knox was one of about two million English-speaking Canadians who emigrated to the United States from 1840 to 1930, the year the United States applied immigration restrictions to Canada. A limited agricultural base, population pressures that led to an unfavorable population to land ratio, slower industrialization in Canada than in the United States, and industrial wages that were up to 60 percent higher in the United States than in Canada at the turn of the twentieth century were the leading causes of emigration for Anglo-Canadians. Most English-speaking Canadians settled in communities relatively close to their home provinces, the largest numbers concentrating in such states as Michigan, New York, and Massachusetts, while French-speaking Canadians settled predominantly in the six New England states. Unlike French-speaking Canadians, Anglo-Canadians did not form enclaves, according to the scholarship to date, which shows no evidence of such grouping. The geographer Randy William Widdis argues, however, that, although English-Canadian immigrants may have appeared "invisible or not clearly discernable" in the United States, their high rates of endogamy, reluctance to acquire U.S. citizenship, and continued interest in Canada imply that they had some distinctive traits.[35] One such trait may have been their transnational support of the Ku Klux Klan.

In the end, there apparently was no love lost between the former transnational migrant Farnsworth and the Klan, for the *Rochester Courier* in New Hampshire indicated in May 1924 that he had made some negative and surprising comments about the KKK, "which, but a few weeks ago, he was lauding to the very skies." The newspaper pointed out that Farnsworth contended that the KKK "spread terrorism" with its robes and masks. Although his new organization, the Crusaders, would not allow its members to wear regalia to disguise themselves, it is clear they were working on behalf of Protestants against Catholics. While touting the organization after the Maine primaries in 1924, Farnsworth admonished the 150 people who gathered to hear him in Portland, "Let us eliminate the terms Republican and Democratic and think in terms of Romanism and Protestant." How much time and energy Farnsworth devoted to his new organization is not known. After Farnsworth died in Boston in March 1926, following surgery for intestinal cancer, his obituary reported that he had formed the Maine Booster Club, based in Portland, with the goal of promoting summer tourism in Maine among people who lived in the southern United States.[36] Farnsworth apparently remained a promoter until his death.

Farnsworth's strong marketing skills undoubtedly helped the Ku Klux Klan to acquire its large membership in Maine in the 1920s.[37] But his actions also suggest that the KKK as an organization did not suit him. His inclusion of Anglo-Canadian and other foreign-born Protestants in the Klan movement of the northeastern United States reveals a contradictory dimension to this avowedly nativist organization, and it demonstrates that the KKK's ideology was not transferable to the borderlands region. More specifically, the Klan's idea of nation and nationalism did not fit Maine and the other New England states. Farnsworth's creation of an auxiliary for Anglo-Protestants from Canada and other Commonwealth nations underscores this inherent problem. For Farnsworth, who had himself emigrated from Canada to the United States, anti-Catholicism superseded national origins. As white Protestant Canadian immigrants supported the KKK in the 1920s to assert control over French-Canadian and other Catholics in their New England communities, they undermined the Klan's emphasis on Americanism. Even as the Klan tried to demonstrate its civic-mindedness by supporting prohibition in Maine and municipal reform in Portland, it undercut its own role in the polity, as we will see in the next chapter, through its confrontations with Franco-American Catholics in the state.

3

Confronting Franco-Americans in Maine

NINETEEN TWENTY-FOUR was the Ku Klux Klan's most active year in the state of Maine. In February forty Klan members threatened union leaders who were attempting to organize French-speaking lumbermen in the town of Greenville; in August the Klan celebrated a political victory by detonating a bomb in the city of Lewiston, home to Maine's largest Franco-American population; in September the Klan threatened to parade across bridges separating Saco from the city of Biddeford, the site of Maine's second-largest Franco-American population. Despite such conflicts, Maine escaped the violence that characterized encounters with the Klan in other areas of the country, even in other New England states, and by the end of 1924 the Klan's influence in Maine was on the wane. Internal conflicts, decreasing membership, and financial problems within the state organization along with scandals within and the decline of the national Ku Klux Klan led to its collapse in Maine.[1] Although a number of factors combined to bring about the Klan's eventual demise, in taking a stand that was firm and consistent yet not overly combative, the state's Franco-American population modeled an appropriate resistance to the organization's message of unyielding Americanism and nativism.

In 1920, 33 percent of Maine's foreign-born population was of French-Canadian descent, but in such industrial cities as Lewiston, French-Canadian immigrants made up nearly three-fourths of the foreign-born.[2] King Kleagle F. Eugene Farnsworth's broad attacks against Catholics and the foreign-born described in the last chapter of course represented indirect attacks against Franco-Americans, whose numbers were growing throughout the twenties, thanks both to new immigration and to a healthy birthrate.

A January 1927 article in the Klan-sympathetic *Fellowship Forum,* a weekly Protestant fraternal newspaper published in Washington, D.C., detailed some of the concerns and fears that Protestant Americans had of French speakers in New England. "In the manufacturing centers of Maine,

34

New Hampshire and Massachusetts are hundreds of thousands of French Canadians who are separated from their compatriots on the St. Lawrence by a belt of Protestants," the newspaper remarked. "Remove that belt and the two branches of Romanists will become one." This would be problematic, contended the newspaper, because "French Romanists in Canada and the United States, like other Romanists of various races, are more devoted in their allegiance to the papal system than they are to the governments under which they reside." Holding up Canada as an example of what might happen in the United States, the newspaper asserted, "Quebec Romanists regard Ontario Protestants, citizens of the same country, as pagans and aliens, while they regard Romanists of other countries as compatriots and fellow citizens."[3] Such religious arguments undoubtedly motivated some Protestants to join the Ku Klux Klan.

In addition to religious prejudice, economic concerns drove some citizens into the Klan. Compared with other states in the 1920s, Maine's economy was in decline. Its textile industry, for example, faced stiff competition from southern mills. In August 1924 the *New York Times* reported that the cotton mills of several industrial cities in Maine were operating only a few days a week, shoe factories were not running at capacity, and the Bath shipyards had closed. Proceeding to comment on demographic shifts, the newspaper noted that Maine's rural youth were leaving for other states in the hope of improving their circumstances at the same time as Irish and French-Canadian immigrants were entering Maine. As a result, anti-Catholic Yankees, the *Times* commented, have "taken refuge under the Klan, which has mobilized the prejudices, and to some extent the business rivalries of many of the voters of Maine." The Klan's appeal in the state, according to a Protestant minister from Portland, was easy to explain: *"It's the rising of a Protestant people to take back what is their own."*[4]

In 1923 a fifteen-year-old girl from the small manufacturing town of Dexter, near the geographic center of Maine, wrote a poem that captured the community's economic and social tensions as well as Yankee Protestants' response to them:

> *There is an organization started called the K.K.K.,*
> *Members are joining by thousands every day;*
> *Every true American surely ought to go,*
> *If they do not like it, they can just say so.*
>
> *But if you go once, you'll a member be.*
> *It's nice to be a 'white man,' you'll very soon agree;*
> *Don't stand back and just say,*
> *'I think I'll join the KLAN some other day.'*

Is it money, or are you afraid?
The Catholics won't come to you to trade,
But, never mind, do what you can,
You'll gain the trade of the Ku Klux Klan.

The Catholics are trying to destroy the Klan,
The lodge that belongs to the honest white man,
But do as they might, or do as they may,
The Ku Klux Klan is here to STAY.

The *New York World* elaborated on the antagonisms the teen identified. When a Catholic priest in Dexter learned that a bank clerk had attended a meeting of the Ku Klux Klan, he insisted that the bank fire the offender; if it did not, he threatened, his parishioners would withdraw their funds from the institution. Unwilling to yield to the dictates of the priest, the Protestants in town mobilized the bank's large depositors, who demanded that the bank rehire the clerk, and it did.[5]

In its reporting the *New York World* defended Dexter's French Catholic population by highlighting its qualities. "These French people are thrifty, honest and law-abiding citizens, the majority of whom own their homes and have substantial bank accounts," and it emphasized that they would be "a credit to any town." The newspaper pointed out that this ethnic population sent its children to the public schools and that many of them completed high school, and some even attended college. It further underscored the group's community involvement and business acumen, noting that "French citizens take an active part in town affairs and some of them are merchants who have been eminently successful." The Catholic faith and the economic success of Dexter's Franco-American population, the *World* suggested, had led to their adversarial relationship with the town's Protestants.[6]

The Dexter directory provides some insight into the rising economic status of the community's Franco-American population relative to that of Klan members in the mid-1920s. Of the men with French surnames listed in the directory, 3.6 percent were woodsmen, none were farmers, 69.1 percent were industrial workers, 12.7 percent were self-employed or nonindustrial blue-collar workers, and 14.5 percent had white-collar occupations. Of 112 Klan members named in the 1924–25 meeting minutes and 1925 charter of Dexter's Leif Ericson Klan, exactly half could be traced in the town directory. The directory shows that men with occupations as varied as farmers, machinists, mill workers, carpenters, clerks, accountants, and managers joined the klavern in Dexter. In all, 14.3 percent of the town's Klan members were farmers, none were lumbermen, 51.8 percent were industrial workers, 14.3 percent were self-employed or nonindustrial blue-collar workers, and 19.7 percent had white-collar jobs.[7] Well over half of the Klansmen, then, were members of the working class. Scholars who have examined the socioeconomic profile of Ku Klux Klan members in other locales in the United States have generally found that they came from all social and economic groups but largely represented the lower middle and working classes; as in Dexter, KKK members nationally often reflected a cross-section of the population of their communities rather than the socioeconomic margins.[8] Although Protestant Klansmen in Dexter held better jobs than the Catholic Franco-American men, it is also evident from the occupational rankings that Franco-Americans were gaining access to some of the better jobs in nonindustrial and white-collar occupations.

As animosity between Catholics and Protestants mounted in Dexter, local government officials banned the Klan from meeting in the town hall, but when Klan sympathizers petitioned, the officials reversed themselves. The activist priest called on his congregation to boycott the establishments of Klan sympathizers, and Protestants responded in kind by boycotting Catholic merchants. During the boycotts, the Klan burned a cross atop a hill in Dexter, and antagonisms between Catholics and the Klan grew. "Things have come to such a pass that a Klansman—and there are many of them—does not dare walk down Main Street unaccompanied at night," reported the *New York World*. After one Klan meeting, angry Catholics heckled the departing members; and when Catholics followed and threw rocks at two of them, the Klan members pulled guns. Such incidents led the *World* to report that Dexter's French speakers "constitute one armed camp; the members of the Klan another." The hostilities, which produced no casualties, demonstrate the efforts of Franco-American Catholics to repulse the Klan. Despite Catholic opposition, however, the Dexter Klan paraded regularly in regalia, and it was sufficiently strong to sweep all of its candidates into town office in 1924.[9]

The meeting minutes from 1924–25 give us a glimpse into the Dexter Klan's activities, especially those involving politics. The organization attracted as few as thirteen to as many as sixty-seven members to its weekly gatherings. The best-attended meeting took place in March 1924, when the Klan "naturalized" (that is, initiated) eleven individuals and discussed which candidates to support for local offices. The Dexter Klan subsequently called a special meeting to approve the slate of candidates that its political committee had proposed for town clerk, selectmen, tax collector, town treasurer, cemetery commissioner, school board, fire chief, and water board. The minutes do not shed much additional light on the inner workings of the organization. One might find occasional comments about the group's civic mindedness, such as its decision "to form a 'Poor Committee' to look after the needy" and its placement of an ad in the *Dexter Gazette* to remind local Republicans in advance of the general election to make sure that they were registered to vote. The records of the meetings also reveal that the Leif Ericson Klan decided to invite Ralph Brewster, a Dexter native, to give a talk at the town hall in 1924.[10]

That year, Brewster sought the Republican gubernatorial nomination, and confrontations between Klan forces and Franco-Americans intensified in the political arena. Brewster, a state senator, attracted the Klan's support from throughout Maine, in part because he advocated prohibition, an issue that energized the KKK nationwide, but largely because he had called for a constitutional amendment prohibiting the use of public funds for parochial and sectarian schools. Brewster's proposition, although broadly conceived, targeted French speakers in the rural northern county of Aroostook, particularly those who lived along the St. John River, which divides Maine from New Brunswick. Acadians (descendants from the French maritime colony of Acadia) and French Canadians (descendants from the French colony of New France) had immigrated to the region in the eighteenth and nineteenth centuries.[11] According to the Maine School Report of 1924, Roman Catholic nuns, dressed in religious habit, were teaching in the tax-supported schools of the St. John Valley. In a letter to a Portland Methodist minister, Brewster complained that the nuns were not just offering a public education in their classrooms but giving religious instruction as well. Because this practice was not illegal, Brewster intended to address the issue by finding a way to distinguish parochial from public schools. The Ku Klux Klan supported public education, and its Kreed stated explicitly, "We Condemn the support out of the public treasury of Any sectarian school or other institution not owned or controlled by public authority." The *Maine Klansman* praised Brewster's efforts: "In certain sections of the county French Catholics are in the majority and of course the parochial schools are also in the majority. It has been stated that these schools are not favoring the Catholic religion but were offering education to Protestants and Catholics alike. This sounds good on paper," the newspaper stated, "but the truth of it is that these schools have been, and always will be, no different than any other parochial school. It will be a Godsend when these schools are a thing of the past in Aroostook County." Roman Catholic nuns also taught in tax-supported public schools in Oregon, and the KKK circulated pictures of them doing so in its successful ballot initiative in 1922 compelling all youth between eight and sixteen years of age to attend the state's public schools; the only such measure ever enacted in U.S. history, the U.S. Supreme Court struck it down as unconstitutional in 1925.[12]

Brewster and the KKK attracted the aid of the Orange Order on the schools issue. Protestant Irish had brought the Loyal Orange Institution from Great Britain to the United States around 1870 to oppose Catholic Irish in the country. A Protestant fraternal mutual-aid society, the Loyal Orange Institution's Grand Lodge of Maine met in the town of Mexico in June 1923, during which it approved resolutions in support of the Eighteenth (prohibition) Amendment, Bible reading in the public schools, and a measure to register its opposition to the use of public funds for sectarian institutions. The Orange Order's principles therefore appeared to be perfectly synchronized with those of the Ku Klux Klan. Potential members of the Orange Order had to pledge on their application form that "I never have been, am not now and never will be a Roman Catholic, and I will always uphold the teachings of Protestantism, and maintain the system of FREE PUBLIC SCHOOLS of our Country, and will always oppose the use of the public school fund for sectarian purposes, and any attempt to subordinate the affairs of State to the control of church." The order's membership application form also specified that gambling, selling or consuming alcohol, being Catholic, and supporting Catholic education were all grounds for disqualification.[13]

While the numerical strength of the Maine Orange Order in the 1920s is unknown, the organization did have lodges in such northern communities as Millinocket, Island Falls, and Houlton as well as in the central Maine city of Auburn, home to the Excelsior No Surrender lodge, a name that implies the determination of the group not to yield to increasing Catholic influence. As in Canada, the Orange Order of Maine supported the KKK's activities. Orangemen from Island Falls, for example, marched alongside five hundred Klansmen and Klanswomen in Lincoln's Labor Day parade in 1924. As a representative of the Orange Order, Moses King Jr., who had joined the Know-Nothing movement in 1854 and was now in his early nineties, wrote letters to Brewster from "the Roman City of Lewiston" to encourage him on the schools issue. King pointed out that his anti-Catholicism led him "to cast my lot with the Klansmen of America, to save America from that Hell and Purgatory of the Pope of Rome." Such collaboration between the Orange Order and the Ku Klux Klan was not unique to Maine, as the KKK in Colorado, for example, also recruited members from the Loyal Orange Society.[14]

In addition to the Orange Order, if the letters of Thomas Germon are any indication, Brewster also gained the support of Anglo-Canadian immigrants on the schools issue. Germon was a former Conservative from Ontario, a resident of the United States for seventeen years, and a naturalized U.S. citizen. Religious conflicts in Canada led this expatriate Canadian to write to Brewster in 1923 and 1924 endorsing the lawmaker's efforts to prohibit the spending of state funds on sectarian institutions, efforts that included changing the Maine constitution to ensure that sectarian schools would no longer be eligible to receive state disbursements. Germon alluded in his letters to the ethnolinguistic conflicts that had taken place in Canada when French-speaking minorities in the late nineteenth and early twentieth centuries had struggled to obtain public financial assistance for their Catholic schools in provinces with English-speaking majorities. During that period Ontario, New Brunswick, Manitoba, Alberta, and Saskatchewan enacted legislation either to curb or eliminate bilingual instruction in their schools. In siding with Brewster's legislative agenda, Germon shared with the senator his opinion of Canada's experience with sectarian schools: "I am Thoroughly in accord with The Bill because I am well acquainted with trouble They have with seperate [sic] schools in Canada from East to West and always will have so long as They allow The Hierarchie [sic] of Rome to dominate The Country." Germon inquired of Brewster how he might assist in his Republican gubernatorial bid, even though he had voted only once in the United States and had not registered as a Republican. It is not known to what extent Germon supported the Klan movement, but it is clear that he shared its sympathies, at least on the issue of religious schools.[15]

Whether or not Maine should amend its constitution to prohibit expending public funds on parochial schools emerged as the central issue in the Republican gubernatorial primary in 1924. Brewster's opponent, State Senate President Frank G. Farrington, opposed the measure, just as he had opposed a similar bill that Brewster had introduced in the state legislature the year before. There was no mistaking Brewster's lack of support in northern Maine's St. John Valley. In the towns of Frenchville, Sainte-Agathe, and Van Buren, Farrington gained 880 votes to Brewster's 6.[16]

When Brewster lost the primary to Farrington by 320 votes, he demanded a recount of the 97,000 votes cast. Brewster alleged that, contrary to state law, election officials rather than voters had marked over one thousand ballots in the St. John Valley, and he produced affidavits from town clerks in the valley to substantiate his claim that officials had thereby improperly assisted voters, voters who he implied were unilingual francophones. In the statement Brewster filed with the governor and council he declared, "Our [state] constitution provides that 'no person shall have the right to vote—who shall not be able to read the Constitution in the English language and write his name.' " Not surprisingly, the Ku Klux Klan Kreed supported Brewster and the Maine constitution on the point of English-language ability: "We Demand that no alien shall be naturalized or permitted to vote in any State in the Union who cannot speak and write the English Language." In his complaint Brewster also alleged that the Sainte-Agathe polls had shut their doors at 9:30 p.m., half an hour after the legally ordained closing time, and that during that extra half-hour, election officials had marked an additional thirty ballots in favor of his opponent. Brewster further charged that voting had not been conducted in private in Sainte-Agathe, as legally mandated, because the town had failed to furnish the polls with election booths.[17]

In rendering its decision the Maine Supreme Court voided Sainte-Agathe's entire vote because it had neglected to shield voters from observation. All of the town's 252 Republican votes had been cast for Brewster's opponent, so their exclusion considerably reduced Farrington's 320-vote margin. On a separate matter, the Supreme Court ruled that the homemade ballots some localities had generated when they ran out of official ballots also would not count. Other voting irregularities in Maine's largest city, Portland, further eroded Farrington's lead. In the end, Brewster gained enough votes as a result of the recount to be declared the Republican nominee for governor in 1924.[18]

During that election year, even though the Ku Klux Klan Kreed opposed mob violence, the KKK launched aggressive attacks against Maine's Franco-American population.[19] Confrontations took place in the rural logging town of Greenville, in the small textile mill town of Sanford, and in the larger textile centers of Lewiston and Biddeford. Each confrontation, while unique, sported distinct similarities: Protestants wanted to preserve their ascendancy in economic, social, and religious matters.

This led them to oppose efforts to unionize lumbermen in Greenville. During the late nineteenth and early twentieth centuries, French-Canadian descendants provided much of the labor for Maine's lumber industry. Beginning in July 1923 the Industrial Workers of the World (IWW), or Wobblies, sought to organize Maine's woodworkers within the Lumber Workers' Industrial Union, No. 120. The IWW campaign was part of a broader drive to unionize lumber workers in the northeastern states of Maine, New Hampshire, Vermont, and New York, because those states were major producers of the wood pulp used to make paper. When IWW recruiters arrived in Greenville, the town's selectmen ordered them to leave the area, and the Ku Klux Klan backed the officials' demand. In December 1923 the *Maine Klansman* had declared, "We should enforce an absolute prohibition to the admission of the professional agitator and deport all who have hereto gained admission. I.W.W. and Red agitators must either conform to our laws and customs or go back to the place from whence they came." In February 1924 the head of Maine's IWW, a Finn named Robert Pease, told the press that many union members were French Catholics who simply wanted "good wages, eight hours a day in the lumber camps and clean linen on our bunks." Arguing that they were breaking no laws, the IWW organizers refused to leave Greenville. Confronting them at the boarding home where they were staying, forty Klan members threatened to remove the Wobblies by force if they would not leave town voluntarily.[20]

Word of the Klan's threats quickly reached IWW loggers, who left the lumber camps en masse and marched into Greenville. There they walked the streets in a show of force against the Klan and built bonfires to warm themselves against the frigid winter weather. Greenville's residents feared violence, but none resulted, and most of the 175 lumbermen returned to their camps the next day. IWW organizers remained in the area and continued recruiting woodsmen. But lumber companies screened potential employees to determine if they were affiliated with the IWW, and Wobblies also faced community opposition from the YMCA and local merchants. When the Wobblies organized a boycott against four Greenville establishments for discriminating against its members, three of its leaders were arrested and placed on trial for conspiracy. The jury found Pease, the IWW head, John Lucelle, an IWW organizer, and William Parent, a Québec-born IWW organizer, guilty of conspiracy, and they were given jail sentences ranging from one to two years. Moreover, Parent was deported to Québec on the completion of his jail term. The imprisonment of the IWW leadership, the difficulty obtaining jobs and housing, and the organized community hostility, aggravated by the Klan, led to the collapse of IWW efforts to unionize French-speaking lumbermen in Greenville in 1924.[21]

The Klan and Franco-Americans also clashed in Sanford. In August 1924 an estimated 250 Klan members paraded through the southern Maine town, either riding horseback or marching in their white robes and hoods while carrying U.S. flags. The Klan band from Portland joined the procession, and Klan members' wives and children followed in automobiles. According to newspaper reports, thousands of spectators turned out to watch the parade, hundreds of them cheering the Klan and nearly equal numbers jeering them. An estimated 1,500 people attended the Klan's so-called naturalization ceremony at Sanford's Goodall Park, while another 1,500 gathered outside of the fenced-in area. Some spectators threw stones, and a person or persons pulled fireboxes levers. Arrested for causing disturbances during the meeting were Franco-Americans Henry Gagné and Alfred Fréchette.[22]

Tensions were running high. The *Sanford Tribune and Advocate* did not mask them, nor did it hide its contempt for the Ku Klux Klan; for example, the weekly newspaper had placed the following quote from an unidentified judge above its masthead in July: "The principal difference between the Old Know Nothing Party and the Klan is that the Know Nothings admitted it." In August when Almon E. Garnsey, a Sanford jeweler, ran as a Republican candidate for the Maine state legislature, the *Sanford Tribune and Advocate* commented, "Mr. Garnsey is a dyed-in-the-wool member of the Ku Klux Klan," and it pointed out that "Mr. Garnsey has stated that he has not any — — use for Sanford's French-speaking people." Declaring its opposition to Garnsey's candidacy, the newspaper instructed Republican voters to split their tickets to avoid voting for Republican candidates like him and the Klan-backed gubernatorial candidate. Although Sanford's residents voted against Garnsey, he gained enough electoral support from the nearby town of Springvale to win the election.[23] Even though such reports, gleaned from the local press, remain mere sketches, they nonetheless portray an unmistakable hostility between members of the Ku Klux Klan and the state's Franco-Americans in the vital arenas of education, employment, and politics.

In 1924 the Klan also targeted Franco-Americans in the state's urban centers. Jobs in the textile industry in the southern Maine city of Biddeford had attracted large numbers of French-Canadian immigrants, and they were becoming influential in municipal politics. In 1922 the Democrat Edouard H. Drapeau defeated the Republican incumbent to win the mayor's race, and he won reelection in 1923. In April of that year about one thousand people attended a Klan meeting in Saco, across the river from Biddeford. Addressing the attendees, King Kleagle Farnsworth could well have been speaking about Biddeford when he charged, "This government is now being controlled by aliens, and Catholics." During the mayor's race in Saco in 1924, the Klan threw its support behind the Republican John G. Smith, who defeated a two-term Democratic incumbent. When Smith's supporters visited his home and called him outside to speak, some youths from Saco and Biddeford heckled him, and fistfights broke out; as he gave a victory speech at Saco City Hall, young men again interrupted him and were ejected from the hall. They continued their antics in the streets, engaging in arguments and fights. The press reported no such disturbances when Drapeau won election to a third term as Biddeford's mayor the following week.[24]

In late August Mayor Smith signaled that he would grant the Ku Klux Klan a permit to parade in Saco on Labor Day. Blaming Biddeford's youth for the commotions during his election night, he warned them to stay away, declaring, "If this crowd of Biddeford roughnecks stays at home there will be no trouble." With the mayor's blessing, the Klan secured a permit to march in Saco, but even though it had not sought a permit in Biddeford it informed the press that it would parade there as well. The *Portland Press Herald* portrayed the likely scenario: "They are going to invade Biddeford, covering some of the principal streets of that town, and folk are wondering what sort of a reception the thousand robed and hooded men will meet when they cross the Saco River."[25]

Responding in the press, Mayor Drapeau warned the Klan to stay in Saco and not enter his city. He also took Saco's mayor to task for his characterization of Biddeford youth, asking, "Is this a blanket indictment of the cultural status of the neighboring city of Biddeford?" Drapeau chastised Smith for maintaining his legal office in Biddeford and making a living off its residents while at the same time disparaging them. Drapeau offered additional criticism of his counterpart: "Unquestionably in Mayor Smith's mind the citizens of Biddeford are uncouth and uncultivated because they have not banded themselves together to make cowardly war upon those who differ in race or religion." In his open letter to the press, Drapeau continued his counterattack: "Unquestionably, too, it is elevating to run rampant in ludicrous garb, burn lumber in geometric arrangement, and mouth execrations of one's fellow citizens." Differences in social class as well as in ethnicity and religion, Drapeau insisted, had prompted the mayor's and the Klan's unsavory remarks and behaviors: "Perhaps the distinction between the citizenry of the two cities in Mayor Smith's mind is the result of his personal prejudice in favor of the element found in Saco."[26]

Drapeau did not stop there. He issued an order forbidding the Saco Klan from marching in Biddeford, and he backed up his words with a show of force. On Labor Day Biddeford police and fire crews blocked the bridges over the Saco River. Klan members from throughout New England joined the Saco Klan, with three hundred men and women marching in the parade. According to the *Biddeford Daily Journal,* "The feeling of the crowds which lined the streets of the city ran high during the parade and trouble was imminent from the start of exercises until late in the evening." Apparently the KKK had a healthy fear of Biddeford's Franco-American residents, for it chose not to parade in their city. There were some tense moments, nonetheless. The *Biddeford Daily Journal* reported that Saco officers had their clubs in hand to control the crowds, and at one point a policeman drew his gun and threatened to fire it but did not. The newspaper noted that small conflicts broke out in the evening, but it did not elaborate.[27]

In addition to Biddeford, the Klan set its sights on Lewiston. In January 1924 the *Maine Klansman* observed, "If anyone walks down Lisbon Street in Lewiston, he will certainly think that he is in Quebec, or an alien land, instead of the United States. French is spoken nearly everywhere." In March the Klan newspaper asserted the need for change: "The foreign element have practically every city office within their grip. However, there are a few real Americans in the city and they are working day and night to reclaim the city for those to whom it rightfully belongs." The Klan held organizational meetings in the Lewiston–Auburn area, and local newspapers indicated that it was making gains in its recruitment efforts.[28] Even though one KKK organizer pointed out in April 1924 that the Klan did not dare parade in regalia in Lewiston, the group nonetheless tried to intimidate the city's residents. When Brewster won the Republican gubernatorial primary after a recount in August, the Klan punctuated the coup with a dynamite bomb blast at

1:00 a.m. one Sunday, which in turn called attention to the twelve-foot cross burning atop one of the city's highest peaks.[29]

The gubernatorial campaign between the Republican Brewster and his Democratic opponent, William R. Pattangall, in 1924 should be viewed in the context of Maine and national politics. Maine was a rock-ribbed Republican state. From 1855 to the mid-1920s Republican candidates won the governorship of Maine in all but four elections (1878, 1880, 1910, and 1914), and the Republican Party controlled the state legislature during all but two sessions (1879 and 1911.) Thus, Republicans had dominated the state for nearly seventy years.[30] In this political environment, Pattangall stood little chance of winning.

Pattangall was an attorney, a former newspaper editor and manager, and an experienced politician who had served in the state legislature, as mayor of Waterville, and as Maine attorney general. He had first run for governor in 1922, when he lost to the Republican Percival P. Baxter. In 1925 *Forum* magazine described Pattangall as "a down-East Yankee with a touch of Mayflower blood, a Protestant, and a Mason, . . . the very epitome of the Klan's own definition of a one hundred per cent American of three centuries standing."[31] Yet Pattangall was the Klan's chief political opponent in Maine in 1924.

Although the Maine Democratic Party did not condemn the Ku Klux Klan explicitly during its state convention in March, Pattangall wanted the national Democratic Party to do so at its summer assembly in New York. As Maine's Democratic gubernatorial contender, Pattangall attended the Democratic National Convention and joined the delegates who demanded that it condemn the KKK by name. Among the thirteen members of the resolutions committee calling for the Klan to be named explicitly were delegates from Maine, Massachusetts, Rhode Island, and Vermont. The minority report they ratified would have committed the national Democratic Party "to oppose any effort on the part of the Ku Klux Klan or any organization to interfere with the religious liberty or political freedom of any citizen, or to limit the civic rights of any citizen or body of citizens because of religion, birthplace or racial origin." The Klan issue deeply split the delegates at the national assembly, and Klan and anti-Klan forces exchanged both words and fists. Klan enthusiasts chanted, "Booze! Booze! Booze!" to voice their opposition to the nomination of the New York governor Alfred Smith, a Catholic who opposed prohibition, and anti-Klan forces crowed, "Ku, Ku, McAdoo!" to verbalize their contempt for the nomination of William Gibbs McAdoo, who had Klan support. Neither candidate garnered the two-thirds majority the party required for nomination; not until the 103rd ballot did the delegates agree on a presidential nominee, John W. Davis, as a compromise candidate.

The three-time Democratic presidential contender William Jennings Bryan appealed for national unity when he asked the delegates not to condemn the Ku Klux Klan by name in its platform. For his part, Pattangall spoke out strongly on the convention floor in favor of an anti-Klan plank, contending, "There is more in this matter than the mere naming of a secret organization. There has crept into American life so strong an influence in certain States that United States Senators told me last night that if the Klan was opposed by them they could not be re-elected to their seats in the Senate." Tired after giving his speech, Pattangall left the hall and asked his wife, Gertrude, an alternate delegate, to sit in for him. When the party platform came up for a vote, a brawl broke out on the convention floor, and delegations changed or challenged the reporting of their votes. Mrs. Pattangall decided to follow the example of the Maine Democratic Convention in casting hers. Consequently, she helped the national convention to defeat the issue of condemning the Ku Klux Klan by name by giving opponents of the proposition a one-vote majority out of almost eleven hundred votes cast.[32]

Back in Maine, Pattangall and the Democratic Party tried to make the KKK the central issue in the gubernatorial campaign. The *Portland Press Herald* chided him for doing so, arguing that it was counterproductive: "Talking about the Klan will not aid us in solving any of our problems. It will not assist anyone in giving the State better government." Acknowledging that Brewster had won the Republican primary with Klan backing, the newspaper supported his equivocation on the KKK. "Of course Senator Brewster cannot be expected to come out and say that he regards the Klan as an evil institution," the editor noted. "If he did so he would only be alienating the Klan vote. On the other hand, he cannot be expected to come out and say that he looks upon the Klan as the finest organization in the land, because if he did so there would be many citizens who would not like it."[33]

Brewster's actions were in keeping with the positions of the national Republican Party. During the Republican National Convention, which took place in Cleveland, Ohio, the Committee on Platform and Resolutions considered an anti-Klan proposal but instead presented the following statement, which the convention delegates adopted: "The Republican Party reaffirms its unyielding devotion to the Constitution and to the guarantees of civil, political, and religious liberty therein contained." Republicans nominated Calvin Coolidge on the first ballot, and during the campaign he remained silent on the Klan issue.[34]

When the Republican vice presidential candidate, Gen. Charles G. Dawes, addressed a gathering of about five thousand people at Maine's Island Park on Lake Cobbosseecontee in August 1924, he became the first Republican candidate to speak directly about the Klan in the Maine elections. In his autobiography Dawes noted that Maine's Republican State Committee had prohibited Republican candidates from mentioning the KKK in their speeches during the campaign, and it was apprehensive about Dawes's intention to do so; moreover, the Republican National Committee worried about losing 150,000 votes in the Klan stronghold of Indiana in the national elections and had advised against it. Although the incumbent president Coolidge chose not to denounce the KKK formally, Dawes decided to speak out against the Klan in response to a comment the Democratic contender Davis had made the previous day at a rally in Sea Girt, New Jersey, where he condemned the KKK and then challenged Coolidge to do the same. "I agree with him that it has no proper part in this or any other campaign," Dawes stated. "Let me say at once that I recognize that the Ku Klux Klan in many localities and among many people represents only an instinctive groping for leadership, moving in the interest of law enforcement, which they do not find in many cowardly politicians and office holders. But," Dawes admonished, "it is not the right way to forward law enforcement," and he emphasized, "Lawlessness cannot be met with lawlessness and civilization be maintained." Dawes then denounced the divisions the Klan promoted and advocated religious tolerance.[35]

Thomas Carens, a reporter for the *Boston Sunday Herald,* covered Dawes's speech. "As he reached the words 'Ku Klux Klan' in the very first sentence," Carens stated, "a stir ran through the crowd, and the first reaction was a roar of laughter." Carens explained that the laughter was "probably an appreciation of the general's bluntness in approaching an issue which the Republicans have been educated to believe must be discussed only in whispers." As David M. Chalmers put it, "While the President's silence comforted the Klansmen, Dawes' . . . speech pleased the anti-Klan Republicans." The Republican gubernatorial candidate Brewster followed Dawes to the podium that summer day by the lake. But, as usual, he said nothing about the KKK in his remarks.[36]

Less than a week before the election Brewster finally broke his silence. It was an open secret that he accepted the Ku Klux Klan's support during his gubernatorial bid, but constituents wanted to know if he himself was a member of the secret society. In a letter published in the press Brewster denied he was a KKK member: "I am not now, nor have I ever been, a member of the Ku Klux Klan or of any other secret organization other than the college fraternity which I joined as an undergraduate at Bowdoin." Trying to underplay his Klan support, Brewster went on to insist that he was a Republican candidate, not the candidate "of any other group or organization."[37]

Pundits outside of Maine felt the state's race for governor had implications for the rest of the country. The *Detroit Free Press* commented on the national interest the campaign had generated because it was "a straight Klan and anti-Klan fight." On election day the *New York Times* observed that "Maine will present the first test of Klan strength in the North." The *New York World* wrote that "Maine means very much, whether Pattangall wins or loses. For Maine means to the Nation the surrender of the Republican organization to the Ku Klux Klan." The *World's* editor blamed President Coolidge for this situation because he had not himself condemned the Ku Klux Klan. "He refused only because the Republican Party in Maine and in Indiana and in other States is Klan-controlled. There is no other reason." The editor continued his rant: "No eleventh-hour statement now would alter the fact that the Republican Party has played for the Klan in Maine. No consideration of principle, of loyalty to American ideals, no sense of duty as President of the United States has weighed in Mr. Coolidge's mind against the desire to safeguard the Klan vote."[38]

Bolstered by the Klan, Brewster scored victories in the general campaign in every Maine county except Androscoggin. That county's largest city, Lewiston, had overwhelmingly voted for Pattangall. After Brewster's election, crosses burned and at least a dozen bombs exploded in towns surrounding Lewiston. Around midnight on the Saturday following the election a cross was set ablaze on the Côté farm within Lewiston's precincts, while at the same time others burned and more bombs discharged throughout Lewiston and Auburn.[39] Heralding the Klan's electoral triumphs, the explosions and conflagrations were also intended to strike fear in the French-speaking Catholics who had dared vote against the Klan's interests and candidate.

The Ku Klux Klan's exertions had similarly helped gubernatorial candidates win victories in Oregon, California, Georgia, and Alabama in 1922. When the *New York Times* learned that Brewster had defeated Pattangall in 1924, it expressed the view that other states would be reluctant about confronting Klan organizations. Had Pattangall won, the newspaper maintained, "there can be no doubt that in consequence a concentrated assault upon the Klan and upon Klan candidates in other States would at once have got under way." Instead, capitalizing on Brewster's success, the Republican National Committee enlisted him to campaign for Republican candidates on Long Island, New York, which had an active Klan organization.[40]

Brewster's gubernatorial opponent was mindful of the Klan's influence beyond the political arena. A year after losing his second campaign for governor, Pattangall contended that "the Klan is more than an organization; it is a state of mind," adding, "The Klan's propaganda has caused a tremendous development of anti-Catholic, anti-Jewish, and anti-alien sentiment all through the country." The Klan's influence, Pattangall believed, was far out of proportion to its actual numbers. He offered a balanced assessment of the

Klan. While he agreed that many of the KKK's complaints about Catholics and immigrants were grounded in truth, he charged that the organization "exploits evils and a widespread unrest that are real enough and that need cure, but it makes a fake diagnosis, presents a false cure, gives poisons instead of remedies, and actually increases the evils it claims to relieve." Pattangall challenged the Klan's premise that Catholics and Jews could not be good Americans because of their "religious loyalties," and he pointed out the hypocrisy and inconsistency of the group's "attempts to use its spiritual hold on its members as a means for political control." As the Klansman Charlie York told his biographer, members would decide at their gatherings which candidates to support, not only at the local level but also at the state and federal levels, and "every member was supposed to vote as the Klan voted."[41]

Despite the Maine Klan's political success with the 1924 gubernatorial election of Brewster, various incidents in late 1923 and throughout 1924, many of which were publicized by the press, reveal that it was imploding. Media exposure of the corruption and immorality of the KKK facilitated its decline in Maine, New England, and the rest of the country. The arrest of Rev. Caleb Ridley, a Klan chaplain, for driving while intoxicated in Biddeford in late 1923 undermined the KKK's stance of favoring prohibition and made other Protestant clergy and Klan members uneasy, while no doubt uncovering the hypocrisy of the Klan's ideals before the general public. The strong promotional skills of former King Kleagle F. Eugene Farnsworth had helped the KKK to acquire its large Maine membership by the mid-1920s. After the KKK deposed Farnsworth in early 1924, Dr. E. L. Gayer became King Kleagle of Maine, New Hampshire, and Vermont and moved the headquarters to Rochester, New Hampshire. But Farnsworth's charisma attracted members away from the KKK into a rival organization, and Gayer found himself competing with his predecessor not only to retain members but also to draw foreign-born Klan supporters to an auxiliary society that Gayer reportedly planned to organize.[42]

Internal divisions also plagued individual state klaverns. The press reported, for example, that Klan members in Lewiston and Auburn separated to form rival factions in October 1924. When, during that month, Lawrence Coolidge was punched in the jaw and kicked while selling Klan newspapers in Lewiston, the local press described his assailant as a man "of foreign descent" but did not blame Franco-Americans; in fact, several days after the incident the *Lewiston Evening Journal* implied that Coolidge may have found himself caught in the rivalry between two local Klan factions. The *Lewiston Daily Sun* suggested that the friction had actually begun earlier in the year, following Farnsworth's departure as King Kleagle, when his loyalists opted to form an organization outside of the national Ku Klux Klan.[43]

The Maine Klan also faced financial and legal problems in 1924. In May the Klan was the object of several lawsuits. Edgar L. Hatch and N. T. Fox Company, Inc., each sued the Loyal Realty Company and Maine Savings Bank, its mortgagee, for materials and labor they had supplied to erect the Klan's hall in Portland.[44]

Perhaps the most damaging legal action was that brought by Moses W. Lucas, a brick manufacturer who served as a shareholder and the president of the Loyal Realty Company. Lucas filed a bill of complaint in the Supreme Judicial Court of Cumberland County against Loyal Realty and Maine Savings Bank. He alleged that Loyal Realty had incurred such debts in improving its Portland property that it faced "imminent danger of insolvency," and he asked the court to appoint a receiver to liquidate the Klan corporation's assets. In its reporting of the civil suit, the *Portland Press Herald* informed readers that the KKK's income no longer met its expenses, because "rumor has it that the Invisible Empire has lost half it[s] membership in Portland, with the other half divided over allegiance to various factions." Subsequent press accounts intimated that Lucas had left the KKK to follow Farnsworth into his new organization, and they revealed that the KKK settled the suit with Lucas and Farnsworth by offering them a cash settlement for their shares in Loyal Realty. The *Press Herald* portended dire consequences for the Klan: "It is known that the bringing of this action in equity and the attendant publicity was a very serious blow to the future of the Klan in Portland and vicinity."[45]

When a Klan church in Brewer closed in July 1924 its leaders similarly found themselves the objects of a lawsuit. Rev. Milton C. Bennett of Portland, a preacher and a composer of sheet music for the Klan, sued for the salary he had been promised for the unexpired term of his contract, and he won his case in February 1926.[46]

These lawsuits did not pose the only financial and legal challenges for the Maine Klan. Valued at seventy-five thousand dollars, the organization's new three-story building with its four-thousand-seat auditorium burned to the ground in forty minutes in December 1924. Although initial reports pointed to a faulty boiler, the cause of the fire was not determined. The Klan planned to rebuild the structure, but it could not afford to do so. In 1924 the Portland klavern's property taxes were twenty-three hundred dollars, an amount the Klan had difficulty paying, and in April 1925 Klan officials asked the City of Portland for a property tax exemption, professing that it was a religious, patriotic, benevolent, and educational organization. Citing mismanagement and portending insolvency, four stockholders and creditors of the Loyal Realty Company brought suit against the corporation in November 1925, asking the Cumberland County Supreme Judicial Court to issue an injunction that would restrain it from engaging in any financial transactions without the approval of a court-appointed receiver.[47]

The plaintiffs' specifications to the bill of complaint, advanced in December 1925, described vividly the Portland Klan's decline. When the KKK began its work in Portland, "the association was increasing in numbers, and money was freely offered for building purposes, due to the vigorous campaign for membership, the political issues in which the members were interested, their confidence in the leaders of the movement and the prosperity of the individual members in a period of employment and high wages." They continued, "At the present time[,] however, the contrary is true, a considerable proportion of the membership has lapsed," and they noted further that growing unemployment had adversely affected the level of donations by the members, and that the Loyal Realty had no regular income outside of the contributions of Klan members. The plaintiffs complained that the directors of the company nevertheless planned to rebuild the meeting hall even though the KKK lacked the financial resources to do so. DeForest H. Perkins, the president of the Loyal Realty Company and later the Grand Dragon of the Maine KKK for several years, denied the allegations.[48] Portland city officials had apparently turned down the Klan's request for a property tax exemption, for Klan officials claimed that the restraining order placed upon it as a result of the lawsuit prevented the organization from paying its taxes, causing it to lose title to its Portland estate. The Loyal Realty Company settled the lawsuit out of court in March 1926 by assigning its property so that it could be sold, the creditors paid, and any remaining proceeds distributed among stockholders or returned to the corporation. In June 1926, the assignee sold the Klan property to a Portland real estate company to settle the Klan's financial obligations.[49]

Despite its financial and legal challenges, the Klan nonetheless tried to maintain a visible and political presence in Maine during 1926. In August it organized a three-mile-long procession in Portland of twelve hundred men and four hundred women, some of whom traveled from Massachusetts and Rhode Island to participate. Besides the parade the Klan organized a field day, and Imperial Wizard Hiram W. Evans reportedly was on hand to naturalize five hundred new members into the organization.[50]

The Maine KKK also tried to influence the outcome of the U.S. Senate race held in 1926, but the results underscored the extent of the society's decline. When Sen. Bert M. Fernald died in office in 1926, Maine held a special election to complete his unexpired term. Four candidates sought the Republican Party's nomination. Although the Klan favored Hodgdon C. Buzzell, Arthur R. Gould won his party's nomination. The KKK tried to derail his candidacy. Grand Dragon Perkins accompanied Rev. Arthur F.

Leigh, a Klansman, when he filed papers with the Maine Secretary of State's Office, alleging that Gould had exceeded his campaign spending limits and should be disqualified as the Republican nominee. The *New York Times* implied the KKK opposed Gould's candidacy because his wife reportedly was Catholic. The secretary of state dismissed the Klan's charges for lack of evidence. The Ku Klux Klan and Governor Brewster thereafter crossed party lines to throw their weight behind the Democratic nominee, Fulton J. Redman. Maine's election attracted nationwide attention because it would affect the balance of power in the U.S. Senate, where Republicans and Democrats each held forty-seven seats. Gould carried a majority of the vote in every city and county of Maine, including the home city and county of his Democratic opponent, to win the special election. The *New York Times* wrote that "Democratic cities like Lewiston, Biddeford and Rockland all went against Mr. Redman, many of his own party voting against him to punish the Klan rather than for any particular animosity toward their candidate." The *Lewiston Evening Journal* interpreted the election result as a repudiation of both Brewster and the KKK, suggesting tongue-in-cheek that their efforts had backfired: "The election, most agreed, proved that the Ku Klux Klan has a great power in Maine if one could only get it against him."[51] The *Journal's* words poignantly highlighted the fact that the KKK no longer possessed the ability to sway the outcome of Maine's elections.

The decline of the Maine Klan mirrored what was happening to the organization nationally. In February 1926, for example, the *New York Times* reported that internal dissent, outside criticism, and the national Klan's inability to achieve its goals all contributed to its downward spiral. As we have seen, divisions within the Maine Klan stemmed from the split in leadership following Farnsworth's departure as King Kleagle and over the Klan corporation's misuse of financial resources. Like the national Klan, the Maine branch faced criticism, not only from groups it had targeted and attacked but also from Protestant organizations. The Scottish Rite Masons came out against the Klan and stressed to their members the incompatibility of being both a Klansman and a Scottish Rite Mason. Similarly, Judge Albert M. Spear, a retired Maine Supreme Court justice and the grand master of the Masonic Order of Maine, denounced the Klan and opposed the entry of Masons into Klanhood.[52]

The Maine KKK also faced other forms of resistance. In 1923 the presidents of Bates College in Lewiston and Bowdoin College in Brunswick joined an organization called the National Vigilance Association to curb the then-growing influence of the Ku Klux Klan in the United States by such actions as promoting anti-masking legislation as well as laws requiring the publication of the names of members of secret societies. In 1923 city officials in Bangor, Old Town, and Lewiston, all communities with sizable Catholic populations, denied the Klan's requests to meet in their city halls. In the same year, Clyde Smith, a Republican state senator from Skowhegan, introduced anti-Klan legislation to require secret societies to file their membership lists with town and city clerks, to disallow the wearing of masks and hoods in public without permit when three or more persons gathered together, and to add five years of prison time to the sentences of individuals who committed crimes while disguised. Although the Senate defeated the measure, some municipalities, like Augusta, allowed the Maine KKK to use their city hall and to parade on their streets only if unmasked. In 1926 the organization used this restriction as an excuse for canceling its planned statewide meeting in Augusta. The *Lewiston Evening Journal* viewed the results differently. The Klan had expected Augusta's mayor to turn down its request to parade, and it had planned to generate interest in the KKK with the ensuing fight, the *Journal* suggested. But Mayor Ernest L. McLean, a Democrat running for governor, defused a potentially contentious issue simply by imposing the restriction that the organization march without masks. The *Journal* also saw the incident in the context of the Klan's descent: it noted that the Maine KKK had been on a downward slope over the past two years, and that it was declining even more rapidly during 1926.[53]

While not yet dead in 1926, the Klan in Maine was dying. The *Washington Post* noted the sharp decrease in the number of members in good standing in the second half of the decade: a precipitous drop from 61,136 in 1926 to 3,168 in 1927. During its declension the Ku Klux Klan likely motivated the introduction of an unsuccessful bill in 1927 prohibiting marriage in Maine between white individuals and those of African descent. After 1927, its numbers fell to a mere 226 in 1930.[54]

Bereft of its auditorium and much of its membership, the Klan sought to rent the Portland City Hall auditorium in March 1929 to host the Klan spokesperson, U.S. senator J. Thomas Heflin of Alabama, but city officials denied the request in order to avoid such disturbances as had taken place in Massachusetts when hostile crowds greeted the senator (discussed in chapter 7). When the communities of Bangor and Pittsfield also refused Heflin permission to speak at their town halls, the Pittsfield Klan prevailed upon its allies in Dexter to open their town hall for Heflin's address, which was attended by approximately three hundred people. On another occasion Heflin spoke for nearly two hours at the Pythian Temple in Portland to an audience of eleven hundred people. This event was the last notable public event of the Maine Klan during the 1920s. Yet the correspondence of the Klan reveals that the secret society continued to exist in the state in the 1930s; the letterhead with the slogan "COMMUNISM WILL NOT BE TOLERATED" illustrates that the Maine Klan, like the Klan elsewhere in the United States, was targeting Communism as a key enemy during the Great Depression.[55] But there were no noteworthy Klan events in Maine in the 1930s. The steady devolution of the group in the state after 1925 points to its confrontations with Franco-Americans in 1924 and to its gubernatorial success in that year as the organization's denouement in the Pine Tree State.

Given the number of KKK mob actions in Maine in 1924, it is surprising that apparently no one was killed or even seriously injured. In contrast, virulent clashes between Klan and anti-Klan groups in Massachusetts in the mid-1920s resulted in significant property damage and personal injuries. As we will see in chapter 7, judging by occasional newspaper reports of the names and activities of anti-Klan members, we can infer that in Massachusetts, Catholics of various ethnic backgrounds banded together to launch organized counteroffensives against the Ku Klux Klan.[56]

In Maine, however, Franco-American Catholics eager to preserve their ethnic institutions had been struggling bitterly against the assimilationist policies of the Irish bishop, Louis Walsh. From Walsh's appointment in 1906 until his death in 1924, Franco-Americans in Maine fought with him for control over the finances and ethnic character of their parishes and institutions.[57] In his promotion of American loyalties and the use of English, Bishop Walsh acted like other Irish prelates who dominated the Catholic hierarchy in the United States and who sought to unify the ethnically diverse Roman Catholic Church in the face of nativist hostilities. Walsh would push English-language instruction in his meetings with French teaching orders who taught in the state's Franco-American schools, sometimes citing the Maine law of 1919 prescribing English as "the basic language of instruction," even though the law did not apply to the elementary schools where the nuns taught. The law to which Walsh referred represented part of the intensified discrimination against Franco-Americans that took place in the aftermath of World War I. The Ku Klux Klan surely was on Walsh's mind; on New Year's Eve, for instance, he recorded in his diary that the KKK had contributed to making 1923 his most difficult year. The bishop's actions, from working to Americanize ethnic groups like Franco-Americans to speaking out against the Klan on Columbus Day, serve as examples of Irish clerical leadership against the KKK in Maine.[58] It is important to note, however, that anti-Klan resistance in Maine and the other New England states usually originated in the laity rather than in the Catholic Church hierarchy. As a consequence of their conflicts with Bishop Walsh, Franco-Americans appear not to have joined other Catholic groups to combat the KKK. Instead, the state's Franco-Americans employed strong but not overly aggressive means to resist Klan activity in the communities in which they lived.

Anecdotal evidence reveals that the Ku Klux Klan did frighten a number of Franco-Americans in Maine during the 1920s. Josephine LaBrecque, who grew up in the Westbrook neighborhood known as Frenchtown, said "it was scary" to know that some of her neighbors were members of the KKK. LaBrecque's mother would keep her and her sisters indoors when she learned the Klan planned to parade in their community. After hearing about the fires that devastated Catholic institutions in Québec, and that had been blamed on the Ku Klux Klan, the Ursuline Sisters recorded their fear of being burned out of their Waterville convent by the KKK. Candide Desrosiers recalled seeing Klan members riding on horseback, dressed in their white robes, when she was a young child in Patten. Her mother, aware of the Klan's dislike of Catholics, feared they had come to burn down their home; Desrosiers's mother would draw the shades, bless the windows with holy water, and pray the rosary with her five young children, all of whom she kept indoors when the Klan paraded.[59]

If the experience of Theophile Bernier of Lewiston was at all representative, however, it would appear that the Ku Klux Klan did not substantially intimidate Franco-Americans. According to Bernier's grandson Pierre Vincent Bourassa, Bernier refused to allow the KKK to affect him adversely. Bourassa wrote that Bernier voiced this opinion in English while at a local hardware store, adding that "if the Klan did not like the way he felt they could pay him a visit to settle the problem." Assaulted a week later while returning home from his job at a textile mill, Bernier discovered there was nothing missing from his wallet. The attack, it seems, was the consequence of his antagonizing the Klan. Bourassa writes that his grandfather did not report the incident because of the possibility that local police or judicial authorities belonged to the KKK. The incident made Bernier even more resolute about retaining his French-Canadian identity: "From that day on Monsieur Bernier refused to speak English, associated with few Protestants, and voted for the Democratic ticket."[60] Considering this limited, anecdotal evidence, we can speculate that the effect of the Klan on at least some Franco-Americans may have been for them to assert more forcefully their ethnic identity.

Interestingly enough, that assertion, at least in Bernier's case, found expression at the ballot box as well as in his choice of language and personal relationships. While it signaled a measure of retrenchment (seen in his decision to speak only French and to limit his contact with non-Catholics), it also gave evidence of his civic participation (he was a voter.) Thus, in seeking to retain his ethnic identity and to express it by exercising suffrage, Bernier gave evidence of his decision to pursue political participation and *survivance* (the preservation of the French language, Catholic faith, and French-Canadian traditions) as intertwined goals. Democratic organizers and Franco-American journalists similarly encouraged Maine's French speakers to preserve their heritage and institutions by registering to vote and casting their ballots against the Klan's candidate in the gubernatorial election of 1924.[61]

French speakers in the Northeast were not the only objects of the Klan's intimidation and violence in the 1920s. Native-born Protestants who were non-English speakers in eastern Texas, second- and third-generation German descendants in particular, were subjected to kidnapping and tarring and feathering as well as being shot at and stabbed, according to the historian Walter D. Kamphoefner. As in the case of Franco-Americans like Bernier who continued to speak French, the Klan's efforts appear to have had little effect on curbing the use of German.[62]

During the KKK's heyday in Maine, Franco-American journalists made clear through their discourse that Franco-Americans knew intimately their constitutional rights in the United States. Against the notion of King Kleagle Farnsworth that the United States was a Protestant nation, Louis-Philippe Gagné contended in *Le Messager* of Lewiston: "La séparation de l'Eglise et de l'Etat existe aux Etats-Unis et on n'a pas droit de dire que la nation est protestante" (The separation of church and state exists in the United States and one does not have the right to say that the nation is Protestant). Gagné dismissed Farnsworth's, and the Klan's, assumption that people could not be both Catholic and American. His defense made clear what nativists like the Klan neither could nor would accept: the notion that ethnic retention proceeded hand in hand with participation in American society. The editor of *La Justice de Biddeford* argued in the columns of his newspaper that the KKK worked against the principles espoused by the Declaration of Independence, the U.S. Constitution, and the lessons of such presidents as George Washington and Abraham Lincoln; the editor maintained, "Sa propre existence est une trahison à l'esprit américain" (Its very existence is a betrayal of the American spirit). Franco-Americans understood their legal and personal rights in the host society. Despite pressure from the Roman Catholic Church and the Ku Klux Klan, Franco-American communities worked to preserve their French language and many of their French-Canadian traditions throughout the 1920s, all the while learning English and becoming naturalized citizens and voters, giving evidence of their commitment to and participation in U.S. society.[63]

Another sign that the Klan did not succeed in intimidating Franco-Americans was that they did not feel it necessary to avoid Ralph Brewster. Although Franco-Americans knew that Brewster had been involved with the Klan during his bid for governor in 1924, they had such confidence—and sufficient electoral power—that they could invite him to their events and know he would feel compelled to attend. Hence they invited the governor to their winter carnival in 1925 and to the Saint-Jean-Baptiste Day banquet in Lewiston in 1927, receiving him at the banquet with "une véritable ova-tion." In 1930, when Brewster campaigned for the U.S. Senate, he took out a full-page political advertisement, asking in French for the votes of readers of *La Justice de Biddeford*. In that same year, *Le Messager* reported that Franco-American Republicans met with Brewster in Lewiston and supported his bid for the U.S. Senate.[64]

In short, the Ku Klux Klan's conflicts with Maine's Franco-Americans do not support the interpretations of scholars who have argued that the Klan of the twenties is best understood as an organization promoting social and political causes.[65] While those considerations may have motivated some indi-viduals to join the Klan, in Maine nativist sentiment, religious prejudice, and class differences compelled white Protestants to band together and use the organization as a means of protesting the social, political, and economic advances that French-Canadian immigrants and their Franco-American descendants had achieved in the United States.

The Klan's confrontations with Maine's French speakers illustrate another important point. Accounts written by elites in the late nineteenth and early twentieth centuries have typically portrayed French-Canadian descendants in the northeastern United States as docile and passive, as inordinately dependent upon and controlled by their religious leaders, almost as an ethnic group without agency.[66] As this study documents, however, Maine's Franco-Americans confronted the Ku Klux Klan both physically and politically, thus helping to precipitate the demise of this inordinately powerful reactionary mass movement before the onslaught of the Great Depression.[67] Franco-Americans of Maine proved to be historical agents in their own right.

4

Expansion in the Granite State

WHEN THE Ku Klux Klan made preliminary incursions into New Hampshire in 1921, F. H. Jackson, a KKK organizer from New York, explained that the secret society had as its goal "to inculcate the sacred principles and noble ideals of chivalry and the maintenance of white supremacy." Journalists seized on this comment to ridicule the hooded empire. "There may be citizens who did not know that white supremacy is in jeopardy," Hobart Pillsbury observed wryly in the *Boston Sunday Herald.* "New Hampshire has less negroes than any other state, according to the census, less than 1 per cent. of the whites and only a few more than the Indians. But," Pillsbury continued, "the Klan will undertake to protect the whites, many as they are, from the blacks, few as they may be."[1]

Like the national Ku Klux Klan in the 1920s, the New Hampshire version had broader goals than the promotion of white supremacy. Jackson also described the KKK to the press as "a practical fraternal order pledged to wholesome service, and not merely a flashy social association." Some of the Klan's civic objectives and ideals, Jackson pointed out, included the "suppression of graft by public officeholders; preventing the causes of mob violence and lynchings; preventing unwarranted strikes by foreign agitators; sensible and patriotic immigration laws; sovereignty of state rights under the Constitution; separation of church and state and freedom of speech and press." When George P. Mason, a Klan organizer from Tulsa, Oklahoma, tried to establish the headquarters of the New Hampshire Klan in Manchester in January 1923, like Jackson he stressed the organization's goal of ensuring white supremacy. But Mason also pointed out that the KKK targeted bootleggers, gamblers, drug pushers, and men who abused their wives, and he noted that the organization wanted to promote honest government in the state, suggesting a greater purview in New Hampshire, and suggesting as well the Klan's civic-mindedness and desire to reform New Hampshire communities.[2]

What Jackson and Mason did not say, but the *Boston Sunday Advertiser* pointed out, was that the New Hampshire Klan sought to offset the growing influence of the state's Irish and French-Canadian populations. A former New Hampshire lawmaker, Frank H. Challis, stated this goal explicitly. Although Challis denied being a member of the KKK, he acknowledged that he had been a member of the American Protective Association, an anti-Catholic society, and he vocalized his support for the Klan in New Hampshire, asserting "The Ku Klux [*sic*] is the only thing that will save New Hampshire for the Yankee." Challis continued, emphasizing "And, New Hampshire is going to oust from power the Irish, and Canucks, and Catholics through but one agency—the Ku Klux Klan."[3] Like the Maine Klan, the KKK of New Hampshire saw ethnic Catholics as its primary targets. One of those targets, Franco-Americans, offered through their press an eloquent resistance to the Ku Klux Klan that highlighted the secret society's inherent contradictions, contradictions that contributed to its eventual demise.

As a Klan organizer, Mason recruited in Concord, the state capital, where he also approached Republican lawmakers to join his organization in January 1923. He likely was the unnamed organizer who created a buzz in the press that month by making himself visible in the hallways and lobbies of the State House, despite not being a registered lobbyist. In February Mason attended legislative proceedings and openly consulted with lawmakers when House members discussed a bill that would have imposed some restrictions on the Klan.[4]

Rep. George Sibley, a Democrat from Manchester, sponsored House Bill No. 185, "An Act to Prohibit Parades and Meetings of the Ku Klux Klan Except by Special Permission." The oddly worded bill contradicted itself, for it would have prevented processions, meetings, and demonstrations by the KKK or other organizations wearing masks and bedsheets, while simultaneously making exceptions for them to do so if they had the permission of "the regularly authorized Imperial Kleagles or other officials of such order." Perhaps Sibley's intention was to bring a measure of levity to the House chambers, for the *Manchester Leader and Evening Union* reported that "Rep. George L. Sibley of Manchester caused considerable amusement in the House by introducing a number of bills, one of which regulates the Ku Klux Klan, another gives a vacation to employes [*sic*] of the Manchester Traction, Light and Power company and another provides that every person shall have a minimum of eight hours sleep." Unsurprisingly, the House Judiciary Committee found Bill 185 "inexpedient to legislate." Sibley nonetheless spoke in favor of the measure on the House floor, but lawmakers accepted the committee's report and rejected it. Incidentally, Sibley also spent a half-hour on the House floor defending his bill to require eight hours of sleep;

according to the *Manchester Leader and Evening Union,* "Mr. Sibley said the great trouble with this country right now was a lack of sleep, and declared the Legislature could do better work if it went home and slept for six months." Laughing lawmakers accepted the Judiciary Committee's recommendation not to pass the legislation.[5]

Anti-masking legislation introduced in January 1923 by Rep. Alfred O. Mortenson, Democrat of Gorham, met the same end. Aimed at the Ku Klux Klan, House Bill No. 265, "An Act Prohibiting the Wearing of Masks and Disguises in Public," would have punished offenders with a fine and imprisonment. In March, the Committee on Revision of Statutes decided the measure was "inexpedient to legislate"; the House of Representatives accepted the committee's report, and its adjournment led to the indefinite postponement of the bill. Although ten states enacted anti-mask and anti-Klan legislation during the 1920s, none was in New England.[6] Mortenson's anti-Klan bill likely failed because Jackson and Mason had not established a solid Klan presence in New Hampshire.

In late 1923 Maine King Kleagle F. Eugene Farnsworth tried yet again to start a Klan organization in the Granite State after the KKK had gained a foothold in Maine. Farnsworth lectured to over five hundred men at the Grange Hall of Rochester in October 1923, speaking out against Catholics, Jews, and blacks. As in Maine, the Roman Catholic population in New Hampshire far outnumbered Jews and blacks: there were 146,646 Catholics in 1926 (about 33 percent of the state's population in 1920), compared to 2,129 Jews in that same year (less than half of 1 percent of the state's 1920 population), and 621 blacks (0.1 percent of the total population) as of 1920. Farnsworth's audience included businessmen, professionals, and city council members as well as police and fire personnel. As he tried to make inroads in New Hampshire, *L'Avenir National,* the French-language newspaper of Manchester, offered a crisp commentary of Farnsworth's actions. When the newspaper learned that Farnsworth planned to return to Rochester to give a talk on Americanism and the KKK, it said that, given the organization's public pronouncements, "la conférence projetée de M. Farnsworth devrait plutôt s'intituler l'anti-Américanisme et le Ku Klux Klan" (Mr. Farnsworth's planned lecture should instead be titled anti-Americanism and the Ku Klux Klan).[7]

In mid-November Farnsworth spoke to a gathering of five hundred to eight hundred women and men at the Odd Fellows Hall in Rochester. The admission tickets distributed by a local physician, Leon G. Verrill, described Farnsworth as "The Old Man, the Most Loved and Most Feared Man in New England." Such words garnered press attention as well as the curiosity and interest of potential new members. Farnsworth and his supporters likely drew the appellation of Old Man from D. C. Stephenson, the powerful Grand Dragon of the Klan realm of Indiana, who fashioned himself in those terms. As he had done in Maine, Farnsworth promoted public education over parochial schools in New Hampshire, and he expressed the Klan's desire to prevent Catholics from teaching in public schools or from serving on public school boards.[8]

Back in Rochester in early December 1923, Farnsworth spoke to 250 women at the Odd Fellows Hall about the town's upcoming elections. "The Ku Klux Klan is not a political organization, but we vote. We get in our dirty work at the polls," Farnsworth stated unashamedly. He went on to implore the women, "I want you ladies to get into harness and elect all Protestant officials. . . . Don't vote for a Jesuit. Vote for clean 100 per cent. men." These words belied Farnsworth's comment, made at the same event, that "we have no hatred in our hearts. We are not anti-Catholic." The Catholics who made up approximately one-third of New Hampshire's population in the 1920s must surely have recognized the hypocrisy and the contradictions inherent in such pronouncements by one of the leaders of the Ku Klux Klan.[9]

Catholic electoral support had helped Frederic E. Small to unseat his Republican opponent, a seven-term incumbent, in the Rochester mayoral contest in December 1922. When Mayor Small twice turned down the Klan's request to allow Farnsworth to give lectures at the city opera house, the KKK mobilized to ensure his defeat. The Klan also worked to prevent the election of Catholics, reported *Le Courier de Lawrence,* the French-language newspaper of Lawrence, Massachusetts. Democrats renominated Small for the mayoralty in November 1923, but his Klan-backed Republican opponent defeated him in the general election in December. In fact, the Klan supported all the Republican candidates in Rochester's municipal elections, and Republicans won all but one seat—the school board seat that the Franco-American Gustave Lanoix secured with a nineteen-vote margin.[10] Overlooking the one loss and gloating about Small's defeat, the *Maine Klansman* proclaimed, "Rochester now has an all-American city government." Stephen H. Goetz gives the Klan little credit for the election results, however. Republicans dominated Rochester politics, he explains, and Small's loss of the mayoralty represented primarily a return to Republican control.[11]

In contrast to Rochester, Portsmouth had a larger population and greater financial resources, and in early 1924 Farnsworth redirected some of his organizing efforts toward that city. But newspaper accounts reveal that he was not warmly received and drew little applause. Although at least six hundred people attended the Klan meeting in January, some of them from nearby Kittery, Maine, they occupied only about one-third of the available space at Freeman Hall. The *Maine Klansman* misinformed its readers by claiming that the hall had been filled to capacity and that Farnsworth had delivered "one of his stirring Protestant American lectures."[12]

Apparently one Portsmouth KKK member was so inspired by the spirit of Protestant Americanism that he wrote the following poem:

> *There's no land like America*
> *And none more grand or free,*
> *No freedom like American,*
> *In lands beyond the sea.*
>
> *Who ever becomes an American,*
> *No matter from what sod,*
> *Are guaranteed full liberty,*
> *In the way they worship God.*
>
> *This is the spirit we would impart,*
> *To each free born woman or man,*
> FREE FLAG, FREE SCHOOLS, FREE WORD OF GOD
> *Are the watchwords of our Klan.*[13]

Ironically, while the Klansman's poem extolled religious liberty, the organization to which he belonged discriminated against New Hampshire Catholics and Jews, underscoring the wide gap between the Klan's words and its deeds.

In addition to Portsmouth, Farnsworth held organizational meetings in Farmington, Somersworth, and Concord in January 1924 in an effort to expand Klanhood in the Granite State. In Concord he told an audience of seven hundred to eight hundred people that "America was built upon the foundations laid out by the Protestant Bible," and he asserted further, "The Ku Klux Klan intends that this country shall be continued in the control of Protestant mentality." Farnsworth discussed immigration history with his audience, telling members it could be divided into two periods. Without specifying time frames, he indicated that during the first period Protestants from northern Europe emigrated to the United States and during the second period individuals emigrated from southern Europe, resulting in "the dumping of millions of illiterates onto our shores who have found their way into our jails, and our prisons, our institutions for the helpless." Reflecting the Klan's vision of a white, Protestant polity, Farnsworth contended that Catholics, Jews, and Negroes could never be assimilated into American life, the Catholics because they could not exercise independent judgment, the Jews because they did not accept Christianity, and the Negroes because races cannot be mixed.[14]

When Farnsworth stumped again in Rochester in late January 1924 there was a Republican mayor in office, and he secured permission to speak at the city opera house, the very site that former mayor Small had not allowed the Klan to use for its meetings. Farnsworth and another Klan speaker argued that the constitutional principles of free speech and free assembly had returned to the opera house that evening. Farnsworth seized the occasion to speak out against immigrants. Perhaps without realizing the contradictions in his speech, Farnsworth advocated immigration restrictions while championing the admission of Anglo-Saxons to the United States; in making the veiled threat that "every hyphenated American or politician will be set out on the sidewalk," he probably did not consider the hyphenation implicit in his promotion of Anglo-Saxonry.[15] Klan leaders like Farnsworth unwittingly laid open the hypocrisy of their organization.

They also made it plausible for crimes to be attributed to the hooded empire. Late one Saturday evening in February 1924 Moses Goldberg, a merchant, was beaten and strangled at his clothing store in Concord. Born in Russia, Goldberg had lived for thirty years in Concord and had been active in the city's Jewish community. The *Concord Daily Monitor and New Hampshire Patriot* reported that Goldberg's demise represented "a distinct community loss" and noted that he had had friends "of his own race and many of other nationalities." After Goldberg's murder, the editor of the *Concord Daily Monitor*, a city marshal, and Goldberg's wife each received a short letter written in the same handwriting and signed "Ku Klux Klan." The letter sent to the editor and the marshal both indicated that a Jew had been "eliminated," and they threatened, "We'll get more." The one sent to Goldberg's wife contained the ominous message, "We got your husband. Look out." The police were uncertain whether the letter writer may simply have been trying to frame the KKK. In defending Goldberg's Americanism, most likely from the KKK's version, the *Concord Daily Monitor* observed that "he mastered the English tongue quickly so far as its meaning went[,] though he never learned to pronounce its words without an accent." The newspaper emphasized that Goldberg was an American who had helped Jewish and other immigrants in Concord: "To him they looked for instruction in American ways."[16] Whether or not the Ku Klux Klan was responsible for Goldberg's murder, the secret society created a climate in New Hampshire that made it possible to implicate it.

A few weeks after Goldberg's death, anti-Klan leaders met at the Rochester opera house to denounce the organization. Chaired by the former mayor Small, the speaker's platform included Rev. Stoddard Lane, pastor of the First Congregational Church of Manchester, as well as local and state politicians. Speaking to an audience of about twelve hundred people, Small contended that the KKK went against the teachings of Jesus Christ. As the keynote speaker, Lane pointed out that Christ, a Jew, would not have been admit-

ted to the Ku Klux Klan. He characterized the KKK as "un-Christian" and
maintained that the hooded empire was "a menace to our unity as a nation
and our membership in the Kingdom of God." Lane insisted the Klan "must
be repudiated by all men who call themselves Americans and Christians."[17]

On the evening following the anti-Klan meeting, the KKK gathered again
at the Rochester opera house, and leaders from Indiana and Ohio lectured at
the event. Arriving in New Hampshire after engagements in Maine, William
H. Kline of Ohio spoke out against racial intermarriage, Roman Catholic
convents, and Jews. In complaining about immigrants, Kline specifically
pointed out that large numbers of Mexicans and Canadians had entered the
United States illegally. Few Mexicans lived in New Hampshire during that
period, but Canadians constituted 57.2 percent of the state's foreign-born
population in 1920, and French-speaking Canadians made up 41.9 percent of
the Granite State's immigrant population.[18]

French-Canadian descendants were present in sufficient numbers to support two French-language newspapers, *L'Impartial* of Nashua and *L'Avenir
National* of Manchester. These newspapers occasionally reported on national
and local Klan activities, interpreting them for their readership. When Imperial Wizard William J. Simmons told an audience in Oklahoma that New
England's French-Canadian population illustrated the problem of immigration because it spoke French, supported parochial schools, and reproduced
in large numbers, the two newspapers translated his remarks and offered
some commentary. *L'Impartial* gave a brief history of the KKK and told its
readers about the various groups the society targeted, mentioning that even
naturalized immigrants could be subjected to the hooded empire's hostility. *L'Avenir National* offered a spirited rebuttal of the Imperial Wizard's
comments. It pointed out that Catholic soldiers from France had assisted
George Washington in securing the independence of the United States from
Great Britain, and it underscored the message that these French Catholics
had not constituted a danger to the fledgling country. "Aujourd'hui les
Français établis en Nouvelle-Angleterre ne sont pas plus un danger," (Today
the French established in New England are not any more of a danger,) the
newspaper insisted. "Ils ne croient pas être des étrangers en ce pays; ils sont
aussi Américains que les membres du Klan et ils n'échangeraient pas leur
américanisme, qui est fait de respect pour la loi et l'ordre et les institutions
du pays, contre celui du Klan, qui fait appel aux passions, aux préjugés
et au fanatisme" (They do not believe [themselves] to be strangers in this
country; they are as American as the members of the Klan and they do not
swap their Americanism, which is created from respect for law and order and
the country's institutions, for that of the Klan, which appeals to passions,
prejudices and fanaticism). Turning the sarcastic comment about the healthy

birthrates of Franco-Americans back on the Klan, *L'Avenir National* wrote, "Leur multiplication est la meilleure preuve qu'ils contribuent à la grandeur et la prospérité du pays, ce dont leurs détracteurs ne peuvent se prévaloir, heureusement" (Their multiplication is the best proof that they contribute to the greatness and prosperity of the country, of which their detractors cannot pride themselves, fortunately).[19] Through their own press, the Franco-Americans of New Hampshire defended themselves against the ideology of the Ku Klux Klan: they fought its prejudices and uncovered its contradictions.

The sources do not reveal what role, if any, New Hampshire's Franco-American bishop played in combating the KKK in the 1920s. George A. Guertin was born in Nashua of French-Canadian parents and had served as the pastor of a Franco-American parish in Manchester prior to his elevation in 1907 to the bishopric, a position he held until his death in 1931. Most records of Guertin's tenure as bishop of Manchester have not survived.[20] For their part, the French-language newspapers of New Hampshire offered no commentary on the possible role of Guertin in working against the Klan in his home state.

Having a Franco-American at the helm of New Hampshire's Roman Catholic Church who was unlike the assimilationist Irish bishop Maine had did not result in a push to anglicize or to Americanize the Franco-American parishes of the Granite State at a faster rate than they preferred. In fact, the Americanization movement in New Hampshire appeared not to have been as strong as it was in Maine. Nonetheless, like Maine, New Hampshire passed legislation in 1919 to promote the Americanization of immigrants. Although not identifying French-Canadian immigrants by name, House Bill No. 262, "An Act in Amendment of the Laws Relating to the Public Schools and Establishing a State Board of Education," singled out the French-Canadian population centers of Nashua and Manchester as examples of cities with large foreign-born populations that could not read, speak, or write English. Bishop Guertin intervened on behalf of the state's French speakers and reached an agreement with the chair of the Governor's Advisory Committee on Education by which the wording of the legislation preserved the teaching of French in New Hampshire's elementary schools. As enacted, the legislation did not "prohibit the conduct of devotional exercises in private schools in a language other than English." In addition the law stated, "A foreign language may be taught in elementary schools *provided* the course of study (or its equivalent) outlined by the state board of education in the common English branches, that is, in reading, writing, spelling, arithmetic, grammar, geography, physiology, history, civil government, music and drawing, be not abridged but be taught in compliance with the law of the state." The French Catholic schools complied with the legislation by instituting bilingual instruction for their students, teaching religion classes and the history of Canada in French and all other courses in English.[21] This arrangement possibly mitigated the Klan's confrontations with the Franco-American communities of New Hampshire, unlike what happened in Maine.

After Farnsworth was ousted as the head of Maine's Klan, the New Hampshire Klan also lost the skills of this organizer; as we will see, despite some gains under new leadership, the Granite State Klan began to lose momentum and subsequently declined. E. L. Gayer of Indiana, the new King Kleagle, established the Maine–New Hampshire–Vermont Klan headquarters in Rochester. Through the efforts of George J. Barber, a chiropractor in Rochester whom a Boston newspaper identified as "the most important Klansman of the city," the KKK purchased in early 1924 a twenty-room colonial-style mansion as a base for its northern New England operations.[22] In June an estimated ten thousand Klan members from Maine, New Hampshire, and Vermont gathered at a farm in the town of Farmington, outside of Rochester, to celebrate the merging of the Klan realms under Gayer's leadership. During the festivities a national Klan speaker delighted his audience by proposing the creation of a new Klan order to be called "Who's Through in America" for such anti-Klan politicians as the former mayor of Rochester Fred Small, the mayor of Boston, James Curley, and Gov. "Alcohol" Smith of New York.[23]

Such events increased the KKK's visibility in the Granite State and surely made credible the allegation of Nelson B. Burrows in July 1924 that the Ku Klux Klan had abducted him in Dover and subsequently branded him with the letters *KKK*. Burrows believed that his conversion to Catholicism upon remarriage, and his work in founding a Knights of Columbus council at Rochester, where he served as Grand Knight, had motivated the Klan's actions. The police officers who interviewed him found his account to be a "very plausible story." Klan leaders denied, however, any involvement in Burrows's kidnapping and branding. Under intense questioning by law enforcement officials Burrows later confessed he had branded himself and had fabricated the tale of his abduction. Vindicated by Burrows's confession, the Klan from its Rochester headquarters issued a public statement that asserted, in part: "We want the public to know that we stand four square for law and order, for everything that is in the best interests of communities and this great nation and that we will always, as we have done in this case, exert every effort and use every resource of this organization in our attempt to see that justice prevails and that every man shall have the right to worship God according to the dictates of his conscience."[24] In the Granite State such assertions must have given little consolation to the Catholic and Jewish populations, the very people often singled out by Klan officials in their polemical speeches. As we will see in the next chapter, the actions of Rochester-based

Klan leaders contradicted their own words when they helped a Klan law-breaker flee from Vermont authorities.

As the result of its activities and rhetoric, the KKK engendered some opposition at the state level in New Hampshire. When Democrats held their convention at Concord in September 1924, they chose to denounce the KKK by name, unlike their counterparts in Maine. In doing so, the Democrats acknowledged that they were following the lead of their presidential nominee, John W. Davis. The platform's anti-Klan resolution stated, "If any organization, no matter whether called the Ku Klux Klan or any other name, raises the standard of racial or religious prejudice or attempts to make racial origins or religious beliefs the test of fitness for public office, it does violence to the spirit of American institutions and must be condemned by all those who believe in American ideals."[25]

The KKK also met some local opposition, and tensions periodically flared up between the hooded society and groups that contested it. When the body of James Travis, an anti-Klan activist and past Grand Knight of the Whitefield Council Knights of Columbus, was found weighted down by logs in a pond, County Solicitor M. J. Ryan was required to investigate rumors that the Klan was responsible. Travis, along with other unidentified individuals, had allegedly knocked down a burning cross on the evening of Columbus Day 1924. After speaking with some of Whitefield's residents, the county solicitor determined that the Klan was not responsible for Travis's death. Nonetheless, the *Boston Herald* reported rumors that Klan and anti-Klan groups planned to clash in Whitefield, but the violence never materialized.[26]

Eager to prevent possible clashes, other New Hampshire municipalities took it upon themselves to place restrictions on the Ku Klux Klan, because the New Hampshire state legislature had proved unwilling to enact anti-Klan legislation. Citing a desire to preserve the peace, the mayor of Concord, Willis H. Flint, denied the Klan permission to parade in the city in 1924, and he asked the police chief to arrest any individuals who attempted to march in regalia. Two years later, Fred N. Marden, the subsequent mayor of the city, relaxed this stricture by agreeing to let the Klan parade in the community, but he turned down the society's request to wear masks during its procession. Although the Portsmouth City Council issued the KKK a permit to parade on Independence Day in 1927, the council reversed itself the next day.[27] The Klan did not have free rein in the Granite State.

This resulted, in part, because the New Hampshire Klan never achieved the size or the strength of its counterpart in Maine. According to figures from the *Washington Post*, the New Hampshire Klan admitted a total of seventy-five thousand members from its founding to the year 1925—half of what the Maine KKK had admitted by that point. If the experiences the Klan had in Manchester and Keene are any indication, it had difficulty organizing in the Granite State. In March 1924, when KKK recruiters visited Manchester, a city with a large Franco-American Catholic population, the *Manchester Leader and Evening Union* reported there was little interest in the organization, and it noted, "There is little talk on the streets and no open drive for members." In late April the newspaper reported that KKK organizational meetings had attracted few people and that Klan organizers had departed for other venues. A lack of interest in Klanhood in Keene led to the cancellation of a planned August 1924 parade in the city.[28] Because of its smaller size and difficulty in organizing, the Granite State Klan did not achieve the social or political results of the Maine Klan, and it did not confront Franco-American and other Catholics in New Hampshire in the same ways that it did in the Pine Tree State.

As in Maine, the Klan struggled financially in New Hampshire. In March 1925 the Klan staved off until May a public auction of its estate only when several Portsmouth Klansmen stepped forward with sufficient cash and signed notes to cover the balance of mortgage instruments held by the former owner and the Rochester Trust Company. In May Klansmen in Portsmouth had to come up with another large cash payment to halt the postponed sale of the headquarters. Probably seeing he had no future in the financially troubled New Hampshire Klan, Gayer left the Granite State in August 1925 to resume the practice of medicine in his native state of Indiana, home to one of the largest and most politically powerful Klan organizations in the country. A year after his departure, when the Klan again faced difficulty in making its mortgage payments, it lost its estate through foreclosure proceedings.[29]

The New Hampshire Klan declined precipitously from the mid to late 1920s. In 1926, according to the *Washington Post,* the Granite State Klan had only 2,101 members in good standing, and that figure fell to a mere 95 in 1928. Membership rose to 296 in 1929 but dropped again, to 124, in 1930. Judging by brief reports in national Klan publications, at least two New Hampshire Klan organizations, the Androscoggin Klan No. 4 from the state's White Mountain region and Johns River Klan No. 7 of Whitefield, survived at least into the 1930s.[30]

Despite its decline, the New Hampshire Klan continued to make its presence felt. In November 1925, it burned a thirty-five-foot cross in Keene, and in February 1926 a ten-foot cross at a park in Nashua, reportedly the first time the organization had burned a cross in that community. Around 8:00 p.m. on St. Patrick's Day in 1926 a dynamite bomb exploded in Milford, and terrified residents witnessed a fiery cross. The following month the Klan set off dynamite at the base of the fifteen-foot cross it had erected in East Wilton.[31] Like the frenzied conclusion of a fireworks display, the series of fiery crosses and dynamite bombs the KKK ignited in that two-year period represented not the regeneration of the New Hampshire Klan but rather its grand finale.

While the New Hampshire Klan might be dismissed as having had "only a superficial significance," as Stephen Goetz argues, it did serve to perpetuate discrimination against Jews in the Granite State and especially Catholics, including the large Franco-American population.[32] Judging from the reports of French-language newspapers, Granite State Franco-Americans recognized and publicized the Klan's inherent contradictions, contradictions that ultimately led to the organization's collapse as a social movement not only in New Hampshire but also throughout the United States.

5

Rebuff in the Green Mountain State

THE Ku Klux Klan created a stir in and beyond Vermont in 1922 by recruiting students from Norwich University, a military college in Northfield. In December the *Montpelier Evening Argus* reported that an unspecified number of cadets who attended a meeting of the Political Science Club acknowledged that they had joined the secret society. Astounded that the Klan had infiltrated the school, the *Boston Daily Advertiser* in February 1923 stated, "The fact that the Ku Klux Klan has burrowed so deeply into Norwich University is already a national scandal." The *Advertiser* elaborated: "As one of the institutions from which the government may draw trained officers in time of war, Norwich is almost a part of the War Department."[1]

From the Ku Klux Klan's formation in Vermont until 1925 it admitted 80,301 members, according to the *Washington Post*. That figure slightly exceeded the New Hampshire Klan's numbers and represented a little more than half of Maine's.[2] To understand the social and intellectual climate of Vermont in the 1920s that made possible this significant rise of the Klan in the Green Mountain State, one need only to recall that U.S. senator William Paul Dillingham of Vermont led national efforts to impose stricter immigration laws in the 1920s, and President Calvin Coolidge, a native son of the state, signed the discriminatory National Origins Act of 1924 to limit immigration. In addition, the University of Vermont zoologist Harry F. Perkins organized the Eugenics Survey of Vermont, the results of which recommended social reforms, including a sterilization law so that only the fittest Vermonters would procreate. Like the Ku Klux Klan movement that preceded it, the Vermont eugenics movement targeted French Canadians, the state's largest immigrant population, for Yankees saw them as an inferior group.[3]

"The 'hard-shell Yankees,' who are the larger part of the population, are inclined to favor the Klan and its mission, while the Irish and French

Catholics are bitterly opposed to it," reported the *Boston Daily Advertiser,* underscoring the ethnic tensions that existed when the Ku Klux Klan established itself in Burlington in 1923. The KKK worked to bolster prohibition in Vermont. In September 1924, for example, E. L. Rash, a Klan organizer, testified at the Burlington Municipal Court that he had given the deputy sheriff information that led to the seizure of liquor in the Agel family rum-running case, a case in which Max Agel was found guilty of possessing illegal alcohol and sentenced to prison. In Vermont, as across the country, the Ku Klux Klan also engaged in extralegal tactics to enforce prohibition because its enforcement was not adequately funded and, importantly, because of the Klan's nativism. The KKK, for instance, allegedly sent a threatening letter to the French-surnamed E. LaFrance, owner of the LaFrance Hotel in Burlington, warning him that bootleggers (ostensibly affiliated with his hotel) had to leave the city.[4]

In 1920 French Canadians constituted close to one-third (31.8 percent) of Vermont's foreign-born population, followed by Anglo-Canadians (24.0 percent), Italians (9.1 percent), and the Irish (6.5 percent.) As was true in Maine and New Hampshire, the Ku Klux Klan in Vermont had Catholics, particularly Franco-Americans, as its primary target. But to a much greater degree than in the other two states, the concerted opposition of the press and local communities in Vermont made much of the Green Mountain State inhospitable terrain for the hooded order and served to rebuff its efforts to get rooted there.[5]

During the 1920s Klan orators often emphasized that they did not oppose Catholics or other groups, even Jews and blacks. "That same statement has been made to me over and over again," noted Roy L. Emery, a native of Randolph, Vermont, who wrote to the editor of the *Bethel Courier* from Pence, Indiana, where he had made his home for the previous seven months. Emery indicated in his letter, published in June 1924, that he had friends who were KKK members and that he had attended a public meeting of the Klan "out of curiosity" in December. "Regardless of what they say," he emphasized, "their feeling against the Catholic, the Jew, and the Negro, is very strong indeed." In 1926 Vermont Catholics numbered 89,424 (about 25 percent of the state's population in 1920), while there were 1,433 Jews (less than half of 1 percent of the state's 1920 population), and 572 blacks (0.2 percent of the total population) in 1920. Based on his observations in Indiana, Emery contended that Vermont would be better off without the Ku Klux Klan.[6]

Later in the year the editor of the *Bethel Courier* argued that "the Klan has an animus rather than an aim; that it is founded upon prejudice; that it fosters bigotry and intolerance in religion; that it seeks to proscribe those to whom the federal constitution guarantees equal rights regardless of race or religion." The brunt of the Klan's energies, the editor stated unequivocally, was directed against the Catholic population: "In this part of the country—Vermont in particular—the K.K.K. has only one strong appeal to prejudice, and that is the disfavor in which the Roman Catholic church, priesthood and people are held by a portion of the non-Catholics."[7]

That anti-Catholic sentiment found expression in Vermont, as elsewhere in the United States, in the post-World War I Americanization movement, of which the Ku Klux Klan was part. Like other New England states, at the conclusion of the world conflict, Vermont tried to pass legislation mandating English as the sole language of instruction in schools. But unlike Maine and New Hampshire, Vermont failed in this endeavor. The legislature's two unsuccessful attempts at enacting English-only laws prior to the arrival of the Ku Klux Klan foreshadowed the opposition the hooded order would encounter as well as its eventual demise in the Green Mountain State.

In March 1919 the Vermont state senator Henry L. Ballou, a Republican and a former minister of the Congregational Church of Chester, introduced S. 84, "An act requiring the exclusive use of the English language in schools." The Vermont Senate approved the measure after its third reading. When the Vermont House of Representatives debated S. 84, Rep. Harry W. Witters, a Democrat from St. Johnsbury, mindful of Vermont's sizable Franco-American population, offered an amendment to allow "the combined use of French and English in the instruction of children" in schools that did not receive state funding. His colleague Benjamin Williams, a Republican from Proctor, suggested replacing the word *French* with the phrase *any foreign language,* an idea the House accepted before sending the bill back to the Committee on Education. The committee rejected Witters's amendment and proposed instead to modify S. 84 by exempting "a private school whose course of study in English complies substantially with that prescribed by the state board of education," and the full House then accepted the committee's report. The Senate rejected the House amendment, however, and when a conference committee could not reach a compromise between the two versions of the bill the measure died.[8]

Undeterred, Ballou in February 1921, then representing Chester in the House of Representatives, introduced H. 243, "An act to promote Americanism in schools." While the bill stated explicitly that "the English language shall be used exclusively in the instruction of children . . . in all public or private schools in the state," it had provisions allowing the teaching of foreign languages and the saying of prayers in languages other than English.[9] The measure aroused considerable opposition.

The Sisters of Providence who taught in Winooski recorded in their chronicle the concerns of the parish community and of the nuns to the proposed legislation, which they viewed as an attack on their language and, consequently, their faith: "Une résolution qui a soulevé nos bons paroissiens et qui est pour nous d'un intérêt douloureux, vient d'être soumise devant nos gouvernants. On voudrait abolir l'enseignement de la langue maternelle dans les écoles primaires, mais, ce qu'on vise à travers l'école, c'est l'Eglise: la langue et la foi sont intimement liées" (A resolution that has stirred up our good parishioners and which is for us of distressing interest has just been submitted before our government. They would like to abolish instruction in the mother tongue in the primary schools, but, what we aim at through the [parish] school, it's the Church: the language and the faith are intimately tied). The Sisters thus expressed the connection between language and faith that French Canadians considered inseparable. The Sisters, in fact, were not averse to English-language instruction. In 1917 they had modified their curriculum to introduce one hour of English in grade two and to increase the amount of English-language instruction they offered from one hour to half a day in grades three and four. While not specifying whether the change in 1917 was motivated by internal or external pressures, the Sisters commented, "Les enfants se familiariseront plus jeunes avec la langue anglaise, et cela, espérons-le, sans nuire au français" (The children will acquaint themselves at a younger age with the English language, and that, we shall hope, without prejudicing the French).[10] Like the Franco-American community they served, the Sisters of Providence promoted bilingualism but not the elimination of the French language.

The Sisters also noted in their chronicle the opposition of Franco-Americans and members of the Jewish community to the 1921 legislation. The Sisters' notations imply that the Franco-American Catholics and Jews of Vermont set aside their religious differences to join forces against the language bill: "Une forte opposition vint des représentants des Canadiens-français. Les Juifs ont aussi bien défendu la langue d'Abraham, d'Isaac et de Jacob" (A strong opposition came from some of the representatives of the French Canadians. The Jews have also defended well the language of Abraham, Isaac, and Jacob). Franco-American leaders appeared before the Committee on Education of the Vermont House of Representatives to testify against H. 243, contending that they could maintain their French language and still be loyal U.S. citizens.[11] Joseph Cauchon, a mill worker from Winooski, stated unequivocally, "We want to continue to teach the language of our people in our schools, while continuing [to be] loyal to our chosen country." To illustrate the Americanism of French-Canadian immigrants in Vermont, J. B. E. Chevrier, who operated a shoe store out of his home, told the committee that he had helped prepare 850 men to become naturalized U.S. citizens during the twenty-five years he had lived in Winooski. As early as 1913 Chevrier had served as president of a statewide Franco-American organization that promoted naturalization, and in 1921 he was serving as an officer in several Franco-American organizations, including the Saint-Jean-Baptiste Society, Club Canadien, and Les Artisans Canadiens. Other Franco-Americans from Winooski, St. Johnsbury, and Montpelier also spoke against the proposed legislation, as did a representative of the Hebrew Free School of Burlington, who stressed the value of children being schooled in their mother tongue and who remarked on problems they would have in communicating with their own parents if they lacked such training. Rep. Learned R. Noble, a Republican from West Rutland, captured the sentiments of H. 243's opponents, the *Burlington Daily Free Press* reported, when he stated, "The English language comes from the French. Why even the name 'Vermont,' is French and 'Montpelier,' too. Then why should we prohibit the teaching of French in the State[?] I don't think we need this bill."[12]

The Roman Catholic bishop Joseph J. Rice, a supporter of bilingualism, also opposed H. 243. Rice communicated in a letter to the state senator Ira Lafleur that the bill did not advance education and was not in fact rooted in patriotism. In 1919 Rice had written to Lafleur to oppose the pending English-language legislation of that year, arguing that the measure targeted Franco-Americans, an ethnic group he considered loyal and patriotic residents of Vermont. Rice had studied theology and canon law at the Grand Séminaire in Montréal, had served in French-speaking parishes in Massachusetts, and had even joined the mutual-aid association Société des Artisans canadiens français prior to becoming the bishop of Burlington. His ties with French speakers undoubtedly encouraged him to endorse the education of children in their mother tongue. When, in February 1921, Rev. L. Albert Vezina of Sacred Heart of Mary Parish in Rutland wrote to Rice that increasing numbers of parishioners, particularly those under the age of twenty-one, did not understand French, he asked Rice's permission to introduce English into the Masses he preached. Rice apparently waited several months after the defeat of the English-language bill by state lawmakers before responding to Vezina's request. Rice granted Vezina permission to introduce English in the Masses but made it clear he wanted Vezina, a Québec-born and ordained priest, to work toward helping the parish community to preserve its French-language skills, even stipulating that the French sermon had to precede the English sermon, the English sermon "must never exceed in duration the French sermon," and the Gospel as well as announcements could be read in English so long as the French version came first. Rice continued beyond the 1920s to promote French-language use in other Franco-American parishes that sought to introduce English into the Mass.[13] Given his advocacy of the use of the French language in Vermont's Franco-American parishes, it is unsurprising that he would oppose legislation requiring English as the language of instruction in the state's schools, especially the Catholic parochial schools.

While the Sisters of Providence recorded in their chronicle that the initial results of the opposition to the English-language legislation had been favorable, as of February 20, 1921 they expressed their concern that "chaque session est une menace" (each session is a threat). Subsequent events validated their concerns. On March 7 the House Committee on Education reported out H. 372, a substitute bill for H. 243. The measure specified that most courses would have to be taught in English, among them "citizenship, reading, writing, spelling, English grammar, geography, arithmetic, free hand drawing, the history and constitution of the United States, elementary physiology and hygiene, . . . special instruction in the geography, history, constitution and principles of government of Vermont, and such other subjects including manual training and domestic science." When bill H. 372 reached the floor of the House, Representative Ballou argued in favor of the legislation by pointing out that large numbers of men drafted during the recent world conflict had not been able to read or write English. Likely persuaded by the Franco-American opponents of the English-language legislation, Rep. Henry Chase, a Republican from Bennington, reasoned that the bill amounted to an attack on the French-language parochial schools of Vermont and that the legislation was unnecessary, because those schools taught American principles. The House closed debate on H. 372 after its second reading and on March 8 overwhelmingly defeated a motion to reconsider its decision not to allow a third reading of the bill.[14] The strong resistance of Franco-Americans, of their Roman Catholic bishop, and of members of the Jewish community all contributed to the bill's defeat, making Vermont one of only two New England states (Massachusetts was the other one) that did not require elementary or high school instruction to be conducted in English.

It was no coincidence that a Protestant minister sponsored the aforementioned English-language bills in Vermont and that some Protestant clergy backed the Ku Klux Klan in the Green Mountain State, for these ministers stood with the KKK in its opposition to the Catholic Church and its diverse ethnic membership. All across the country, the Klan worked through Protestant clergy to become a mass movement in the 1920s. Rev. E. E. Robbins, the pastor of the First Congregational Church of Rochester, Vermont, commented on the Klan's appeal to Protestant ministers in October 1923 by noting, "They often fill a church where before there was but a handful in attendance." Robbins sermonized in favor of the KKK, asserting, "The Klan stands for one hundred per cent Americanism; it stands for the sacredness and the purity of the home; it stands for the maintenance of our public schools and the Bible in the same; it stands for the Protestant Church and the Protestant religion. Is there any organization," he questioned, that "can stand for higher or better things?"[15]

When the KKK held its first public meeting in Vermont in May 1924, Robbins gave the opening prayer to the five hundred people who gathered at the Springfield town hall to hear the Klan speaker A. O. Henry of Akron, Ohio. Henry told the audience that the Klan "movement is not a movement of hatred, of animosity and strife, but of love and belief in the Golden Rule. But," the Klan spokesperson emphasized, "this is a Protestant movement."[16]

The obstructionism of the Klan and Protestants in the Green Mountain State occasionally made it difficult for the Catholic Church to expand its institutions to meet the needs of its growing membership in different communities. In Barre, where the Klan reportedly sold memberships on an installment basis ("$1 down and the rest when they catch you"), the KKK worked to block the sale of a school on Summer Street to the Roman Catholic Church. The Diocese of Burlington owned property near the structure and wanted to open a parochial school in the village. At a special meeting in July 1925 the townspeople voted by a slim majority to sell the property to the diocese. But the board of aldermen subsequently received a petition to reconsider that decision and it agreed to do so. "I understand that the [Protestant] churches and the K.K.K. are behind the movement," wrote Rev. Patrick M. McKenna to Bishop Rice. "Excitement is running pretty high, and I would not be surprised if the second meeting would vote not to sell," he informed the bishop. Rice decided to withdraw the purchase offer to avoid "any ill feeling among the citizens of Barre." But in order to circumvent anti-Catholic sentiment in the community, the Catholic Church acquired the property through a conduit: Joseph B. Sanguinetti, a granite manufacturer, purchased the school property in February 1927 and two days later conveyed the deed to the Roman Catholic Diocese of Burlington. As a result of this purchase St. Monica Parish opened its parochial school in the former public school building in 1927.[17]

Barre was not the only Vermont community where Catholics experienced tension due to the Klan's presence. After Rev. W. P. Crosby visited the community of Marshfield he wrote the bishop, "I find that since I was there last that the Ku Kluxers have been going strong there and I do not know what we can do about a place to say mass. I am afraid that the best we can do is to use the home of one of the families up there at least for a while." Crosby also informed the bishop that "the poor Catholics up there are scared stiff. . . . They say that practically all the non-Catholics are Kluxers and that very much bitterness is shown toward them."[18]

In nearby Montpelier, St. Augustine Catholic Church was the target of

Klan activity. Around 10:30 p.m. one Saturday in July 1924 a cross blazed at the parish cemetery, the first cross burning witnessed within the city limits. The parish publication implicated but did not blame the Ku Klux Klan. "The cross is the particular religious emblem of the Catholic church from long usage," declared the *Bethel Courier,* before proceeding to condemn the cross burning outright: "Burning it anywhere may be interpreted as an indignity aimed at that church. Burning it in a Catholic cemetery cannot be regarded as anything else."[19]

Frances Emmons Carver, a Montpelier resident, was a young girl at the time. Many years later she wrote to Governor Richard Snelling of the terror she had experienced as a ten-year-old witness to the Klan's activities in Montpelier: "My bedroom window faced the hill on which St. Agustine's [*sic*] cemetary [*sic*] rested," she stated. "One night I reached to draw the curtain before retiring and was terrorized by a massive cross in raging flames and white hooded maniacs prancing around it." Carver screamed and ran to her parents. "It was many years before the nightmares ceased; I was a Catholic and in my childish mind I relived the horror and felt sure they were coming after me," she revealed. Then she emphasized, "Fifty[-]five years have not erased the agony of that night nor its aftermath." Carver urged Governor Snelling to combat the Klan's reappearance in the Green Mountain State in the early 1980s (discussed in chapter 11).[20]

Carver told an interviewer in 1989 that the Klan was a "silent enemy." Klan members lived and did business in the community, which included Catholics and Jews, yet they engaged in anti-Catholic and anti-Jewish behavior, she pointed out. "No one knew who the enemy was," Carver asserted. Consequently, "all the Catholics and Jewish people played dumb" about the Klan during the 1920s. Like Carver, Frank Haley had little idea who the Klan members in the community were when he moved to Pownal after marrying his wife in 1924. "You could be going along and be talking with this man and even though he was your friend, he'd never let on he was a Klansman. You'd find out maybe five or six years afterwards."[21]

That level of secrecy, of course, made it difficult to arrest and convict individuals for crimes attributed to the KKK. In November 1925, nearly one and a half years after the cross burning in the cemetery of St. Augustine, another was burned on the church steps at two o'clock one morning. The following February Wesley Lewis and Harold Warren, railroad employees from Montpelier, stood trial for the incident in a courtroom packed "with interested spectators," the press reported. "The case created an awful lot of angry division in Montpelier," noted Deane C. Davis, one of the attorneys who defended the men and who many years later (1969–73) served as governor of Vermont. "It took days to get a jury, because if you found anybody who said they had no opinions one way or the other about the Ku Klux Klan, he had to be a liar or living under a haystack," Davis observed. "We finally ended up with six Catholics and six Protestants on the jury, and when the case was over we had a hung jury." According to the *Burlington Free Press and Times,* the defendants denied setting the fire but admitted to being present when crosses blazed in another section of Montpelier during the same evening that one burned on the steps of St. Augustine. "A large part of the evidence was circumstantial and some of the testimony was contradictory," explained the newspaper.[22] The jury quite likely split evenly along religious lines.

Efforts to rebuff the Klan through the political process did not meet success either. In early 1923 the state senator William A. Root, a Republican from Bennington County, introduced an anti-Klan bill to the Vermont legislature, but the measure failed to pass. S.41, "An Act Relating to the Wearing of Masks and Disguises in Public," stipulated that males over twelve years of age could not conceal themselves with masks or disguises in public places, and individuals who committed misdemeanors or felonies while masked or disguised could face the maximum penalties allowed by law. While Root's bill did not mention the KKK specifically, the *Burlington Free Press and Times* pointed out that it served to put the Klan on "official notice in the Legislature . . . that the organization was not wanted in Vermont." Because Root was the only person to appear before the General Committee to discuss the bill, the *Montpelier Evening Argus* surmised that "evidently Vermont has no K.K.K. problem." After considering amendments to allow children to wear masks at Halloween and to permit masked balls to take place, the General Committee chose not to rewrite the bill and reported it out unfavorably. The Vermont Senate subsequently rejected the bill "without comment."[23]

Two years later, in February 1925, after being presented with a petition signed by one thousand Vermont residents, most of whom were from Burlington and Winooski, the state senator Martin S. Vilas, a Republican from Chittenden County, introduced anti-Klan legislation. The measure, S.74, "An Act Requiring Secret Associations to File with the Secretary of State Their Names and a List of Their Officers and Members," could have resulted in KKK officers receiving fines and prison sentences for noncompliance or for the filing of false statements. The measure would have exempted college sororities and fraternities, "associations of a purely social nature," and labor unions. The bill died in committee. Like all the other New England states, Vermont failed to pass any anti-Klan legislation in the 1920s.[24]

Despite the Green Mountain State's failure to enact anti-Klan laws, the Ku Klux Klan did not go unchallenged, for individual towns and cities of Vermont objected to its presence in their communities. When about twenty-five men attended an organizational meeting of the KKK at the G.A.R. Hall in St. Johnsbury in May 1924, the editor of the *Caledonian-Record* wrote, "We don't know of a community in the United States that has less need of a hooded organization than St. Johnsbury." The editor continued, "The people of this town have lived in peace and harmony; have obeyed the laws pretty effectively; have shown unstinted pride in their town; [and] have worked together patriotically irrespective of religion, race, social or financial standing." Consequently, "no Klan can exist in St. Johnsbury," observed the editor. "The people are too well educated; too law abiding; too self-respecting. The Klan thrives where there is ignorance, prejudice, intolerance, bigotry." The editor then advised readers: "Don't make the Klan an issue and there will be no Klan." Rev. Ambrose C. DeLapp, the pastor of the South Congregational Church in St. Johnsbury, spoke out against the Klan at his church's weekly prayer meeting. "I cannot see my way clear to align myself with an organization that is liable to appeal to the lower instincts of prejudice[,] hatred and bigotry," he stated. "Neither do I care to give encouragement to an organization that fosters intimidation."[25]

In similar fashion the *Bellows Falls Times* editorialized against the Klan for the negative impact it would have. "Bellows Falls without the Klan is a live, prosperous contented community, made up of all kinds of persons with all kinds of creeds," stated the newspaper. "Bellows Falls with the Klan would be a community split up the middle with creed opposing creed, with all hope of future co-operation for the common good abandoned." The editor advised those who might consider joining the Klan to read the U.S. Constitution and to reject the group's "doctrines[,] which will bring us all unhappiness and perhaps ruin."[26]

As an alternative to the Ku Klux Klan, the *Caledonian-Record* encouraged readers to consider joining the Elks Club instead. "In Elkdom they will find only 100 per cent Americans and they will not find their faces hidden behind a mask," wrote the editor, challenging the Klan's patriotism as well as its secrecy. Rather, "they will find loyal, patriotic American citizens: Protestants, Catholics and Jews; Englishmen, Scotchmen, Irishmen, Italians, or men of other origins, but all naturalized Americans, all working as 100 per cent Americans should for religious and racial tolerance, for charity to women and children and brotherhood among their fellow men, and always for The American Flag."[27]

Disputing the Klan's version of patriotism, the editor of the *St. Albans Weekly Messenger* stated, "It seeks to capitalize one of the very highest and holy emotions—for that is what patriotism is—for an unworthy and unpatriotic end." Moreover, the organization sought to undermine the U.S.

Constitution, contended the editor: "Not until it is accepted that defiance of the Constitution constitutes patriotism can the Klan with honesty claim that it is patriotic."[28]

Some newspaper editors expressed their opposition to the secret society with characteristically dry New England humor. "As yet we have seen no signs of hooded activities in Waterbury," reported the *Waterbury Record*. "One of the Vermont State Hospitals for the Insane is located here. Guess we needn't worry."[29]

The press in Vermont also criticized the Klan for its clandestine ways and hinted that it was to blame for incidents for which it might not have been directly responsible. When C. R. Rice of Springfield received a letter signed "K.K.K." telling him to leave town, he confronted a Klan organizer, Thomas Chilcote of Indianapolis, Indiana, at the Springfield Klan headquarters. Chilcote denied that his outfit had sent the letter. "Criminals, blackmailers and those having private feuds follow in its [the Klan's] wake, so that the plan and insignia of the order are used for purposes of private war," the editor of the *Rutland Daily Herald* wrote. "Many outrages charged to the modern Ku Klux Klan are no doubt perpetuated by imitators, but the lawless methods of the organization are to blame for that," the editor insisted. "Institutions which work in the open have no such embarrassments."[30]

The KKK received no less criticism when it acted in the open. In September 1924, after more than two thousand Klan members from Maine, New Hampshire, and Vermont had assembled on a farm five miles north of St. Johnsbury, and stood in a circle around the American flag, the editor of the *St. Albans Daily Messenger* commented, "What a shame to prostitute the flag to such a cause." The editor elaborated: "To see the Stars and Stripes floating over a gathering called under the auspices of an organization known to be hostile to certain races and creeds to which under our Constitution are guaranteed Liberty and Equality, is enough to make any red-blooded American blush with shame and rage." Challenging the Klan's brand of Americanism, the editor held that the KKK did not serve a useful purpose and asserted, "We are one big family under the American flag. As such we must live in harmony and concord if this great nation is to survive."[31]

Reflecting local opinions in statewide venues, both Democrats and Republicans in Vermont voiced their opposition to the Ku Klux Klan when they held their state conventions in 1924. Unlike Republicans in most New England states, Vermont Republicans meeting in Rochester in late September denounced the KKK by name. Democrats, who met in Rutland several days later, followed suit by condemning the Ku Klux Klan by name in their party's platform.[32] Although the KKK had its supporters in Vermont, anti-Klan sentiment seemed to pervade much of the Green Mountain State in the

1920s. Well-touted by the state's newspapers, the intensity of the opposition to the Ku Klux Klan in Vermont appears to distinguish it from the borderland states of Maine and New Hampshire during the third decade of the twentieth century.

Local opposition to the KKK persisted throughout 1924. In October an estimated 150 Protestant men attended a Klan meeting at Mechanics Hall in Windsor. H. F. Blake of Claremont, New Hampshire, opened the meeting, and a Reverend Gilmore of Rochester, New Hampshire, took the floor to speak out against African Americans, Jews, and Catholics. "The audience was not really representative of the townspeople of Windsor," the *Vermont Journal* insisted, "and the probability is that the organization of the Ku Klux [*sic*] will be slow in growth here where there are no parochial schools and where people of all colors, races and creeds have managed to live together in a spirit of goodwill."[33]

In Rutland, after a police officer named Kenneth Preston attended a Klan meeting on his own time while out of uniform in October 1924, Commissioner of Public Safety Fred C. Roberts initially suspended him and then dismissed him from the police force. Mayor James C. Dunn told the press that Preston, a two-year veteran of the force, had erred in attending the meeting of a society that promoted prejudice: "Here we are in Rutland, a peaceful community with all nationalities working together in harmony. I deeply resent any outside agency coming in here to create prejudice and ill feeling." The editor of the *Rutland Daily Herald* was more blunt about his view of the KKK: "What the Klan wants from Rutland is merely enough silly clowns to pay their ten dollars and guarantee big commissions to organizers and Klan officers. It is a money-making scheme, first and last, with violence, intimidation, crime and blackmail as by-products. It has no place in any law-abiding community." Two days after Preston was fired, a cross allegedly erected by the KKK was burned in Rutland.[34]

In nearby East Clarendon, Klan members held an outdoor meeting on the Prescott farm in November 1924. When an unidentified individual started recording the license plates of the twenty-two vehicles parked near the gathering, a Klan member confronted the person, "and one word led to another, so that another innocent bystander presently 'took a poke' at the klansman, who sat down very suddenly and took no further interest in the proceedings," the *Rutland Daily Herald* noted wryly. The Klan dispersed when residents of Rutland encircled the Klan members and began marching toward them. Anti-Klan individuals in Rutland subsequently distributed a list of individuals they believed were members of the secret society, and they urged members of the community to boycott the establishments of the businessmen and professionals on the list. "We are going to smoke these klansmen out into the open," one antagonist stated emphatically in the press. "If they are not members of the society let them come out openly and repudiate it. Otherwise their business will feel the heavy pressure of boycott."[35]

Some municipalities took direct action against the Klan. In mid-November 1924 Rutland's board of aldermen passed an ordinance banning parades and meetings of people wearing masks and hoods on the city's streets and highways. The ordinance went into effect after the city council adopted it and Mayor James Dunn approved it. Several months later the Burlington board of aldermen adopted a similar measure, an ordinance prohibiting individuals over twenty-one years of age from wearing disguises in public.[36]

The KKK encountered some additional maneuvers to thwart them at the state level in late 1924. When the men's and women's national organizations, the Knights of the Ku Klux Klan of Georgia and the Women of the Ku Klux Klan of Arkansas, respectively, applied for charters to do business in Vermont, Secretary of State Aaron H. Grout denied their applications because they did not define precisely the nature of the businesses they wanted to conduct in the Green Mountain State. Grout determined that the applications were incomplete and did not conform to the spirit of Vermont law, and he returned them to the organizations.[37] Thus the Ku Klux Klan in 1924 met considerable resistance in Vermont, some of it at the state level but most significantly from the municipalities that rejected the group's efforts to foment division within their communities.

Opposition at the local and state levels alone did not defeat the Ku Klux Klan in the Green Mountain State. It imploded as a result of its own folly. The Klan created a disturbance that reverberated beyond the state's borders in August 1924 when it carried out the armed robbery of the Cathedral of the Immaculate Conception in Burlington. The police pursued the Klan candidates William E. McCreedy, a thirty-four-year-old wire chief at the Burlington telephone exchange, and Gordon F. Wells, a twenty-seven-year-old drug salesman, for two blocks down Pearl Street after midnight on August 8. As McCreedy and Wells, both residents of Burlington, were arrested for the break-in and burglary, the Klan organizer and Kleagle William C. Moyers fled the Green Mountain State. Within days officials arrested the twenty-four-year-old Moyers in his native Tennessee and extradited him to Vermont.[38]

After Wells's arrest, he told the attorney general that Moyers had created a story about the cathedral storing poisonous chemicals and rifles in order to get him and McCreedy to join in a raid on the church. During the subsequent trial a witness named Eugene White testified that he had been drinking whiskey with McCreedy, Wells, and Moyers on the night of the break-in, and he confirmed that Moyers had told the men that "enough ammunition, acid, gas and guns are concealed under the Cathedral Church to blow up all the Protestants in New England." White indicated that McCreedy and Wells then challenged Moyers to show them the munitions, and he agreed to do so. But White did not go with the men, and he returned to his home around 9:00 p.m., as the others proceeded to carry out their plan.[39] Through his testimony White divulged the Klan members' violation of prohibition laws as well as their premeditated plans to the trespassing that led to the church burglary.

The *Burlington Free Press and Times* blamed the Ku Klux Klan for the actions of the men. "It makes little difference whether or not the Klan was directly responsible for the desecration of the Cathedral. It is hard to understand how this thing could have happened without the propaganda which the Klan has spread in this city and vicinity," the newspaper insisted. "Certainly there was no spirit evident in Burlington before the Klan came which would have led to entering the Cathedral on any such mad pretext as Wells confessed to. If the Klan did not foster it," the *Free Press and Times* questioned, "where did it come from?" The *Hyde Park News and Citizen* also deplored the break-in: "We believe all people who believe in religious liberty and the protection of property, especially church property, hope that the severest penalty will be given the guilty ones." The newspaper expressed its hope that the punishment the Klan associates would receive would have an effect on the larger Klan organization, "putting a check on the spread of this un-American order, especially in Vermont."[40]

In November 1924 one of the Klan associates, Moyers, surprised the Chittenden County Court by pleading guilty to grand larceny. McCreedy and Wells opted instead to stand trial for stealing a crucifix, tools, vestments, and candles from the church. During the cross-examination of the state's first witness, the defense attorney asked the priest who had initially contacted the police the very question the KKK had tried to answer on the evening of the break-in: "Are there any arms or ammunition in the basement of the Church?" But the state objected, and Judge Harrie B. Chase sustained the objection. "And thus the alleged curiosity of the respondents as to what was in the basement of the Church went unsatisfied," the *Burlington Free Press and Times* noted with subtle humor.[41]

At the conclusion of the trial, the jury found McCreedy and Wells guilty of petty larceny. At their sentencing Judge Chase voiced his disagreement with the jury's verdict, claiming that the two men, like Moyers, were "guilty of grand larceny," and he sentenced them to four to six months of hard labor at the Windsor House of Correction. During Moyers's sentencing the state's attorney argued that his Klan principles had led him to undertake the forcible entry and burglary at the cathedral. Moyers's defense attorney responded, "First, it is no crime to be a member and kleagle of the Ku Klux Klan. There is no law against it," and he pleaded: "I ask [that] the court not condemn him because he is a member of the K.K.K." Nonetheless, Judge Chase sentenced Moyers to two to three years of hard labor. For reasons that went unrecorded, the outgoing Republican governor, Redfield Proctor, pardoned McCreedy and Wells in January 1925, and the new Republican governor, Franklin S. Billings, secretly pardoned Moyers in August 1925.[42] Consequently, not one of the men served his full prison term.

The burglary at Burlington's Cathedral of the Immaculate Conception and the subsequent arrests and sentencing of the KKK associates received widespread publicity and served to highlight for many—individuals both outside of and within the KKK—the corruption of the organization in the northeastern United States. When Klan members from Vermont, New Hampshire, and Maine learned that E. L. Gayer and Paul Blackburn, leaders of the northern New England realm, had hidden Moyers from authorities following the break-in at the cathedral and that the two Klan officials had refused to assist law enforcement personnel in apprehending the fugitive, they recognized that their own officers had chosen not to obey the law. Consequently, according to the *Boston Herald,* up to 38,000 rank-and-file members (out of a reported 127,000 members in Maine, 40,000 in New Hampshire, and 11,000 in Vermont) threatened to leave the hooded society for violating its own principle of supporting law and order. Vermont's citizens were aware that events taking place outside of their state similarly challenged the professed law-and-order stand of the Ku Klux Klan, such as the group's assaults on men and women in Oklahoma and the resulting civil disorder that led to the imposition of martial law by the governor of that state.[43]

Corruption within local Klan organizations also led to its decline in Vermont. A South Barre man who had been a KKK member for five years during the 1920s told an interviewer nearly half a century later that the Barre Klan lost membership after one of its own disappeared with funds he had collected from other members to purchase Klan regalia. Additionally, the men who burglarized the Burlington cathedral probably were not the only Klan associates in the state to violate the prohibition laws that the Klan purported to obey. The Ku Klux Klan's corruption and lack of respect for the law contributed to its demise in 1924–25 not only in northeastern states like Vermont but nationally as well.[44] The kidnapping and rape by the Indiana Grand Dragon D. C. Stephenson of a woman named Madge Oberholtzer, who later died either of poison she ingested to end her life or of an infection from the bite wounds that Stephenson had inflicted on her body, constituted the most sensational incident of Klan immorality in the 1920s. Well publicized in the press, examples of Klan improvidence hastened its decline in northeastern communities as well as across the nation.

Figures published in the *Washington Post* document the Klan's precipitous decline in the Green Mountain State from the mid to late 1920s. According to the *Post*, by 1926 there were only 2,982 KKK members in good standing in Vermont, and that number dropped to 140 in 1930.[45]

Even as it disintegrated the Vermont Klan made its presence felt in the state. In May 1925 about 2,500 Klanswomen and Klansmen of northern Vermont gathered at the Lamoille Valley fairgrounds, where they marched in a parade, listened to a lecture, held an initiation ceremony, burned three crosses, and set off fireworks. Businesses in the area did not rebuff them, for the *News and Citizen* reported, "The leading business houses received the visiting klansmen in a spirit of fair play, the majority of them decorating their stores for the occasion." In August 1925 members from Vermont, New Hampshire, and Massachusetts met on the Montpelier farm of E. E. Hill, and over four thousand cars were parked in the field for the evening fireworks. Thousands of Klan members from Vermont, New Hampshire, and Massachusetts gathered again at Montpelier to celebrate Independence Day on the Towne Farm in July 1927. A religious service on Sunday afternoon launched the two-day event, which included a baseball game, tug of war, an exhibition drill, a lecture, a parade of a half mile in length, and a fireworks display to cap the festivities.[46]

National Klan publications reveal that the organization continued to hold events in the Green Mountain State at least until the early 1930s. *Kourier Magazine* reported in December 1930 that Klanswomen and Klansmen from northern New Hampshire and Vermont had assembled in early November for a meeting and oyster supper served by the women in the Vermont town of Island Pond, "located on the Canadian border near the strongly Roman Catholic Providence [*sic*] of Quebec." Other Klan meetings took place in Derby, Newport, and Hartland in 1930 and 1931.[47] Derby and Newport are also located on the Canadian border that Vermont shares with Québec.

Canada shared not just the border but also its population with the Green Mountain State. When the *Burlington Free Press and Times* reported on the trial of Gordon Wells for the incident at the cathedral, it revealed without comment that he was a KKK "probationer" from Canada who had lived there for eleven years before emigrating to the United States.[48] Perhaps the newspaper missed the incongruity of the fact that this Canadian-born man wished to join a nativist organization in the United States. This is a little-known and virtually unexplored aspect of the KKK movement in the United States. As we saw in chapter 2, it was not unusual for Anglo-Canadians to support the Ku Klux Klan in the northeastern United States.

Another Vermont sympathizer with Anglo-Canadian roots, William Roderick Cameron, was a songwriter for the Klan. His work sheds additional light on Anglo-Canadians' promotion of the KKK in the United States. In a song titled "A Call to Colors: American Parody to Wearing of the Green," probably written in the early 1920s, Cameron disparages Catholic immigrants in the United States. The third stanza of his song reads in part as follows:

> *After many years of peace,*
> *Through America's unguarded gates;*
> *There came an alien element*
> *Of liars, crooks and fakes.*
> *They want to burn our Bible up,*
> *Tear down our public schools,*
> *Pull down old Glory,*
> *And give us Roman rule.*

Cameron warns that Catholic immigrants must subscribe to the principles of law and liberty enunciated in the United States Constitution or they will be returned to their native lands. In another song, called "A Klansman's Prayer," Cameron implies the mechanism by which such deportation might take place as he promotes Klanhood:

> *Why don't you be a Klansman,*
> *Loyal, just and true*
> *Standing for Law and Order*
> *As other Klansman [sic] do?*
> *Stand up for love and justice*
> *And everything that's right.*
> *They stand for Right as Jesus did*
> *That's why their robes are white.*

As the author of songs illustrating affinities with the Ku Klux Klan and its principles, Cameron was not himself a native-born U.S. citizen. Born in Canada of Scottish ancestry, he emigrated from Sherbrooke, Québec, to the United States in 1911 and became a naturalized U.S. citizen in 1917. During the 1920s Cameron made his living by selling groceries in Barre, a town known for its granite production. In the late nineteenth and early twentieth centuries, jobs in the granite quarries attracted European immigrants, some of whom brought left-wing Socialist traditions to the town. French-Canadian immigrants from Québec also found work in the quarries, often gaining their foothold in the industry as strikebreakers.[49] These French speakers surely were among the Catholic immigrants whom Cameron targeted with his songs. During the 1920s Protestant Anglo-Canadian immigrants such as Cameron supported the KKK's efforts in New England, efforts to denigrate French-Canadian and other Catholic immigrants in the region.

Anglo-Canadians may have been introduced to the Ku Klux Klan movement before emigrating to the United States. Reports in American newspapers suggest that KKK organizers in Canada hailed from various Klan realms in the United States. The Saskatchewan King Kleagle Hugh F. "Pat" Emmons, for example, had worked as an evangelist and Exalted Cyclops (klavern president) in South Bend, Indiana, before moving to Canada. After he was tried and acquitted in July 1928 for the misappropriation of Klan funds in Regina and for receiving Klan funds under false pretenses in Moose Jaw, Magistrate J. H. Heffernan situated the group's presence in Saskatchewan in the context of Canada–U.S. relations: "We have a very poor manhood when we allow this gang from the United States to come here and collect money and have the audacity to tell the people of this Province what the principles of British nationhood are," stated Heffernan. "They have had the audacity to tell us what the Union Jack stands for. Imagine a few Canadians going over to the United States and starting in on a campaign to tell the people what their flag stands for and what the Constitution of the United States means!"[50] Little did Heffernan know that Canadian immigrants in the United States—people like Cameron in Vermont—had been doing just that during the 1920s.

Their efforts may not have been unique to the Northeast. In the western states of Washington, Oregon, and Colorado expatriate Canadians who became naturalized U.S. citizens supported the KKK by joining an auxiliary called the Royal Riders of the Red Robe, an organization for Protestants of foreign birth. The Royal Riders wore crimson rather than white robes. The Canadian-born Carl DeLochte headed the Colorado Royal Riders in the 1920s. Montana, Illinois, and Ohio had their own associations of Royal Riders, and given the location of these states near the border with Canada, these organizations surely included Canadian immigrants as well.[51] Other than offering passing references to the Royal Riders of the Red Robe, the existing scholarship offers no insight either into this KKK-affiliated organization or into the important role played by Anglo-Canadians in their championing of the principles of the Ku Klux Klan in the United States during the 1920s. Because Anglo-Canadians could not join native-born Americans in the KKK, the willingness of the organization to accept Anglo-Canadian support demonstrates an inherent contradiction in the ideology of the Klan while also revealing that its anti-Catholicism was more meaningful to the group than its notion of nationalism.

Thus Anglo-Canadian immigrants in the northeastern United States, people like the burglar of the Burlington cathedral and the songwriter in Barre as well as the members of Farnsworth's Christian Crusaders in Maine, joined forces in the 1920s with native-born Protestants to promote the ideals of the Ku Klux Klan, just as Canadian natives did in the western United States. Ethnoreligious tensions in Canada, to which Anglo-Canadian immigrants had been exposed before emigrating to the United States, undoubtedly propelled some to back the Klan movement in the United States to thwart the growing influence of Catholics in American society. In the northeastern United States, English-speaking Canadian immigrants worked to assert a Protestant character in the region they cohabited with their French-speaking former compatriots. Seeing the role of Canadian immigrants as targets of or participants in the Ku Klux Klan in the United States during the 1920s therefore challenges our previous understanding of this organization.

Also visible in the Ku Klux Klan experience in Vermont—a factor that distinguishes it from Maine and New Hampshire, which were part of the same Klan realm as Vermont—was the extent of opposition the KKK faced in the state. The Klan "is an importation and not at all native to our ways of thinking or acting," emphasized the *St. Albans Weekly Messenger* in April 1924. Demonstrating prescience, the newspaper continued, "This is not its native soil and even if it were to gain a foothold it would soon wither and perish under the biting blast of Vermont common-sense." Underscoring the anti-Klan sentiments of Vermont newspapers and of the general public, the editor of the *Burlington Free Press and Times* in June 1924 stated, "As a matter of fact, Klan organizers in Vermont have received no bouquets, but instead a number of brickbats from the press of the State. And the general feeling has been entirely opposed to the Klan."[52] The efforts of newspaper editors plus the good sense and, indeed, the apparent tolerance of many of Vermont's citizens for ethnoreligious diversity served effectively to fend off the KKK as it attempted to storm the Green Mountain State in the 1920s.

But Vermont's slow population growth and its small proportion of non-English speakers may in part explain its aversion not only to English-language legislation for its schools but also to the KKK movement in the state. Of the six New England states, Vermont experienced the smallest increase in population during the early twentieth century. From 1900 to 1920 the southern New England states witnessed the largest growth in population: Connecticut, 52 percent; Rhode Island, 41 percent; and Massachusetts, 37.3 percent. The northern New England states expanded much less rapidly: Maine, 10.6 percent; New Hampshire, 7.7 percent; and Vermont, 2.6 percent. Vermont, therefore, was the state least affected by immigration during the opening decades of the twentieth century. Compared to the other New England states, Vermont in 1920 also had the lowest proportion (7.2 percent) of foreign-born whites ten years of age and older who could not speak English.[53] Of all the New England states, Vermont appears to have been the least affected by the social tensions that typically arose from the influx of non-English-speaking immigrants, the very kinds of stresses on which the KKK capitalized in the 1920s. The apparent lack of social tension among the state's residents, often commented on in the press when the Ku Klux Klan attempted to recruit members in various communities, made it easier for Green Mountain residents of Anglo-Saxon heritage to rebuff the white-robed society.[54]

6

Confronting Irish Catholic Politicians
in the Bay State

WHILE LECTURING in New Hampshire in November 1923, the King Kleagle of Maine, F. Eugene Farnsworth, also set his sights on the Bay State: "We are going to form in a semi-circle. We are going to join hands and march to the sea. Then we will march into a place called Dublin, but known to us as Boston in the state of Massachusetts." Farnsworth made it clear that the Ku Klux Klan was prepared to do battle with Boston's Irish Catholic population and its mayor, James M. Curley: "We are going to beard the Curley lion in his den. We'll march on City Hall if necessary. This means a big fight. We'll present an embattled square to the enemy that will be impenetrable." Although Farnsworth softened his rhetoric somewhat as the lecture progressed, he continued to employ military metaphors. "This doesn't mean we shall use guns and bullets," he noted. "I mean an embattled square of ballots that will drive the Roman Catholics out of office there. . . . Arrayed in our armor of righteousness we shall form a solid phalanx that will sweep away all these thugs, porch-climbers, bootleggers and gunmen that are opposed to us." In contrast to this negative view of Catholics, Farnsworth projected an unblemished (and inaccurate) view of the Ku Klux Klan: "All the criminal element is on the other side and sponsored by the Roman Catholics. There is no man on our side who is connected with the nefarious rum business or who has a criminal record."[1] As the Klan made incursions into Massachusetts and confronted Irish Catholic political leaders there, the hooded society discovered that politicians would not hesitate to use all legal means and even some extralegal ones against it.

Home to 3.8 million residents in 1920, Massachusetts had the largest population of any New England state. While its African American population far exceeded that of the other New England states, the 45,466 blacks living there made up a mere 1.2 percent of the state's population. More than 1 million Bay State residents in 1920 were foreign-born whites; in descending order, Canada (24.2 percent), Ireland (16.8 percent), Italy (10.7 percent), and Russia and Lithuania (10.4 percent) contributed the largest proportions of immigrants to Massachusetts. But immigrants were not the only ethnic stock: over one million second-generation Massachusetts residents were whites whose parents had been born outside of the United States, and more than 400,000 were whites of mixed parentage, that is, whites one of whose parents was born in the United States and the other abroad. Thus, in 1920 two-thirds of the entire population of Massachusetts was composed of first- and second-generation ethnic stock. As noted in chapter 1, most of the ethnic population of Massachusetts consisted of Catholics, who by 1926 numbered over 1.6 million members (over 40 percent of the state's population in 1920), while Jews, in 1926, numbered 213,085 persons (over 5 percent of the population in 1920.)[2] Given how radically the demography of the Bay State had changed from its colonial origins as a Puritan haven, it is small wonder that Klan leaders like Farnsworth wanted to invade the Commonwealth during the 1920s to reassert Protestant control.

Prior to the arrival of the Ku Klux Klan in Massachusetts, state lawmakers passed legislation to assimilate immigrants as part of the Americanization movement that swept across the United States during and after the Great War. In 1917 the state formed the Massachusetts Bureau of Immigration "to bring into sympathetic and mutually helpful relations the commonwealth and its residents of foreign origin." To this end the bureau sought to help immigrants learn English, "to develop their understanding of American government, institutions and ideals, and generally to promote their assimilation and naturalization." In 1919 lawmakers passed "An Act to Promote Americanization through the Education of Adult Persons Unable to Use the English Language," which provided for reimbursement by the state of one-half of the expenses that municipalities incurred by offering English-language instruction to individuals over twenty-one years of age. The legislation stipulated that the "instruction shall be given in the English language, in the fundamental principles of government, and in other subjects adapted to fit the scholars for American citizenship." The immigrant education program therefore served to facilitate the integration of foreign-born adults into American society. Massachusetts funded the program through the 1920s, but, unlike Maine, New Hampshire, Connecticut, and Rhode Island, it did not feel compelled to pass English-only legislation during the early twentieth century for youth attending elementary and secondary schools in the state.[3] This was the political context the Ku Klux Klan found when it arrived in the Bay State.

The Klan tried establishing itself in Boston as early as 1921, according to army intelligence officials. As described in chapter 1, the KKK gained its institutional origins in Massachusetts through the efforts of the Loyal Coalition. The group, which maintained its national headquarters in Boston, promoted "American principles" and opposed the Irish Republican movement, the movement for Ireland's independence. The offices of the Loyal Coalition in Boston served as the state headquarters of the KKK, as state senator William I. Hennessey discovered when he tried to join the Klan and was rebuffed on account of his Irish surname.[4]

The KKK intended to address forcefully the changing demographics of Massachusetts. In a four-page pamphlet titled "A Mobilization of Americans!" the Klan lamented "The Problem": "The old order has changed and we have now a conglomerate mass of diverse ideals and inheritances, instead of the old unified nation." The proposed "solution" was "to oppose the mounting tide of foreign influence!" and the publication stressed that "only native-born citizens of the United States can feel for her that final, fiery loyalty!" Among the objectives of the KKK, as indicated in the pamphlet, were the formation of a "secret, militant organization" of people of similar race, color, and religion to join together in fraternity: "The kind of men we want are American, native-born citizens of the United States, white, Protestant, Gentile, intelligent, honest, loyal, and fearless." To recruit such men, the organizer T. A. Jackson would send a letter from Boston to each individual who had been identified by his office as "an American who is zealously devoted to his race, his country, and his home," and he would request that the person complete and return the questionnaire he enclosed. That document, a standard form produced by the national Ku Klux Klan office, consisted of twenty questions about the place of birth, race, principles, and allegiance of the applicants. For example, question 13 queried, "Do you believe in White Supremacy?" and question 20 asked, "Do you owe ANY KIND of allegiance to any foreign nation, government, institution, sect, people, ruler or person?"[5]

The Ku Klux Klan tried to attract individuals from throughout Massachusetts who shared its principles. Besides Boston, Worcester emerged as an early center of Klan activity and influence in the Bay State. In June 1922 an unidentified robed Klansman addressed 150 members of the Exchange Club of Worcester on the society's aims and goals. *L'Opinion Publique,* the French-language newspaper of Worcester, reported the next month that the KKK had established a branch in the city that was "l'un des plus importants de l'Etat" (one of the most important of the state) and reportedly had a membership of 125, a number that would climb to at least 4,000 by the mid-1920s. After remaining quiet for over a year, the KKK of Worcester, over the objections of Mayor Peter F. Sullivan, organized in September 1923 a public meeting of 2,500 Klan members and their friends, 2,000 of whom packed Mechanics Hall while the overflow crowd of 500 moved to nearby Washburn Hall. Bertram Priest, a printer and member of the Orange Order, rented Mechanics Hall under his name for the KKK meeting and distributed tickets to the event. Priest claimed not to be a member of the Klan, which likely was true because he was not a native-born U.S. citizen; but, as we have seen, white Protestants born abroad could and did support the KKK movement in the United States, as did the Orange Order. During the Klan gathering in Worcester an estimated 25,000 to 30,000 protesters appeared on Main Street, but they "confined their opposition to jeers and cat calls and the occasional dropping of stench bombs," reported the *Boston Herald*. More than a hundred police officers were on hand to manage the crowds, and no violence erupted.[6]

King Kleagle Farnsworth served as a keynote speaker at this first public event of the Klan in Massachusetts. The selection of Worcester as the venue is perhaps unsurprising given that its multicultural population in the 1920s included people of Irish, French-Canadian, Italian, Polish, Lithuanian, Albanian, Syrian, Greek, and African descent as well as people of Jewish and Roman Catholic faith traditions—in short, precisely the groups targeted by the Klan because of their religious background and/or national origins. Farnsworth's nativist comments echoed those he was making in other New England states. "This country is teeming with alien enemies who do not believe in our form of government or our institutions, nor our public schools," he contended in Worcester. "To my way of thinking, an American is one who owes entire allegiance to his flag and country. I am tired and sick of this hyphenated Americanism," Farnsworth complained, "because no man is a good American if his allegiance is divided." One month later Farnsworth returned to Worcester to preside over a meeting of one thousand individuals at Mechanics Hall, where he encouraged those present to become involved in city politics, just as the KKK had done in Portland, Maine.[7]

Interestingly, after Swedes lost political power in Worcester, they joined the Ku Klux Klan movement. Despite the fact that the Klan screened immigrants and their children through the membership application forms, the hooded knights accepted white Protestant Swedes as native stock because they were Nordic peoples, the geographer Kevin L. Hickey speculates. The Ku Klux Klan provided individuals of Swedish descent with a forum through which to address ethnic and religious rivalries in Worcester. According to Charles W. Estus Sr. and John F. McClymer, following the defeat in 1919 of the three-term Swedish Republican mayor Pehr Holmes and the election in 1923 of an Irish Catholic Republican, Michael J. O'Hara, who had formed a coalition of Irish and Yankee supporters to gain office, Swedes joined the KKK in the

effort to recapture political and social power in the city and to promote Protestant values. In the past, the Yankees had sided with the Swedes in elections,
but they no longer backed the temperance movement as strongly as Swedes.
Although Swedes made up only about 10 percent of Worcester's population,
they represented nearly half of the city's Klan membership; consequently, the
Worcester Knights of Columbus, largely composed of Irish Catholics, came
to view the local Klan as a Swedish society. The KKK did not come primarily
from either the highest or lowest strata of Worcester society. Hickey's analysis
of the membership ledgers reveals that a large majority of Worcester's Klan
came from middle occupational groups, with the smallest proportions representing high white collar or unskilled job categories: high white collar, 5.3
percent; low white collar, 30.0 percent; skilled, 27.9 percent; semiskilled and
service, 28.0 percent; unskilled and menial occupations, 8.8 percent. By the
1920s, notes Hickey, most Swedes had lived in Worcester for less than forty
years and thus would have been first- or second-generation U.S. residents.
Hickey does not offer evidence that first-generation Swedes became Klan
members, but his findings on the presence of Swedes in the movement help
to illustrate that the KKK's definition of Americanism did not prevail in New
England. White Protestants from Sweden as well as from Canada and other
Commonwealth nations could become part of this avowedly nativist movement in New England. Similarly, in Buffalo, New York, up to 40 percent of
the city's Klan members had German ancestry, estimates the historian Shawn
Lay, who speculates that they wanted to show evidence of their assimilation
into white Protestant U.S. society.[8]

Scattered accounts in the press provide additional, if limited, information
on the Klan's origins in Massachusetts. Among the reports were the Klan's
ties to universities. In June 1923 50 Boston University students apparently
used their connections in athletic clubs and other university organizations to
form a Klan branch on their campus. By October 1923 an estimated 150 to
200 Harvard University students had joined the KKK and were holding Klan
meetings in their rooms. Both Klan and anti-Klan newspapers intimated
that administrators at the university sanctioned the Klan's presence and
influence on their campus. The *Dawn,* a Klan newspaper published in Chicago, reported that Harvard officials had denied the request of the National
Association for the Advancement of Colored People that the university expel
students who joined the KKK. In fact, the *Republic,* a Catholic weekly in
Boston, and the *California Eagle,* a paper based in Los Angeles, had both
complained that Harvard yielded to the influence of the Ku Klux Klan when
it chose not to allow the son of the black Civil War veteran Roscoe Conkling
Bruce to live in the dormitory reserved for first-year students because of his
race.[9]

The *Boston Sunday Advertiser* identified one Harvard-educated individual, Lothrop Stoddard, as "the most prominent member" of Boston's Ku Klux Klan in 1923. Holder of a doctoral degree from Harvard, Stoddard wrote *The Rising Tide of Color against White World-Supremacy,* published in 1922, in which he expressed concern about the situation of whites throughout the world in the aftermath of World War I. "The prospect is not a brilliant one," Stoddard contended. "Weakened and impoverished by Armageddon, handicapped by an unconstructive peace, and facing internal Bolshevist disaffection which must at all costs be mastered, the white world is ill-prepared to confront—the rising tide of color." In addition to promoting white supremacy, Stoddard advocated restrictions on immigration, arguing that throughout "the white world, migrations of lower human types like those which have worked such havoc in the United States must be rigorously curtailed. Such migrations upset standards, sterilize better stocks, increase low types, and compromise national futures more than war, revolutions, or native deterioration."[10] Stoddard's views of nonwhites and immigrants accorded well with those of the KKK. That the *Advertiser* identified him as one of the leaders of the Klan movement in Massachusetts is therefore unsurprising.

Newspapers are a source of insight as well into some of the other early leaders of the Ku Klux Klan in the Bay State. One such leader was the former Grand Goblin of New England, A. J. Padon Jr. (see chapter 1). Another was Frank H. Cook of Dorchester, who remained only one month with the Klan organization. Cook told the *Boston Sunday Advertiser* in 1923 that he had joined the KKK in July 1921 after responding to an advertisement for salesmen. As a Kleagle, his job was to recruit individuals to the organization and sell them memberships. Although Cook liked the fact that the KKK stood for Americanism, he found that its virulently anti-Catholic and anti-Jewish stances conflicted with his own views of freedom of religion. "It was not the type of Americanism I had been taught to believe in," he stated. The former Kleagle elaborated: "I resigned because I believed that the racial and religious prejudices against Catholics, Jews and Negroes are menacing, disloyal and untrue to the best traditions of this great country." Cook also acknowledged that he left the Klan because he objected to the organization's financial transactions, but he did not elaborate.[11]

In addition to such internal dissension, the Ku Klux Klan of Massachusetts encountered opposition from outside its ranks. When the Suffolk County district attorney Joseph C. Pelletier of Boston, who also served as the Supreme Advocate of the Knights of Columbus, learned that the Klan was trying to establish itself in Boston in 1921, he asked the public for assistance. He implored Bay State residents: "The Ku Klux Klan are not only un-American, but rabidly anti-American, and it is the duty of every good

citizen not to take the law into his own hands, but to report to the proper
officials the formation, wherever it occurs, of a branch of this society that
with dastardly hand contemplates the destruction of the dearest and best of
American principles." Pelletier asked Massachusetts residents to be as dutiful
in informing officials of the Klan's activities as they had been in disclosing the
actions of anti-American groups during the war.[12]

When Pelletier ran for mayor of Boston in 1921, his candidacy served as a
lightning rod for the Klan. "The fact that Mr. Pelletier was Supreme Advocate of the Knights of Columbus gave the Klan an issue," stated Padon. Klan
leaders capitalized on Pelletier's improprieties as district attorney and painted
other members of the Knights of Columbus with the same brush in order to
recruit members to the KKK. "They pointed out that he had not defended
himself against the charges of graft and extortion in office," Padon remarked.
"And they claimed to prospective candidates that his action was the action
of every Knight of Columbus in New England. This was unjust and untrue,
nevertheless it was done." Moreover, according to Padon, "the argument
was wonderfully timely and skilful. It fanned into flame the embers of religious bigotry. Hundreds who would probably not have joined the order on
any other argument were inveigled into the Klan on this issue." The KKK
undoubtedly gained additional fodder when the Massachusetts Supreme
Court unanimously found Pelletier guilty both of malfeasance and of malfeasance in office in 1922 and removed him from his post as district attorney,
a position he had held since 1909. Although Pelletier is a French surname,
"[Joseph C.] Pelletier is an Irishman, with a nation-wide reputation," noted
the *New Republic*. As Padon's statements imply, Pelletier served as an example
of the kind of corrupt Irish Catholic officeholder the Klan wanted to replace
in Massachusetts.[13]

Besides shedding light on the political machinations of the Massachusetts
Klan, Padon supplied the *Boston Daily Advertiser* with information about
the inner workings of the organization and its extralegal functions. Padon
revealed that each Klan lodge had a Mystic Circle, a secret committee known
only to the members of the circle itself and to the Exalted Cyclops (president)
who appointed them. "Their mission is to investigate and punish wrongdo-
ing in their community," Padon said. "They are superpolicemen working
above the law of their community and their country, to take the law into
their own hands." Padon told the *Advertiser* that one of the early objectives of
Boston's Mystic Circle was to reduce the role of Catholics in politics, and he
revealed that the Imperial Wizard, William J. Simmons, had stated explicitly
that he wanted the inner circle to "put the fear of God into the hearts of our
enemies." Padon explained how the Mystic Circles operated. If a local Klan
organization felt an individual deserved to be tarred and feathered, whipped,

run out of town, or even murdered, for such offenses as adultery, bootlegging, or the appointment of a black to political office, the Mystic Circle of
another klavern would perform the task, allowing local Klan members to
"establish a perfect alibi, and the crime would be blamed on irresponsible
hoodlums masquerading as Klansmen." That way Klan members from other
klaverns would not be suspected. When needed, he further explained, local
Klan members would be asked "to 'return the courtesy,' with the result that
the job would be done by out-of-town men without leaving the slightest
trace of their identity."[14]

After newspapers in Boston published such accounts of the KKK's operations in Massachusetts, state lawmakers proposed a number of anti-Klan
measures. They undoubtedly had read widely circulated press reports that
U.S. government officials maintained that jurisdiction over the Ku Klux Klan
resided with individual states rather than with the federal government. In
January 1923 Rep. Coleman E. Kelly, a Democrat from Boston, introduced
House Bill No. 219, by which members of the Massachusetts House or Senate would lose their seats if they filed legislation "for the purpose of injuring
any religious organization" or that originated with "any member of the Ku
Klux Klan organization." Kelly also introduced legislation asking for a grand
jury probe of the Klan's activities in Boston. "The Ku Klux Klan should be
told that beneath the mud of Flanders many American youths are sleeping
the eternal sleep—and, many of them, thousands of them are Catholics, Jews
and Negroes," Kelly stated. The contributions of the immigrants who had
died in the war effort, Kelly emphasized, demonstrated their devotion to the
United States, "and these men built their own Americanism, and the Americanism they built is imperishable."[15] Unlike the KKK's rhetoric, Kelly's words
embraced African Americans, Jews, and Catholics as Americans.

Besides Kelly, several other lawmakers introduced anti-Klan measures in
January 1923. Rep. John H. Logue, a Democrat of Boston, presented House
Bill No. 566, a resolution calling for the governor to order state and municipal police to work together "in suppressing all unwarranted violation of law,
or threats thereof, by the Ku Klux Klan, so called, or its sympathizers." Rep.
J. Frederick Curtin, also a Democrat from Boston, introduced House Bill
No. 189, which would have fined and/or imprisoned individuals who promoted "klans or clubs or societies" that targeted people on the basis of their
religion or birth as well as those who organized meetings at which masks
or disguises were worn; in addition, the measure would have required the
officers of societies organized in opposition to racial or religious groups to
submit a list of their officers to the town or city clerk of the municipality
where they formed. The Law and Order League filed a bill, introduced by
Rep. John H. Drew, another Democrat from Boston, as House Bill No. 190,

a measure that would have made it illegal to wear masks in public places and for individuals to congregate while wearing masks. In addition, Rep. Hugh J. Campbell, yet another Democrat from Boston, introduced House Bill No. 265, an act that would have required all societies, except labor unions, to file lists of members with the secretary of state if the membership exceeded one thousand persons.[16]

In February 1923 the Rules and the Legal Affairs committees asked for "leave to withdraw" bills 189, 190, 219, and 265, and the House of Representatives accepted the reports of the two committees. According to the *Boston Herald,* lawmakers felt that there was insufficient evidence of Klan activity in the Bay State. Boston's Catholic weekly newspaper, the *Republic,* pointed out that there was no need for anti-Klan legislation in Massachusetts because the group was not establishing a strong foothold there and was, in fact, disappearing from the Commonwealth.[17]

Instead, lawmakers chose to take milder action against the Ku Klux Klan. After the resolutions of Kelly and Logue were referred to the Rules Committee, it opted to draft House Bill No. 803 to condemn the Klan. The measure noted that the KKK was committing violent acts in other parts of the United States and that it might also do so in Massachusetts. It resolved "That the House of Representatives of The General Court of Massachusetts regards any such organization as a danger to American institutions, as a threat to that freedom of thought and speech guaranteed to the American people by the Constitution of the United States." The resolution expressed "complete confidence" that the KKK would not gain a "foothold among the law abiding people of Massachusetts, that our public officials will be able to protect all our citizens in their constitutional rights, and that the Commonwealth will maintain its tradition of ordered liberty under the Constitution." During the floor debate Rep. Andrew P. Doyle, a Republican from New Bedford, told his colleagues, "The Catholics of this State will extend to you their gratitude for your prompt action in this matter. The Catholics have the utmost faith in their Protestant fellow citizens to protect them in their constitutional rights." The House of Representatives unanimously passed the resolution in January 1923.[18]

Within days Sen. Wellington Wells, a Republican from Boston, presented resolutions similarly condemning the Ku Klux Klan and pledging the Senate to preserving the constitutional rights of the state's citizens. The resolutions stated, in part, "That the Senate of Massachusetts hereby expresses its firm opposition to any secret organization whose aims and activities are inimical to the rights and liberties guaranteed to our citizens by the Constitutions of the United States and of this Commonwealth." The Senate unanimously approved the resolutions.[19]

In 1924 several lawmakers introduced anti-Klan legislation, but none of the measures gained passage. Rep Patrick J. Sullivan, a Democrat from Boston, presented on behalf of the Law and Order League House Bill No. 22, a measure that stipulated that organizations with twenty or more members who are required to take oaths must file their membership lists, their bylaws, and their loyalty oaths with the secretary of state. Labor unions and fraternal organizations that had existed for more than ten years were exempted. In addition, the bill would have required the regulated organizations to file the meeting minutes they had approved containing resolutions intended to defeat legislation or political candidates, and it would have required the societies to desist from mailing literature to nonmembers. Representative Logue also presented House Bill No. 54, proposed legislation that would have compelled social and other organizations, except fraternal benefit societies and political or charitable groups, to file with the secretary of state a list of their officers and the names of their societies. In addition, the regulated organizations would have been required to submit their true name when renting halls or face fines and/or the imprisonment of their officers. But the Legal Affairs Committee asked leave to withdraw bills 22 and 54, and in late January the full House of Representatives accepted the committee's reports. Efforts to squelch the KKK apparently did not end there. In August the *Boston Herald* reported that Representative Kelly filed legislation to prohibit people without permits from wearing masks in public places and gathering for meetings, but there is no record that the House took up this legislation.[20]

Bay State lawmakers proposed additional anti-Klan legislation in 1925 and 1929, but those measures also failed. Representative Sullivan reintroduced the petition of the Law and Order League of Boston, recorded in 1925 as House Bill No. 154, and he introduced the petition of Mayor Curley as House Bill No. 962, a measure containing the same wording as Bill No. 154. The Legal Affairs Committee asked for leave to withdraw both bills 154 and 962, and the full House accepted the committee's reports.[21] In 1929 Rep. Timothy J. McDonough, a Democrat from Boston, introduced House Bill No. 895 on behalf of himself and Francis J. Finneran, a prominent figure in the Massachusetts Democratic Party. The legislation would have required secret societies to submit the names of their members to the secretary of state. Again, the Legal Affairs Committee asked for leave to withdraw Bill No. 895, and the full House accepted the committee's report.[22] In the end, Massachusetts lawmakers proposed a number of anti-Klan bills from 1923 to 1929 but succeeded only in passing resolutions condemning the Ku Klux Klan.

In contrast to state lawmakers, Boston's mayor chose to act directly and forcefully against the Klan. James Curley proved to be a formidable opponent of the KKK. Indeed, the *Fiery Cross,* a Klan newspaper published in

Indianapolis, called Curley "one of the alien oppositions' most powerful
henchmen." Curley was a crafty strategist who learned to manipulate the
Klan for his own political ends. Like Pelletier, Curley ran for mayor of Boston in 1921. Although Curley had served in the U.S. Congress from 1911 to
1914, and as mayor from 1914 to 1918, he was the underdog in the 1921 race
because he had lost the two previous elections; in addition, his chief opponent, John R. Murphy, had the backing of reformers like the Good Government Association as well as the endorsements of politicians who could deliver
substantial votes. In his 1957 autobiography, *I'd Do It Again: A Record of All
My Uproarious Years,* Curley admitted that he had paid a KKK member two
thousand dollars to convince a Congregational minister named A. Z. Conrad
to speak out against him during the campaign. "There are those who think
the 'sympathy votes' I siphoned from Murphy because of this attack won the
election for me," Curley stated unashamedly. He freely acknowledged that
the election would have turned out differently if voters had learned of his
underhandedness: "If any Irish Catholic had found out I even talked to 'the
Black Pope,' [KKK] I would have been doomed." In a political career span-
ning four decades, Curley went on to serve as mayor of Boston from 1922 to
1926, 1930 to 1934, and 1945 to 1949; he also won election as Massachusetts
governor and held that office in 1935–36 before returning to Congress from
1943 to 1946.[23]

In January 1923 Mayor Curley declined an invitation by the Loyal Coalition to attend the lecture of the retired U.S. naval officer Rear Adm. William
S. Sims, whose pro-British sympathies the American Association for the
Recognition of the Irish Republic had denounced at its statewide convention
in 1921. Curley responded to the unwelcome invitation by publicly attacking
the Loyal Coalition, the KKK, and Sims: "As I consider the preachments and
practices of your peculiar society detrimental to the peace and welfare of the
city of Boston and repugnant to the principles of civil and religious liberty,"
Curley wrote to Telfair Minton, the secretary of the Loyal Coalition, "and
since the published president of the Loyal Coalition, Lothrop Stoddard, is
said to be a member of a lawless, vicious aggregation of cowardly, nocturnal scoundrels known as the Ku Klux Klan, I am amazed that you have the
impudence to send such an invitation to me or any other loyal American
citizen. Moreover," the mayor stated, "I have no desire to sit on any platform
with Admiral Sims, retired, whose best service to the American navy was his
retirement from it." Ever colorful, Curley elaborated on his negative remarks
about Sims: "I would suggest that when he is done shooting off the only
weapon he is expert at—his mouth—he be escorted to the Cunard or White
Star dock and given an opportunity to follow the trail and example of his

ante-type, Benedict Arnold." Curley pithily concluded his bombastic letter, "Your tickets are herewith returned."[24]

The *Dawn* also remarked on Curley's "caustic and scurrilous" comments and indicated that the Loyal Coalition had filed a complaint with the president of the United States and had sent a copy to the U.S. secretary of the navy to protest Curley's lack of etiquette, including his denigration of a former leader of the U.S. Navy and, by extension, of the navy itself. When Curley was away on vacation later in the month, his office received a letter threatening his six children, after which the superintendent of police set up round-the-clock protection of his home as well as a police escort of his children to and from school. The *New York Times* observed that Curley had recently denounced the Ku Klux Klan and had adamantly insisted that "unless we destroy it, it will destroy us, and destroyed it must be as pitilessly as rabid dogs are destroyed." The threatening letter Curley had received, the *Times* suggested, served to avenge his attacks on the KKK.[25]

When Curley learned that Farnsworth had made a deprecating remark about him during a speech in Portland, Maine, in September 1923, Curley did not shy away from lambasting the King Kleagle. "And now the New Brunswick barber, mesmerist, stock peddler, lecturer, pseudo-patriot and bogus American, is recruiting sergeant for the Ku Klux Klan," Curley charged, "filling the ears of rural Maine with slanders of the good citizens of the Pine Tree State, bringing the blush of shame to the face of decent Protestantism, vilifying the officials and Government of the State, and its cities, and doing his pestilential best to control elections and foment civil war." Curley then challenged Farnsworth to a public debate in any meeting hall the Klan leader chose in the Commonwealth.[26]

The issue of the Klan's use of meeting halls in Massachusetts became contentious for individuals and communities. As early as 1922 the mayors of cities near Boston, including Brockton, Lawrence, Lowell, Lynn, Medford, Newton, Salem, and Woburn, publicly voiced their opposition to the KKK and vowed to drive it out of their municipalities, particularly by preventing the organization from holding meetings in their communities. Newspaper articles hint at the influence of Franco-Americans and the Irish in opposing Klan gatherings. When aldermen in Springfield denied the KKK permission to use the high school building for a public meeting, the *Dawn* in October 1922 cited Alderman Aimé H. Côté as the chief opponent, as he had complained that the Klan would "incite religious prejudice or bigotry." The Klan was shunned in Springfield despite the fact that the Exalted Cyclops, according to the Klan newspaper, was "said to be an important official of a municipal department." In 1923 the Salem City Council unanimously adopted a resolution drafted by the Ancient Order of Hibernians to prohibit Klan parades and meetings in their city. By January 1923 no klavern had yet formed in Salem, noted the *Boston Daily Advertiser,* because "a strong civic spirit to keep the Klan out of Salem has developed."[27]

As orchestrated by Mayor Curley, the same was true in Boston. In September 1923 King Kleagle Farnsworth antagonized Curley by announcing from Worcester that he planned to launch a membership drive in Boston. With his typical bravado Farnsworth told reporters that Boston's halls were not capacious enough to seat all of the people he would attract to the Klan's meetings there. Farnsworth bantered with the journalists: "I'd like to have you newspaper fellows arouse a great antagonism to my going to Boston, and then I'll be sure of getting a fine reception. Of course, if you will not arouse the town, there's no need of my going there." In response to Farnsworth's publicly stated intentions, Curley threatened to revoke the license of any establishment that allowed the Ku Klux Klan to meet on its premises, arguing that the Klan meetings "would tend to public disturbance and public disorder."[28]

In an editorial titled "Why Worry about It?" the *Boston Telegram* implicitly suggested that Curley was overreacting to the Ku Klux Klan. The newspaper dismissed concerns about Farnsworth, for it viewed him merely as an opportunist "who has made a living in many peculiar trades, from barbering to hypnotizing" and who "finds organizing the Ku Klux Klan more profitable than any of his other enterprises." The *Telegram* recognized that the King Kleagle would profit from the Klan's expansion in Massachusetts. Exploring Farnsworth's psyche, the *Telegram* editorialized: "Freud might be able to tell us just what complex F. Eugene suffers from, but, unable to get Freud's diagnosis, we will rest on the opinion that as long as $10 notes may be had for the asking, F. Eugene will be found shouting and screeching for America for Americans." The newspaper also commented that "klan organizing will remain profitable for Eugene as long as there is a lot of noise made about the klan," implying that Mayor Curley should tone down his anti-Klan rhetoric.[29]

The American Civil Liberties Union (ACLU) itself called into question Curley's rhetoric and opposed him on the issue of revoking the licenses of halls that rented their facilities to the Ku Klux Klan. John S. Codman, an ACLU representative, wrote to Curley to state that, while the organization was not sympathetic to the Klan, it wanted to protect the right of free speech. Curley challenged the ACLU's interpretation of the U.S. Constitution. "The difference between the views of the A.C.L.Union and mine is one of latitude, of where freedom ends and treason, sedition and disloyalty begin," Curley wrote to Codman. The mayor maintained that he, too, supported the constitutional rights of assembly and speech, but he went on to explain why he opposed them for the Klan. "Any organized body or society whose avowed purpose is to persecute and restrict the liberties of other citizens, which fosters race and religious hatreds, foments civic dissensions, disturbs the peace, overrides the law and presumes to engage in activities that are noxious, nocturnal and lawless," Curley insisted, "places itself clearly outside the constitution and the law and is a threat to the peace and integrity of the state. It cannot expect to shelter itself behind the rights it denies and the guaranties it repudiates, because admittedly it is a public enemy." The ACLU wrote in its report of October 13, 1923, that Curley had "recently restated his refusal to allow the Klan to hold a meeting in a licensed hall." Consequently, the ACLU wrote to Curley again to demand that he respect the civil rights of the Klan. "If your interpretation of the rights and principles you claim to defend were to obtain acceptance," Curley responded, "public meetings of thieves, burglars and other lawbreakers to discuss and formulate plans for assailing and plundering the public" would deserve sanction as well, he implied. Harry F. Ward, an ACLU officer, subsequently informed Curley that his organization was prepared to take the mayor to court if he revoked hall licenses as a means of preventing the society's meetings in Boston. Curley responded to Ward in part by stating he would not allow the KKK to gain sway in Boston as it had in other parts of the country, such as "Texas or Oklahoma or a section of the back-lots of Maine."[30]

The Ku Klux Klan defied Curley, and he struck back. When Curley read in the press that the KKK had rented the lower level of the Shawmut Congregational Church in Boston's South End, under the alias of the Protestant League of Massachusetts, he wrote the board of assessors to question whether the church should continue to enjoy its tax-exempt status as a religious institution if it engaged in the commercial practice of leasing its property. Curley's efforts and the negative publicity generated by newspaper stories of the Klan's meetings led the church's board of trustees to deny the group further use of its premises.[31]

The ACLU and the KKK were not the only ones who opposed Curley's tactics. When Boston officials broke up a KKK meeting of 150 people at the Caledonian building in March 1924, the *Nation* protested, "This is succumbing to Klanism." It contended that "the lawlessness of the hooded order is not to be cured by more lawlessness, official or unofficial." The *Nation* further implored, "Nor are 'strong measures' necessary," explaining, "The Klan is already disintegrating."[32]

In spite of Mayor Curley's strong opposition, the Klan did not give up. It continued to hold secret meetings to establish itself in Boston, the *Maine Klansman* claimed in March 1924. The newspaper took exception to the mayor's pronouncements that the KKK would not find a home in the city. "The descendants of the Minute Men have stated that the Klan is needed here and here it shall remain," the newspaper contended. It further asserted, "Right thinking citizens realize that unless they win back their heritages [sic] through the Klan that Protestantism will find no place in 'New Dublin.'"[33]

Mayor Curley was not deterred by the *Nation,* the ACLU, or the Klan. In September 1924 when he learned that the KKK planned to hold a meeting at the Neponset Hall in Hyde Park, he sent the fire and building commissioners to inspect the premises. When they arrived, they were denied entry. A fireman climbed in through a window and let the building and fire commissioners into the hall; they then proceeded to find enough municipal code violations to prevent the building from being used as a public meeting place.[34]

The Ku Klux Klan proved to be an expedient political issue for Curley, particularly as he campaigned for governor in 1924. In September he blamed the KKK for tearing down posters promoting his gubernatorial bid that campaign workers had placed along busy roads. In October *L'Etoile,* the French-language newspaper in Lowell, reported that, just as Curley and other Democrats arrived at Leominster, an explosion could be heard and a twelve-foot cross burst into flames. The incident gave Curley ammunition, the newspaper claimed, pointing out that Curley vowed in his speech to chase the KKK out of the Commonwealth after his inauguration as governor, a promise he repeated on the campaign trail.[35]

In late October the editor of *L'Etoile* cautioned readers against putting too much faith in politicians who used the KKK as the central issue of their campaign. "Méfions-nous des politiciens qui dénoncent sans cesse le Ku Klux Klan" (Let us beware of politicians who denounce incessantly the Ku Klux Klan), the newspaper warned, while acknowledging that the Klan deserved condemnation. "Mais un candidat qui fait toute sa campagne sur cela en ignorant les questions sérieuses n'est qu'un vulgaire charlatan désireux d'arriver au pouvoir en flattant les passions, mêmes justifiées, du peuple" (But a candidate who builds his whole campaign on that while ignoring serious questions is nothing but a common charlatan who wishes to gain power by pandering to passions, even justified, of the people). The editorial implies an unwillingness on the part of Franco-Americans to accede to Irish political leadership to combat the Ku Klux Klan in Massachusetts, for the editor undoubtedly was making a dig at Curley, who focused on the KKK as the central issue of his campaign for governor in 1924.[36]

That year the Ku Klux Klan attracted considerable attention throughout Massachusetts by setting crosses ablaze. Fiery crosses that burned in Brookfield, Fitchburg, Holden, Lynn, Malden, Melrose, North Grafton, Swampscott, Watertown, and Worcester one evening in April were all believed to be the work of the KKK, as was an accompanying explosion in Brookfield. Some of the burning crosses set off brush fires, including one in Worcester near the convent of the Sisters of Notre Dame that firemen had to extinguish. Curley capitalized on this visible symbol of the Klan's presence during his gubernatorial bid. J. Joseph Huthmacher notes that crosses "seemed to burn more frequently as the campaign progressed." Joseph F. Dinneen made the same point: "Wherever he spoke in central and western Massachusetts a fiery cross appeared on a hillside within sight of his gathering, and with pointing finger Curley became dramatically emotional." On each occasion Curley's comments were remarkably similar, and the cross burnings took place with such regularity that "the charge was made that one of Curley's lieutenants was deliberately touching them off," an allegation never proven, Dinneen pointed out.[37]

Curley came clean in his autobiography. He indicated that he had alleged during the 1924 gubernatorial campaign that his Republican opponent, Alvan T. Fuller, was the candidate of the Ku Klux Klan. Curley acknowledged that he would point to burning crosses on hillsides "as evidence of the Klan's interest in the Republican candidate." As he did so, Curley wrote, he would utter, " 'There it burns,' I said, 'the cross of hatred upon which our Lord, Jesus Christ, was crucified—the cross of human avarice, and not the cross of love and Christian charity. . . .' I went on to excoriate the Klan, whose pagan disciples trailed me around the state, seeking to knife me as they were already knifing Al Smith of New York." Feigning indignation, Curley continued, "They burned cross after cross in an effort to intimidate the people while my opponent sought to minimize the danger, even having the temerity to accuse Curley of deliberately erecting these flaming crosses as stage props." Then he confessed parenthetically and named the aides who were responsible: "(They were [stage props], of course. Among my fire-lighters were Mike Ward and Frank Howland)."[38]

Because Curley succeeded in making the KKK a campaign issue in 1924, the Republican State Committee had to withdraw the invitation that the Republican National Committee had extended to Maine's governor-elect, Ralph O. Brewster, to campaign on behalf of Massachusetts Republicans. Given Brewster's Klan sympathies, the state committee felt that "Brewster would do more harm to the Republican cause in Massachusetts than he would good." Instead, Republicans in the Bay State enlisted the support of the Maine congressman John E. Nelson, an opponent of the Ku Klux Klan. "By this bold stroke the Republican organization has riddled Curley's Klan issue full of holes and has emphatically demonstrated that the Ku Klux Klan and the Republican party of Massachusetts not only have nothing in common," asserted the *Boston Evening Transcript*, "but, in fact, are travelling along different roads." Furthermore, contended the newspaper, "it eliminates Curley's only talking point and leaves him stranded without political issues which can be of any benefit to him."[39]

Republicans planned to send Nelson to campaign in New Bedford and Fall River, communities with large Franco-American populations. Those communities tended to vote Republican because of their conflicts with the Irish, but Curley had gained support in those communities for his Democratic gubernatorial bid on account of the Klan issue. Republicans hoped Nelson, by making speeches that attacked the KKK, could persuade Franco-Americans to remain with the Republican Party rather than support Curley.[40]

After losing his bid for governor, Curley continued to serve as mayor of Boston, and he persisted in his efforts to root the Klan out of the city. In June 1925 the building commissioner, the police superintendent, and the fire commissioner together prevented the KKK from assembling in Boston by closing the hall where it gathered because it did not meet fire regulations. The city officials cited problems with the fire extinguishers and pointed to the barred and screened windows that prevented egress from the basement meeting room. The actions of these officials forced the Klan to relocate its meeting to Reading and thus foiled its plans in Boston. The assembly had been organized to test the city officials, confessed C. U. Lewis, a national Klan organizer. "We had two attorneys present to fight our case. But when the officials said they would be obliged to close the building because of the fire menace, of course we could do nothing. We had to submit," lamented Lewis.[41]

"As mayor of Boston, in the interest of the public peace, the welfare of the city and in defense of law, order and the preservation of Americanism, I will endeavor to squelch Ku Klux Klanism," Curley proclaimed the following day. He vowed to persevere in his efforts against the Klan, declaring that he would continue to send fire and building officials to close the meeting halls of the KKK, if conditions warranted. Curley did acknowledge, however, that if the Klan's meeting places met city codes, he would not be able to prevent their gatherings. Those halls that did not meet all municipal codes but that disallowed Klan meetings would be spared, he candidly revealed.[42]

George Bradlee, a former Boston resident, felt Mayor Curley's efforts to repel the Ku Klux Klan deserved "metrical mention." In July 1925 the *Boston Herald* published the following poem by Bradley:

> *Said Mayor Curley to the Klan,*
> *'Just try to come in, if you can!'*
> *Said the Klan to Mayor Curley,*
> *'We can wait, if it's too early.'*

'But you can't come in, at all,'
Said His Honor, 'There's no hall.'
Said the Klan, 'We'd like to meet,
But we don't want Tremont street,
For, although we like fresh air,
We'd not find it healthy there.'
So the cautious Klan crept in;
But Jim Curley with a grin,
Took down his trusty old Red Tape,
And fired 'em out by the Fire Escape.[43]

Not until 1926, after Curley had left office, did the Klan succeed in holding a public meeting in Boston. The KKK met at the American House Hotel, and the Boston mayor, Malcolm E. Nichols, said he could do little to prevent the assembly, for hotels came under the jurisdiction of the state licensing board, unlike public halls, which were granted their licenses through the mayor's office. At the meeting approximately one hundred members of the Boston Tea Party Klan No. 11 received their charter from national Ku Klux Klan headquarters.[44]

After James Curley lost his bid for governor in 1924, a clergyman told him, "You won something more than the election—you have flushed the Ku Klux Klan into the open and have driven them out of Massachusetts." Curley, however, graciously shared the credit with the Republican challenger who defeated him and with the citizens of the Bay State who opposed the Klan. "Governor [Alvan T.] Fuller ruled against providing [state] police protection for open meetings of the Klan. This action, plus a shower of brickbats and other appropriate missiles, marked the demise of the Klan in Massachusetts," Curley wrote in his autobiography.[45] As we will see in the next chapter, Catholics in the Commonwealth of Massachusetts launched an effective, if extralegal, counteroffensive against the KKK during the 1920s.

7

Counterattack by Commonwealth Catholics

OPPOSITION TO the Ku Klux Klan in Massachusetts came from many different quarters, from both societies and individuals. The most significant and effective anti-Klan activities in the Bay State were the grassroots efforts undertaken by residents, many of whom were the Catholic targets of the Klan. Perhaps coming as a considerable surprise to the KKK, Catholics in over twenty communities of the Commonwealth of Massachusetts did not hesitate to use extralegal means, including violence, in their counterattack against the hooded society. Consequently, the culture wars between the Protestant Klan and its Catholic opponents erupted into numerous riots in the Bay State in the mid-1920s.

Among the societies that spoke out against the Ku Klux Klan was the Masonic order. In June 1922 Grand Master Arthur D. Prince of the Massachusetts Grand Lodge of Masons sent all of the order's state lodges a message denouncing the KKK as "an unmasonic organization." Prince stated that the Klan's "avowed principles violate Masonic law at every point and it would be impossible for me to conceive of a Mason who could so far forget his Masonic teachings as to affiliate with an organization which advocates taking the law into its own hands, condemning men and women in secret trials, and imposing the punishment of the whip, the tar bucket or unlawful banishment." Prince further stated that he would not allow Masons to use the organization's temples for KKK purposes.[1]

Other Masons similarly worked to oppose the Ku Klux Klan in the Bay State. In 1923 Rev. Dudley Hays Ferrell, Grand Master of the Grand Lodge of Massachusetts, Ancient Free and Accepted Masons, condemned the Klan and asked fraternalists to keep the hooded society out of the Masonic order. As the KKK worked to recruit Masons into its organization, Frederick W.

Hamilton, the supreme council deputy for the Masonic Order of Massachusetts and the head of the Scottish Rite Masons, warned in 1923 that the organization was incompatible with Klanhood. "No Scottish Rite Freemason can consistently be a Klansman," Hamilton stated unequivocally.[2]

Another organization, the Executive Committee of the Massachusetts Federation of Churches, adopted a resolution in December 1922 against the KKK, a resolution it borrowed from the Federal Council of Churches of Christ in America. "This committee records its strong conviction that the recent rise of organizations whose members are masked, oath-bound and unknown, and whose activities have the effect of arousing religious prejudice and racial antipathies is fraught with grave consequences to the church and society at large," the resolution stated. "Any organization whose activities tend to set class against class or race against race," it continued, "is consistent neither with ideals of the churches nor with true patriotism, however vigorous or sincere may be its profession of religion and Americanism."[3]

Not only organizations but also individuals spoke out against the Ku Klux Klan in Massachusetts. Some Protestant ministers voiced their opposition to the secret society. For example, Rev. Henry Wilder Foote, a member of the Harvard Theological School faculty, declared at a November 1922 vesper service, "Any secret organization or 'invisible empire' like the Ku Klux [*sic*] is a danger to the republic, since it sets in private, secret judgments above the government." Foote expressed his concern that the KKK's vigilantism subverted "the principle of our forefathers that we should have a 'government of laws and not of men,'" for its practices could only result in "oppression and tyranny," he insisted. Other Protestant ministers from the Boston area, including Methodist Episcopal, Universalist, and Congregational churches, among others, also publicly denounced the Klan as early as 1922.[4]

In December of that year the *Boston Herald* editorialized against the Klan, challenging its self-appointed role as the spokesperson of white Protestants. "If it were not for the fact that, in many cases, they have actually usurped some of the functions of government, we might laugh at them or ignore them. Their pretensions are ridiculous," the newspaper asserted. Questioning the mental stability of the Ku Klux Klan, the editor asserted, "One of the commonest forms of insanity is that of persecution. The Klanners have it in aggravated form. They think the United States is being persecuted by everybody from the Pope to [the Irish Catholic New York City] Mayor [John F.] Hylan, and they are unable to tell the difference between themselves and the United States." The *Herald* editor also suggested the way to deal with the Klan: "Orderly processes of law, applied with more than the customary vigor and dispatch, are the obvious remedies." Although Suffolk County District Attorney Thomas C. O'Brien announced in October 1922 that he would prosecute members of the KKK who violated any state laws and asked citizens to notify him of any violations, Massachusetts residents, as we will see, chose instead to take the law into their own hands to meet the challenge of the KKK in the Bay State.[5]

In Massachusetts, as in Maine, some college presidents and state officials joined a national anti-Klan organization to try to bring about an end to the KKK. The National Vigilance Association sought to promote anti-masking legislation by state legislatures and the public filing of the membership lists of secret societies. It also advocated having the federal government assume jurisdiction over, and the prosecution of, mob action.[6]

Opposition to the Ku Klux Klan also came from the Bay State's political parties, which denounced the KKK at their conventions. In August 1924 the Socialist Party of Massachusetts passed a resolution condemning the society because it "raises false racial and religious issues to the end that the working class may forget its historic mission to build a new social order."[7]

Unlike the national Democratic Party, Massachusetts Democrats at their state convention in September 1924 chose to denounce the group by name: "The Ku Klux Klan is a menace to the peace and security of the country and its free institutions. It should be driven from American public life." Bay State Democrats went even further in their platform, criticizing Calvin Coolidge, the incumbent Republican president and former governor of Massachusetts, for his reticence in speaking out against the Klan: "We are confronted with the spectacle of the President of the United States, the leader of the Republican Party, afraid to raise his voice against a society of masked men who are striking at the constitutional guarantees of liberty and religious freedom and who will, if not checked and dispersed, prove deep disunion and disorder." The platform lauded the Democratic presidential nominee, John W. Davis, for taking a public stand against the KKK.[8]

Massachusetts Republicans were much more cautious, for the Klan's association with the Republican Party in the northern states posed a problem for them. "The state committee took cognizance of the Ku Klux Klan issue in making up the personnel of the resolutions committee," noted the reporter Thomas Carens, as Republicans planned their state convention. Several committee members represented groups that opposed the Klan: "Judge [R. H.] Boudreau [of Marlboro] is one of the leading Franco-American Republicans of the state"; Joseph T. Zottoli of Boston "is a leader among the Italians"; and Matthew W. Bullock "is a prominent negro lawyer in Boston," Carens wrote. Despite the presence of these individuals on the resolutions committee, Massachusetts Republicans only mildly and indirectly condemned the KKK at their convention in September 1924, stating in their platform merely that "we deplore any organized effort to create racial or religious prejudice."[9]

The Republican Party's stance cost it some black voters. William H. Lewis of Boston, a former assistant attorney general of the United States, switched his party allegiance on account of the Klan issue to support Davis's presidential bid. Lewis hoped to lead other blacks, who had largely voted with the Republican Party since the end of slavery, to back Davis. "As a colored American, I propose to vote for Mr. Davis because he is opposed to the Ku Klux Klan, the greatest menace to American democracy today," Lewis stated.[10]

In the Commonwealth of Massachusetts, then, a strong anti-Klan climate existed among certain elites. But, as demonstrated in the previous chapter, state lawmakers chose not to take definitive action to proscribe the Ku Klux Klan, not even along the lines of what Massachusetts members of the National Vigilance Association were advocating throughout the country. In this political climate and social context, grassroots vigilante associations sprang up in local communities to repulse the hooded empire in the Bay State.

After the KKK founded branches in Lawrence, Methuen, and Haverhill, an anti-Klan group calling itself Les Vigilants formed, as reported in the French-language press. The society, also known by the letters PPP for "Progrès, Protestation, Punition," claimed to have organized four hundred members by mid-January 1923. *L'Etoile* and *Le Citoyen* indicated that they did not know the identity of the organizers, but their coverage, along with that of *L'Impartial* and *La Tribune,* implies that many of the society's members were probably Franco-Americans from northeastern Massachusetts. Newspaper accounts in the French- and English-language press intimated that young men made up the anti-Klan group and that it recruited among Catholics, Jews, and blacks. *La Tribune* reported that Les Vigilants claimed to be protective as well as punitive in that the group planned to hinder the Klan but, if unsuccessful, would seek to avenge the acts of the hooded society. An organizer of the group informed the *Boston Daily Advertiser* that the PPP planned to bring "to justice all persons who commit outrages against Catholics, Jews and the colored people." His rhetoric points to a level of cooperation among Franco-Americans and Jews that departed from the anti-Semitism of French-Canadian intellectuals in Québec in the 1920s. The PPP organizer further indicated that "the P.P.P. would feel justified in interfering with the Ku Klux Klan even to the extent of breaking up their meetings if possible." He stressed that the vigilante society, like the Klan, would operate under a cloak of secrecy: "Because we are fighting a secret organization we must of necessity keep our work secret." Officers also mimicked the Klan by donning robes and hoods but placed the letters "P.P.P." on their regalia. The *Imperial Night-Hawk,* a Klan newspaper published at the Imperial Palace in Atlanta, Georgia, informed its readers that "the letters stand for Progress,

Protection, Punishment" and summarily dismissed one of the goals of the organization with the quip "The protection part of it presumably applies to bootleggers."[11]

Various press reports attest to the PPP's identification of Jews, blacks, and Catholics as the intended victims of the Klan and its sympathizers in Massachusetts. In October 1922 someone threw a brick through the window of the home of Leo Simmons of Revere with a note signed "K.K.K." that read, "Jews are not wanted. Must vacate within 48 hours." When J. Levine, who operated a shoe business out of his modest home in Wakefield, planned to move to a more upscale neighborhood, he received a note in January 1923 signed "K.K.K." threatening a visit from the Klan on the very first night he stayed in his new abode. Levine naturally worried that he and his wife would lose everything they had worked for over the course of many years. When William W. Bryant, a black postal worker, moved with his wife to a home they had purchased in a white neighborhood in Arlington, they received a threatening letter in September 1924 signed "K.K.K. of New Hampshire." The letter read, "We learn you have deliberately moved into a white neighborhood," and it warned Bryant: "Unless you move away immediately more drastic measures will be taken against you."[12] The social and economic gains of these above individuals apparently inspired the jealousy and threats of the KKK or its sympathizers.

Catholic institutions were also Klan targets in Massachusetts. In January 1923 a worker found a note inside of the new Immaculate Conception High School building in Malden that stated, "No Katholic high schools or colleges for this district while a Klansman lives." Because the KKK threatened to bomb the structure, hundreds of former students began guarding the building during the evenings. In the same month Rev. James T. O'Reilly, the pastor of St. Mary's Catholic Church in Lawrence, received—as did some of his parishioners—a letter signed by the KKK stating that the hooded society planned to destroy their church and other parish buildings. Also in January 1923, Rev. James Donnelly, the pastor of St. Bernard's Church in Fitchburg, received a letter from the KKK that it planned to blow up his church with dynamite. Given this menacing climate, the KKK was suspected of causing the fire that destroyed the Catholic school of St. Anthony Parish in Shirley in 1923. In November 1924 a young boy witnessed two people dressed in Klan robes setting fire to St. Gregory's Roman Catholic Church in Dorchester. Charles H. Smith, a member of the Knights of Columbus and the manager of the Smithsonian Bureau of Investigation, a Boston detective agency, contacted the premier of Québec, Louis A. Taschereau, to alert him of the similarities between the church fires in the Boston area and those that had taken place in Québec. Smith subsequently received a chilling letter signed

"K.K.K." and stating, "We are dead wise to your game, furnishing dope to the Canadian government about the church fires. We will shove your body through the murder machine. Beware of the fifth day after this—Leave town."[13]

The PPP formed in reaction to this hostile climate. As an anti-Klan organization, the PPP wanted to be proactive in northeastern Massachusetts, and its actions resembled those of the KKK. When the PPP suspected the Klan of holding a meeting on property owned by the Deaconess Fresh Air Home in Haverhill, fifteen PPP members dressed in their robes surrounded the building in January 1923 and threatened to burn it down. The PPP also drew the letters *KKK* on the home. The *Boston Daily Advertiser* reported that "Haverhill citizens deplore the acts both of the Ku Klux Klan and the P.P.P.," yet it acknowledged "Meanwhile the Ku Klux Klan is growing rapidly."[14] No other articles about the PPP were found. If the society continued its anti-Klan activities, it did so under a much lower profile, without regalia and without crediting itself for its tactics.

Despite the possible disappearance of the PPP, anti-Klan sentiment continued to run deeply in the greater Franco-American community of Haverhill. In a column from September 1923 published in English, likely for the benefit of the KKK and its supporters, *Le Citoyen* issued Klan members a warning: "They may be able to thrive in the South where colored folks are afraid of the whites, but in this section of the country they are going to have casualties." In August residents of the Belvedere district of Lowell had been awakened before midnight by the sound of a cannon, only to be confronted by both a twenty-foot cross burning atop Fort Hill Park, visible for miles, and by the firing of a second cannon. *L'Etoile* reported that this incident marked the first visible sign of the Klan's presence in Lowell. *Le Citoyen* promised repercussions for the Lowell men who joined the Klan: "If you are in business and value it keep your face out of the K.K.K., for you are going to be shown up in the end." *Le Citoyen* concluded its English-language editorial by threatening members of the Ku Klux Klan with violence: "These fanatics, if they try to pull their stuff in this territory, should first arrange with the undertaker for a decent burial, for, believe us, they are going to get all that's coming to them."[15]

The editor's prediction came true the following year. In 1924 the Ku Klux Klan met violence in the northeastern and central Massachusetts communities of Bolton, Berlin, Byfield, Salisbury, Wilmington, Haverhill, Lancaster, Spencer, Millbury, and Worcester. After selectmen in Berlin, fearing disorder, refused to allow the KKK to meet at the city hall in May, one hundred Klan members turned out for a meeting in Bolton and were met there by four hundred Klan opponents. Anti-Klan members hurled rocks at their adversaries, but there were no reported injuries. When two hundred Klan members met in a field near Berlin in July, young men hiding behind trees and stone walls attacked them as they departed. Indulging in a little Bay State humor, the *Boston Daily Advertiser* joked, "The Klansmen emulated the British in their famous retreat from Lexington, as their autos dashed back along the road they had come, amid a bombardment of rocks."[16]

When nearly one thousand Klansmen and Klanswomen met on the fenced ball field of Byfield in July, one hundred young men armed with bats and other clubs demanded access to the meeting. Klan members called the state police for protection and received it; the KKK had a permit to use the ball field, officers informed the Klan's opponents and told them they would break the law if they forced their way into the meeting. Tensions dissipated when Klan opponents withdrew, and the meeting resumed. At its conclusion the KKK burned a thirty-foot cross to symbolize the purifying of American politics, a national goal of the organization, as a Klan leader informed the *Boston Herald*.[17]

Five hundred Klan members also met in July in the field of Harry E. French in Salisbury and burned a forty-foot cross. As they left the site, two hundred youths from Amesbury threw stones at their vehicles. Police did not report any injuries.[18]

While fifteen hundred Klan members gathered on the farm of Dr. Bradford Powell in Wilmington in July, hundreds of anti-Klan sympathizers prepared to ambush them. After the Klan had burned a twenty-foot cross and were starting to leave the farm, bird calls went out, and Klan opponents emerged to hurl stones, clubs, and other objects at the departing vehicles, breaking windows and denting cars. Glass, nails, and tacks strewn onto the roadway punctured tires as well. The Klan members at the meeting covered their license plates to prevent onlookers from determining their identity. There was no indication that they fought their attackers; instead, they drove off as quickly as they could to escape harm and possibly to escape identification.[19]

The small clashes that took place in Massachusetts between the Klan and its opponents from May to July 1924 appeared to give anti-Klan forces both experience and confidence. This led to more violent confrontations in the Bay State from late July through October, resulting in more serious consequences, including some casualties.

In late July 1924 an estimated three thousand to five thousand Klan members assembled on a farm in Groveland but did not burn a cross, at the request of police, who undoubtedly anticipated trouble. When the Klan finished its meeting around midnight, sweepers had to clear the road of nails and glass that anti-Klan forces had placed there to puncture the tires of Klan vehicles. State police, with the assistance of police from nearby municipalities, escorted the Klan from their meeting. One member of the KKK drove each of the one thousand vehicles while other Klansmen, "all armed with rifles, revolvers, shot guns, black-jacks and pieces of iron pipe," walked alongside the automobiles, noted the *Boston Herald*. "Large numbers of the Klan group were apparently former service men, wearing army uniforms," reported the *Biddeford Daily Journal*. The Klan members moved peacefully through Groveland, but when they crossed the Merrimac River into Haverhill four hundred to five hundred people attacked them with rocks and other projectiles at White's Corner. These opposition forces, armed with baseball bats, revolvers, and rifles, had also come from Boston, Lawrence, Lowell, Lynn, and Newburyport. The Klansmen fought their attackers, and three to five anti-Klan members (newspaper accounts vary on the actual number) suffered gunshot wounds. Twenty-four men, Klan and anti-Klan members alike, were arrested by state and Haverhill police during the riot. Among the anti-Klan sympathizers arrested were Francis Cotter and Edmund Lucy, both of whom suffered gunshot wounds, along with James Connolly and Eugene Lemiere, the latter from Haverhill.[20]

Le Courier de Lawrence remarked with evident pride that a Franco-American officer of the law, Olivier Leblanc of Haverhill, had single-handedly arrested eleven rioters. In an attempt to mock the negativity commonly directed toward such hyphenated Americans as Leblanc during the 1920s, *Le Courier de Lawrence* pointed out that "Leblanc appartient à la race dégénérée des franco-américains" (Leblanc belongs to the degenerate race of Franco-Americans). At the court hearing State Trooper Leblanc testified that Klan vehicles had been traveling single file when a car with individuals hostile to the KKK pulled up alongside the procession and exchanged gunshots; the Klan fired the first shots, Leblanc pointed out, and he stopped both vehicles.[21]

Judge John J. Winn of the central district court in Haverhill criticized both the society and its antagonists for taking the law into their own hands. He fined eight Klansmen who had been riding in vehicles where weapons were found for disturbing the peace, and he sentenced another Klan member, who had been found in possession of a lead pipe, to thirty days in jail. Winn dismissed the charges against two teenage members of the society from Worcester, and he ordered the remaining arrestees to stand trial. Several weeks later Judge Daniel J. Cavan found eight Klan and five anti-Klan members guilty of disturbing the peace, and he sentenced each to thirty days in jail.[22] Through such prosecutions and convictions, Massachusetts authorities sent a message aimed at deterring vigilante groups from organizing either on behalf of or against the Ku Klux Klan.

Following the Haverhill riot, newspapers in the Bay State commented on the influence of southern and midwestern Klan members in New England. The *Boston Daily Advertiser* noted, for instance, that the fifty-six-year-old William Y. C. Humes, "a Southerner" from Miami, Florida, had ridden in the Klan vehicle that had reportedly fired gunshots after the Klan meeting in Groveland. Humes had been in Massachusetts during the summer to promote Florida real estate investments, and the newspaper pointed out that he was not a person of high moral character, for he had previously been arrested for the murder of a young man who had given "undue attention" to his twenty-four-year-old wife. When 500 Klan members met in Oxford and 150 met in Lunenberg in August *L'Opinion Publique* observed that a number of Klan autos had license plates from Ohio and Texas, something the newspaper interpreted to mean that the local branches lacked sufficient organization and needed to rely on outside speakers.[23] These brief accounts, like those discussed earlier, provide some insight into the presence of Klan members from the South and Midwest in Haverhill and other Massachusetts communities, but the full extent of their involvement in New England is not known.

Haverhill was not the only site of violence between Klan and anti-Klan groups in Massachusetts in the summer of 1924. In May the KKK had held meetings on farms and fields in Lancaster and Spencer, located in Worcester County. In late July clashes between the two forces in these locales left over fifty people hurt, with five of them seriously injured as the result of fractures of the back and skull and bullet wounds to the head, chest, arms, and legs. At least one of the wounded was a police officer. In Lancaster alone five hundred men and boys confronted two hundred Klan members with sticks and stones and held them under siege for nine hours until police were able to escort them away from their meeting place.[24]

The number of individuals involved in the confrontation in Spencer went unreported but police intervention there prevented a riot. "Des noms français parmi les adversaires du Klan" (some French names among the Klan's opponents), noted *L'Etoile* in its description of the event. Arrested for throwing stones at Klan vehicles as they departed from their meeting on the Wilson farm in Spencer and thereby causing an estimated fifteen thousand dollars in damage were the Spencer residents Léo Gagnon, John Daoust, Julius Durnomski, Charles McGrail, William J. Sullivan, and John Demetre. Each received a three-month jail sentence at the Worcester House of Corrections.[25]

Several individuals involved in the Lancaster clash were also arrested. Charles A. Schumacher Jr., who owned the land where the riot took place, admitted firing his gun into the air to dispel the rioters, and police charged him with disturbing the peace. Arrested on the same charge for throwing stones were Louis Draleaux, David Salvatore, and Constantino Sommi.[26] Unfortunately, the available evidence sheds little light on the men who constituted the opposition to the Ku Klux Klan in Massachusetts. But the last names of the arrested opponents in Lancaster and Spencer suggest that Franco-American, Irish, Italian, and other ethnic Catholics joined forces to combat the Klan in their communities. The variety of ethnic surnames also suggests that the Irish were not the Klan's primary opponents (or targets) in the Bay State.

Following these encounters, *L'Etoile* observed that the Klan members who had been carrying firearms at Haverhill and Lancaster had had permits to do so. The newspaper said that the state representative Roland D. Sawyer, a Democrat from Ware, complained that many civic authorities who were authorized to grant gun permits were either Klan members or individuals sympathetic to the society, and he announced plans to introduce legislation to restrict the issuance of permits. Sawyer's bill, as amended, stipulated that licensees keep detailed records of the firearms they leased and sold and of the individuals who acquired them; it also required licensees to share their records with licensing authorities as well as the commissioner of public safety and police. Approved in April 1925, the legislation called for prison sentences for those who carried without permit such dangerous weapons as "a pistol or revolver, loaded or unloaded" and "any stiletto, dagger, dirk knife, slung shot [*sic*], metallic knuckles or sawed[-]off shotgun."[27]

After the Lancaster and Haverhill riots, the state police cut short or postponed the department's vacations so that all officers could be called to duty and at least fifty could react within an hour's time to disturbances in any part of Massachusetts. In addition, Commissioner of Public Safety Alfred F. Foote issued orders on August 1 requiring state police to disarm all Klan members attending meetings along with those who were watching the gatherings. "I have pointed out that we cannot forbid the Ku Klux Klan from lawful assemblages, under the Constitution," Foote stated, "but we can and will prevent any and all assemblages of men bearing arms." The individuals with permits would be able to retrieve their firearms the following day, and those without permits would face arrest. "These instructions apply equally to klansmen and anti-klansmen," Foote announced. "I want it understood from one end of this state to the other, that Massachusetts will not tolerate armed warfare between any factions whatsoever," he emphasized.[28]

When some thirteen hundred Ku Klux Klan members gathered at a farm in Shrewsbury on August 1, state and local police searched all vehicles within one mile of the meeting site and confiscated the weapons they found.[29] The final take included five loaded revolvers, eleven clubs, one lead pipe, and an unspecified number of rifles, shotguns, slingshots, blackjacks, and rocks. The police arrested two Klansmen, one of whom had a rubber hose filled with zinc filings in his car and another who had two clubs in his. Police averted a riot by keeping anti-Klan sympathizers, estimated at half the number of Klan members, some distance away from the highway so the KKK could leave the premises without being attacked.[30]

In September seventy-five Klan opponents showered over seven hundred Klan members with rocks as they met in the field of Arthur Mystrom in Millbury. Only after the police arrived and Klan foes took off did members of the hooded society leave the site. There were no known injuries.[31]

Such hostilities did not deter the Ku Klux Klan from gathering about the state. In October an estimated fifteen thousand Klansmen and Klanswomen from throughout New England assembled at the New England exposition grounds in Worcester, where they initiated up to twenty-six hundred candidates into Klanhood. The hooded society thrilled its members with an air show. The hired pilot flew a Curtiss biplane over the crowd that was painted with the letters "K.K.K." on its underside and the words "100 per cent American" on its topside. When the plane descended suddenly and disappeared, a Klan spokesperson purportedly announced that the aircraft had been "forced down by a rifle bullet which punctured the fusilage [sic] and crippled the engine." This announcement must have created high drama at the fairgrounds and stirred up sentiment against the Klan's opponents. Called to the scene, the police discovered a bullet hole in the plane's hood. But the pilot claimed the hole had been made prior to the event and that a clogged fuel line had instead caused the engine to fail that day, so the police chose not to investigate further. The plane was quickly repaired and flew again over Worcester that evening. Decorated with red lights in the shape of a cross, the plane created a brilliant show, delighting the assembled Klan members.[32]

Anti-Klan violence surfaced only after the Klonvocation ended. When Ku Klux Klan members left the fairgrounds, "a hostile mob numbering several thousand" attacked them and their vehicles. While some young men threw stones as the vehicles passed through Worcester, others jumped onto the running boards and assaulted the occupants. A number of automobiles sustained damage, and individuals reported injuries. Two Klan members were arrested for possession of revolvers, but the district court subsequently dismissed the charges against them. Arrested for throwing stones, Michael Burke, a sixteen-year-old Worcester anti-Klan member, had to appear before the juvenile court, for the district court judge chose not to dismiss the charges against him.[33]

All throughout 1924 Klan members in Massachusetts faced intimidation, if not violence. In October over three hundred Klan opponents surrounded the Methodist Church in Upton, where the KKK was holding a meeting, and remained there until the police dispersed them. Some of these foes of the group then chased a couple of Klan vehicles through Upton and threw stones at one of them. When the KKK rented the Southboro Town Hall for a meeting in December 1924, anti-Klan demonstrators filled the hallways outside of the room to prevent KKK members from entering it.[34]

Even people not ostensibly associated with the KKK might mistakenly be singled out for assault. In late October 1924 nearly half a dozen bands preceded Republicans, who were dressed in blue and red uniforms, as they marched through the streets of Clinton in a torchlight parade. The party stalwarts were demonstrating in favor of the Coolidge-Dawes ticket in that year's presidential campaign. A burning cross on a hill appeared to signal the start of the parade, and anti-Klan forces emerged to throw rocks and rotten fruit and vegetables at the marchers. While the Republicans may have suffered indignities, none suffered injuries.[35]

As the above events suggest, the Klonvocation on the New England exposition grounds represented the last major event of the Ku Klux Klan in Massachusetts in 1924. The gathering also represented the last public appearance of the organization in Worcester in the 1920s. After the Klonvocation's violent conclusion, the Worcester Klan virtually disappeared as a force to be reckoned with. This fact, in addition to the Klan's inability to establish a foothold in Boston, as revealed in the last chapter, demonstrate that its strength in the Bay State did not lie in urban areas. Instead, the Massachusetts Klan found its strongest support primarily in rural areas of the state, as was true throughout much of New England.

Perhaps nothing illustrates the KKK's rural Massachusetts origins better than the locations of the violent attacks by anti-Klan forces on the hooded knights in the countryside towns of Billingham, Northbridge, Gardner, South Upton, Millbury, Berlin, Clinton, Medfield, Leicester, Westwood, Sudbury, Reading, North Reading, and North Brookfield in 1925. In mid-April men and boys stoned the automobiles of 15 members as they left a meeting in Billingham. In late April confrontations took place between the Klan and its foes in Northbridge and Gardner. Over 200 Klan opponents prevented 150 Klan members from leaving a field in Northbridge. The anti-Klan forces amassed large piles of rocks by the gates to the field and used them to smash windshields and headlights and to hold the Klan at bay from ten o'clock at night until four thirty the next morning. Police officers on the scene felt there was little they could do to stop the rioting; when Patrolman Charles H. Harriman tried to disperse the anti-Klan group, he "was stood on his head and his face was rubbed in the dirt by the crowd of anti-Klan sympathizers," wrote the *New York Times*.[36] When the Ku Klux Klan paraded in Gardner without a permit, word of the procession spread through town, and 300 people quickly gathered on Conant Hill to attack the marchers with stones and thus prevented them from reaching the summit. Of the three Klansmen dressed in robes and hoods who were arrested for parading without a permit, one may have been a Protestant Anglo-Canadian because the French-language press published the fact that he hailed from St. Stephen, New Brunswick.[37]

In early May 150 anti-Klan sympathizers threw stones at KKK members as they left the field on the Swanson farm in South Upton where they had assembled, and Klan members responded in kind. Windshields were smashed, but no individuals were reported injured. "Si c'est le cas il faut admettre que ni les Klannistes, ni les Anti-Klanistes qui ont pris part à la lutte, ne feraient bonne figure sur une équipe de base-ball" (If that is the case one must admit that neither the Klan nor the anti-Klan who took part in the fight would make good players on a baseball team), *L'Opinion Publique* commented, tongue-in-cheek. The police arrested Eugène B. Tétreault for throwing stones at the Klan; he had been sought since the Northbridge clash earlier in the week for having hit Constable Harriman. Given that the South Upton clash constituted the third one that week, *L'Opinion Publique* wondered, "Où aura lieu la prochaine assemblée et sera-t-elle aussi intéressante? Nous verrons" (Where will the next gathering take place and will it be as interesting? We shall see).[38]

Not unexpectedly, the answer to the first part of the question was rural sites, where several other clashes took place in May. About 200 anti-Klan forces gathered in Millbury after witnessing a burning cross, and they proceeded to shower Klan members with rocks as they left the farm of M. E. W. Witter. In the same month stone-throwing anti-Klan forces damaged fifteen automobiles as they left a KKK meeting in Clinton. Also in May, as 250 to 300 Klan women, men, and children left a meeting in the field of Frank Brewer near Berlin, up to 500 Klan assailants threw stones at them. Klan members responded in kind. "Men were falling from the impact of stones. Women were trampled under foot. Children, separated from their mothers, began to scream and cry. There was the crash of clubs on heads and impact of stones on heads and bodies," reported the *Boston Daily Advertiser*. As the local police tried to halt the riot, an officer was hit in the head and badly injured, and the police chief was knocked to the ground. In addition, "several of the Klansmen were seen to be staunching the flow of blood from their wounds," indicated the *Daily Advertiser*. Local police remained powerless to stop the fighting for two hours until state police arrived and assisted them in quelling the riot. In perhaps one of the lighter moments of the fracas, one of the attackers managed to snatch the robes of the Klan guard whose job it was to turn spectators away from the meeting.[39]

Ku Klux Klan parade in Portland, Maine, c. 1923. Courtesy of Special Collections Department, Raymond H. Fogler Library, University of Maine.

KKK parade in Milo, Maine, c. 1923. Courtesy Milo Historical Society.

Witham Klavern, headquarters of the Maine KKK, Portland, c. 1924.
Courtesy Maine Historic Preservation Commission.

KKK parade in Dexter, Maine,
c. 1924. Courtesy Dexter
Historical Society.

Ku Klux Klan Field Day, Montpelier, Vt., Fourth of July 1927. Courtesy Vermont Historical Society.

F. Eugene Farnsworth, King Kleagle of Maine, and Klansmen in Rochester, N.H., planning their "invasion" of the Irish Catholic city of Boston, governed by Mayor James Curley. *Boston Sunday Advertiser*, 18 November 1923.

Initiation ceremony of the PPP, an anti-Klan vigilante society formed in Haverhill, Mass., 1923. *Boston Daily Advertiser*, 18 January 1923.

Sample stones used by anti-Klan forces to form barricades against Klan members at whom they lobbed projectiles near Worcester, Mass., 1924. *L'Etoile*, 6 August 1924.

One month later up to ten thousand Klan members from Rhode Island, Connecticut, and Massachusetts participated in a Konklave (secret gathering) organized in a cow pasture on the Arnold farm in the southwestern Massachusetts town of Southwick. The pasture formed a natural amphitheater, and the Klan erected a sixty-foot iron cross there. Journalists were allowed to attend the gathering so long as they took no notes and did not name the speakers. One of the speakers commented on the recent clashes in central Massachusetts and threatened, "We may have to kill someone yet, but if we start, I can tell you we have the numbers and the qualities to do it right," the *Boston Herald* quoted him as saying. "Yet is an indeterminate expression," averred the *Republic,* "but unless the Klan should devote itself to the useful labor of going down to kill in some rat-infested cellar, which is unlikely, though not unfit, we don't know just what they propose to kill." The *Republic* also seized on the occasion to warn the KKK, "If they are merely looking for a fight, the residents and the local police will be enough to set them running."[40]

That fight happened in June, when six hundred to seven hundred Klan members gathered again at a field near Berlin. As nearly half of the Klan passed through the neighboring community of Clinton under state police escort around midnight, they encountered several hundred male opponents. Rioters threw flowerpots, porch chairs, and anything they could grab. The skirmish led to broken windows in homes and several injuries, including of police officers. The police recovered fifteen clubs, a revolver, and twelve lead pipes from the scene. No Klan opponents were arrested because their friends protected them by descending on the police and forcing the officers to release them. Klan members were not so fortunate. The police arrested close to forty members of the hooded society, one for intent to kill (he had fired a revolver at three individuals), several for possession of illegal weapons, one for driving without a license, and the rest for disturbing the peace and parading without a permit. Judge Allen Buttrick of the district court in Clinton held the Klan responsible for parading in violation of town regulations, and he asked the grand jury to investigate the actions of both groups of adversaries. During the four-hour hearing Buttrick remarked on the detrimental effects of Klan members from other regions of the country on the town of Clinton: "It is strange that after all these years that this peaceful and quiet community has been aroused by orators from the South and Middle West," he stated, "bringing to the citizens a gospel of hate and distrust for those who practice or profess a different religion."[41]

In the aftermath of the riot the police chief of Clinton, Michael J. Kittredge, complained about the state police escort of the KKK during the parade though his town, and he accused them of favoring and protecting the society, an allegation that Lieutenant Roy Kimball of the state police denied. Boston Mayor James Curley also argued that the state police should not provide protection at rural Klan meetings. In his inimitable style, Curley asserted, "Withdraw the constabulary protection of the state from these treasonable and strife-provoking meetings and the wholesome fear of public indignation and outraged Americanism will keep the skulking and cowardly members at home in their cellars and put an end to the mercenary activities of the klan's recruiting sergeants." Commissioner Foote responded to Curley by noting that the state police had appeared at Klan meetings only at the request of public officials and claimed that they remained neutral, insisting that they were not taking sides between the Klan and its opponents. Capt. George Parker, the head of the Massachusetts state police, also defended his forces: "We are not protecting the klan; we are simply maintaining law and order by preventing the throwing of stones."[42]

Stones were not the only weapons used against the Klan. In July riots between Klan members and their opponents in Medfield and Leicester resulted in twenty injuries. In Medfield Klan foes launched unspecified projectiles at 150 members, and in Leicester they pummeled 500 members with rotten eggs, tin cans, and bricks, knocking two Klansmen unconscious. L'Opinion Publique noted wryly, "Nombre de Klanistes étaient revêtus de robes immaculées avant la bataille. Inutile de dire que ces robes ne présentaient plus le même aspect après la bagarre" (Numbers of Klan were adorned in immaculate robes before the battle. Needless to say that these robes no longer display the same appearance after the fighting).[43]

In early August seventy-five Klan members and their friends gathered in a field in Westwood. Word of the meeting had circulated for weeks in advance, and anti-Klan groups from surrounding communities made plans to attend. On the night of the meeting three hundred to five hundred Klan opponents and up to one thousand spectators appeared. The foes pushed their way past the Klan guards and stormed the meeting, "ripping off hoods and gowns," and raced toward the speakers' platform. Some Klan members fled to their cars and were cut on their face and hands by broken windshield glass. "From the cars, klansmen reached out with club or fist to rap the hands or the heads of men who gripped the sides of the automobiles and tried to tip them over," the Boston Herald wrote. Several hundred persons chased thirty Klan members out of the field, and they tried to take refuge in the home of the farm owner, Stephen Illsley, where they remained hostage from thirty minutes to three hours (the newspaper accounts vary.) When a Klan member inside the Illsley home reportedly shook a club through a window at the opponents encircling the residence, the latter lobbed stones through all of the windows, damaging the furnishings, and threatened to burn down the abode. Only through the intervention and protection of the local and state police were the hostages able to leave the premises in their automobiles. At least twenty people, including a boy and three women, suffered cuts from broken glass, back pain from a thrown stone, and injuries to their teeth, but some Klan members opted not to seek hospital treatment in order to conceal their identity. The police arrested three alleged KKK members during the riot for carrying concealed weapons in violation of a law that had gone into effect in late July; although convicted, the men won their cases on appeal. The homeowner Illsley did not face prosecution. He claimed not to be a member of the KKK but had hoped to earn money selling sandwiches and beverages to the hooded society; the damage to his home likely far surpassed whatever profits he made that day.[44]

In August another violent clash took place in Sudbury. During the confrontation between the Ku Klux Klan and two hundred opponents, five Klan foes were seriously injured. Alonzo Foley of Saxonville took a bullet to the temple and received last rites from a Roman Catholic priest; an x-ray revealed three buckshot lodged in his head, but doctors expected him to recover once they operated. Thomas Silney of Saxonville and William Bradley of Framingham both were shot in the thigh, Edward Purcell of Framingham had his ear "blown off by buckshot," and Francis Maguire of Saxonville also suffered a bullet wound. "Friends of the men wounded in the riot declared that the 'antis' carried no guns, rifles or revolvers last night," reported the *Boston Herald,* "but that the klansmen were fully armed and evidently willing to shoot on the slightest provocation."[45]

Lieutenant Charles T. Beaupré of the Framingham state police barracks ordered the arrest of approximately eighty persons at the scene. One wore a steel helmet, something which piqued the curiosity of journalists, for he also wore it at his court appearance the next day. "Asked why he assumed such warlike headgear, he said he had been whacked over the head at previous Klan meetings," the *New York Times* informed readers. The Klansman had been well-prepared. Following the riot, the state police collected forty to fifty wooden clubs, two rifles, a revolver, a shotgun, an iron pipe, and pieces of brass. Among the arrestees were anti-Klan members. *La Tribune's* listing of alleged Klan foes includes several individuals with Irish surnames and one with a Franco-American family name, which suggests that Catholics from both cultural groups united to defeat the Klan in their locale. In the end the judge released all the opponents and subsequently discharged the fifteen alleged Klansmen who had been arraigned because of a lack of evidence to present to a grand jury on their role in the shootings.[46]

Shortly after the battle at Sudbury the Ku Klux Klan met in the nearby community of Ashland and lit crosses on Cape Cod from Hyannis to Provincetown. *La Tribune* interpreted these actions as reprisals against the Klan's opponents in the aftermath of the conflict at Sudbury. "Cape Cod was a stronghold of the American Protestant [*sic*] Association movement a generation ago, and when the K.K.K. entered the region a few years back the adherents of the old A.P.A. joined the newer movement," offered the *Providence Journal.*[47]

Displaced from urban settings, Klan members had to opt for rural environments in which to hold their meetings. When 500 Klan members from the greater Boston area planned to assemble in May at a structure owned by the National Motion Picture Bureau near the Malden-Medford town line, 175 police officers acting at the behest of the bureau prevented the meeting, and the Klan regrouped at the Batchelder estate in Reading. As the Klan left the Batchelder farm after their gathering in June, 40 youth stoned twenty Klan automobiles. The Klan members waved clubs and revolvers at their attackers but did not use them. No one suffered injuries, and no windshields were broken. But in August guns, stones, and tear gas bombs used in a clash in North Reading between 700 Klan and "a hostile crowd" (the estimates in the press ranged from 100 individuals all the way up to 1,000) ended with injuries on both sides. Police from Reading and nearby communities, along with state police from nearby barracks, tried to contain the crowd. Although police arrested two supposed members of the KKK, one for assault on an officer as he held another Klan member and the latter for carrying a dangerous weapon (a club), the judge set both men free.[48]

Such arrests of Klan members as well as the attacks by their opponents provoked the ire of one sympathizer, who complained in a letter to the editor of the *Boston Post* in mid-August that Klan members were not being treated fairly in Massachusetts. "Hasn't the organization a right to assemble for a meeting as they choose and if there were no attempt of the opposition to interfere is it reasonable to suppose that the members would stir up a riot amongst themselves?" the writer questioned. "The antis disturb and exasperate almost to the verge and then our police hunt around and seize a K.K.K. who may have an unloaded revolver which he carries to protect himself." The individual, who signed the letter "COMMON SENSE," grumbled further that the wrong people were being arrested by law enforcement officials and that the newspapers "make a great splurge over it."[49]

The American Civil Liberties Union (ACLU) also came to the defense of the Ku Klux Klan. John S. Codman, a Boston-based member of the ACLU, wrote to Governor Alvan T. Fuller after learning from newspaper reports that the president of the Law and Order League had asked the governor to prohibit Klan meetings in Massachusetts because they resulted in riots. While asserting that the ACLU was neither favorably nor disfavorably inclined toward the group, Codman argued that his organization wanted to preserve the right of free assembly. The ACLU had expressed similar sentiments a year earlier after the Haverhill riot, when it sent a letter to Hiram W. Evans, Imperial Wizard of the Ku Klux Klan, indicating that it would be willing to assist the society in any legal proceedings brought to ensure its right to meet in Massachusetts. "As the representative of the Union, I respectfully submit that the recent disturbances at Klan meetings in Massachusetts have been due to the attacks of unsympathetic outsiders," Codman wrote to Fuller, "and that to forbid lawful meetings on account of the possibility of such attacks is not only to deprive citizens of their civil rights but is directly subversive of law and order since it is a plain invitation to the disorderly elements in the community to break up by force any meetings which to them may be distasteful." Codman then asked the governor to use the state constabulary to assure "lawful meetings in Massachusetts" and to arrest those who interfere with them—in short, to offer state police protection so that the KKK could meet. The governor eventually chose, however, to withdraw state police protection for Klan gatherings and to leave this task to local police.[50]

Exactly when the state police stopped protecting the Ku Klux Klan from its adversaries is not clear. In mid-September they escorted the KKK from its gathering in North Brookfield. On the town square a riot broke out between an estimated 1,000 to 1,500 KKK members and several hundred of its opponents. As two hundred Klan vehicles traveled to the Bergin farm, anti-Klan members threw rocks, and an alleged Klan member fired two shots. In response, antis standing in front of the town hall threw eggs. When Klan members left their meeting, the state police and town selectmen escorted them, but foes again lobbed rocks and eggs as the vehicles passed through the town square. A stone hit a state policeman in the head as he tried to rescue two men the mob had thrown into a watering trough. The North Brookfield police chief found himself overpowered by the crowd, which took his night stick, handcuffs, and revolver from him. The police arrested one Klan member and one adversary, both of North Brookfield, for rioting. *L'Etoile* reported that one man had been shot, and the headlines above its column on the mêlée made clear that it blamed the KKK: "DESORDRES CAUSES PAR LES KLANISTES" (DISORDERS CAUSED BY THE KLAN).[51]

Not all measures taken against the KKK in 1925 were extralegal. When Newton M. DeBow and Melvin Dame, Klan members and operators of a printing shop in Lowell, sent Postmaster Xavier A. Delisle a pamphlet they had written titled "The Danger Signal," they were arrested for misusing the mails. The pamphlet threatened to attack such prominent Bay State Roman Catholics as William Cardinal O'Connell, the archbishop of Boston, and Mayor Curley. The two men pleaded guilty to misusing the mails and were placed on probation. In yet another indication of how the northeastern

KKK differed from the national Klan, "The Danger Signal," the *Boston Globe* stated, described DeBow as "a '100 percent American,'" but testimony in the case revealed that he was originally from Nova Scotia and had lived in the United States for only seven years.[52]

During the tumultuous year 1925 the Ku Klux Klan reached its peak in Massachusetts. According to the *Washington Post,* from the Klan's arrival in the state until 1925, it admitted 130,780 members. In 1926 the Klan had 91,324 members in good standing, revealed the *Post.* In February 1926 the *New York Times* commented that internal dissent since 1923 had plagued the Massachusetts Klan, and its numbers were declining. While the leaders had claimed a membership of 100,000 several years earlier, the *Times* noted that former officials contended the numbers had never exceeded seven thousand. Thus, figures from the *Times* differed substantially from those of the *Post.* Saying that the paying members numbered about 1,500 in early 1926, the *Times* flatly declared, "The Klan is dead politically in Massachusetts." The *Post's* figures confirm the Klan's demise in the Commonwealth: membership in good standing plummeted to 11,545 in 1927 and to 720 in 1930.[53]

Despite its decline the Ku Klux Klan continued to make its presence felt in the Bay State. When Catholics and Protestants of Leominster left Friday evening Lenten services in March 1926, bombs exploded and at least five crosses burst into flames on the hills of the Nashua River valley. During the same evening crosses burned on hills around Fitchburg.[54]

Klan members also maintained a visible presence in the Commonwealth by holding outdoor meetings in 1926. In July Klanswomen held an open-air assembly in Springfield that attracted Mrs. Robbie Gill Comer, their Imperial Commander, who was based in Arkansas. The Women of the Ku Klux Klan decided to form a Klan haven in Massachusetts, and its work served as an extension of their matronly role, for they decided to make weekly contributions to support two homeless children. In September up to fifteen thousand KKK men, women, and children from various states gathered at the Bailey Farm in Agawam, near Springfield, over a period of several days to hear speeches given by state and national Klan leaders and to participate in sports events. Six thousand Klan autos encircled the KKK, "shielding its activities from view," as the *Boston Herald* described the scene. Obviously fearing trouble, Klan guards wore uniforms like those of the Springfield Military Police Reserves and reportedly represented themselves as state police officers to all who tried to gain access to the grounds.[55] The state police protection of the KKK had apparently ended by that time.

The last armed altercation between the Klan and its adversaries in Massachusetts took place in 1926. As four hundred Klan members met in a field in Groton in October, one hundred anti-Klan forces cut down trees to form barricades along the highway; they then attacked the Klan in an armed conflict in which over one hundred shots were exchanged from rifles and revolvers. While the police knew of no casualties, they suspected that friends of the individuals who were hurt in the conflict simply carried them away.[56] Such violent clashes undoubtedly helped precipitate the Klan's decline in the Bay State.

In spite of its decline, the KKK nonetheless tried to exert its influence in the political arena by advocating anti-Catholic legislation. In February 1927 Telfair Minton, the former secretary of the Loyal Coalition and an individual who was "friendly to the Ku Klux Klan," according to the *Boston Daily Advertiser,* proposed a bill to ban prenuptial agreements that stipulated the kind of religious training any children of the marriage should have. The measure targeted the Roman Catholic Church, the *Advertiser* noted, because the church required such agreements before granting its approval for inter-faith marriages. Minton argued before the Legal Affairs Committee of the Massachusetts legislature that marriages and homes were breaking up "by the demand that future children shall be brought up in the Roman Catholic faith." The attorney Nils J. Kjellstrom of Westboro represented the national Ku Klux Klan at the hearing and told the committee that the Klan was introducing similar legislation in every state in the country. The Legal Affairs Committee "killed the bill by giving Telfair Minton leave to withdraw," noted the *Advertiser.*[57]

Despite this legislative defeat, the national Ku Klux Klan continued its attempts to stir anti-Catholic sentiment in Massachusetts in 1927. In June Imperial Wizard Evans spoke to an estimated seven thousand Klan women and men from throughout New England who gathered in Springfield. Evans took the occasion to denounce the pope and others in the Catholic hierar-chy; he also beseeched the Klan to work against the 1928 presidential bid of the Catholic governor of New York, Alfred E. Smith, and to defeat a Catho-lic U.S. senator from Massachusetts named David I. Walsh. Walsh attracted negative Klan attention because he had served as the first Irish Catholic governor of the Bay State and, as a delegate to the 1924 national Democratic convention, had pushed to condemn the Ku Klux Klan by name.[58]

The KKK had misgivings as well about the role of Catholic educators in Massachusetts public schools. In 1927 *Kourier Magazine,* a national Klan newspaper operating from Atlanta, published an article written by a member of the Mayflower Klan No. 2 of Brockton that lamented the decline in the quality of elementary schoolteachers as women moved into more remunera-tive occupations, such as clerical work, after the world war. Moreover, the writer protested, Roman Catholic women were filling the resulting empty teaching positions in the elementary schools. Without citing a source, the individual contended that 50 percent of public schoolteachers were Catholic and that the proportion ranged as high as 95 percent in cities such as Boston and Lowell. The Brockton member's worry was that the infusion of Catholic teachers into the public school system was having an adverse effect on the "patriotic temper" and thus undermined the Klan's vision of Americanism.[59] In their attacks on Catholic educators Klan members and sympathizers continued their cultural war against their religious and ethnic rivals.

Perhaps it was no surprise that U.S. senator J. Thomas Heflin of Alabama was chosen to address the Mayflower Klan of Brockton in March 1929. Heflin had gained a reputation during his political career as "the long-time exponent of Ku Kluxery," noted one journalist a decade later. His visit to Brockton sparked a physical confrontation with anti-Klan forces in Massachusetts. As Heflin approached Vasa Hall, where an audience of about eight hundred awaited him inside the building, "a group of about 100 irate persons" jeered him outside the structure. As Heflin gave his speech, a rock crashed through a window near the stage. When Heflin left the building, he encountered more heckling, and Klan opponents slung mud at him. The next evening Heflin spoke for over two hours at a Klan meeting in the Campello section of Brockton, during which he addressed the crowd about the anti-Catholic measures he championed in Washington, including immigration restrictions. As Heflin left the meeting a bottle thrown by a protestor nearly hit him but instead struck a police sergeant, knocking him unconscious. Although stones were also thrown, no other injuries were reported.[60]

Following the bottle-throwing incident at Brockton, Heflin tried to get his colleagues in the Senate to pass a resolution condemning those responsible, contending that their actions interfered with his constitutional rights.[61] He asked the Senate to "stand firm at all times in its support and protection of the American citizens' sacred right of free speech and peaceful assembly." During the floor debate Sen. William E. Borah of Idaho reasoned that voting for Heflin's resolution would be tantamount to voting for his anti-Catholic activities, and Borah further alleged that the resolution would make the Brockton incident a "contest between Roman Catholicism and Americanism." Stated Borah: "When he presents a resolution which puts the Senate in the position of denouncing those he says were Catholic criminals, he allies the Senate with his attack upon the Catholic people of the United States." The Senate sided with Borah and soundly defeated Heflin's resolution.[62]

Heflin's speeches in Massachusetts, as in Maine, served as the last notable public events of the Commonwealth Klan in the 1920s. Reports in *Kourier Magazine* reveal that the KKK nonetheless continued to maintain some level of organization in the Bay State during the 1930s. The newspaper published stories about the activities of these Klan groups, many of which tried to portray their Americanism by adopting the names of patriots and patriotic events, such as the Paul Revere Klan at Leominster and the Boston Tea Party Klan; other groups highlighted their Protestantism by taking the name of Protestant explorers, as did the Viking Klan of Lynn.[63]

Although the Massachusetts KKK continued to promote Protestantism during the 1930s, it increasingly directed its attention and energy against Communism, following the example of Klan groups in other states. "We denounce it [Communism] as an enemy of the American government and of American institutions, and American social order," stated one unnamed Massachusetts Klan group in the *Kourier*. "We will make war on Communism by every lawful method," it asserted. In 1931 the Bay State Klan went on record with a formal resolution in favor of having public school educators swear loyalty oaths, pointing out that high-ranking federal and state officials took oaths of allegiance to their respective constitutions. In advocating state legislation for this purpose, the Massachusetts Klan undoubtedly hoped to alleviate its concerns about Catholics and possibly Communists influencing young minds in the state's public schools. Ironically, the governor who in June 1935 signed into law "An Act Requiring that an Oath or Affirmation Be Taken and Subscribed to by Certain Professors, Instructors and Teachers in the Colleges, Universities and Schools of the Commonwealth" was none other than James Curley.[64]

To summarize, the Massachusetts experience reveals the efforts of Irish Catholic civic leaders, especially Boston mayor James Curley, in working against the Ku Klux Klan in the Commonwealth during the 1920s. One might wonder if Franco-Americans in the Bay State acceded to Irish political leadership, such as Curley's, in the face of the Klan threat. While Massachusetts Franco-Americans tended to vote more Democratic than Republican before 1920, the historian Ronald Petrin has found that they supported whichever party offered them the influence they sought; political pragmatism rather than ethnic conflict thus determined the political party affiliation of Franco-Americans, he contends.[65] The KKK threat does not appear to have solidified Franco-Americans' backing of the Democratic Party in the Commonwealth. As noted in chapter 6, for example, while some Republican Franco-Americans may have endorsed James Curley's 1924 gubernatorial bid, which took place at the height of the Klan's popularity in Massachusetts, others did not.

Unlike Irish Catholic politicians, Irish Catholic religious officials, such as Archbishop William O'Connell, appear not to have taken a leadership role in resisting the KKK in the Commonwealth. Newspaper accounts and archdiocesan files, for example, are silent on any possible role O'Connell may have had in fighting the KKK. Archdiocesan records do intimate, however,

O'Connell's interest in the Americanization movement.[66] This fact, along with conflicts between Franco-Americans and their Irish bishops, including the Sentinelle crisis in Woonsocket, Rhode Island, in the twenties (described in chapter nine), and the bitter memories of earlier conflicts in Fall River (1884–86) and North Brookfield (1897–1900), may well have prevented greater cooperation between Franco-Americans and the Irish in the political realm during the 1920s.[67] To the extent that Franco-Americans and the Irish did cooperate in combating the KKK, the Bay State experience suggests that they did so at the grassroots level.

Thus the Massachusetts experience particularly highlights the work of ordinary individuals to rid their communities of the hooded society. Catholics of diverse ethnic backgrounds banded together at the local level in an impressive show of unity against a common enemy. In the process they adopted the Klan's tactics of secrecy and violence and, in the case of the PPP, even robes that resembled those of the KKK. Massachusetts Catholics mounted an effective, if extralegal, counterattack against the Ku Klux Klan. Their actions helped to make the former Puritan haven a more hospitable environment for those who brought different religious traditions to the Bay State. In addition to Massachusetts, anti-Klan riots took place in Indiana, Pennsylvania, Ohio, New Jersey, and West Virginia during the 1920s; ethnic groups in those states, such as the Irish and the Italians, united to form anti-Klan organizations like the Knights of the Blazing Ring or Knights of the Flaming Circle to resist the hooded society through violence. Like other minority groups in the United States, in countering the Ku Klux Klan, Catholic ethnic groups in Massachusetts may have helped the nation to avert the fate of some European countries of the 1930s, in which similar right-wing organizations changed adversely the course of world history.[68]

8

Attempt to Americanize the Ocean State

In August 1924 *La Tribune,* the French-language newspaper of Woonsocket, Rhode Island, published a sensational story about one of its reporters being branded with the letter *K* on both his forehead and left arm before he managed to wrestle free of his attackers. The branding incident exemplified the potential physical threat the Ku Klux Klan posed in the state. The Klan's presence in Rhode Island created other problems for the Ocean State's Franco-American Catholics. The KKK supported the Americanization movement, under way since the Great War, and threatened parochial schools. Unlike in most other New England states, Franco-Americans of Rhode Island tended to vote with the Republican Party, leaving them in the awkward position of potentially having political ties to the Ku Klux Klan, which also favored the Grand Old Party. Not only Franco-Americans but also other Catholics as well as Jews were targets of the Klan in Rhode Island, which resisted the social, economic, and political gains these religious groups had made. In 1926 Catholics in Rhode Island numbered 325,375 (more than half of the state's population in 1920) and Jews, 24,034 (about 4 percent of the population in 1920.)[1] Individually and collectively, these non-Protestant groups worked to resist the KKK's influence and its version of Americanism in their communities and throughout the state in the 1920s.

Like other New England states with large immigrant populations, Rhode Island passed Americanization legislation in the early twentieth century. In 1919 the Ocean State enacted a law providing free public evening schools so that immigrants could learn English; individuals between sixteen and twenty-one years of age who could not speak, read, or write English were required to attend. As a result of this law factory classes established with state aid to accommodate working youth began in 1920. Rhode Island passed other Americanization measures through the 1920s, often with the support of the Ku Klux Klan.[2]

In 1920 Mother St. Jean de Dieu of Highland Park, New York, visited the convents of her order, Religious of Jesus and Mary, to inform the sisters of the antagonism of secret societies to Catholic schools. In the face of postwar Americanization efforts Franco-Americans wanted to preserve their French Catholic schools. Recording the substance of the Mother Superior's visit, a nun at Our Lady of Lourdes convent in Providence wrote, "On essaie de détruire les écoles catholiques ou d'en assimiler l'enseignement avec celui des écoles publiques" (They are trying to destroy Catholic schools or to make the teaching similar to that of the public schools).[3]

The Peck Bill was one such assault on the Franco-American parochial schools of Rhode Island. In 1922 Frederick S. Peck, a Republican farmer from Barrington, introduced in the Rhode Island legislature H 823, "An act to Secure More Adequate Economic Support and More Efficient Administration of Public Education." Private schools, under Peck's bill, would be required to obtain the approval of the state board of education, which would ensure that all instruction, except for the teaching of foreign languages, was conducted in English. The legislature ultimately passed H 823 Substitute A, which contained virtually the same language as the original bill Peck had introduced. Franco-Americans led the opposition to the measure, but an Irish American bishop and an Italian American community leader also spoke out against the legislation. Orchestrated by the mutual-benefit society l'Union Saint-Jean-Baptiste d'Amérique, based in Woonsocket, Franco-Americans called on Rhode Island's governor to veto the legislation.[4]

In 1922 the governor of Rhode Island was Emery J. SanSouci, a Franco-American Republican. The alliance of Franco-Americans and Republicans had much to do with Rhode Island ethnic politics in the early twentieth century. Before the advent of the New Deal, Franco-Americans in New England sided either with the Irish in the Democratic Party or with the Yankees in the Republican Party, depending on which group posed a lesser threat to their interests. In Rhode Island, Franco-Americans perceived the Irish as the greater threat. "It should be noted that from time to time there have been deep rivalries in the Catholic Church of Rhode Island between Irish and French-Canadian clerics and laymen. While these disputes have no direct bearing on politics," Duane Lockard points out, "the indirect implications are obvious." Another reason Rhode Island's French-speaking population leaned toward the Republican Party in the early twentieth century, Lockard submits, was the success of the Franco-Americans Aram J. Pothier and SanSouci in holding the governorship of the state for eleven of the first twenty-eight years of the century. When the Québec-born Pothier won the Republican gubernatorial nomination in 1908, it divided Rhode Island's Democrats. "The continued dominance of the Democratic party by Irish politicians had already produced grumbling among Franco-Americans," writes Lockard, "and the nomination of Pothier postponed the consolidation of the ranks of the immigrant groups." The leaning of Franco-Americans toward the Republican Party in Rhode Island led to notable political results, for Pothier and SanSouci were the first two Franco-Americans to become governor of any New England state, a feat not repeated in the region until Philip Noel became governor of the Ocean State in 1973.[5]

French speakers prevailed on the Franco-American governors to protect the interests of their ethnic group, as in the case of the Peck bill, which SanSouci vetoed, arguing that it introduced "fundamental and radical changes in the educational system of Rhode Island" that required more thorough discussion. Elie Vézina, the secretary general of l'Union Saint-Jean-Baptiste, promptly thanked SanSouci on behalf of Franco-Americans for his "courageous attitude in a matter of such importance to their faith, their institutions and their language," and he complimented the governor for "remain[ing] true to your duty as a Roman Catholic and to the race from which you are descended." Vézina pointed out to SanSouci that there were forty-two thousand members of l'Union Saint-Jean-Baptiste, and he informed the governor that he could count on the political support of the Rhode Island members, who were concentrated in the Blackstone Valley, in the future: "They clearly realize your true desire to protect all their interests, when necessary, and it is most certain that their help shall not be wanting when needed." Such admiring remarks turned to disappointment, however. Torn between loyalty to his political party and to his ethnic group, SanSouci did not veto the legislation within ten days of its passage. The Rhode Island Supreme Court therefore declared the veto invalid, allowing the Peck bill to become law. Opposition to the Peck Act caused many Franco-Americans from Woonsocket and the rest of Rhode Island to move from the Republican Party to the Democratic ranks from 1922 on.[6]

The Peck Act was but one element of the Americanization movement in Rhode Island. Another was the arrival of the Ku Klux Klan, whose presence some Rhode Island citizens felt as early as December 1922. Louis Gross, a furniture peddler from Providence, received a card in the mail, signed "K.K.K.," stating, "This is warning No. 1." Gross had lived in the Providence area for twenty years and had become a naturalized U.S. citizen fifteen years earlier. Nonetheless, he received a second note in the mail later that month, telling him to leave Rhode Island. In January 1923 Rabbi Jacob Goldman of Pawtucket received a letter, written in red ink and signed by the KKK, threatening not only to burn down his synagogue but also to harm him personally.[7]

Numerous Woonsocket residents also received ominous threats that month, and prominent Catholics were the initial targets. The pastor of

Sacred Heart Church, Rev. Edward O'Donnell, received a letter written in red ink and signed "K.K.K." notifying him that the clandestine organization stood "100 Strong." The writer portended: "Warning. You dirty Irish. We'll get even with you yet. Watch your step. We will burn down your old wooden church." The state senator Patrick J. Cox, a Democrat from Woonsocket, received a letter asking him for one hundred dollars, but it gave no indication of where or when to deliver the funds, and a second letter warned him that his life was at stake and that he needed to "take heed, and do as we say." Lawrence Hand, a druggist, and John Smith, a meat market owner and the newly appointed police commissioner of Woonsocket, found letters threatening to burn down their homes and stores because they were Catholic. On an even more sinister note, Smith and Cox were told that their daughters would be violated.[8]

Several days after this initial round of letters was received, at least ten more persons in Woonsocket, including Reverend O'Donnell, were the objects of menacing correspondence, purportedly from the KKK. This time not only Catholics but also Jews as well as Protestant merchants received letters from the "Invisible Empire, Klan 56, Woonsocket Order." It is curious that Protestants would be recipients of such letters, but the *Providence Journal* noted that not all of the messages were written on Klan stationery, and the authorities questioned whether the KKK had indeed produced all of them. Some businesses were also targets. Warnings signed "K.K.K." announced that the Smith, Park, and Strand theaters of Woonsocket would be blown up if they did not close. (The Ku Klux Klan, like the Roman Catholic Church, opposed modern motion pictures.) Albert Cote, a clerk who worked for the Texas Oil Company in Woonsocket, found a note that had a large *K* in each corner was addressed to him and signed, "Woonsocket Klavern No. 56." Attached to an oil barrel, the note contained the following cryptic message: "Catholics unbearable. Tanks ideal place for havoc."[9]

Another series of letters written in January 1923, eleven of them signed "K.K.K.," reached businesses and institutions in Woonsocket, including the St. Francis Orphanage, Holy Family Church, coal companies (threatening that they would be burned down, if they did not deliver coal to Klan members), drugstores, the Woonsocket hotel, Postmaster Thomas F. Cavanaugh, and a Jewish shoemaker surnamed Levin. Levin's letter read, "We will get you – Jews yet. We will make the penalty if we have to kill you. It will be easy to burn your store down in the night."[10]

Some of the letters attributed to the Ku Klux Klan may not have been authentic. This was the case in Newport. The police discovered that three young boys had sent notes to four or five Jewish residents signed "K.K.K." and telling them to leave the city. When the authorities brought the boys into police court, Judge Max Levy scolded them before sending them off with a warning.[11]

The wide distribution of supposed Klan letters raised fears among Rhode Island's residents. They especially worried the personnel associated with French-Canadian institutions in Woonsocket, particularly in light of the fires blamed on the KKK at Catholic properties in Canada. "The burning of many French Catholic churches and nunneries in Canada recently has led the heads of the organizations here to fear that the klan may transfer its wrath to Rhode Island," reported the *Boston Daily Advertiser*. The newspaper went on to assert that Woonsocket's large French Catholic population would defend itself from any attacks by the secret society: "If an atrocity of this sort should happen it is freely predicted that this city will flame with violence, for the hotblooded French population will see red and start a reign of terror of their own."[12]

Franco-Americans of Rhode Island worked against the Americanization movement—and its hooded proponents—primarily through the legislative process, however. They tried to amend the Peck Act in 1923. Representatives Albert J. Lamarre, a Democrat from Pawtucket, and Edouard B. Belhumeur, a Democrat from Woonsocket, introduced H 699, which would have required school committees in any given town to approve private schools if their attendance requirements and English-language instruction matched those of the town's public schools; the bill also would have allowed the teaching of foreign languages if they supplemented the educational requirements of a town's public schools.[13]

As an effort to overturn the Peck Act, the Lamarre-Belhumeur bill encountered opposition. The Rhode Island Sons of the American Revolution came out against the legislation, and they adopted a resolution stating, "The society views as un-American any proposal to substitute any other language for English as the language of instruction and urges the General Assembly to keep intact the educational legislation of 1922." The Rhode Island Daughters of the American Revolution adopted similar resolutions favoring English-language instruction in the state's schools. When it became aware of this opposition l'Union Saint-Jean-Baptiste, in March 1923, encouraged its Rhode Island councils to send delegations to the capitol to lobby for the Lamare-Belhumeur bill.[14]

The House of Representatives passed the proposed legislation the following month. Unlike the House, the Rhode Island Senate did not support measures to amend the Peck Act and stalled action on the Lamarre-Belhumeur bill for nearly two months. When Sen. Adelard J. Fortier, a Democrat from Pawtucket, moved that the Judiciary Committee report out the bill, a majority of the committee's members voted not to do so, thus letting it die. Another measure which would have amended the Peck Act by allowing instruction in grade six in a language other than English for up to sixty minutes daily, proposed by Sen. James T. Caswell, a Republican of Narragansett, similarly died in the Senate.[15]

Opposition to the Peck Act amendments took an ominous turn. After the Rhode Island House of Representatives passed the Lamarre-Belhumeur bill in April 1923, three Franco-American lawmakers received threatening letters signed "K.K.K." Representatives Belhumeur, Lamarre, and their colleague Wilfred L. Vandal of Pawtucket, who had also spearheaded legislative efforts on behalf of the bill, each received messages telling them to leave Rhode Island and not to return to the state. In addition, Lamarre found a note nailed to the front door of his home criticizing him for his work in trying to overturn the Peck Act.[16]

Besides language legislation Representative Lamarre sponsored two anti-Klan bills in 1923, thereby giving the Klan another reason to keep him in its sights. He introduced Bill H 520, "To Make It Unlawful to Wear in Public Places or on the Streets Masks or Devices for Covering the Face in Order to Conceal Identity." The measure would have made exceptions for Halloween and New Year's Eve. Lamarre subsequently introduced H 590, a bill to prohibit the formation of groups that opposed others on account of their religion or race. The proposed legislation called for fines and/or imprisonment for persons who recruited others to "klans or clubs or societies which have for their aim and purpose the organized opposition to any individual because of his membership in any religious organization, or because of his birth." The bill also sought to punish those who furnished such klans or clubs with a meeting place. Newspaper articles about Lamarre's proposal do not reflect any public statements against the KKK at the time he introduced his anti-Klan bills. But at a meeting of the Franco-American Social Circle held at the Jacques Cartier Hall in Pawtucket later in the year, Lamarre called the Klan "a heinous and venomous organization and a debased mob, the product of fanatical minds." He also observed, "It attempts to control the political life of the State and nation through dividing the country along religious and racial lines. It has sown wherever it has gained power the seed of discord, disorder and strife."[17] Despite Lamarre's efforts to deal with these problems, neither of his anti-Klan bills passed.

In spite of the lack of legislative success in combating the KKK, individuals and groups spoke out against the organization. The Rhode Island governor William S. Flynn, a Democrat, denounced the KKK in a speech he gave at a meeting of the Holy Name Society of the Holy Trinity Catholic Church in Central Falls. Flynn characterized the group as being "un-American" and praised the men being installed as members of the religious society: "You

men are true Americans and true Catholics, willing to fight and die for lawfully constituted authority. These men of the Klan are fanatical groups that
seek destruction of unity among Catholics." In East Greenwich a leader of
the American Legion of Rhode Island condemned the Ku Klux Klan as an
un-American entity and argued that it was the duty of American Legion
members to oppose the organization. The executive committee of the veterans' group subsequently passed a resolution bolstering legislation to combat
the KKK, claiming that the Klan's activities "are resulting in contempt for
law and order and causing the destruction of American ideals and institutions." In adopting this statement, the American Legion of Rhode Island
acted differently from its counterpart in Indiana, noted the *Providence Evening Bulletin.* Indiana was the epicenter of the Ku Klux Klan movement in
the United States in the 1920s, and the executive committee of the American
Legion that met at Indianapolis chose neither to endorse nor denounce the
secret society.[18]

Like the Rhode Island American Legion the state branch of the Ancient
Order of Hibernians (AOH) condemned the Ku Klux Klan. At a meeting
in Woonsocket in September 1923 the AOH resolved to "denounce the un-
American methods pursued by that organization which is even now working
its way after numerous floggings and lynchings and murders from the South
and West into our New England, the citadel of liberty and the birthplace of
the Revolution." The Irish Catholic society deplored the racial and religious
divisions the KKK fomented, and it praised unnamed Protestant newspapers
that "are openly standing by freedom of religion and the Constitution of the
United States." The Rhode Island Hibernians also vowed to work against the
KKK in their state. When the Newport branch of the AOH met in December
it singled out by name the KKK's "official spokesman in New England, that
heterogeneous mass of inconsistency, King Kleagle F. Eugene Farnsworth,"
and it praised Mayor James Curley in Boston for his anti-Klan efforts.[19]

Like the Hibernians, the executive committee of the Democratic State
Party of Rhode Island adopted in October 1923 a resolution condemning
the Ku Klux Klan, contending that its "proscription of American citizens
by reason of race, color or creed is diametrically opposed to the essential
doctrines of the Democratic party." Moreover, charged the committee, the
Klan "is opposed to the fundamental principles of our country, and . . . it is
particularly opposed to the aims and ideals which inspired Roger Williams
and those who came with him." The Democratic state committee called on
Rhode Island residents to use lawful means to resist the Klan's intrusion into
their state.[20]

When the Ku Klux Klan distributed promotional literature in Rhode
Island in November 1923, showing evidence of a recruiting drive in the state,

the *Providence Journal* brought this information to the attention of its readers and called on them to oppose the society. "There is no room in American life for a cowardly organization of this sort, which stirs up racial and religious strife, sets citizen against citizen in a bitter and unnecessary antagonism, and attempts to undo the good work of amalgamation and tolerance that so many stout-hearted Americans have been laboring to accomplish during the last few years," the newspaper opined.[21]

The next month, when Ku Klux Klan propaganda appeared in Providence city schools, it faced similar resistance. The public schools subscribed to a circular titled "People and Places in Current Topics," and one of the issues focused on Klan principles and promoted the organization. Mayor Joseph H. Gainer, an Irish Catholic Democrat, objected to the pamphlet's distribution in the city's schools, charging that it constituted propaganda. The mayor pointed out that the circular used the letters *KKK* as an example of alliteration and recommended that young readers "use it." Gainer noted in his letter to the school committee chair that the circular read in part, "The Ku Klux Klan does not want the negroes, Jews and Catholics to stop paying taxes or to stop going to school, it simply wants to out-vote them, so that they will not hold office or be hired for public work." The Providence school committee subsequently banned the publication "People and Places in Current Topics" from the city's schools and replaced it with another called "Current Events," which school officials had previously authorized.[22]

In December 1923 the *Providence News* wrote that opposition to the KKK was sufficiently strong in Rhode Island that the organization had not yet held public meetings or ceremonies in the state. The newspaper also indicated that the Ku Klux Klan numbered "more than 5000 members" and that it planned to work through the Republican Party to elect members to public office, "where more effective pro-Klan work can be carried on, if possible, without notoriety."[23]

Such information likely inspired members of the Rhode Island legislature to propose several bills to combat the KKK in 1924. Rep. Harry Horovitz, a Republican from Providence who had been born in Russia and educated in Providence's public schools, proposed H 510, a "Resolution Disapproving the Activities of the so-called Ku Klux Klan." There is no evidence that the measure passed, but a subsequent bill Horovitz proposed did succeed: Resolution H 737, "Condemning the Principles of the Ku Klux Klan, and Discouraging the Spread of Its Activities throughout the Country." The resolution pointed out that the KKK "is un-American in its objects, criminal in many of its activities and is dedicated to the creation of race hatred and religious prejudice," and it called on Rhode Island residents as well as all American citizens to oppose the group. Both the House and the Senate unanimously approved Horovitz's resolution.[24]

Members of the House introduced two other anti-Klan bills in 1924, but neither one passed. Rep. William F. Brown, a Democrat from Providence, introduced H 749, a bill "Affirming a Faith in Fundamental Principles of Our Government and Condemning any Appeals to Religious and Racial Prejudice." Brown's measure condemned those who functioned within or were sympathetic "with an invisible Super-Government" that eroded the rights of Americans espoused in the Declaration of Independence and the United States Constitution. The bill also denounced the KKK by name as well as its "racial and religious bigotry." The other unsuccessful bill, H 841, introduced by Rep. Joseph A. Potvin, a Democrat from Pawtucket, would have required organizations with twenty or more members, not including labor unions or benevolent societies, to register with the secretary of state their membership roster, constitution, bylaws, regulations, membership oath, and list of officers.[25]

After the KKK organized a chapter in West Warwick, the city's American Legion post passed resolutions to condemn the hooded society. Sen. Robert E. Quinn of West Warwick was prepared to introduce anti-Klan legislation with provisions similar to those of Potvin's bill, but there is no record that he followed through on his plans. Lack of legislative backing did not discourage other groups from going on record to oppose the KKK. The Providence Central Federated Union did so partly as a defensive measure because of allegations that the Broad Street car barn of the United Electric Railway Company was a distribution point of KKK propaganda, a notion that the Car Men's Union denied. The Coventry Democratic town committee, the Newport post of Veterans of Foreign Wars, and the Italian societies of the Pawtuxet Valley all spoke out against the Klan. The Italian societies used the opportunity to affirm their Americanism while challenging the Klan's version. "Be it resolved that all the societies of American citizens of Italian extraction of Natick composed of members who have shown and who are showing continuously that they are 100 per cent. American by having in their ranks over a hundred boys who served in the American Army and Navy during the World War and by being law-abiding citizens in time of peace and by believing in the fundamental principles of this nation of ours," emphasized the resolution, "vigorously condemn the activities of the Ku Klux Klan." The Italian societies further stated that they stood prepared to do all that they could to rid the Pawtuxet Valley of the white-robed society.[26]

The *Providence News* kept an eye on the association, and in February 1924 alleged that its members had been holding secret meetings throughout

Rhode Island in preparation "for an open assault on the free institutions of the State founded by Roger Williams as the center of freedom in thought and speech." In addition the *News* asserted that Klan members included "not only men from all walks of life, but some leaders in the financial, political and religious life of the State." Indeed, the Ku Klux Klan worked to recruit members of the Rhode Island legislature to the cause, inundating them with literature—all signed "100 percent. American"—that denounced Jews, Catholics, blacks, and non-Nordic European immigrants. Blacks were the smallest target, numbering 10,036 individuals, or 1.7 percent, of the Rhode Island's population in 1920.[27]

The Rhode Island organizers of the white knights included the New Jersey residents Morris S. Westervelt and Leslie C. Sparks. The two men rented a home in East Greenwich, where the Klan initially established its state head-quarters. Westervelt, "a paid national organizer," according to the *New York World,* served as the Kleagle of the Providence Kounty Klanton and became the acknowledged leader of the Rhode Island Klan.[28]

Meetings organized by these New Jersey Klansmen aroused the curios-ity and even the animosity of outsiders. When Westervelt spoke at a Klan meeting in Coventry in February 1924, "Scores of automobiles wended their way through the Pawtuxet Valley during the evening attracting considerable attention from the peaceful but aroused French-Canadian, Polish and Italian mill workers in the mill villages of West Warwick and Coventry," reported the *Providence News.* The newspaper also noticed that five armed constables patrolled the area where the Klan met, and a dozen more watched the high-ways "to protect both the persons and the identity of those who attended the meeting." When Westervelt and Sparks tried to speak at a KKK meeting at the Odd Fellows Hall in Newport, three hundred members of the Newport post of the American Legion broke up the session, and only police interven-tion "prevented a serious riot and saved the organizers from bodily harm."[29]

Following the incident, Mayor Mortimer A. Sullivan ordered the city police not to allow the KKK to meet in Newport again, and he held a special session with the city's board of aldermen, during which the board backed a resolution calling for the revocation of the license of any hall that allowed the group to meet in the city. "This historic city, prominent as it always has been in every cause for the advancement of liberty and justice," stated the mayor, who continued by using undiplomatic language, "will not be allowed by its citizens to become a sewer for the filth, foulness and dirt which issues from the diseased and polluted mouths and minds of a per-verted and disreputable organization or its abominable and contemptible representatives." Sullivan vowed to protect Newport's historic reputation as a city of religious tolerance.[30]

Other individuals also decided to take their own steps to combat and to intimidate the KKK. Westervelt and Sparks found themselves constantly followed. One evening in March 1924, eight men paraded around the East Greenwich home that the two organizers shared. Someone telephoned Mrs. Sparks to inform her that the parading men were overheard saying that they planned to kill the Klansmen when they exited the home. Westervelt was not at home at the time, but he spotted the group of vigilantes when he arrived there with his family and chose to drive off, only returning at 3:00 a.m. the following day under police escort.[31]

Shortly after this incident, George William Gill, a mill worker, called into question the Ku Klux Klan's Americanism in a thoughtful and well-written letter to the editor of the *Rhode Island Pendulum.* "One of the duties of the public schools is the diffusion of enlightenment, particularly and especially on the fundamental Document of our national structure, the Constitution of the United States. Any Americanism that is Americanism will be in accord with this Constitution," Gill maintained. "But how can we teach the much maligned 'Alien' element the rudiments of Americanism when we have within our midst a Klan claiming a conservatively estimated membership of some five millions," Gill commented, "who spend their excess energy in nocturnal convocations, and, hooded, evince such misguided and unconstitutional zeal for the maintenance of a Document with the contents of which they are, most evidently, unfamiliar." Underscoring the KKK's inherent contradictions, Gill emphasized, "The Klan pretends to stand for the Constitution, but if they did STAND FOR THE CONSTITUTION THEY COULD NOT STAND FOR THEMSELVES."[32]

Whereas Gill used the power of the pen, others used brute force to demonstrate their opposition to the hooded society. In April 1924 an estimated 150 to 200 people attended a Klan assembly at Hart's Hall in Shawomet, and "a threatening crowd" of up to 100 men formed outside of the meeting place. One person threw a stone as the attendees left the hall, but no one was hit. As four individuals made their way to their vehicles, which were some distance from the meeting place, seven or eight anti-Klan members chased and attacked them, leaving them with bloodied noses and bruised eyes. The victims chose not to give their names to the police in order to keep their identities secret. Unlike these Klan members, Westervelt appears to have escaped harm.[33]

Opposition to the KKK played out in Rhode Island and national political conventions as well. In April 1924 the Rhode Island Republican State Convention unanimously adopted a resolution presented by Col. G. Edward Buxton Jr. to condemn the Ku Klux Klan. Buxton prefaced his remarks by sharing the definition of Americanism he had presented to his regiment before departing with them for France to serve in the world war, a definition which stood in contrast to the Klan's: "An American is anyone, native born or naturalized, who cares enough for the institutions of America to uphold these institutions while alive or to die for them if necessary." Buxton pointed out that his regiment consisted of people of different religious and ethnic backgrounds, and he noted, "All these groups furnished their heaps of dead without discrimination upon a common field."[34]

The Democratic State Convention challenged the genuineness of the Republican convention's anti-Klan stance. The Democrats charged that KKK members "hold prominent positions in the G.O.P. of this State" and that Republicans in the state Senate had blocked a Democratic anti-Klan bill. Democrats therefore resolved "that, in the opinion of the delegates here assembled, the Republican convention was not sincere in its pretended opposition to the Ku Klux Klan, but was simply angling for the votes of certain peoples after having made their peace with the Klan."[35]

At the Democratic National Convention in New York City, Rhode Island delegates joined the demonstrations against the Ku Klux Klan that took place on the convention floor. The state senator Patrick H. Quinn, a national committee member and Rhode Island's representative to the resolutions committee, led the contentious minority fight to have the Democratic Party denounce the KKK by name in its platform. "The debate on the Klan issue was tremendously exciting," Harvey Almy Baker, a Rhode Island delegate, wrote to his wife. "It was a scene the like of which had not been seen in a Convention in the country since the Civil War," he exclaimed. All ten of Rhode Island's delegates voted in favor of condemning the KKK by name, but, as noted in chapter 3, the resolution failed by one vote. The defeated measure was the Klan's gain, in the view of the *Providence Evening Bulletin,* which chafed, "If there was any victory at all the other night it was for that organization of hooded bigots who ignore the true lessons of American citizenship and history and line up on the side of racial and religious prejudice for the pursuit of their own threatening purposes."[36]

While Democrats were preparing to assemble in New York City to debate the Klan issue at their national convention, an estimated eight thousand Klansmen and Klanswomen from throughout New England gathered in the village of Foster Centre in late June 1924 to enjoy field day activities as well as a clam chowder dinner and lectures by KKK spokespersons. Rhode Island's Klan leader, Morris S. Westervelt, organized and spoke at the gathering. The *Providence News* situated the event in a political context: the open-air ceremony, the first of its kind in Providence and Kent counties, took place "under the protective and friendly atmosphere of rock-rib[b]ed Republican Foster Centre," quipped the newspaper.[37]

Highlighting the Klan's Republican base, the *News* pointed out that the Klan's strength came from areas of Rhode Island "where there is a high percentage of illiteracy and where Republicanism is a religion." The newspaper explained that the KKK drew support from country towns. The *News*'s account should not be interpreted as an indication that the Klan was strictly a rural movement, however, because 97.5 percent of the Ocean State's residents lived in urban areas, making Rhode Island the most urbanized state in New England in 1920.[38] The newspaper's comment underscores the fact that the Klan's strength in Rhode Island came largely from its towns rather than its cities.

As Republican leaders promoted the Klan in Rhode Island's towns, they risked losing ethnic Catholics from their ranks. Italians and French Canadians were the largest immigrant groups in the state. Immigrants from Italy made up 18.4 percent of Rhode Island's foreign-born population in 1920, and those from French Canada, 16.5 percent; they were followed by immigrants from England, who amounted to 14.7 percent of the state's foreign-born population, and those from Ireland, who made up 12.7 percent. As the *Providence News* pointed out in June 1924, the Republican Party "now fears that the elements in the population of Rhode Island, especially the French and Italian Catholics, plan to retaliate."[39] Nonetheless, the KKK continued to organize open-air celebrations in country towns, which afforded them the physical and cultural space to attract additional members to the organization.

Westervelt convened another open-air ceremony to initiate new members in Rhode Island on the Austin farm in Exeter in late June. After a screening process, the men admitted into the Klan would each receive a membership card indicating that he "has been found loyal and worthy of advancement in the mysteries of Klankraft." That entailed a formal ceremony. About one hundred residents of Washington County, dressed in full regalia, formally joined the Ku Klux Klan in an initiation ceremony observed by upward of one thousand Klan members from Rhode Island and Connecticut. The new members knelt on the ground encircling the U.S. flag, illuminated not only by three blazing crosses but also by the beaming headlights of hundreds of Klan vehicles. "The Klan has shown its fangs in Rhode Island," commented the *Providence News*.[40]

The next day the *News* signaled that the Klan now had its sights set on Woonsocket. "The northern [Rhode Island] city has been the backbone of the fight against the Peck Educational Bill, a measure plainly aimed at the French parochial schools of Rhode Island," explained the newspaper. "The Klan stands solidly back of the Peck Bill, although they think it does not go far enough." The KKK wanted to inspect Catholic schools and convents, the *News* further alleged. The Klan's stated goals for Woonsocket were religious and ethnic. "Organize the Klan in Woonsocket and thus make a breach in the citadel of Romanism in Rhode Island," a Klan speaker at South County (the common name for Washington County) stated. "Let's go to that city and Americanize it," the speaker said of Woonsocket. "Put their schools and French daily newspapers out of business and the victory is ours," he asserted. The KKK was correct in identifying Woonsocket as an ethnic enclave. By 1930 the city's thirty-six thousand Franco-Americans would constitute 70 percent of the population, making it numerically and proportionally "la ville la plus française aux États-Unis" (the most French city in the United States). The KKK held its first meeting in Woonsocket in late July 1924, but no anti-Klan attacks took place as had happened in Massachusetts, noted *La Tribune*.[41]

At least fifty people from Woonsocket attended another large Klan gathering in Foster Centre in late July. Approximately eight thousand Klan members assembled, and two thousand automobiles, nearly all from Rhode Island, provided lighting in the evening, after a day filled with activities such as a baseball game and races. An unidentified national Klan speaker and an unidentified Klanswoman from Massachusetts gave talks. A robed Klan member on a white horse led the two hundred Klan initiates to the ceremony at which Westervelt administered the Klan oaths.[42]

Intrigued by the practices of the hooded society, one Franco-American journalist was determined to observe a meeting of the Ku Klux Klan in the Woonsocket area. When Lucien Sansouci overheard a small group discussing on the street the Klan's plans to assemble at nine o'clock one evening in the woods near the Massachusetts border, he decided to investigate. At the site Sansouci discovered nearly twenty individuals wearing white robes and hoods, but—curiously enough—not bearing the emblems commonly associated with the Ku Klux Klan. The group spotted Sansouci and interrogated him, and then five hooded members tried to brand him. As this happened Sansouci observed that the person hoisting the branding iron had an emblem resembling that of the Knights of Columbus. One of the attackers "était de notre origine" (was of our [national] origin), *La Tribune* alleged, for the individual reportedly told Sansouci in French, "Ce n'est rien qu'une leçon qu'on te donne de ne pas être espion" (This is nothing but a lesson we are giving you not to be a spy). The newspaper also said that Sansouci thought the voice sounded familiar and believed he might be able to identify it. As a result of the branding Sansouci suffered superficial wounds, which the *Woonsocket Call* described as "slightly blistered, . . . apparently only skin deep," and which would quickly heal.[43]

Press reports suggested that Sansouci's branding was the work of the Ku Klux Klan. Kleagle Westervelt denied that the KKK was responsible, and he assured the press that the organization had had no meeting in the area where Sansouci had been. "Je ne sais pas si ce sont des Klansmen qui m'ont fait cela" (I do not know if Klansmen did that to me), Sansouci himself admitted. "Il se peut que ce soit le fait de quelques-uns de mes amis qui ont voulu me jouer un bon tour" (It may be the act of some of my friends who wanted to play a good trick on me), he suggested. Contributing to Sansouci's impression that he was the victim of a practical joke, he received a mysterious telephone call on the evening of the attack, before he had informed anyone of it, asking him if the KKK had captured him. Sansouci acknowledged, "Tout ce que je sais c'est que mes agresseurs portaient des robes blanches et des capuchons blancs et ressemblaient beaucoup aux portraits de membres du Klan que j'ai vus" (All I know is that my assailants wore white robes and white hoods and looked much like the pictures of Klan members that I have seen).[44]

After learning of Sansouci's branding, the ACLU contacted the journalist to verify the accuracy of press stories. Sansouci confirmed that he had "been branded on the forehead with the letter *K* by hooded men" and, he added, "on my left arm." Sansouci went on to express doubts that his attackers were members of the KKK, even though they were wearing robes and hoods, explaining, "One spoke to me in French and one was wearing an emblem ring which appeared to me as being the emblem of the Knights of Columbus, though I could not swear it was." Sansouci complained in his letter to the ACLU that local authorities were making light of the incident: "They beleive [*sic*] and insist in beleiving [*sic*] that this adventure was nothing but a joke, and they seem to ignore that a criminal joke of this kind is punishable." Sansouci expressed a desire to prosecute his attackers, and the ACLU stood ready to assist him.[45] There is no evidence that they were ever found. Sansouci, the press, and the investigators do not appear to have considered the possibility that the PPP (described in chapter 7) or a similar anti-Klan organization may have been responsible for the branding.

La Sentinelle found Sansouci's story amusing. A French-language newspaper based in Woonsocket, *La Sentinelle* was the rival of *La Tribune,* Sansouci's employer. In its version of the branding, *La Sentinelle* chastised Sansouci by calling him "Sanschagrin" (without sorrow) and it suggested that the incident was simply a ploy to help *La Tribune* sell papers. *La Sentinelle* went even further, suggesting tongue-in-cheek that Sanschagrin deserved a monument for having risked his life to investigate the KKK.[46]

Sansouci's branding was not the only sensational Ku Klux Klan story to emerge from Rhode Island in the summer of 1924. In late August the *New York World* reported on the abduction of the drugstore owner Ernest S. Louis of Freeport. Two weeks before the kidnapping, a thirteen-year-old girl named Dorothy Shedlock had alleged that Louis "had fondled her and kissed her after sprinkling perfume on her." After Shedlock's mother went to the police and was prompted by them not to pursue legal action to avoid bringing undue attention to the child, the KKK apparently took matters into its own hands. Ten unmasked Klan members accosted Louis at his drugstore and demanded that he leave town. Louis refused, and he received a threatening letter several days later urging his departure. Louis told some friends that the leader of the Klansmen who confronted him was Wilford Van Riper, a stonemason with whom he had served in a volunteer fire company; the mason's brother, Clarence Van Riper, was a lieutenant on the police force, and Louis believed that connection explained why the police denied him protection after the Klan had threatened him. On the day District Attorney Charles B. Weeks convened a grand jury investigation to hear Dorothy Shedlock, her mother, and a fourteen-year-old girl named Hazel Rasmus, who also maintained she had been fondled by Louis, the drugstore owner was kidnapped while walking home with his pregnant wife and another family member. Three to five men (the accounts differ) jumped Louis, knocked down his wife, shoved Louis into an automobile, and told him they were Klansmen; the men drove Louis around for two hours, and, before dropping him off at a hotel in Hicksville, warned him again to sell his business and leave Freeport. Louis's reaction to the episode intimates that the KKK had succeeded in frightening him. Louis told District Attorney Weeks he could not identify his captors, he retracted his previous statement identifying Wilford Van Riper, and he told Weeks his abductors had "treated me fine and if they'd had a box of cigars along and a bottle of champagne it'd been a regular party."[47]

The ways in which the KKK handled Louis highlight the Rhode Island Klan's attempts to assert control over individuals who violated standards of morality in the community. All across the United States the Ku Klux Klan of the 1920s dealt harshly with individuals who committed adultery, deserted family members, engaged in bootlegging, and other actions that violated its conceptions of probity. But the Klan's public focus on issues of morality also led to its downfall, argues the sociologist Kathleen Blee, who points to the highly publicized case of Grand Dragon D. C. Stephenson of Indiana, a philanderer who eventually served twenty-five years of a life sentence for the kidnapping, rape, and second-degree murder of Madge Oberholtzer, a social worker.[48] The negative publicity generated by that case greatly undermined the national Klan's righteous stance as a defender of morality, as publicized in the KKK's interventions with Louis.

Besides the accounts of the Louis case, other press stories suggested the Klan's potential interest in local governance. For example, in September 1924 the *Providence News* indicated that community organizations such as the

Warwick Town Civic Club served as fronts for the Ku Klux Klan. Following the November elections, the *Rhode Island Pendulum* editorialized that
the Klan had functioned as a catalyst for reform in the state: "Among the
many forces at work in Rhode Island to secure victory for the reform forces
one of the most powerful was the Ku Klux Klan." Such narratives of the
Klan's involvement in civic clubs and its work as a reform movement reflect
ways in which the organization tried to improve Rhode Island communities
during the 1920s. Such conduct appears to stand in sharp contrast to the
KKK's anti-Catholic, anti-immigrant actions in Rhode Island as well as to
its extralegal abduction of and threats to the alleged pedophile Ernest Louis.
But the historian Nancy MacLean cautions against the practice of scholars of
using "false polarities" to analyze the Klan's activities. "It was at once mainstream and extreme, hostile to big business and antagonistic to industrial
unions, anti-élitist and hateful of blacks and immigrants, pro-law and order
and prone to extralegal violence," she contends. "If scholars have viewed
these attributes as incompatible, Klansmen themselves did not," MacLean
argues.[49] As earlier chapters have suggested, the Klan's opponents and some
of its own New England members did recognize such apparent contradictions within the society, contradictions that hastened its decline in the New
England states.

How the *Providence News* discovered the Rhode Island Klan's involvement
in civic clubs underscores the organization's difficulties in the Ocean State.
When the Warwick Klan did not keep up payments on the office that Kleagle
Morris Westervelt had rented, the landlord evicted the society and tossed its
possessions out the door in September 1924. Westervelt left town, according to the *News,* and it found papers blowing about in the wind near the
Klan's former office, including those that documented the KKK's role in civic
clubs. Not only financial challenges, but also internal dissension plagued the
Rhode Island Klan. Westervelt and C. S. Cleasby, who served as the treasurer or secretary of the Providence Kounty Klanton, had rented an office
in Providence under the guise of conducting an insurance business, but they
did not recruit enough new members or adequately manage their finances
because the building's owner similarly evicted them the previous month for
nonpayment of rent. The press also reported that some Klan members challenged Westervelt's leadership style and argued for more open management,
which Westervelt resisted out of fear that the Rhode Island Klan would be
harmed if more people knew how strong it was in the state.[50] Despite the fact
that some of Rhode Island's citizens saw the KKK as an avenue for change,
the circumstances of the Klan leader's abrupt departure from Warwick and
Providence served to illustrate the organization's decline in the Ocean State.

One way in which the Rhode Island Klan tried to stanch its declension was to allow foreign-born individuals to attend its meetings. This represented an effort to expand its influence among Protestants who were not native-born residents of the United States. "They are being allowed to attend Klan meetings so that they may be instilled with the spirit of the Klan and so the Klan can tell them how to vote," speculated the *Providence News*. In December 1924 the former Maine King Kleagle F. Eugene Farnsworth stumped in Rhode Island to attract foreign-born Protestants to the Crusaders, an organization with a broader membership than the KKK that included foreign-born Protestants as well as women.[51] While there is no evidence that the Crusaders inspired the imagination or interest of enough Rhode Islanders to become a social movement of its own, the attempted inclusion of non-native-born Protestants in the activities of the Ku Klux Klan in the Ocean State provides further evidence to illustrate that the KKK, as it operated elsewhere in the country, did not work in the Northeast.

Although there is little information on women's participation in the Rhode Island Klan, occasional newspaper items disclose that they were active in the movement and even had their own organization in the state. When the *Providence Journal* informed its readers that an estimated four thousand Klan associates had gathered in Westerly in July 1924 for a ceremony initiating four hundred new Klan members, it wrote, "A large number of women as well as men attended the meeting." In September 1924 the *Providence News* pointed out that the Klan auxiliary Kamelia was functioning in the Ocean State. While the newspaper said little about the women's Klan, it did observe, "It is well known that the Kamelias are a thriving institution here." The *Rhode Island Pendulum* noted in mid-September that thirty Klanswomen had met the previous week in East Greenwich. When the *Providence News* reported that three thousand Klan members gathered in Greenville in late October to support the bid of the Republican Jesse H. Metcalf for the U.S. Senate, it cited the presence of five hundred women.[52] Unfortunately, little additional information exists on the impact or the role of women in the KKK movement in Rhode Island. It seems clear, however, that the Klanswomen cast their lot with Klansmen as proponents of the Republican Party.

The elections in the fall of 1924 in which Klanswomen and Klansmen endorsed Republican candidates such as Metcalf troubled Franco-Americans. The *Providence News* featured an article in French that declared, "Le Ku Klux Klan déclare la guerre aux candidats catholiques. Il se ligue avec le parti républicain" (The Ku Klux Klan declares war on Catholic candidates. It is in league with the Republican Party). The *News* chastised the Republican Party for embracing the KKK in its search for votes, and it expressed its disappointment in the Franco-American Republican Aram Pothier, who was vying for another term as Rhode Island governor, because he appeared willing to accept Klan votes as well. Because Pothier did not repudiate the KKK, the French-language article stated unequivocally that "M. Pothier, un Franco-Américain, [est] le candidat des Ku Klux Klan, qui ont juré la disparition de l'élément de langue française, qui ont juré la mort de l'Eglise catholique" (Mr. Pothier, a Franco-American, [is] the candidate of the Ku Klux Klan, who have vowed the disappearance of the French-language element, who have vowed the death of the Catholic Church). The *News* further contended that Pothier put Franco-Americans in the awkward position of having to side with the KKK if they chose to support his candidacy.[53] Pothier's 1924 Republican gubernatorial bid therefore led to an odd fusion of Franco-American Republicans and their social and cultural nemesis, the Ku Klux Klan. Joining ranks with the Klan must have been a bitter pill for Franco-Americans to digest to help the standard-bearer of their ethnic group win another race for governor. As we will see in the next chapter the Ku Klux Klan in the mid- to late 1920s became implicated in a fractious ethnic conflict that further divided Franco-Americans, and it also infiltrated the militia to boost its declining membership in the Ocean State.

9

Infiltrating the Rhode Island Militia and Implication in the Sentinelle Affair

IN MARCH 1928 the *Providence Journal* alarmed its readers with the news that two hundred Klansmen had joined Rhode Island's First Light Infantry, which equipped them with Springfield rifles as well as a machine gun.[1] This account jarred residents of the state, forcing them to consider the potential power the Klan could wield and the probable harm it could still cause in their state. From the mid to late 1920s the Ku Klux Klan remained more active in Rhode Island than in the other New England states. During this period the hooded knights also implicated themselves in the Sentinelle controversy, which divided Franco-Americans from the Irish Catholic hierarchy and created internal discord in Franco-American communities in the Ocean State and throughout New England.

Despite the lack of success in overturning the Peck Act during the 1923–24 legislative session Franco-Americans were undeterred. When a new legislature convened in 1925, the Franco-American representatives Edouard B. Belhumeur of Woonsocket and Henri G. Nesbitt, a Republican from Pawtucket, sponsored H 745 to amend the Peck Act.[2] Their bill would authorize school committees of Rhode Island to approve private schools if they met certain conditions, including that "reading, writing, geography, arithmetic, the history of the United States, the history of Rhode Island, and the principles of American government shall be taught in the English language substantially to the same extent as such subjects are required to be taught in the public schools." The bill also "provided, however, that nothing herein contained shall be construed or operate to deny the right to teach . . . in any other language in addition to the teaching in English as prescribed herein." The bill thus allowed for the teaching of French in Rhode Island parochial schools. While the Nesbitt-Belhumeur bill may appear to be similar to the Peck Act, Richard Sorrell emphasizes that it gave local school boards, which were likely more sympathetic to the needs of local ethnic groups, control over private schools, and it recognized officially the right to teach in a foreign language. Reelected governor in 1924, Aram Pothier signed the Nesbitt-Belhumeur bill into law on April 29, 1925. Franco-Americans were pleased. In addition to thanking the bill's legislative sponsors, *L'Union,* the French-language newspaper of l'Union Saint-Jean-Baptiste d'Amérique, gave credit to the work of *La Tribune* of Woonsocket, la Fédération Catholique Franco-Américaine, l'Ordre des Forestiers Franco-Américains, and its own organization, l'Union Saint-Jean-Baptiste d'Amérique, for advocating this legislation to allow instruction in languages other than English: "A tous ceux qui ont aidé à réparer l'erreur du bill Peck, l'Union offre ses compliments et ses félicitations" (To all those who helped correct the error of the Peck Bill, l'Union offers its compliments and congratulations).[3]

In spite of this legislative setback, Frederick S. Peck, who was active in both the state and the national Republican Party, continued to push Americanization bills through the Rhode Island legislature. In 1925 he sponsored H 691, a bill authorizing the State Board of Education to visit, inspect, and supervise the state's day and evening schools "for the promotion of Americanization." The measure became law in March 1925. Lawmakers also enacted other successful legislation to fund Americanization measures, particularly instruction in English and in American government, through the 1920s.[4]

During this Americanization push *L'Union* commented that discrimination continued to exist against Franco-Americans in the United States and that the spirit of intolerance still reigned supreme. "La haine du nom français n'a pas entièrement disparu et l'instinct d'intolérance à l'égard des citoyens d'origine étrangère, de ceux surtout qui appartiennent aux races latines et qui pratiquent la religion catholique," the newspaper insisted, "est encore très fort parmi ceux qui s'arrogent, à l'exclusion de tous les autres, le titre d''Américain'" (The hatred of the French name has not entirely disappeared and the instinct of intolerance regarding citizens of foreign origins, those above all who belong to Latin races and who practice the Catholic religion is still very strong among those who claim, to the exclusion of all others, the title of "American"). While *L'Union* did not name the Ku Klux Klan, the implication is clear that it spoke to the kinds of intolerance the KKK promoted. In this social context, *L'Union* informed Franco-American readers in June 1925 that they should view the Fourth of July as their own holiday, not only because France had assisted the Thirteen Colonies in their revolution but also because Franco-Americans had developed institutions in the United States, such as schools, parishes, and mutual-aid societies, that served the country. *L'Union* advised readers, "Fêtons de tout coeur la fête de l'indépendance des

Etats-Unis et crions dans les deux langues de Lafayette et de Washington: Vive la République Américaine!" (Let us celebrate wholeheartedly the birthday of the independence of the United States and let us cry out in the two languages of Lafayette and Washington: Long live the American Republic!).[5] Reflecting this American spirit, pictures from the 1920s of the women's councils of l'Union Saint-Jean-Baptiste from such northeastern communities as Lewiston, Maine, Winooski, Vermont, Spencer, Massachusetts, and Taftville, Connecticut, typically portray them holding American flags.

Among the leading proponents of Americanization, the Ku Klux Klan made Providence its official Rhode Island headquarters in 1925. When the Knights of the Ku Klux Klan of Rhode Island and Providence Plantations filed articles of association with Secretary of State Ernest L. Sprague, it fashioned itself as a fraternal organization that encouraged its members to be active in community and civic affairs. The charter, which Sprague granted, indicated that the KKK sought both to educate "members in the duties of American citizenship" and to facilitate "teaching respect for and obedience to the Constitution of the United States and the Constitution and Laws of the State of Rhode Island."[6] The charter thus contained language that hardly anyone would have found objectionable.

Yet the Ku Klux Klan had difficulty attracting new members, and its numbers declined steadily in Rhode Island from the mid to the late 1920s. According to the *Washington Post,* in 1926 there were 4,666 members in good standing in Rhode Island, and that number dropped to 2,121 in 1927. That year T. W. Stevens, the Grand Dragon of Connecticut and Rhode Island, wrote to former Klan members to invite them "back on the firing line again" and to let them know the organization needed their assistance "to help the Imperial Wizard save our Country in this, our most perilous time since the Civil War." Imperial Wizard Hiram W. Evans alluded to the KKK's opposition to Al Smith, the pope "and his agents," and to the anti-Klan lawsuits and negative propaganda of former Klansmen that plagued the hooded society, when he sent a letter of his own to those with lapsed memberships, inviting them to rejoin the Ku Klux Klan. "I note that you have been suspended in your local organization," Evans wrote. "You need a part in our great program. We need you to win the war. Re-enlist for new and greater service," he urged. "We cannot LOSE this war," Evans insisted. As we will see, some Klansmen decided to join the battle by enrolling in Rhode Island's First Light Infantry. The appeals of Klan leaders did not succeed in attracting more numbers to the cause, however, for Rhode Island's overall Klan membership fell to 593 in 1928 and dwindled to 174 in 1930.[7]

As the Rhode Island Ku Klux Klan declined, it faced little overt opposition. Pranks occurred, nonetheless. In February 1925 four KKK members who attended a church service did not find their vehicles where they had left them, something they interpreted as an anti-Klan action, an explanation partially corroborated by police, who pointed out that "all of the cars were found in a conspicuously anti-Klan section of South Providence." But there appear not to have been the kinds of physical confrontations with Klan members that had taken place in prior years. In December 1925 the *Rhode Island Pendulum* editorialized that the Ku Klux Klan was gaining acceptance not only in Kent County but also throughout the state. Opposition to the organization was declining, the editor contended, while illustrating the newspaper's pro-Klan sympathies by stating that, despite the expulsion of the Kent County KKK leader (unnamed, but most likely Kleagle Morris S. Westervelt), the society "is a powerful organization standing for definite and stated principles." When forty Klan members rode through East Greenwich in their hoods and robes in July 1926, the *Pendulum* suggested the lack of protest signified growing acceptance of the hooded society: "A few years ago there would doubtless have been a disturbance had the Klansmen appeared in uniform on the streets."[8]

In 1927 the KKK felt sufficiently comfortable with the social climate of Rhode Island to organize a new church in Providence. Guy Willis Holmes, a Klansman, became the president general of the American People's Church of Providence. Clarence Cleasby, a former Klan officer and an incorporator of the new church, denied it was a KKK church but emphasized instead that it existed of, for, and by the American people.[9] Thus even if the Klan organization was no longer ascendant in Rhode Island, it appears that its principles continued to find expression in the Ocean State.

In fact, several bills introduced in the Rhode Island Senate in 1927 likely had the Ku Klux Klan stamp on them, as Sen. Albéric Archambault, a Democrat from West Warwick, suspected. S 55 provided that it would be contrary to Rhode Island public policy for residents to have memberships in societies whose center of government was a foreign country or whose chief executive officer was not a U.S. citizen. One effect of this legislation would have been to prevent French-Canadian descendants in Rhode Island from maintaining memberships in mutual-benefit societies based in Canada. As described in the press, one of the bills targeted miscegenation, while another addressed nuptial contracts that contained provisions about the education of children (most likely similar to the Klan-inspired bill that Massachusetts lawmakers took up the same year.) When the bills reached the Senate floor, Archambault moved that his colleagues adopt the recommendation of the Judiciary Committee to postpone indefinitely action on each bill, and the Senate voted unanimously to do so, thus defeating each measure.[10]

Despite the efforts of Franco-American leaders like Archambault to repulse the Ku Klux Klan and it principles, the secret society became implicated in the intra-Catholic Sentinelle affair, not only by Franco-Americans caught up in the controversy but also by the KKK's own actions. The account that follows casts new light on one of the most contentious intra-Catholic controversies to take place in New England in the early twentieth century. During the five-year Sentinelle crisis, which lasted from the mid to the late 1920s, militant Franco-Americans led by the attorney and editor Elphège J. Daignault fought against what they perceived as attempts by the Irish Catholic hierarchy to anglicize the Franco-American population of Rhode Island.[11] They also resisted the centralizing efforts of Irish prelates, which they felt threatened the autonomy of Franco-American parishes. The Sentinelle dispute centered around Bishop William Hickey's demand that Franco-American parishes help pay for the construction of Mount Saint Charles Academy, a diocesan Catholic high school in Woonsocket. Militants refused to contribute, even though a majority of the academy's students would be Franco-American, because Hickey envisioned creating a bilingual high school in which French-Canadian descendants would mix with youth of other backgrounds. "The problem," wrote Richard Sorrell, "was that Sentinelles wanted exclusivity rather than a majority." As a diocesan rather than a parish school, Mount Saint Charles could become anglicized at the bishop's whim, militants believed. Founded in 1924 as a direct result of this dispute with the Irish bishop, the French-language newspaper, *La Sentinelle* (the Sentinel), gave the controversy its name.[12]

The Sentinelle affair divided moderate Franco-Americans, who supported the bishop's plan, from the militants, who did not. *La Sentinelle* took a combative stance in the dispute, in contrast to its Woonsocket rival, *La Tribune,* which adopted a moderate position. *La Tribune* and other moderates, "including almost all parish priests and most lay community leaders," according to Sorrell, felt that the Roman Catholic Church trumped ethnicity in this conflict with the Irish bishop. The mutual-benefit society l'Union Saint-Jean-Baptiste led the opposition of moderate Franco-Americans against Sentinellism, thus positioning itself against the other large Franco-American mutual-aid society, l'Association Canado-Américaine, based in Manchester, New Hampshire, and led by Daignault. The Sentinelliste dispute spread beyond Rhode Island's borders, attracting support from French-Canadian descendants in communities like Worcester, Massachusetts, and Manchester, New Hampshire, as well as in the Province of Québec.[13]

Some Franco-American professionals (such as doctors, lawyers, priests, and journalists) from throughout New England believed they were under siege during the 1920s. "The nativism of Yankee employers and legislatures, the seeming collaboration of the Roman Catholic hierarchy and the rising violence of the Ku Klux Klan made the Franco-American élite feel even more like an embattled minority," writes the historian C. Stewart Doty. "Under that three-part threat, some Franco-Americans turned to French fascism for solutions, not just influences, led by the Sentinellist movement of Woonsocket, Rhode Island." As the controversy escalated, Sentinelles petitioned the pope to forbid Bishop Hickey from co-opting a percentage of the funds raised by individual parishes; when the pope sided with Hickey, sixty-two militants filed a civil suit against the bishop. They stopped making financial contributions to the church, an action that extended to the nonpayment of pew rentals. The Catholic Church responded in April 1928 by excommunicating all Sentinelles who had signed the civil suit, not only for bringing the matter to civil courts but also for their rebellion against the Church hierarchy. Church officials placed *La Sentinelle* on an index of forbidden works. In addition, the Sentinelles faced another blow when the Rhode Island Supreme Court turned down their appeal to deny bishops the right to exercise authority over parish funds. Following the condemnation of their newspaper, the Franco-American militants changed its name to *La Vérité* in May 1928; when the retitled newspaper was also condemned, they changed its name to *La Bataille* in November 1928 and then to *La Défense* in December 1928, before ceasing publication in February 1929. Only in that year, when the agitators in the Sentinelle affair signed repentance forms with Catholic Church officials, did the five-year controversy finally come to an end.[14]

"In its beliefs and tactics," Doty writes, "Sentinellism seemed to be a Franco-American version of French fascism." Some Franco-American journalists equated Sentinellism with the apparent fascist movement they were witness to in their New England communities, that of the right-wing Ku Klux Klan. J. Lussier, the editor of the French-language newspaper, *La Justice* of Holyoke, Massachusetts, was one of them. "Le Rhode Island semble être devenu le refuge des Clans" (Rhode Island seems to have become the refuge of the Clans), he wrote. "En effet, l'on y trouve pas seulement le Ku Klux Klan dont les occupations principales consistent à se réunir, à la nuit tombante, dans quelqu'enclos pour tramer contre la paix et l'ordre et y brûler des croix" (In effect, one finds there not only the Ku Klux Klan whose principal occupations consist of meeting, at nightfall, in some enclosure to plot against peace and order and there to burn some crosses), he commented, continuing, "Il y existe un autre petit clan qui . . . [est] caché à l'ombre de la croix" (There exists another little clan which . . . [is] hidden in the shadow of the cross). Militant Franco-Americans constituted the latter group, and it was time to break the silence and denounce them to end the silent complicity with them, Lussier insisted. He argued further that the bishop and various clergy the Sentinellistes were attacking deserved to be respected for the positions they

held in the Catholic Church. If the Sentinellistes were so concerned about
Mount Saint Charles, Lussier insisted, they should take charge of the institution themselves. He contended that they were a misguided lot who were
causing unnecessary harm to the Church. After *La Justice* published Lussier's
editorial, *La Tribune* reprinted it, thus breaking its silence on the Sentinelle
affair, and from the summer of 1925 on it openly criticized *La Sentinelle.*[15]

The Klan-sympathetic *Fellowship Forum* offered its own comments on
the dispute between the Franco-Americans and the Irish of Rhode Island.
"From the standpoint of the Protestant American, Bishop Hickey may be
correct in refusing to make French the principal language taught in his
schools—as this is certainly not a French nation," the newspaper wrote in
February 1927. The *Fellowship Forum* noted that long-standing tensions
existed between Franco-Americans and the Irish, and it acknowledged,
"There seems to be rank discrimination against the French papists in and
around Providence."[16]

But in its issue of April 1927 the *Fellowship Forum* openly complained
about the apparent lack of acculturation on the part of French-Canadian
descendants: "The French-Canadians have resisted Americanization stub-
bornly, relying on French newspapers, French priests and nuns, and French
parochial schools to perpetuate their native language and customs against
any adoption of American customs or the English language." Commenting on demographics, the newspaper charged that Rhode Island's French
speakers lived in ethnic enclaves where "they dwell apart from the American
population, and form 'little Quebecs' entirely unlike American communities." In its article on the Sentinelle crisis in the same issue, the *Fellowship
Forum* maintained that "the quarrel has developed into a bitter feud between
Irish and French Roman Catholics—with no consideration for Americanism on either side, although the bishop does have on his side the laudable
purpose of forcing some instruction in English and some compliance with
the school laws of Rhode Island." Yet that did not sufficiently appease the
newspaper, for it highlighted its central objection: "Neither side has any love
for the Public Schools, and Americanism is not an issue, as both sides of the
controversy are Romanists—not Americans."[17]

Hooded proponents of Americanism paraded in Woonsocket, the center
of the Sentinelle crisis, around midnight in late July 1927. The Ku Klux Klan
carried a fiery cross at the head of its procession, passed in front of Précieux-
Sang (Precious Blood) Church, the Franco-American mother church of
Woonsocket, and traced the same Court Street route that Catholics had used
the previous week. While *La Tribune* did not specify why the Catholics had
marched, it interpreted the Klan's actions as a demonstration of hostility
against the French Catholic population.[18]

But the hooded society was not the only "klan" that concerned Franco-Americans. At the height of the Sentinelle crisis, *La Tribune* published a daily front-page article critical of Daignault and the Sentinelliste movement. On September 3, 1927, for example, *La Tribune's* headline read, "Le Klan Daignault est reconnu" (The Daignault Klan is recognized). The newspaper informed its readers that the Ku Klux Klan and the anti-Catholic newspaper *The Menace* had congratulated Daignault for his work against the Catholic Church. *La Tribune* deplored this action, stating, "La chose la plus terrible qui puisse arriver à des catholiques, c'est d[']être félicités et encouragés par les ennemis avoués de l'Eglise dans leur travail" (The worst thing that could happen to some Catholics is to be congratulated and encouraged by the avowed enemies of the Church in their work). *La Tribune* indicated that the *Fellowship Forum,* which it identified as a Klan newspaper, had published in its issue of July 4 that Daignault's efforts against the Catholic Church no longer made it necessary for the KKK to continue organizing in Rhode Island and that Daignault and his followers had done more to destroy the influence of the Roman Catholic Church in the state than the Klan had done in five years of work there.[19] In this way, *La Tribune* acknowledged the fascist tendencies of the militant Franco-Americans embroiled in the Sentinelle affair.

In April 1928, after Roman Catholic Church officials excommunicated Daignault and banned *La Sentinelle,* the newspaper he edited, U.S. Sen. J. Thomas Heflin of Alabama argued on the Senate floor that this action "vitally concerns the liberty of the citizen and the freedom of the press in the United States and presents a sharp and vital conflict between two governments—the Government of the United States and the government of the Pope of Rome." Heflin questioned, "Aye, which one of them is supreme in its authority in the United States?" It was the same question that local and national Klan leaders had been raising throughout the 1920s. Heflin went on to explain his understanding of the Sentinelle controversy, a version he obviously exaggerated and embellished. He stated that French-Canadian descendants in Rhode Island had contributed large sums of money to the Roman Catholic Church that it did not use for the intended purposes and, when a priest and bishop refused to provide an explanation of how their funds were dispensed, they resorted to a civil rather than an ecclesiastical court to resolve the matter. "Instead of commending them for their willingness to have the matter fairly and lawfully determined by a court of justice in the United States," Heflin complained, "the Catholic authorities condemned and denounced them for exercising their rights as American citizens." He added that "the Rhode Island French-Canadian Catholic American citizens involved in the matter" had "refused to put Rome first." In other words, they had done what the KKK typically accused Catholics of not doing, namely, of exercising independent judgment. "Why, these citizens of the United States have been tried in a Roman Catholic ecclesiastical court in Italy, a foreign country, under the jurisdiction of the Pope of Rome, and without regard to their rights as American citizens," Heflin contended, "and while their case is still pending in the Supreme Court of Rhode Island; [*sic*] they have been denounced, repudiated, and excommunicated by the highest authority in the Catholic Church." Heflin criticized the Church's banning of Daignault's newspaper, holding that such an act also represented interference in U.S. internal affairs by a foreign leader. The senator interpreted the actions of the Roman Catholic Church in the Sentinelle controversy as a blow to "civil liberty and religious freedom in America," and he concluded his remarks on the Senate floor by taking a political potshot at the Catholic presidential candidate, Governor Al Smith of New York, for having "not said a word of protest against this denial of American rights and liberties to American citizens."[20] It is curious that Heflin referred to Rhode Island residents of French-Canadian descent as Americans, a usage inconsistent with past declarations made by the Ku Klux Klan and Klan-sympathetic newspapers. As a KKK spokesperson, Heflin apparently did so to seize the opportunity to attack the Church. Heflin's tirade demonstrates that to the Ku Klux Klan and its supporters religion trumped national origins when it came to events in the northeastern borderlands region.

La Tribune perceived this attitude in its interpretation of Heflin's remarks. The French-language newspaper situated the senator's religious intolerance in the context of Rhode Island's history: "C'est une semblable intolérance qui a amené Roger Williams, à quitter la colonie du Massachusetts pour venir fonder celle du Rhode Island où la liberté de conscience fut immédiatement établie afin que personne n'eût à endurer ce que le fondateur de notre Etat eut à souffrir" (It is a similar intolerance that caused Roger Williams to leave the colony of Massachusetts to come found that of Rhode Island, where the liberty of conscience was immediately established so that no one had to endure what the founder of our state had to suffer).[21]

Through *La Tribune*, Rhode Island's Franco-Americans continued to challenge the KKK during the Sentinelle controversy. In May 1928 the paper derided the Klan for thinking it had a monopoly on Americanism: "A les entendre, ces fils de l'Amérique sont les seuls à pouvoir s'appeler 'Américains' avec un grand A; tous les autres humbles habitants de ce beau pays ne sont que des avortons indignes de délier les cordons de souliers de ces parangons du patriotisme" (To hear them, these sons of America are the only ones capable of calling themselves 'Americans' with a capital A; all the other humble inhabitants of this beautiful country are only unworthy little runts [fit] to untie the shoelaces of these paragons of patriotism).[22]

The Roger Williams Klan in Providence invited one of those paragons, Sen. J. Thomas Heflin, to speak in Rhode Island. Heflin addressed an estimated eight thousand people at Grant field in Georgiaville in July 1928; six thousand paid fifty cents' admission to the event, and the rest remained outside of the rock wall that surrounded the field. Heflin praised the Sentinellistes for using a U.S. court rather than a Roman Catholic one to adjudicate their dispute with church leaders. As he did on the floor of the U.S. Senate, Heflin criticized the church authorities for excommunicating the Sentinellistes and for banning Daignault's newspaper. "If I were President," Heflin declared, "I would issue a proclamation that nowhere under the shining sun should any foreign potentate have jurisdiction over any American citizen."[23]

Roman Catholic officials based in Rome were not alone in opposing Sentinellism and its leader, Daignault. *La Tribune* reported on the resistance within the Franco-American community. In October 1928 the newspaper pointed out that two thousand Franco-Americans of Woonsocket and Pawtucket had applauded the Democratic political leader Edmond Talbot, the former mayor of Fall River, Massachusetts, for two long minutes when he accused Daignault at a public rally of fomenting anti-Catholicism in ways not unlike those of the Ku Klux Klan and John W. Perry, the Grand Titan of the organization. *La Tribune* reported that Daignault encountered hisses and jeers in Manchester, New Hampshire, when he verbalized his support of Herbert Hoover for the presidency over Al Smith. "Je ne puis imaginer le peuple franco-américain assez naïf pour voter pour le gouverneur Smith" (I cannot imagine the Franco-American people being so naïve as to vote for Governor Smith), Daignault intoned. "Nous aurions alors un Irlandais pour président et un cardinal à Washington" (We will then have an Irishman for president and a cardinal in Washington), he warned. *La Tribune* hinted that Daignault had acquired that idea from the *Fellowship Forum,* a newspaper, it informed readers, that opposed Smith because of his Catholic faith. *La Tribune* appeared to delight in pointing out that Daignault's detractors at the rally were louder than his supporters.[24]

When Daignault spoke at a Republican rally in New Bedford, Massachusetts, that drew five hundred Franco-Americans in November 1928, he argued that the GOP had been helpful to their ethnic group. Daignault again promoted Hoover's candidacy over Smith's. According to the *New Bedford Times,* he told his audience in French, "We can't expect anything from the Democratic party[,] which is controlled by men of the same race as those with whom we are having trouble in Rhode Island."[25] Daignault's stumping for the Republican Party and the Sentinelliste controversy itself reveal that the Franco-Americans of southern New England appeared to be unwilling to accede to Irish leadership in the face of the Klan threat in their region.

Following the presidential election in 1928, the *Fellowship Forum* wrote that Irish leaders in the Catholic Church were upset at how Franco-Americans had cast their votes. "Outcome of the recent election, in which the papal candidate for the presidency was defeated and in which most of the French Catholics refused to be lined up by the whip of Bishop Hickey, but voted for Herbert Hoover, has only served to further enrage the Irish prelate," the newspaper opined. It implied that tensions between the Irish and the Franco-Americans were exacerbated when the French Catholic Felix Hebert, "supported by the dissenting French Catholics," defeated incumbent U.S. senator Peter Gerry, who was favored by "the Irish under Bishop Hickey." The newspaper went on to explain in detail the Sentinelle controversy to its readers.[26]

The *Rhode Islander* refuted the *Fellowship Forum*'s claims as well as its version of the Sentinelle affair. "Those at the head of this agitation do not represent the French Catholics of Rhode Island. Neither do they speak for any considerable number of them," the newspaper argued. It maintained that the large majority of Franco-American and Irish residents of the state were neither involved nor interested in the Sentinelle controversy. "So far as the *Rhode Islander* knows, Bishop Hickey took no part in the campaign either directly or indirectly," indicated the newspaper. "The statement that he did so is only the product of Daignault's versatile imagination." The *Rhode Islander* also disputed the *Fellowship Forum*'s claim that Hoover and Hebert had won the votes of French Catholic Rhode Island citizens, pointing out that Smith and Gerry carried such towns as Woonsocket, Central Falls, and "in fact every voting district in the State in which the voters of French blood predominate." The paper concluded by equating the Ku Klux Klan with the Sentinelliste movement. Both the *Fellowship Forum* and Daignault "work for the same objective, the weakening of authority in the Catholic Church and the gathering of simoleons for their respective newspaper treasuries," it contended.[27]

In summary, the Sentinelle affair divided Franco-Americans from their Irish leaders in the Roman Catholic Church. The controversy prevented the possibility of forging a united front between them to counterattack the Ku Klux Klan. As we have seen, this discord carried over into politics as well, preventing interethnic political cooperation between the Irish and the Franco-Americans.

The Sentinelle controversy also divided Franco-Americans from each other. It brought into conflict their two leading mutual-benefit societies, l'Union Saint-Jean-Baptiste and l'Association Canado-Américaine. It separated militant Franco-Americans from moderate ones not only in Rhode Island but also throughout New England. The appeal of French fascism to some Franco-American élites propelled them to act during the Sentinelle controversy in ways that other Franco-Americans compared to the right-wing Klan movement. The appeal to French fascism, C. Stewart Doty has observed, particularly divided the Franco-American élite from the Franco-American working-class population.[28] Perhaps the most salient consequence of these internal and intra-Catholic divisions, all of which continued well beyond the conclusion of the Sentinelle affair and well beyond the borders of Rhode Island, was that Franco-Americans found themselves lacking the social and political cooperation and unity necessary to exercise greater political influence in the northeastern United States, a problem that persisted throughout most of the twentieth century.

About one year before the Sentinelle affair ended, the *Providence Journal* broke the story that two hundred Klansmen had infiltrated Companies E, F, and H of Rhode Island's First Light Infantry (FLI). The newspaper suggested that the KKK saw enlistment in these units as a recruitment strategy, for the men who wanted to join companies E, F, and H had to complete application forms both for the Rhode Island militia and for the Ku Klux Klan. Domination of the three companies of the Second Battalion of the FLI allowed the KKK to gain control of the Cranston Street Armory in Providence.[29] This episode, unique in Klan history, helps illuminate the inner workings of the KKK and the character of its local leaders, while also underscoring the tremendous gap between the organization's projected image and the reality of its actions.

The connection between men in the armed services and the Ku Klux Klan was not new in Rhode Island. In February 1924 twelve men in U.S. Navy uniforms, including ensigns, a lieutenant, and a captain, attended a Klan meeting in Anthony. In May 1924 ten to fifteen men in U.S. Navy uniforms distributed KKK literature at a restaurant on Westminster Street in Providence. Klan representatives held a meeting in the same month at the Providence Marine Corps Armory. When the Rhode Island governor William S. Flynn learned of this event, he ordered the adjutant general and the quartermaster general not to allow the KKK to rent state armories. "It is to be deplored by all good citizens that this organization is attempting not only to propagate its vicious principles of racial and religious hatred in the State founded by Roger Williams upon the broad principles of religious tolerance," Flynn stated, "but is even perverting the people's property to its nefarious ends and purposes."[30]

Four years later the KKK tried to achieve the same objective through its work to enlist its members in the First Light Infantry of Rhode Island, as disclosed in documents that Adjutant General Arthur C. Cole presented to Attorney General Charles P. Sisson. According to the *Providence Evening Bulletin,* Klan members wore U.S. Army uniforms with an FLI button on their collars and caps, and wealthy donors contributed funds for arms for the FLI without knowing the regiment was affiliated with the KKK. The FLI relied on private contributions because it was not a federally recognized unit of the National Guard. For its part, the national headquarters of the Ku Klux Klan denied having knowledge of or assuming responsibility for the recruitment of Klan members into the Rhode Island militia. To deal with the situation, the adjutant general asked Rep. William J. Thibodeau, a Republican from North Smithfield and a member of the National Guard, to introduce legislation that would give the governor authority to disband chartered commands in specific cases. The bill, H 832, would also prohibit chartered organizations from exceeding one hundred officers and from discharging members without the prior approval of the adjutant general. Cole wanted to deny independent companies the authority to set up military organizations in Rhode Island. "The independent companies are relics of the past. They are still governed by their individual charters, subject to very limited control by the State military authorities," Cole stated. He went on to express his "hope that the system is corrected and that those chartered units that desire real military training will become a part of the National Guard, and that those units who do not desire to connect with the National Guard take steps to become more social than military." Col. Harold A. Braman, the commanding officer of the First Light Infantry, immediately relieved the unit from duty and asked it to relinquish all arms and uniforms pending an investigation, and its members complied.[31]

After learning through the press that the FLI was "being used for purposes other than provided by law," Rep. Thomas P. McCoy, a Democrat from Pawtucket, introduced H 952, "Providing for an Investigation of the First Light Infantry and Other Chartered Commands of the State by Legislative Committee." The measure pointed out that the state legislature had made appropriations for armories, "not for the purposes of propagating the Ku Klux Klan in Rhode Island." It called for the speaker of the House of Representatives to appoint a special committee to investigate all chartered commands and departments of the militia in the state. Instead, the House voted unanimously on March 23 in favor of H 952 Substitute A, "Authorizing the Militia Committee of the House of Representatives to Investigate the Military Organizations of this State."[32]

McCoy also sponsored H 953, "Directing the Governor to Investigate Klan Activities in the Chartered Commands and the Militia of the State." The bill would have allowed Gov. Norman S. Case, who succeeded Pothier after the latter's death in office, to investigate chartered commands "with a view to ascertaining to what extent said commands are impaired and injured by the activities of the Ku Klux Klan." There were eight chartered commands in Rhode Island: the First Light Infantry, Newport Artillery, Warren Artillery, Cranston Blues, Kentish Guards, United Train of Artillery, Bristol Train of Artillery, and the Kentish Artillery. McCoy's resolution was unnecessary, claimed Rep. Herbert Bliss, a Republican from Newport and chair of the House Militia Committee, because the governor did not require the approval of the General Assembly to investigate the state militia.[33]

As the House Militia Committee prepared to conduct hearings on the KKK in the First Light Infantry, Governor Case, in his first executive order, demanded that the adjutant general, along with the FLI commanding officer Harold A. Braman, discontinue their investigation of the activities of the KKK in the militia. Case told them to prepare to testify before the House Militia Committee, and he ordered them to turn over relevant papers to the committee.[34]

Adjutant General Cole was the first to testify at the legislative hearings. He reported to the committee that Austin C. Barney of Troop F Cavalry had told him that he was a former member of the Ku Klux Klan; Barney also told Cole that Frederick Remington, the secretary of the Roger Williams Klan number 16, had shared information about the recruitment of KKK members to the FLI. The plan, Barney told Cole, "was a part of a wide spread [*sic*] attempt to secure military control throughout this area," Cole testified. Cole's testimony disclosed as well that Barney had also spoken to Grand Titan John W. Perry, who told him that modern rifles were being purchased for the FLI. By the end of 1927 enlistments in the First Light Infantry had jumped from 75 to 240, an increase of 165 men.[35]

Barney was not Cole's only informant. Cole attested that R. A. Calen, a second lieutenant in the United Train of Artillery, had informed him that he had been a KKK member. According to the adjutant general, Calen had told him that "the Klan was keenly interested in getting a foothold in the military circles of the state, that they hoped to first pick up the chartered men, get the officers into the guard, get commissioned officers in the guard, and do practically as they pleased around the armory every way, shape or manner." During an illness of Colonel Braman, Capt. Grafton G. Greenleaf ran the FLI and actively recruited Klan members. Greenleaf admitted to Cole that Klansmen had joined the FLI, but he denied organizing a recruiting campaign or that one needed to be a KKK member to join the infantry, Cole told the committee.[36]

A written report Cole prepared for the General Assembly sheds further light on what Cole learned during his preliminary investigation of the First Light Infantry. Cole wrote that in 1927 the FLI had been in decline and that its membership had dropped to 25 men. Then, during the summer, 75 men from seventeen to seventy years of age showed up for training. By Armistice Day there were more than 100 members in the infantry. The FLI's recruiting drive had expected to attract from 40 to 60 men but drew 225, Cole reported. When he learned that the KKK was selling tickets to a public function held by the FLI, he decided to conduct a secret investigation. In Cole's written review, he confirmed to lawmakers that "the Klan does control three companies of the First Light Infantry; that applicants for enlistment in the First Light Infantry have been required to sign an application that ex-Klansmen swear is the regular Klan application form; [and] that most of the officials of Roger Williams Klan No. 16 are in the First Light Infantry." He went on to recount that FLI members came from all parts of Rhode Island and that "the First Light Infantry has 250 U.S. Army rifles secured without the approval of the military authorities." While Cole expressed his belief that the regiments' activities had been lawful, he had taken the precaution of calling in state-owned firearms and of keeping under surveillance the activities taking place at the state's armories. He also noted in his report that he had apprised the governor of the situation by letter.[37]

Appended to Cole's narrative was his memorandum to Gov. Aram Pothier. In the letter, Cole informed the chief executive that "an organization desiring to upset the tranquility of this State could legally acquire organization, training, arms and ammunition that would otherwise be forbidden them." Cole let the governor know that this had happened in the First Light Infantry and that "during a so-called recruiting drive over 200 members of the K.K.K. and Crusaders joined" the militia and that they continued to sign up. Cole warned the governor that the unit could spread throughout Rhode Island, as permitted under its current charter. He also mentioned having received information that "active steps are being taken to secure control of other independent commands and of the National Guard, if possible." While Cole doubted that the KKK could actually take over the National Guard, he believed that it could gain control over chartered commands, and he recommended amending their charters to prevent this from happening.[38]

In testifying before the Militia Committee, Adjutant General Cole informed the members that, after he had sent the letter to Pothier, the governor invited him to his office to discuss the matter, and a meeting followed. Cole told the lawmakers that Pothier expressed confidence in the adjutant general's ability and advised that he handle the matter as he saw fit. In response to a question from a committee member, Cole admitted he had supplied information about the Klan joining the First Light Infantry to the *Providence Journal,* which published it.[39]

Appended to Cole's written statement to the state assembly was the response of Attorney General Sisson to a letter Cole had sent him. Sisson indicated that he saw nothing illegal on the part of the KKK's attempt to establish a military organization through the First Light Infantry. Nonetheless, Sisson recommended condemning the practice. "Any military organization which predicates its qualifications of membership, in fact if not in form, upon race or creed is not a fit body in times of emergency to administer the laws of the state dispassionately and without prejudice," Sisson wrote to Cole.[40]

When the Militia Committee hearing reconvened the next day, on March 28, Cole told the committee that a *Providence Journal* reporter had conducted an investigation of his own. To join the First Light Infantry he had to enroll in the Ku Klux Klan. The individuals who wanted to join only the FLI and not the KKK were assigned to a different company, Cole stated. In addition, the Klan screened recruits for their religious affiliation and race, he pointed out, and it assigned to Company A those recruits it did not want.[41]

When Austin C. Barney was sworn in before the Militia Committee, he confirmed Cole's testimony, which was unsurprising. As a member of the National Guard, Barney had turned to the adjutant general as his superior officer and had shared information about the KKK's scheme "to place it in the proper hands." Barney subsequently worked as an investigator in the adjutant general's office from December 1927 until March 1928. Barney shared with the committee the substance of his conversation of December 10 with Frederick T. Remington. By that time over two hundred Klan members had joined the FLI, Remington told him. "I asked him what their aims were there and he said they were going to get control and charge of the armories of the State of Rhode Island, the independent organizations, and the National Guard insofar as the commissioned officers were concerned," Barney told the committee, continuing, that "they would be in line then to be placed upon the militia commission at the State House and thereby be in a position to control all movements of military forces." Barney indicated that John W. Perry similarly expressed to him the Klan's desire to "be in control of all the military organizations in the State." Remington also notified Barney that "this wasn't a local affair, that it was broader than a State affair" and that the KKK also set its sights on Connecticut's militia. Remington "stated at that time the Connecticut Grays, the Governor's Foot Guards of Connecticut, were ninety percent members of the Klan, and that they had received their rifles also." Remington further cited the Klan's interest in controlling militias throughout the country, Barney stated. He also informed the committee that Perry made addresses to Klan members that suggested why the KKK wanted to take over military organizations. "On several occasions he has intimated that the United States Government was at a crisis," Barney noted, "and that sooner or later there would be a religious war and that this movement I was told by one of the klansmen was to put the Klan on a firm basis."[42]

As the hearings continued, the *Providence Evening Bulletin* contacted Major Pierrepont B. Foster, the commander of the Second Company in New Haven, Connecticut, to verify the accuracy of the information Barney had shared about the Klan's infiltration of the Connecticut militia. Foster denied Remington's assertion (relayed by Barney) that 90 percent of the Connecticut Grays were Klansmen; while he declined to speak for the First Company of Hartford, he said that he knew of no Klan members in the Second Company. "The roster of the footguard here contains such names as Fitzsimmons, McGrail, Dougherty, Breen, McLaughlin, Weibel, Sullivan and Cox, all of whom," Foster pointed out, "at first blush, would indicate anything but favoritism of the hooded order."[43] According to Barney, Remington's estimate of Klan strength in the Connecticut militia appeared grossly overstated, if not simply inaccurate.

Called before the House Militia Committee, Remington proved to be a defiant witness. He gave evasive responses and refused to answer some questions about the Ku Klux Klan's membership. Remington did deny, however, having told Barney that he had been recruiting Klan members for the First Light Infantry. He admitted to the committee that Colonel Braman was not a member of the Klan and that Captain Greenleaf had been a KKK member until January.[44]

When Perry took the stand, he too testified that Braman was not a Klan member and had never attended the organization's meetings. Perry claimed he had no knowledge of Ku Klux Klan recruitment for the First Light Infantry. He likely would have known, for he headed the Klan organization of all of Rhode Island and the Connecticut counties of New London and Windham. The *Providence Evening Bulletin* wrote that lawmakers questioned Perry about his past while he was on the witness stand. In response to their questions, Perry said that when he served as a police officer in New London, he had gone into a hotel room to pursue a woman who had committed a crime, and that she claimed he had had improper relations with her. Perry stated that he had resigned after his suspension was lifted, and he asserted before the Militia Committee, "I have never in my life violated the laws of God or man."[45] As we will see, the press and one committee member decided to probe the Klan leader's salacious history in order to discredit him.

As the hearings progressed, the Militia Committee read into testimony various documents, called new witnesses, and recalled others who had appeared previously. As expected, Colonel Braman denied that, as commanding officer of the FLI, he had any knowledge of the Klan's efforts to join the unit. Braman also denied having had any involvement with the KKK or any agreement with the organization to allow only Klansmen into the FLI. In early April the committee read into testimony reports that Barney had made to the adjutant general. One of these disclosed that the Pacific Arms Company of San Francisco stood ready to supply the FLI and that this company had supplied weapons to gangsters in Chicago and Mexico. Roswell A. Calin, who had served in the FLI in 1917 and had been a member of the Roger Williams Klan in 1926–27, testified that he found the KKK's social activities acceptable but deplored its military aims. "The Rhode Island Militia can be called out by the Governor in case of riots or strikes while the National Guard is under Federal Government jurisdiction elsewhere," Calin observed. "If the militia is under the control of the Klan, it wouldn't be able to protect the State of Rhode Island in the proper way," he argued, underscoring the fact that "this State is made up of all nationalities and all religions." Calin said he left the Klan when he heard rumors of its designs on the FLI and added that he had told Adjutant General Cole that three-fourths of the FLI were Klansmen. In addition, Calin stated that Cole had secured his commission in the Inspector General's Office for three months in order to keep him from exposing the KKK's affiliation with the FLI to the public. Recalled by the Militia Committee, Remington proved more cooperative the second time around, acknowledging in response to questions from Attorney General Sisson that certain individuals whose names Sisson read from a list of FLI members belonged to the KKK.[46]

During the course of the hearings, newspapers in Rhode Island made inquiries of their own and printed their findings. The *Rhode Islander* featured a front-page picture of Grand Titan John Perry and raised the question, "100 Per Cent American?" The paper reported that Perry was a former Roman Catholic who had served as an altar boy at St. Mary's Roman Catholic Church in New London. It also said that his parents were not native-born U.S. citizens but had been born in islands belonging to Portugal, his father in Madeira and his mother in the Azores. The *Rhode Islander* also challenged the reliability of Perry's testimony before the Militia Committee by indicating that he had resigned from the New London police force in 1922 after some officers, who did not see him on his beat, found him partially undressed in the closet of a room belonging to a married woman. The newspaper pointed out other seeming inaccuracies in Perry's testimony and ended its lengthy article by saying, "And that is John W. Perry, Great Titan of the Knights of the Ku Klux Klan, for the Realm of Rhode Island and Connecticut, proponent of 100 per cent Americanism, advocate of white Protestant supremacy and protector of the virtue of American women."[47] In its exposé the newspaper underscored some of the inherent contradictions of the Ku Klux Klan organization.

As the hearings progressed, the Militia Committee heard from other individuals about the Klan's affiliation with the First Light Infantry. John E. Schlemmer, a former Klan member who had joined the chartered command, pointed out that in recent years businessmen and individuals with political interests had been leaving the Klan organization. He went on to indict KKK members for lacking independent judgment: "Easily led, the rank and file that go to make up the Klan." When a member of the Militia Committee asked if these members might have been "led into a movement to overthrow the established government of a state or country," Schlemmer responded, "Why yes, it is possible."[48]

The committee also heard testimony from Sgt. Clifford B. Hawes, an automobile mechanic who was a member of both the FLI and the KKK. Hawes's testimony was unremarkable, except for the spirited exchange he had at its conclusion with the two Democratic members of the committee, James H. Matthews and J. Frank Sullivan, the other nine being Republicans. When the committee asked Hawes if he would be willing to return to testify again, if needed, he agreed. But Hawes voiced concern about losing time from work and insisted that he receive enough notice so that he could clean himself up and change his clothing before reappearing at the capitol. He objected to the possibility of having to present himself before the committee on a half hour's notice. If that happened, Hawes said, "I will be pretty well mussed up. I don't want you to make pictures of me and make fun of me because I will be all dirtied up in torn clothes. I am not ashamed of being dirty, but I want to look well here," Hawes insisted. "To cover up the soiled spots why don't you wear your white uniform?" Sullivan questioned. "Just a minute. I believe the Knights of Columbus wear black uniforms," Hawes shot back. "I would like to state I have got some respect. I have got lots of good friends in the Knights of Columbus and I like them," Hawes stated. "They don't wear any masks," quipped Matthews. "The Klan don't wear a mask either. I never had one on in my life," Hawes responded. At that point, Chairman Bliss interrupted the badgering by his colleagues and tried to redirect the questioning, cautioning members of the committee not to treat witnesses as "criminals on the stand" and expressing his expectation that all witnesses be treated "as gentlemen."[49]

One of the redirected solons, Frank Sullivan, was unsatisfied with the statements of Perry and other Klan members. When John T. Kenyon, a carpenter's helper and a member of both the First Light Infantry and the Ku Klux Klan, testified that only fifteen or twenty of the two hundred plus FLI members belonged to the KKK, Sullivan interjected that Kenyon and other KKK witnesses were not making an honest effort to assist the committee. Sullivan then turned the committee's attention back to Grand Titan Perry, and he produced evidence to demonstrate that Perry had made misstatements under oath. Sullivan pointed out, for example, that Perry had indicated he had been wounded during the war, but he had in fact "attempted suicide previous to his service in the army, following an affair with a woman when he thought he would [be] exposed, and a volunteer fireman badge deflected the bullet into his foot." The committee read into record the letter of Charles A. Pinney, a captain of police in New London, Connecticut, to Sullivan, in which Pinney informed Sullivan that Perry had been suspended from the police department on October 9, 1922 "for conduct unbecoming a police officer." Pinney stated, "The specific charges were that he, while on duty, entered a room in the Fourneir [*sic*] House in this city and had sexual intercourse with one Mrs. Billie Frank, the wife of a Chief Petty Officer in the Navy who was at that time stationed near here." Pinney went on to indicate that Perry "was caught in the room with the woman by Lieutenant Beebe and Sergeant Murphy of this department and the charges were proven to our satisfaction by their testimony and the admission of the woman." Perry resigned during the period of his suspension, and the charges were dropped. He could not be reinstated to the force, as he had told the committee. Pinney included corroborating evidence with his communication in the statement of the New London city manager, J. E. Barlow, which the Militia Committee read into the record. It also included information from the death certificates of Perry's parents, which proved that his mother was born in the West Indies and his father in Madeira. Citing church records, Representative Sullivan pointed out that Perry had been baptized a Roman Catholic. Sullivan's revelations contradicted statements Perry had made about his religious tradition, ancestry, and war record.[50] Moreover, the lawmaker's revelations, along with the *Rhode Islander*'s exposé, demonstrated that the leader of the Rhode Island Klan, because of his Catholic background, his nonnative and possibly nonwhite origins, and his apparent lack of morality, was the very sort of individual against whom the KKK of the 1920s stood in opposition.

When Perry did not appear before the committee for further questioning, but claimed through his attorney that he was under a doctor's care in New London, Sullivan asked Attorney General Sisson, who was serving as the attorney for the investigating committee, to issue warrants for Perry's arrest for contempt and perjury. On the recommendation of the Militia Committee, the House of Representatives passed by unanimous voice vote a resolution citing Perry for contempt. The House, however, defeated Sullivan's resolution to direct the attorney general to convene a grand jury to indict Perry for perjury, because the attorney general already had that authority, the press related.[51]

When the Militia Committee hearings continued, representatives heard evidence from Rev. Orio Brees about the inner workings of the Ku Klux

Klan and about the position of Crusaders, foreign-born Protestants, in the
KKK organization. Brees joined the Klan in July 1925, became a lecturer
for the society, and served as Kleagle and then as secretary in Washington
County before leaving the group in July 1927. During testimony Brees bitterly denounced the KKK and told the committee that he left it because
he felt it was inconsistent with its principles. Brees alleged that the Klan
would procure new prospects by trapping their children in compromising
positions, and it organized boycotts of businesspeople who would not join
the secret society. Brees also said that the Klan blacklisted him when he left.
Brees identified by name Rhode Island government officials and lawmakers
who were members of the Ku Klux Klan of Washington County. In 1927
nearly one-third of Rhode Island's Klan was concentrated in Washington
County, even though the county contained less than one-twentieth of the
state's population, notes Joseph W. Sullivan. The 681 names Brees read from
the Washington County KKK roster included state senators, representatives,
and sheriffs. Sullivan tracked down 437 of the names that Brees supplied and
classified them by occupation, research that yielded the following socioeconomic portrait of the Rhode Island Klan: business and professional, 26.8 percent; skilled, 44.4 percent; semiskilled or unskilled, 28.8 percent. Although
Brees carried a roster of Crusaders, he did not read aloud their names. Brees
contended that Crusaders were not given a meaningful place in the KKK
organization: "The Crusaders are used as a dishrag by the Klan, whose stunt
is to get $10 out of them and then kick them out in the cold." By this Brees
meant the Crusaders were marginalized, he clarified to the committee.[52]

Two weeks after Brees testified before the Militia Committee, the *Rhode
Islander* published a letter written by three members of the Bradford Baptist Church in Westerly, where Brees had served as pastor. The parishioners
wrote that Brees had been dismissed as the leader of the church in November
1927 "because of charges of improper conduct with a married woman whom
he had brought into the church membership." Brees had left his wife and
young child for the married woman. The *Rhode Islander* published the letter,
it explained to its readers, to illustrate that the Ku Klux Klan portrayed an
untrue image of itself. Members did not exhibit the morality they professed
to promote in the larger society. Brees later went on to become a member of
the New York state assembly and, during his bid for the Republican nomination for state senate in 1952, had to defend his role in the Klan from his
opponents who brought it to light. "I thought I could sell that bunch some
tolerance and understanding," Brees stated about his tenure with the Rhode
Island Klan in the 1920s, and he defended his record as a New York lawmaker
by proclaiming that he stood "for fairness for everybody—Jew, Gentile,
Catholic, Protestant."[53]

After three weeks of hearings, the House Militia Committee concluded its investigation of the alleged Ku Klux Klan infiltration of the First Light Infantry. The majority report contended that the KKK achieved substantial influence in companies E, F, and H of the chartered command. Point five of the report stated "that the Klan activity in the First Light Infantry was to further the interests of the K.K.K., and not because of any desire to make the F.L.I. a more valuable part of the State militia." The document concluded that the Klan's collection of dues and the requirement that FLI applicants simultaneously complete KKK questionnaires at the state armory violated the law (specifically, chapter 418, section 27, of the General Laws.) A majority of the committee found that the FLI "would have become in substance an organization almost wholly composed of members of the K.K.K." had not the scheme come to light. The majority report exonerated Colonel Braman, specifying that he did not know of the Klan situation and was above reproach for his handling of matters once he learned of the Klan's scheme. It also exonerated Adjutant General Cole as well, despite the fact that he had not followed military protocol in dealing with the matter.[54]

The minority report of the House Militia Committee differed from the majority report only in its conclusion about the adjutant general. The minority report criticized Cole for the way he handled matters, stating that he should have consulted Governor Case after the chief executive took office in February 1928. Members in the minority also felt that Cole should have contacted the governor after the press broke the story on the Klan's affiliation with the FLI and before consulting with the House of Representatives. The lawmakers who signed the minority report concluded it by rebuking the adjutant general for actions they deemed to be "unmilitary" and demonstrated "a lack of proper courtesy to the Commander-in-Chief."[55]

The Militia Committee voted to recommend to Governor Case that he call upon Colonel Braman to discharge all KKK members from the First Light Infantry, for testimony had revealed that over two hundred individuals in the regiment were members of the Ku Klux Klan. The governor subsequently announced that he would rescind the executive order he had earlier given that prevented Braman from conducting his own investigation into the KKK in the First Light Infantry while the Militia Committee investigated the matter, and Braman made known his intention "to purge the First Light Infantry of the unsuitable elements." A military tribunal began its investigation shortly thereafter. Adjutant General Cole obliquely summarized in his end-of-the-year report to the General Assembly what transpired after the military tribunal's investigation. "This office has been informally notified that action has been taken to eliminate an unhealthy condition previously referred to in a special report to the General Assembly," he wrote in a paragraph on the FLI. "The membership now, while much smaller than last year, appears active and interested, and drills are held regularly at the Cranston Street Armory."[56]

Two lawmakers tried to pass legislation to prevent groups like the KKK from gaining control of state militias and armories in the future. Rep. Thomas P. McCoy introduced H 985, a bill "Relating to Independent Chartered Military Organizations of the State," which provided that chartered commands could not use Rhode Island state property or aid unless they accepted the authority of the commander in chief and that the governor could disband organizations that did not follow his regulations and orders. The House passed McCoy's bill, but the Senate defeated it. Besides the McCoy bill, the state assembly considered legislation by Representative Bliss to fine or jail "conspirators in militia," that is, any two individuals who joined a state military organization with the intention of diverting it from its lawful ends. Bliss's bill also passed in the House but died in the Senate.[57]

Following the defeat of the McCoy and Bliss bills, both of which were aimed at the KKK, and the refusal of the assembly to indict Perry for perjuring himself before the Militia Committee, Democrats went on the offensive and accused the Republican members in the legislature of protecting the Ku Klux Klan. The *Providence Journal* characterized the General Assembly's debate over the KKK as "bitter" and reported that Democrats blamed the Republican Party for the Klan's continued existence in the state. "The G.O.P. leaders, who were in such full control of the Legislature that they were able to force an adjournment that was almost entirely stripped of the usual trading over bills in committee," explained the *Providence News,* "killed both of two bills which would have forced the immediate purging of Klan influence in the militia forces of the State."[58]

Unlike the state assembly, the attorney general apparently decided to pursue the Grand Titan of the Ku Klux Klan of Rhode Island and Connecticut for perjury. In June 1928 Perry was arrested in New London and arraigned at the Rhode Island Superior Court in Providence. During the trial the state argued that Perry was still under suspension from the New London police force when he resigned, contrary to the testimony he gave to the Militia Committee that there were no charges pending against him at the time. But jurors heard testimony that there had been an understanding that Perry would receive a letter from the New London city manager lifting his suspension before he submitted his resignation. In January 1929, after deliberating for three hours, the jury, which reportedly included one member of the Knights of Columbus, found Perry not guilty.[59]

Although discredited, Perry was not defeated, and he did not disappear. Six months later he established the First United Protestant Church in East

Greenwich, Rhode Island, not only for KKK members but also for women and men who did not belong to an organized church, and he planned to become the first pastor of the new church. Although Perry told the press in June 1929 that he had left the KKK in December 1928, he got back into harness and led the Ku Klux Klan's battle against Communism in the 1930s. During that decade the Klan in the Ocean State continued to organize social activities for members and their families, such as a clambake and field day activities in Georgiaville in August 1931. But the Rhode Island KKK now had Communists in its sights, just like the Klan in the other New England states and across the country. A 1932 Klan meeting notice from Perry, then serving as Grand Dragon of Connecticut and Rhode Island, contained a header in red capital letters: "THE KLAN RIDES AGAIN," followed by "COMMUNISM MUST BE DESTROYED," also in red capital letters. "The growth of Communism in the United States of America has caused many of our leading citizens to become pessimistic as to the future of our form of Government," the notice stated. It quoted Imperial Wizard Hiram W. Evans, who was scheduled to speak in Providence in October, emphasizing the Klan's opposition to altering the U.S. government and arguing that "COMMUNISM MUST BE DESTROYED if our form of Government is to continue." The tear-off portion of the letter, to be presented at the door of the meeting site, asked attendees to pledge their support to fight Communism in the United States.[60]

As Rhode Islanders contemplated the Ku Klux Klan's presence in their state in the early twentieth century, they often invoked the memory of their founding father, Roger Williams. Rhode Island's governor, its Franco-American population, and the English-language press all countered the KKK's anti-Catholic and anti-Jewish rhetoric and actions by extolling the religious tolerance that Williams exemplified. For its part, the Providence Klan overlooked that historical memory and idealized Williams's white, Anglo-Saxon Protestant origins by naming Rhode Island's sixteenth klavern after him. Perhaps the memory and spirit of Williams help explain why the state's residents did not counterattack the KKK as energetically as did the neighboring state of Massachusetts. Intra-Catholic and intraethnic divisions stemming from the Sentinelle affair help explain this disparity as well.

One effect of the Ku Klux Klan in Rhode Island was to push Catholics into the ranks of the Democratic Party. David Patten has observed, for example, that while Republicans emerged victorious in Rhode Island's elections for state and congressional offices in 1928, their achievement masked the bolting of Italians from the Republican Party to the Democratic, a switch he attributed to the issues of prohibition and religion.[61] Both issues had been at the center of the KKK's agenda in the 1920s.

The historian Evelyn Savidge Sterne finds that opposition to the KKK and to the Peck Act led to greater political unity among Rhode Island's ethnic Catholics in the 1920s as well as to political realignment. Al Smith's presidential candidacy contributed to that realignment in 1928. In that year the Democratic presidential contender carried Rhode Island with slightly over 50 percent of the vote; Rhode Island was one of only two states Smith carried outside of the solid South, the other being Massachusetts. Smith's campaign, Sterne argues, aligned within the Democratic Party the larger ethnic groups of Providence, such as the Franco-Americans and the Italian Americans, with the smaller groups, such as Jews and blacks. The movement from the Republican to the Democratic Party ranks of Italian- and Franco-American Catholics was further solidified by the New Deal of the 1930s.[62] As we have seen, the appeal of the Franco-American Republican gubernatorial candidates Aram Pothier and Emery SanSouci, and especially the conflicts between the Irish and the Franco-Americans within the Roman Catholic Church during the Sentinelle affair, complicated this political transition during the 1920s.

Finally, the Ku Klux Klan's involvement in the Sentinelle affair as well as its efforts to take over the First Light Infantry allowed it to permeate the consciousness of Rhode Island residents for longer than was the case in other New England states, where the organization was a fading memory after peaking in the mid-1920s. The House Militia Committee hearings demonstrated that, at least in Rhode Island, the KKK continued to exert itself in a tangible way into the late 1920s. Testimony heard by the legislative committee made apparent the potential for violence that the Klan still posed in the northeastern United States. In addition, the revelations about the backgrounds of Grand Titan John W. Perry and the former Klan leader Orio Brees underscored the inherent contradictions between what the Ku Klux Klan stood for (or against) and its actual practice, further undermining its credibility as an organization. As we will see in the next chapter, contradictions within the Ku Klux Klan organization led to the secession of a major KKK chapter in Connecticut.

10

Encountering Secession in the Constitution State

CONNECTICUT joined Rhode Island to form a Klan realm in the 1920s. In many respects the Klan's history in Connecticut during that decade closely resembled what took place in other parts of New England, where the white-robed society directed its energy toward thwarting the social, economic, and political gains of ethnic Catholics. Like other states in the region, Connecticut had a large Catholic population that dwarfed the other minority groups in the state. Roman Catholics in 1926 numbered 557,747 (about 40 percent of the population in 1920), while Jews in 1926 numbered 90,165 (almost 7 percent of the population in 1920), and blacks in 1920 numbered 21,046 (1.5 percent of the population). As in other New England states, the KKK of Connecticut also faced opposition, not all of it external to the organization. While internal divisions plagued the Klan in other parts of New England and the country, a schism dealt the Connecticut and national KKK a serious blow in 1926 when six hundred members from New Haven voted to secede from the Ku Klux Klan and to disband Connecticut's oldest and largest Klan organization.[1] This event presaged the hooded society's decline in the Constitution State and in the nation at large.

Immigrants constituted 27.4 percent of Connecticut's population in 1920. Foreign-born residents made the Roman Catholic Church the largest religious denomination in the state. In descending order, the top countries supplying Connecticut's immigrants were Italy (21.2 percent), Russia and Lithuania (13.3 percent), Poland (12.3 percent), Ireland (12.0 percent), and Canada (6.5 percent.) Connecticut was the only New England state in 1920 to which Canada was not the largest sender of immigrants. In fact, the proportion of Connecticut's foreign-born population made up of French-Canadian immigrants (3.9 percent) constituted the smallest percentage of any New England state in 1920.[2] Despite this, French-Canadian descendants actively and effectively resisted some of the Constitution State's Americanization efforts.

To deal with its large foreign-born population Connecticut established institutional structures to promote Americanization, and it advocated changes in the language of instruction in its schools. In April 1918 U.S. Secretary of the Interior Franklin D. Lane convened a meeting of governors in Washington, D.C., to lay the foundations of a national Americanization program to unite the diverse population of the country during the world war. The Republican governor of Connecticut, Marcus H. Holcomb, attended the meeting out of which emerged the recommendation to promote English-language instruction in the schools. On his return to Connecticut, Holcomb decreed that all of the state's public and private schools would have to teach in English but that private schools could hold religious exercises in another language. Franco-Americans protested against this measure, and the government of Connecticut relented by allowing instruction in a non-English language for one hour daily.[3]

The next year, in 1919, Connecticut established a Department of Americanization that worked through state education networks to generate posters, a motion picture, bulletins, circular letters, and a speaker's bureau to promote Americanization. The Department of Americanization became subsumed under the state's Bureau of Education in 1926.[4] But it was not Connecticut's sole means of advocating acculturation into U.S. society.

Connecticut sought to enact stricter English-language measures to help anglicize its foreign-born population. In 1923 Sen. Charles M. Blackwell, a Republican from New Haven, sponsored Senate Bill (S. B.) No. 29, "An Act concerning the Teaching of Foreign Languages in the First Eight Grades," legislation that would have prohibited the teaching of any language other than English in elementary schools receiving state funding. The bill died in committee, but a similar House bill gained momentum. H. B. 381, "An Act Concerning the Medium of Instruction and Administration in Elementary Schools," stipulated that Connecticut's private and public schools would have to teach in English up to grade six, after which students could receive instruction in another language, but for no more than one class period. Franco-Americans perceived the bill as a threat to their parochial schools, and nearly all of the state's Franco-American population centers, which were concentrated in eastern Connecticut, sent delegations to the state capitol to urge lawmakers to modify the legislation. Franco-American pastors surnamed Bédard of Putnam, Mathieu of Wauregan, Bellerose of Taftville, and Papillon of Willimantic joined the secretary of l'Union Saint-Jean-Baptiste, Alma Forcier, and other Franco-American leaders to express their concerns about this legislation before the Connecticut General Assembly's Joint Standing Committee on Education.[5]

Franco-Americans succeeded in persuading lawmakers to modify the language bill of 1923 so that they could provide one hour of French instruction daily in their parochial schools. During the education committee hearing on the substitute bill for H. B. 381, Rep. Luther M. Keith, a Republican from Putnam, stated that he opposed the wording of "the original Bill because of our Canadian population." Sen. Frank P. Fenton, a Democrat from Windham, favored the revised bill, arguing, "The French people and others should have the opportunity to teach their own language a certain period each day." Two Franco-American representatives, Hector Duvert, a Republican from Putnam, and Pierre J. Laramee, a Democrat from Windham, also expressed their support for the revised bill. The amended bill read as follows: "The medium of instruction and administration in all public and private elementary schools in this state shall be the English language and not more than one hour in any school day may be given to instruction in any one language other than English." As the representative of a Franco-American organization numbering forty thousand individuals, Forcier voiced his approval of the modified legislation. "In the name of the French[-]speaking Clergy we wish to extend to the Committee our thanks for the change in the Bill," chimed in Reverend Bellerose, who added, "We feel that we now can do as we have been doing in the past." What Bellerose meant, of course, was instructing Franco-American children in French to preserve their French Catholic lifeways. An individual surnamed Hamilton, the commander of the Meriden American Legion, also spoke at the hearing. "One of the principles of the American Legion is to foster and perpetuate 100% Americanism," Hamilton said. "The Legion is composed of men from the Protestant, Catholic and Jewish Churches. It comprises every race, probably represented in our American life," he continued. "The Bill as altered meets with the approval of the Legion. One hour a day instruction in [a] foreign language does not hinder, in any way, the development of children as 100% American," Hamilton emphasized. The revised English-language measure became law in May 1923.[6]

It is not clear what role, if any, the Ku Klux Klan played in promoting English-language legislation in Connecticut, for the organization's origins in the state are somewhat obscure. As early as September 1921 the *New York Times* reported that Connecticut state police had evidence of Klan activity in Derby, Naugatuck, and the Connecticut Valley, but it was not more specific than that. The Connecticut Klan captured greater public attention in 1922 as a result of its various gatherings. In May the *Boston Sunday Herald* reported that Klan members from different cities of Connecticut and from throughout New England participated in an open-air meeting and initiation ceremony near New Haven. During the event several thousand members of the secret society gathered on a hilltop to initiate hundreds of new members, and they concluded their ceremony by burning an eighteen-foot cross. In August the *New York Times* informed its readers that KKK guards at a midnight rally near Middletown allegedly wore army uniforms and a Klan leader displayed on his person the badge of a Bridgeport police officer. This connection between the KKK and law enforcement attracted media attention, but the Republican governor, Everett J. Lake, summarily dismissed the reports. "While there has been quite a little comment about this organization in Connecticut, notably a comic opera midnight initiation near one of our cities," he said, "I can find no evidence of a serious or semi-serious nature in this State." In November seven Klansmen dressed in regalia attended the funeral of former U.S. Deputy Marshal Edson S. Bishop, "one of the oldest Klan members in the state." That news, published in the *Dawn,* a Klan newspaper from Chicago, underscored the Connecticut Klan's connections to law enforcement.[7]

But not all officers of the law were enamored of the secret society. Fourteen members of the New Britain police department, representing half of the evening force, refused to attend their weekly physical drill at the YMCA, because two of them had witnessed the drill instructor leaving a Klan meeting. Angelo Paonessa, New Britain's Italian Catholic mayor, was sympathetic. When the KKK held a meeting in New Britain in December 1922 at which the national lecturer Silas E. Newton of Oklahoma spoke against Catholics, Jews, and blacks, the Klan also verbalized its opposition to Paonessa, because he had threatened to fire city employees who belonged to the hooded society. But Paonessa decried the actions of the men in not following the orders of the police chief to attend their physical drill, which was their duty, and they had to appear before the board of police commissioners to answer to charges of insubordination.[8] The anti-Klan sympathies of the policemen could not override their obligations as city employees.

Measures to oppose the Klan through the legislative process proved unsuccessful in Connecticut. In January 1923 Sen. Thomas F. McGrath, a Democrat from Waterbury, introduced S. B. No. 130, "An Act concerning Clandestine Organizations," which sought to imprison or fine individuals who disguised their identity when appearing in groups of more than two persons on public highways. McGrath also introduced a separate anti-Klan bill, S. B. No. 587, "An Act concerning Associations Inimical to the Government," which stipulated that societies whose members were known only to themselves had to file the names of their officers every quarter with the secretary of state. There is no evidence that these bills became law.[9] Like other

New England solons, Connecticut lawmakers contemplated but did not enact anti-Klan legislation in the 1920s.

One measure that did circumscribe the Connecticut Klan somewhat was the decree made by State Fire Warden A. F. Hawes in 1924 that no crosses be burned without written permit during the period from September to December. Cross burnings regularly took place in Connecticut that year and captured the attention of the French-language press of New England. When the KKK burned a thirty-two-foot cross in Norwich it left a signed placard saying that, just as Christ had died on the cross to save humankind, so the Klan stood ready to die to save the United States, reported *La Sentinelle* in April 1924. The French-language newspaper also noted in May that the KKK had burned a cross on one of the highest hills in New London. That month, six thousand Klan members gathered on Bethany Hill to initiate one thousand recruits at the farm of Nelson J. Pock in New Haven, reported *L'Etoile,* and they performed their ceremony in front of three blazing crosses, added *La Justice de Biddeford.* In July police officers allowed three hundred Klansmen to travel on public roads to Birdall's Hill in Watertown in forty vehicles whose license plates were covered by cloth or newspaper, and the policemen prevented journalists from entering the meeting grounds, reported *L'Opinion Publique;* as part of the event Klansmen burned a large cross, indicated *L'Impartial.* During the fall season, these cross burnings could potentially ignite dried grass, brush, and woods, and Hawes would only allow fires at least two hundred feet away from combustible natural materials. "We will arrest any one found starting fires without permits, whether so-called Klansmen or not," Hawes insisted. "Klansmen are subject to arrest like any one else, and if found guilty can be fined $200 or sentenced to jail for six months." The potential hazard of the Klan's burning crosses became clear when, one evening in May 1925, six acres of woods in Haddam were destroyed, causing damage estimated at several thousand dollars, following the KKK's torching of a thirty-foot cross on Brainerd Hill. The Klan typically wrapped burlap around the crosses and doused them with kerosene before igniting them. A state policeman and a fire warden connected the fire damage to the blazing cross when they discovered in the Haddam woods pieces of burlap that apparently had come from the structure the Klan erected.[10]

The Connecticut Klan's burning of crosses may have attracted attention, but the society's aversion to Catholics attracted membership. With its large Irish and Catholic population, New Haven by January 1923 had the largest Ku Klux Klan membership of any Connecticut city, reported the *Boston Daily Advertiser.* The newspaper's comment underscored the connection between the KKK's anti-Catholicism and its numerical strength. Indeed, the Klan's ephemeral material highlights the organization's anti-Catholic efforts.

To screen out Roman Catholics, the KKK application form directly asked, "Have you ever been a member of the Roman Catholic Church[?]" and "Are any of the members of your immediate family members of the Roman Catholic Church[?]"[11]

In its discrimination against Catholics and other non-Protestants, the Ku Klux Klan targeted the very individuals who provided the labor to operate the factories of the Connecticut Valley. Nighttime travel in certain sections of the valley between Springfield, Massachusetts, and New Haven posed dangerous risks for Catholics as well as Jews, indicated the *Providence News* in June 1924. "Industry flourishes in these communities, and to the textile and the metal trades have been attracted over long periods of years hundreds of thousands of Irish, Poles, French, Italians and others of the European families of races," noted the *News*. "It is the product of their labor that fattens the pocketbooks of some of the very men who have turned against them secretly," commented the newspaper, implying that the individuals who benefited from the work of ethnic populations also confronted them in white robes.[12]

Confrontations occasionally took place in the political arena as well. Duane Lockard points out that Catholics in Connecticut tended to be Democratic, a political tie that the New York governor Al Smith solidified with his presidential bid in 1928. The KKK helped to defeat the runs by the Irish Catholics David E. Fitzgerald for governor and Thomas J. Spellacy for U.S. Senate, asserted the state KKK organizer Charles Nott in January 1923. The following year he focused his political efforts in the state on defeating Catholic and Jewish officeholders.[13]

In Connecticut, as in the other New England states, the Ku Klux Klan found greater empathy among Republicans than Democrats. When Republicans gathered for their state convention in New Haven in September 1924, Mrs. Henry H. Townsend, the vice ward chair of New Haven, introduced a resolution opposing the secret society, but the platform committee soundly defeated it. Delegates subsequently decided not to bring the measure to the convention floor for discussion or debate.[14]

"Let the Republican Party in Connecticut continue its sphynx-like [*sic*] policy of subservient fear of the hooded order," clamored U.S. Congressman Patrick B. O'Sullivan, the temporary chair of the Connecticut Democratic State Convention, in his keynote address to the delegates assembled at Hartford in September 1924. "But let no man or woman in the grand old Commonwealth court the friendship of the Ku Klux Klan and dare to call himself a Democrat," he warned. O'Sullivan spoke out forcefully against the bigotry of this second version of the secret society, the Klan of the 1920s, by pointing out that "this new movement manifests itself as antagonistic to Jew, Catholic, negro and Italian." He went on to highlight the contributions that the

KKK's targets had made to the United States, contributions, he averred, that members of the second Klan had not considered. "Perhaps its sponsors forget that it was a humble Genoese whose caravel, manned by Jews, Portuguese, Spaniards and Italians, laid open the wonders of this hemisphere. Perhaps they overlook the fact that the negro carried a musket in the recent war, and if need be was ready to die for this land," O'Sullivan stated. "Perhaps they have forgotten the part which Catholics have played for greater glory of these United States. Perhaps they deny that the man upon whose teachings rest the dogma of every Christian Church was himself a Jew," he persisted. O'Sullivan challenged the notion that paying homage to one's ethnic origins lessened attachment to the host society, asserting, "Love for America is not so selfish as to banish all thought of the land of one's forbears."[15]

O'Sullivan also seized on the occasion to speak out against the intolerance of the Eighteenth Amendment (the prohibition amendment), thus tackling an issue that motivated the Ku Klux Klan nationally. The Democratic State Convention heeded O'Sullivan's advice and adopted a platform that included an anti-Klan plank. "We condemn the Ku Klux Klan as the most un-American thing in America," the resolution stated. Not only did Connecticut Democrats denounce the KKK, but they also advocated changing prohibition laws to allow for the production and sale of light wines and beers.[16]

Not all of the Klan's challenges came from outside the organization. The Klan realm of Connecticut and Rhode Island appears to have had periodic internal difficulties, for it experienced regular turnover in its leadership. This occasioned comment in the press but often little specific information about the leadership dynamics and divisions within the society. According to newspaper reports, J. W. Scott Sanders of West Haven served as King Kleagle of Connecticut and Rhode Island at least from January 1923 until August of that year. As noted in chapter 8, Morris Westervelt of New Jersey headed the Klan of Connecticut and Rhode Island for much of 1924, and the press cited dissension with Westervelt's leadership when it wrote about his abrupt departure from Rhode Island by early September 1924. When Harry T. Lutterman of Darien, Connecticut, succeeded Westervelt as King Kleagle of the two states, he became the organization's third leader in the short span of two years.[17] Lutterman apparently did not remain long at the helm either.

Newspaper accounts reveal that the Connecticut Klan experienced major internal divisions in 1925 and 1926. In October 1925 five thousand Klan members from Massachusetts, Rhode Island, New York, and New Jersey, along with ten thousand Klan members from Connecticut, attended a Klan ceremony at Double Beach in Branford. As a result of a breach within the Connecticut Klan, Daniel E. Rhoads, a national Klan representative from Michigan who became head of the Connecticut Klan, ordered that those who had defected from the national KKK could not attend the gathering. Those denied entry consisted of the New Haven Klan, the state's first Klan organization. After this incident most members of Provisional Klan No. 1 voted to leave the New Haven organization they had formed nearly five years earlier.[18]

Although the Connecticut Klan in 1926 had twenty-three units, the disbanding of the Constitution State's oldest and largest Klan organization harmed the state KKK. The negative publicity generated by the New Haven Klan's schism with the national Klan and its subsequent secession also hurt the national Ku Klux Klan organization as it declined throughout the country from the mid-1920s on.[19]

Arthur J. Mann, the head of the order department of the National Folding Box Company in New Haven, served as secretary of the New Haven Klan. He made public in January 1926 the letter he had written to Imperial Klaliff (Vice President) Walter Bossert of Indianapolis, announcing that six hundred of the approximately seven hundred Klansmen in the group had decided to quit the Ku Klux Klan organization. "No self-respecting citizen would permit himself to be affiliated with the order as it stands," Mann stated. "We decided to quit because the heads of the organization were after the almighty dollar. They were sending solicitors into this district, signing up riffraff and any one whose $10 they could get," Mann complained. The former Kligrapp therefore alleged that the national Ku Klux Klan existed primarily as a moneymaking scheme, and he lamented its decay throughout the United States. "For every good man" who leaves the KKK, "ten are taken in that would shame a ward leader of Tammany Hall," Mann claimed. Thus corruption within the organization overshadowed that of the unethical politicians it sought to oust from public office. The New Haven defectors became disillusioned with the Ku Klux Klan, Mann suggested, for "it is not only anti-Catholic and anti-Jew, but absolutely anti-American and anti-Protestant." Moreover, Mann asserted in his letter to Bossert, the KKK "has become without question the greatest menace facing the American people today." Consequently, it must be eradicated from U.S. society, he argued.[20]

In a separate letter to the press Mann acknowledged that "hundreds of men in New Haven have made a mistake" in having joined the Ku Klux Klan organization. Weighing in on the defection of the New Haven Klan, the *New York Times* opined, "So New England at last is awakening to its shame and all of the better element in the Klan are quitting it." While complimenting the former New Haven Klansmen for leaving the organization, the *New Haven Journal-Courier* wondered how they could have been deceived into thinking they could improve the country by joining such a society in the first place. "Whatever the evils are which have crept into the life of the United

States—and they are not few—their remedy does not lie in a passionate clash of political, racial and religious prejudices," the newspaper contended.[21]

Following the dissolution of the New Haven Klan, various forms of external opposition to the Connecticut Klan surfaced throughout 1926. As three thousand Klan members met on the exposition grounds of Woodstock in August, three hundred opponents assembled on another section of the grounds, though no trouble was reported. After three young men from Brooklyn, Connecticut, were found guilty of painting the letters "K.K.K." on Wauregan's Sacred Heart Roman Catholic Church and on a public highway in August, they were fined and sentenced to jail for thirty days; although they tried to have their convictions overturned, the superior court denied their appeals. When the KKK made plans to march in Plainfield in September, the selectmen refused to issue the organization a parade permit, holding that it would obstruct traffic and "would tend to incite ill feeling, ill will and resentment upon the part of the remaining populace," because of the recent defacing of highways and church property in nearby Wauregan. When the Klan declared it would march in Plainfield even without a permit, Selectman Henri J. Bessette prevailed on the superior court judge to issue an injunction forbidding the parade and threatening a two-hundred-dollar fine if the Klan proceeded with its plans.[22] There is no evidence that it did.

Such resistance to the Klan in Connecticut undoubtedly helped to precipitate its decline from the middle to the end of the 1920s. In 1926 there were 21,347 Klan members in good standing in Connecticut, as reported in the *Washington Post*. By 1930 a mere 453 remained.[23]

Even as it declined, the Klan continued to make its presence felt in the state. White-robed members ushered in the New Year in 1927 by burning crosses at thirty separate locations. In August 1928 over six thousand members from Connecticut, Rhode Island, Massachusetts, New York, and New Jersey gathered for field day activities at Bruce Park in Greenwich, Connecticut. Klan realms competed against each other in various athletic contests; the Connecticut and New York Klans played a game of baseball, and the Connecticut and Rhode Island Klans faced off in a tug-of-war. Up to four thousand non-Klan members also participated in the day's events, during which the Greenwich police offered protection to the Klan.[24]

In the political realm the KKK may have inspired two distinct pieces of legislation in 1927, legislation similar to what the organization sponsored in other New England states in the same year. In January, Rollin L. Birdsall, a Republican from Willington, introduced H. B. 65, "An Act relating to Marriage, Prohibiting the Intermarriage of Whites and Persons of African Descent, and Prescribing Penalties for violation Thereof," a measure which would have imposed fines or imprisonment or both for miscegenation and for the individual who performed the marriage ceremony of mixed-race couples. Birdsall denied that any society, such as the KKK, for example, had sponsored the legislation. The House Judiciary Committee rejected the bill, followed, in turn, by both the full House of Representatives and the Senate. Rep. Nathan G. Armitage, a Republican from Ashford, introduced in January H. B. 96, "An Act relating to Marriage, Forbidding Certain Contracts, Agreements or Stipulations, Oral or in Writing, by the Parties Thereto, and Prescribing Penalties for Persuading, Enticing or Inducing the Parties to a Marriage So to Do," which would have provided for fines or imprisonment or both for the individual who performed a marriage ceremony, if the person required the couple to "make agreements concerning the religion of future issue." Like Birdsall, Armitage maintained that the bill was his idea and did not originate with any society or organization. The House Judiciary Committee rejected the measure, which ostensibly targeted Catholics with regard to the religious training of children, and the full House accepted the unfavorable report.[25]

Occasional newspaper articles disclose that Catholics were not the Klan's only targets in Connecticut and that the lack of antimiscegenation laws did not discourage its intimidation of blacks. One evening in February 1928 a cross burned on Pillsbury Hill in Rockville after a black man had received both a letter and a phone call warning him not to marry a sixteen-year-old white girl. The couple chose to follow through with their wedding plans the next evening. In January 1929 a cross burned in front of the home of Charles Nichols, a black man from East Norwalk who was married to and had fathered children with a white woman. Nichols also received a threatening phone call from someone who identified himself as a Klan official and who told Nichols that his white boarder, the twenty-two-year-old Fred Cunningham, was "infatuated" with one of Nichols's daughters and had better leave town if he wanted to escape being tarred and feathered. Cunningham chose not to leave, and Nichols vowed to defend his home with two loaded guns in hand. "The scheduled Sunday night raid consequently failed to take place," reported the *Pittsburgh Courier*.[26] These incidents provide impressionistic evidence that Connecticut African Americans exercised their agency and asserted their constitutional and human rights in the face of threats by the Klan or those who implicated the organization.

In Connecticut, as in the other New England states, the reality was that the Ku Klux Klan of the 1920s primarily opposed Catholics. The KKK even formed a new church to proclaim its Protestantism in Connecticut and used the opening celebration to bash Catholics. Drawing from eight thousand to twelve thousand men, women, and children, the dedication in June 1927 of the world's first United Protestant Church, located in Sterling, was the Klan's largest public gathering in Connecticut in the late twenties. The participants came from Klan organizations in sixteen states, including all six New England states, and as far away as Tennessee, Kentucky, and Florida. Together, they formed a parade of two miles in length. Rev. Ernest C. Drake, who had been dismissed as the pastor of Sterling's Methodist Church "because of his advocacy of Klan principles," became the pastor of the new church, half of whose three hundred founding congregants were Klan members. The opening ceremonies for the new church included a collection for the needy, a luncheon, and a cross burning, as well as anti-Catholic speeches. As the leader of the Klan of Connecticut and Rhode Island, Daniel E. Rhoads used the opening celebration to attack the Catholic Church, and he vowed that the Ku Klux Klan would fight Al Smith's presidential bid at the Democratic National Convention, if his candidacy went that far in 1928.[27]

Smith's presidential campaign aroused significant anti-Catholic sentiment throughout the country. Non-Catholics worried about the potential political influence the pope might wield if a Catholic like Smith gained the nation's highest office. In Connecticut, Women of the Ku Klux Klan (WKKK) displayed their anti-Catholicism through their songs. In one, sung to the tune of "Bonnie Lies over the Ocean," Klanswomen opened with the words,

> *Pope Pius is boss over millions*
> *He'll never be boss over me.*

In another stanza, they gleefully chimed together about the role of Protestants in defeating Smith's presidential bid, and in doing so negated what they believed were the pope's intentions:

> *He tried to put Smith in the White House,*
> *The order came over the sea,*
> *The Protestants gave its veto*
> *Real Protestants like you and me.*

The WKKK chanted that the pope was working to place Catholics in political office to extend his influence; their song implied that the WKKK faced declining memberships, and it also suggested that the organization's work against Catholics should compel former members to rejoin their society:

> *Come back, come back: come back all ye faithful, there's work to do.*
> *Come back, come back: Rome's working and we must work too.*[28]

While the songs of the Connecticut Women of the Ku Klux Klan may have stirred anti-Catholic sentiment, there is no evidence they helped to increase membership in the disintegrating society.

Anti-Catholicism nonetheless continued to inspire Klan members through the end of the 1920s. The anti-Catholic U.S. senator from Alabama, J. Thomas Heflin, traveled to Connecticut in June 1929 to address three thousand to six thousand individuals (news reports vary on the numbers) gathered at Marriott's field in Oneco to commemorate the second anniversary of the United Protestant Church. A parade featuring at least fifteen hundred Klan members from Massachusetts, Connecticut, and Rhode Island preceded Heflin's speech. Protected by armed Klan guards, Heflin denounced the Roman Catholic Church from a raised platform erected in the field and decorated with the banners and insignia of the KKK. He objected to what he perceived as the Church's interference with the nation's public school system, and he praised the KKK for its work.[29]

Two years later, shortly before Christmas 1931, fire consumed the United Protestant Church; its charred remains appeared emblematic of the Connecticut Klan's status. However diminished, the Constitution State's Klan continued to organize social activities for its members in the 1930s. Imperial Wizard Hiram W. Evans traveled to Providence and Hartford to address members of the realm of Connecticut and Rhode Island in July 1931, undoubtedly in an effort to stoke interest in the shrinking organization during the Great Depression. In 1932 the Klan celebrated the birthday of George Washington by burning crosses on hills in New London. A burning cross and fireworks concluded the Norwalk Klan's field day activities in June 1932.[30]

Like the Ku Klux Klan elsewhere in the country, the Connecticut Klan particularly directed its energy against Communism during the 1930s. In a Christmas message in 1932, J. W. Perry, Grand Dragon of Connecticut and Rhode Island, told members that "Communism is Christ's most deadly enemy today. Communistic propaganda, disguised in many forms, is rampant in our land." What Perry contended the Communists were doing was exactly what Klan opponents had interpreted the hooded society as doing throughout the 1920s, an irony that must have escaped the Grand Dragon when he stated that Communism's "purpose is to divide our forces, mislead the very elect; destroy our form of government." In his holiday message Perry avowed that the KKK's goal was to root out Communism by exposing its proponents and practitioners.[31]

Despite refocusing its energies on the fight against Communism in the 1930s, the KKK was still interested in religious issues. In January 1933 state representative Benjamin Tonkonow, a Democrat from Meriden, introduced H. B. 677, "An Act prohibiting Inquiry concerning the Religion or Religious Affiliations of Persons Seeking Employment or Official Positions in the Public Schools." The Ku Klux Klan opposed the legislation. The measure would have imposed penalties on those seeking or providing information on the religious affiliation of potential public school employees; the bill sought to end discrimination against Catholics and Jews because of the practice of school officials of questioning the religious affiliation of teachers. Arguing against the proposed legislation, the Grand Dragon of Connecticut contended that 65 percent of the state's school boards and 83 percent of the public school teachers of Connecticut were Roman Catholic. "If there is any discrimination, it is against Protestants and Jews," he alleged. The bill divided lawmakers along political lines, with Republicans comprising most of the bill's detractors and Democrats most of its backers. The House education committee reported unfavorably on the measure, and the full House concurred, resoundingly rejecting it.[32] In this case the KKK's sentiments apparently prevailed.

In summary, the known activities of the Ku Klux Klan in Connecticut did not differ appreciably from those of its counterparts in the other New England states in the 1920s. Women and men of the Connecticut KKK communicated through their ephemeral material, such as song sheets and membership application forms, through their rhetoric, as well as through their burning crosses their fierce opposition to the Roman Catholic Church and its followers, to Jews, and to racial intermarriage. The secession of an overwhelming majority of the New Haven Klan from the national Ku Klux Klan harmed both the Connecticut and U.S. Klan organizations, both of which faced steep declines in membership after peaking in the mid-1920s. For their part, the New Haven secessionists raised the very kinds of criticisms of the Ku Klux Klan that its opponents had been raising since it began spreading throughout the New England states in the early 1920s. As we will see in the next chapter, the lessons that the New Haven secessionists learned were lost on a later generation in Connecticut—as elsewhere in New England.

11

Reappearance in the Late Twentieth Century

SCHOLARS have identified at least four iterations of the Ku Klux Klan. The post-Civil War Klan is typically identified as the first Klan. The second, or 1920s, Klan lost most of its membership in the North by the start of the Great Depression but managed to linger on in the South until World War II by focusing its energies in a struggle against Communism during the 1930s and early 1940s. The third Klan, primarily a southern organization, arose after the Second World War in opposition to the civil rights movement and lasted until the 1970s. The fourth Klan originated in the 1980s and continues to the present day; located primarily in the South, Midwest, and West, it targets such groups as Southeast Asians, Mexican Americans, Jews, blacks, and homosexuals.[1] The Ku Klux Klan all but disappeared from the New England states during the Great Depression. Over the course of the twentieth century the KKK metamorphosed before resurfacing in various northeastern communities from the late 1970s to the early 1990s. While the Klan of New England in the twenties was composed of white Protestants who primarily opposed Catholics, the northeastern KKK of the late twentieth century consisted of whites, including Catholics, who targeted racial minorities, particularly African Americans.

In 1977 P. Bodine, using the alias Karl Baxter, made an appearance on WLBZ television station in Bangor, Maine, and claimed to be Grand Dragon over twelve hundred Klan members he had organized in twelve chapters in the state. Bodine had written to the *Maine Sunday Telegram* in 1968 to say, "I am one of many who feel that the Negro should be encouraged to return to Africa," and now, a decade later, he conveyed to the newspaper the Klan's goal of "anti-mongrelizing," arguing, "When you take the two races and mix them, you get a different race. . . . It's not in the best interests of western civilization." Bodine informed the *Telegram* that the twelve Maine Klan chapters, organized in the state's college communities, were attracting "young men of military age and Vietnam War veterans." The *Telegram* reported that the sixty-two-year-old Bodine was an educator who had taught science at Lincoln High School in the late 1950s but was fired because parents had complained to the school board about his teaching. "In class, he said that even to kill one [African American] wasn't a sin, it was like killing a sick dog," stated one of Bodine's former students.[2]

Claiming harassment by Maine's media, Bodine requested a transfer to another state, news that David Duke of Louisiana, the founder in 1974 of the Knights of the Ku Klux Klan, corroborated in a telephone interview with the *Portland Evening Express.* Without confirming Klan numbers in Maine, Duke acknowledged, "We've got a lot of good people in that area." He went on to comment on Maine's KKK history: "Maine was a very strong Klan state in the 1920s. Our efforts will continue that tradition. The white majority is getting fed up with reverse discrimination." Following the reports, Gov. James Longley, an Independent, asked the heads of several state agencies to monitor the KKK's activities in Maine in order to protect the rights of all of the state's citizens. "We cannot allow one Maine citizen to be threatened or intimidated (by) any group that would place itself above the law," Longley emphasized.[3]

Maine was not the only New England state to attract the KKK in the 1970s. William Wilkinson of Louisiana appeared in white robes at the Seabrook nuclear power plant in New Hampshire in October 1978. He served as Imperial Wizard of the Invisible Empire of the Knights of the Ku Klux Klan, one of a number of competing Klan organizations that emerged in the country in the late twentieth century.[4] Wilkinson indicated that the KKK was recruiting members in the Granite State, and he spoke in support of the controversial nuclear power plant as a means of reducing the country's dependence on Arab oil. Douglas Coen, Grand Dragon of Mississippi, appeared in robes alongside Wilkinson. The two, Wilkinson indicated, had come to New England primarily to attend an upcoming antibusing rally in Boston. Around twelve members of a South Boston antibusing group and twenty-five members of motorcycle gangs from Portsmouth, New Hampshire, Portland, Maine, and Worcester, Massachusetts, all came out to support the KKK. During the rally the motorcycle gangs engaged in a shouting match with members of the Boston branch of the International Committee Against Racism (ICAR.)[5]

After the New Hampshire rally the two KKK leaders from Louisiana and Mississippi appeared in Boston to support the opponents of busing. In 1974 a federal judge ordered the integration of Boston's schools, requiring the busing of 8,500 white children and 9,700 black children out of the city's total of 94,000 students. Racial violence erupted as whites threw stones at buses transporting black children to South Boston and as blacks hurled rocks at buses bringing white children to Roxbury. Duke, then Louisiana Grand Dragon of the Knights of the Ku Klux Klan, stated that Klan members would travel north to Boston to oppose the court-ordered busing; their actions, he indicated, would represent a reversal of the Freedom Rides of the civil rights movement, in which white students from the North traveled south to work for racial integration. Four years later, in October 1978, four Ku Klux Klan members joined an antibusing group, called the South Boston Marshals to speak out against municipal efforts to integrate the schools. From 50 to 125 members of ICAR confronted KKK members outside of Boston City Hall. As Imperial Wizard Wilkinson spoke at the antibusing rally, the protesters, in an action reminiscent of the Massachusetts anti-Klan attacks of the 1920s, lobbed rocks, bricks, eggs, and sticks, injuring eight people, including three Klansmen.[6]

When Duke, serving as Grand Wizard of the Knights of the Ku Klux Klan, planned to make a presidential campaign stop at Boston's City Hall Plaza in December 1979, four hundred to five hundred anti-Klan protesters gathered there to greet him, chanting, "David Duke get the word, Boston ain't Johannesburg." Duke failed to show, and the rally ended after several hours. Duke was touring New England communities as he contemplated entering the presidential primaries of Massachusetts and Connecticut in 1980, in what became the first of his three runs for the Oval Office. Although Duke was constitutionally unable to serve as president because he was only twenty-nine at the time of his first campaign, he hoped his participation in the presidential race would enable him to bring the Ku Klux Klan's principles to the Democratic National Convention. Two months after Duke's scheduled appearance in Boston, state lawmakers enacted civil rights legislation against racially motivated violence and harassment.[7]

During Duke's tour of New England, he also visited Danbury, Hartford, and Waterbury, Connecticut, in December 1979. Two months prior to Duke's arrival in Danbury, Klan literature was distributed at Western Connecticut State College, an action that led the National Association for the Advancement of Colored People (NAACP) and a local group called the Coalition of Black Organizations to sponsor a protest march of three hundred persons who walked from Kennedy Park to Danbury City Hall to demonstrate their opposition to the Ku Klux Klan's presence in their community. While in Waterbury, Duke held a news conference in an effort to organize the KKK of New England, and he claimed that Connecticut had close to one thousand

Klan members, but the NAACP estimated that there were no more than two hundred persons in the state's hooded society.[8]

During the 1980s the Ku Klux Klan of Connecticut made itself most visible in the communities of Scotland and Meriden. In September 1980, 350 members, 35 to 45 of them dressed in regalia, held a rally and cross burning in the rural community of Scotland, forty miles east of Hartford. At the event Imperial Wizard Wilkinson asserted: "We can have equal opportunity, but you cannot make unequal people equal." He also took the opportunity to name Gary Piscottano of New Britain the Grand Dragon of the Connecticut Klan. Up to four hundred protesters, most representing the Committee Against Racism, sang civil rights songs and demonstrated against the Klan. Prior to the event the KKK threatened to use weapons against nonwhites and others who interfered with the rally; consequently, a superior court judge issued an injunction banning weapons from Scotland for the weekend, and state police searched vehicles to enforce the ban. Clashes between Klan and anti-Klan groups nonetheless took place, resulting in multiple injuries but, as a result of the searches, not knife or gunshot wounds.[9]

When the Ku Klux Klan held a second rally in Scotland during the same September weekend, state police arrested the thirty-seven-year-old Wilkinson for possession of a loaded .45 caliber automatic pistol they found in his suitcase. Wilkinson therefore arrived late to the rally. Up to three hundred individuals, most of them men in their twenties, attended the event. One of the men grumbled, "I'm the wrong damn color, that's the thing that I don't like," explaining that federal affirmative action policies promoting the hiring of blacks at factories like the Pratt and Whitney plant in Middleton stood in the way of his gaining employment. He attended the Klan gathering to hear what Wilkinson had to say. No anti-Klan demonstrators appeared at the Sunday evening event, during which the Klan burned a fifteen-foot cross.[10]

In Meriden racial tensions erupted following the fatal shooting in February 1981 of a black man suspected of shoplifting by an off-duty white police officer. The next month Wilkinson led twenty-three Klan members in regalia, along with several dozen sympathizers, in a march from Meriden's war memorial to city hall to show their support for the white policeman. Several hundred individuals came out to oppose the Ku Klux Klan. They represented ICAR (composed in Connecticut of inner-city blacks and Hispanics), the Progressive Labor Party of Boston, and the Revolutionary Socialist League of New York. When forty police officers tried to form a barricade between the Klan and its opponents, black and Latino counterdemonstrators chanted "Cops and Klan work hand in hand." The protesters created noise to interfere with the Klan rally and charged up the city hall steps as Wilkinson spoke. The Klan members escaped inside city hall and emerged by the back door an hour later under police escort, whereupon the confrontation took a violent and bloody turn as protesters threw rocks and bottles and chased the white-robed figures for nearly half a mile. At least twenty-two persons, including seventeen police officers, suffered injuries; four Klan members required hospital treatment. An investigation ensued to determine why forty state troopers stationed two miles from the scene did not receive orders to assist the Meriden police.[11]

In reviewing the events in Meriden, the *New York Times* noted some similarities with the civil rights movement of the 1960s: "Protesters, determined to exercise their constitutional rights, take to the streets, only to be pelted by the rocks and bottles of counterdemonstrators." Paradoxically, the parties had changed. "The marchers in Meriden, Conn., though, were robed and hooded members of the Invisible Empire, Knights of the Ku Klux Klan," wrote the *Times,* "and last week, completing the ironic parallel, they demanded that their assailants be prosecuted under Federal civil rights laws." Kevin Bean, the assistant minister of St. Andrew's Episcopal Church in Meriden, tried to differentiate the recent events in his community from those of the sixties' civil rights movement in the South: "Meriden is not a Greensboro or Biloxi, or anything like a Southern city." With an unemployment rate of 8.2 percent, representing double the state rate, Meriden was experiencing economic hard times, Bean stated, and "a fair number of people have responded with some of the easier answers, in essence blaming the victims," by which he meant economically disadvantaged racial minorities.[12]

The Ku Klux Klan returned to Meriden in July 1981. Seventeen Klan members held a demonstration at the same location as the one in March. Some of the KKK members held placards denouncing the actions of those who had opposed them at the earlier event. The Klan objected to the lack of prosecution by the authorities of those involved in the March confrontation, claiming that the attack violated their civil rights. Nearly 50 individuals showed up to defy the Klan, chanting, "White and black, black and white, workers of the world unite" as well as "What's the plan—smash the Klan, what's the solution—revolution." Counterdemonstrators again hurled rocks and bottles at the Klan, injuring a Klanswoman and a police officer. The state and local police arrested 10 anti-Klan demonstrators for disorderly conduct, inciting a riot, or breach of peace. Several months later the same Klan faction appeared in Windham, where 150 members (22 of them in robes) held a rally and cross burning while protected by 200 state police.[13]

The Klan's activities in Connecticut spurred lawmakers to action. They passed Public Act No. 80-54, "An Act Concerning the Desecration of Property," which took effect in October 1980, and made it a crime to burn crosses either on public or private property without the consent of the owner. The legislation also made it a misdemeanor to deny the constitutional rights of any person "on account of RELIGION, NATIONAL ORIGIN, alienage, color, race, sex or blindness or physical disability," and it stipulated further that violations included the desecration of public property and houses of worship. Another law, Public Act No. 81-243, "An Act Concerning Paramilitary Camps," which was modeled after legislation proposed by the Anti-Defamation League of B'nai B'rith and went into effect in October 1981, took aim at paramilitary groups and made it a felony to teach or demonstrate the use of firearms and explosives to harm or kill people in a civil disorder or to assemble with one or more persons to gain training for such ends.[14]

Local communities also passed ordinances that circumscribed the Klan's activities. When the group planned a return visit to Meriden in March 1982 it learned that city officials had passed an ordinance granting the police chief the authority to ban parades that could lead to violent altercations. The Connecticut chapter of the American Civil Liberties Union worked with the KKK to challenge the regulation. A federal judge allowed the Klan to march, holding that the rights of free speech and assembly guaranteed by the U.S. Constitution had equal weight to worries that city officials had over a potential clash between the organization and its adversaries. On the anniversary of the Meriden clash of 1981, thirty Klansmen and one Klanswoman, all donning white robes and protected by three hundred police officers, organized a White Christian Solidarity Day, at which Imperial Wizard Wilkinson spoke. Upward of one thousand spectators, all searched for weapons, turned out to witness the event. The protesters included ICAR as well as the Committee for Education and Defense Against Racism.[15] No trouble was reported.

Not until April 1983 did the Klan hold another rally in Meriden. Thirty KKK members gathered on the steps of city hall, but four hundred noisy spectators drowned out Wilkinson's words. Three hundred state and local police provided security at the event, including an escort to departing Klan members. While the KKK held other rallies in Connecticut in the 1980s—in New Britain in June 1983 and in East Windsor in August 1986, for example— they attracted less attention from protesters and the press than the Meriden and Scotland events.[16]

But in September 1986 the Connecticut Klan again gained national attention when James Farrands, a tool and die machinist from Shelton, was elected Imperial Wizard. As a result the Invisible Empire of the Ku Klux Klan moved its headquarters from the southern home of the outgoing national Klan leader to Connecticut. This event represented the first time the KKK located its headquarters north of the Mason-Dixon line. Not only was Farrands the first northerner to accede to the national Klan leadership but he was also the first Roman Catholic to do so.[17] His accession suggests the protean nature of the Ku Klux Klan over historical time. That the KKK underwent a metamorphosis from an organization that confronted New England Catholics in the 1920s to one that elected a Catholic New Englander as head of its national organization six decades later is singularly ironic. It boldly marks the declining salience of anti-Catholicism in the United States, particularly among working- and middle-class whites in the late twentieth century.

During the 1980s the Ku Klux Klan also surfaced in Rhode Island. In 1981, when Farrands was leader of the KKK of Connecticut, Rhode Island, and Massachusetts, he accompanied nine other Klan members from Connecticut to distribute KKK literature in Rhode Island along with some Pawtucket residents. That year Rhode Island passed a law making a felony any act of terrorizing individuals or of desecrating property with the intent to terrorize. The appearance of swastikas on the homes of Jews in Providence, on gravestones in a Jewish cemetery, and on synagogues over the course of seven years led to the 1982 conviction of Charles William Sickles, the founder of the Providence klavern. Testifying against Sickles, Patrick C. Labbe, a French-surnamed Klansman from Pawtucket, told the jury that Sickles aspired to overthrowing the U.S. government, "the extermination of the Jews, sending the blacks back to Africa and killing the gays." That Labbe would join the Klan implies that Franco-American identity had declined sufficiently in the late twentieth century that he would not perceive an inconsistency between his ethnic heritage and participation in the KKK. A superior court judge sentenced the defendant, Sickles, to a nine-month prison term for painting a swastika on the wall of the Jewish Community Center to commemorate the birthday of Adolf Hitler in 1979, but the Rhode Island Supreme Court subsequently overturned his conviction because the wrong court had tried the case.[18]

Rhode Island was not the only small New England state in which the Ku Klux Klan reappeared in the 1980s and 1990s. It also emerged again in Vermont, New Hampshire, and Maine in the late twentieth century. In May 1982 seventeen Klan members from Connecticut traveled to Wilmington, Vermont, where two of them reportedly owned property, to hold a rally at the town's ball field. Vermont state police escorted the Klan twenty miles from the Massachusetts border to Wilmington to prevent an ambush. An anti-Klan banner strung across Main Street informed the KKK that "Hatred Does Not Grow Well in the Rocky Soil of Vermont." Prior to the gathering at Baker field, the town attorney, Craig R. Wenk, asked the Windham Superior Court to issue an injunction authorizing "pat down" searches to prevent those attending the rally from carrying weapons. Despite the fact that such searches had been conducted twice in Meriden, Connecticut, the judge turned down Wenk's request, contending it would deny citizens rights guaranteed by the Vermont and United States constitutions, including the rights of free speech, free assembly, and protection against illegal searches.[19]

Attached to Wenk's request as exhibit A was a flyer of the International Committee Against Racism that argued, "The ruling class (capitalists who pull the strings of Gov't.) is using the Klan to split and weaken the working class in this period of U.S. economic decline." ICAR asserted that large corporations, such as General Motors, International Telephone and Telegraph, and Exxon, "are banking on white workers blaming minorities, and all American workers blaming immigrants for the economic disaster they are forcing upon us. Thus, the growth of the Klan and racism presents a real threat to all working people and students." ICAR pointed out that it had worked to stop the Klan in Boston as well as in central Connecticut, and it called for racial unity among workers and students in confronting the Ku Klux Klan with "*militant, direct action.*" This was necessary, underscored ICAR, because "the Klan can only be stopped by the militant refusal of everyday people to accept their poisonous presence and growth," and it called on readers of the flyer to join ICAR's efforts to prevent the Klan from holding its rally in Wilmington.[20]

One hundred and fifty protesters squared off against the white-robed KKK women and men in a nonviolent confrontation; they made sufficient noise to drown out the Klan's efforts to recruit new members and to rail against Communism. In addition to the Boston-based International Committee Against Racism, protesters included the Boston-based John Brown Anti-Klan League, the Keene State College (New Hampshire) Communists, and Vermonters Against the Klan. For approximately one hour seventy-five state police dressed in riot gear kept the Klan and anti-Klan groups apart, after which they escorted the Klan off the ball field and back to the Massachusetts state line. "There was no visible or detectible [*sic*] show of support for the Klan," wrote Mike Sinclair, the Vermont secretary of civil and military affairs, to Governor Richard Snelling. "Likewise, the anti-Klan demonstrators did not appear to have incited the crowd or gained any support for their anti-Klan position," Sinclair added.[21]

Four Connecticut Klan members never made it to the rally. While removing anti-Klan literature from Wilmington's Main Street, Grand Dragon Farrands and three other Connecticut Klansmen were arrested for having a loaded .22 caliber rifle in their vehicle on a public highway, a violation of fish and game laws. Police also confiscated several shotguns and several handguns from their car. Each Klansman was subsequently convicted for the weapons violation.[22]

The Ku Klux Klan returned to southern Vermont in late May, when Imperial Wizard Wilkinson obtained a permit from the Brattleboro police chief, Marcel Leclaire, to hold a two-hour rally on the town common. Wilkinson told Leclaire the KKK would distribute literature on the streets if it did not receive permission to hold its rally; Leclaire subsequently waived the seventy-two-hour waiting period and issued the permit because he felt that the KKK and the attendant crowds could be more easily managed at the common. At least 15 Klansmen and Klanswomen paraded in regalia on the Brattleboro Common and made speeches at the bandstand as part of a drive to recruit new members. From 150 to 250 spectators watched the Klan's activities. While some demonstrators yelled, "Go home!" and from 75 to 100 protesters joined hands to sing "We Shall Overcome," Quakers displayed the banner used earlier at Wilmington, "Hatred Does Not Grow in the Rocky Soil of Vermont," and clergy dressed in their ministerial gowns mixed into the crowd and urged a silent protest. No violence was reported.[23]

Several racial incidents took place in Vermont the same year the Klan held its rallies in the Green Mountain State. Around the time of the Wilmington rally in May 1982, an African American man from Burlington who had dated a white woman received a threatening card in the mail that stated, "You have offended a Klansman. Your activities are being closely watched. For God and Country." The Burlington man also reported receiving over thirty-five telephone calls during which the caller hung up without leaving a message; in one case where the caller did not hang up, the individual threatened him with bodily harm. Also in May a black woman found that her vehicle had been damaged by rocks. In June a cross burned in Concord on the lawn of the town's only black family. The KKK denied responsibility for the cross burning. "While there is no evidence to link these incidents with the Klan," wrote the Vermont Advisory Committee to the U.S. Commission on Civil Rights, "the victims believe that the presence of, and the publicity given to, the Klan gave rise to an atmosphere which encouraged others to act out their racism." In 1982 the KKK also disseminated literature in Saxton's River, and the Brattleboro *Town Crier* complained that the group was using its delivery tubes to distribute literature in rural areas. As a result of the racial incidents and the recruitment efforts in the state, fifty people in Norwich formed the Vermont Anti-Klan Network in June 1982, but it became inactive after Klan activity ceased in the state.[24] Thus in the 1980s as in the 1920s Vermont proved unreceptive to the presence of the Ku Klux Klan in the Green Mountain State.

Citizens of the Granite State likewise resisted the intrusion of the KKK. When residents of Exeter, New Hampshire, learned that individuals interested in joining the Klan organization could write to the local post office for information and a membership application, the owner of the Loaf and

Ladle restaurant put up a handwritten sign to inform KKK members that they were not welcome at his restaurant. Small cards the size of a business card informed New Hampshire residents they could write to national KKK headquarters in Shelton, Connecticut, for free information. "There are thousands of organizations working for the interests of Blacks. How many groups stand up for the cultural values and ideals of the White Majority?" questioned the undated card, which continued with a response and an explanation: "Not many; as a result we are faced with reverse discrimination in jobs, promotions, and scholarships—busing for forced integration—high taxes for minority welfare—a high rate of brutal crime—gun control—anti-White movies and TV programs—in short, a society oriented to the wishes of minorities." The recruitment card then described what the KKK had to offer: "We of the Ku Klux Klan are unapologetically committed to the interests, ideas, and cultural values of the White Majority. We are determined to maintain and enrich our cultural and racial heritage." In 1999 two New Hampshire men distributed Klan literature in the small community of Washington, which had a population of six hundred. The literature pointed to minorities as the source of the country's maladies and tried to portray the KKK as the allies of police in their work to keep youth from abusing drugs. The town residents chose either to ignore the Ku Klux Klan or to focus their energies on organizing a concert titled "Love Thy Neighbor."[25]

From the early 1980s to the late 1990s the KKK resurfaced in Maine on numerous occasions. In January 1981 federal agents entered the home of a Durham resident named Charles S. Anthony, who claimed to be a KKK leader, and seized a .44 caliber Magnum revolver, a .12 gauge shotgun, and a .22 caliber rifle from the convicted felon. Under the alias of Paul Johnson, Anthony had contacted a Portland journalist in 1980 following the acquittal of an African American man for the fatal shooting of a Caucasian during a rock concert at White's Beach in Brunswick. Anthony wrote, "We had faith in the Maine court. That faith was misplaced. In the future the KKK will have to take a more active role in alerting the public as to the problems and solutions."[26]

From May to September 1987 the KKK distributed its newspaper, *The Klansman,* to residents of Gray, Durham, Minot, Falmouth, Bath, Brunswick, Lewiston, and Portland, either in or near their newspaper boxes or simply by leaving copies on their lawns. The newspaper featured articles advocating immigration restrictions and segregation. When contacted by the press Imperial Wizard Farrands of Connecticut acknowledged the Klan's presence in Maine but would not identify who was distributing the organization's literature. As the first Roman Catholic to serve as Imperial Wizard, Farrands illustrated how elastic supposed constructions of religious

and racial prejudice could become as Klan prejudice and targets changed
over time. Farrands told reporters that the Ku Klux Klan stood opposed to
non-Christians and nonwhites. "We're pro-white Christian. If you're black,
if you're Chinese, if you're anything but a Christian, we don't like you," he
stated bluntly.[27]

"All minorities have suffered at the hands of the Ku Klux Klan, but we
realize that blacks have suffered the most," observed L. Evangeline Berry, the
president of the Maine NAACP, who condemned the society's plans to hold
a rally at Rumford. Blacks represented less than 1 percent of Maine's population of 1.1 million residents in 1987. Some had arrived in the state during
labor disputes in pulp and paper mills. The managers of the Boise Cascade
paper mill, Rumford's largest employer, had used replacement workers from
the Alabama company Bolvig, Edmonds, and Kennedy to keep the mill operating during an eleven-week strike in 1986; International Paper Company in
Jay had done the same thing in 1987. When the Boise Cascade strike ended,
342 employees lost their jobs to strikebreakers. Farrands professed not to
know of the Rumford labor dispute, but he spoke by telephone to a reporter
about the problem of blacks taking jobs from whites and about white flight
from cities, which led to the development of cities with predominantly African American populations. "It happened in Gary, Indiana," Farrands noted.
"It can happen in Rumford, Maine."[28]

As the KKK made plans to hold its rally in the small, working-class community of Rumford, with a population of nine thousand, opposition from
political leaders and other groups grew. The Republican governor John R.
McKernan condemned the group, stating "There is no place in Maine communities or with Maine people for the type of violence, hatred and racism
that the KKK practices." Democratic state lawmakers also spoke out against
the planned rally. Similarly voicing opposition were the Maine AFL-CIO,
the Maine board of the National Organization for Women, the Christian
Civic League, the Jewish Federation of Southern Maine, the Maine Council
of Churches, and the Coalition Against Racism, a group that was formed to
oppose the KKK in Maine and included the Maine chapter of the NAACP.
Anti-Klan protesters consisting of blacks, whites, Jews, Catholics, and Protestants thus joined forces to plan counter-rallies in various cities of Maine.[29]

John Day, the political editor of the *Bangor Daily News*, questioned the
publicity surrounding the Klan's planned rally and the public condemna-
tions of it, arguing that Maine's labor problems deserved more attention.
"The real message of what's going on in the Androscoggin Valley will be overlooked," Day complained. "The forces that feed the Klan have been stalk-
ing that region for the past two years. Elsewhere, they've always lurked just
beneath the surface of the Maine mystique," he asserted. Continuing, Day

explained, "During the Boise-Cascade strike at Rumford in 1986 and this summer at Jay during the bitter confrontation between the United Paperworkers International Union and International Paper Co. there have been acts of violence, invocations of class hatred, and the measured use of terror by Maine workers against Maine workers that closely parallels Klan tactics in the South," Day alleged. "It's about time somebody begins defusing Maine's home-grown hatred. That will require a lot more guts than making moral pronouncements about a handful of KKK kooks and their weekend excursion," Day concluded.[30]

Journalists descended on Rumford to cover the rally. Sharing local lore, a town resident named Robert Parker told a reporter that he recalled past conflicts, probably during the 1920s, when Franco-Americans from the community "beat the living hell" out of the Ku Klux Klan. Ironically, in 1987 a Rumford man with a Franco-American name, Gerald Cote, leased the KKK his farm for their rally, indicating that he was using the proceeds to pay his property taxes. Cote told one reporter that he was not "yet" a member of the KKK.[31]

When anti-Klan protesters confronted the Klan on his farm, Cote emerged from his home wearing a KKK T-shirt and carrying a rifle, but police intervened and took it away from him. From twenty to twenty-five Klan members dressed in white robes and "para-military camouflage suits" gathered on Cote's property for a picnic, speeches, and the burning of a twenty-foot cross. Most of the members had traveled to the Cote farm in vehicles bearing license plates from states other than Maine, noted a reporter. One Maine resident, Albert Small of Canton, drove to the KKK rally in a large white car sporting the letters *KKK.* He had worked at the International Paper Company in Jay until the strike, when a strikebreaker from another firm took his job. "They're 90 percent black," Small said of the strikebreakers. "But I'm not prejudiced," he claimed. Small attended the rally because he felt the Ku Klux Klan was "looking out for the little guy." Speaking at the event, Imperial Wizard Farrands underscored the group's white supremacist agenda, when he indicated that the Klan wanted to keep Maine white.[32]

As the Klan held its rally at the Cote farm, some nearby farmers literally raised a stink by spreading manure on their fields, an action one reporter believed was intended "to show their displeasure with the event." An estimated 150 demonstrators came within fifty yards of the rally, burning in effigy a hooded Klan member. Fifteen miles from the rally 350 people attended an anti-Klan gathering in the high school auditorium, where speakers addressed issues of racism and bigotry and the crowd sang patriotic songs. A second-generation Catholic widow of Lithuanian descent told one participant about the cross burnings that took place in Rumford in the 1920s, during which her mother used to tell her, "Don't go outside, it isn't safe." The woman decided to take a stand against the Klan by attending Rumford's counter-rally. Anti-Klan rallies occurred outside of the Rumford area as well, including at Temple Beth-El in Portland, attended by 260 people, and at the South Congregational Church in Kennebunkport, which brought out nineteen objectors.[33]

The following year, in June 1988, four Klansmen tried to march in regalia on Maine Mall Road in South Portland, but one hundred protesters confronted them. They carried anti-Klan signs, grabbed at the hoods of the members, and nearly engaged them in physical altercations. Fearing violence, the police broke up the gathering and escorted away the Klan leader, David White of Shelton, Connecticut, while his three accomplices drove off in a car with Connecticut license plates. The protesters subsequently burned the white hoods they had snatched from the Klansmen.[34]

In September 1988 five men donned Klan regalia and walked to the home of a black woman and her children at Portland's Riverton Park housing development. When police arrived, nearly two hundred people had gathered, and police asked the white-robed men to leave. Three did. The two who did not, William E. Mannette and Mark Bush, both of Portland, were intoxicated, claimed to be Klan members, and were arrested.[35]

These were not isolated incidents. In September 1988 the general manager of a Portland area hotel recounted that, a month earlier, four men who were staying at the hotel put on Klan robes and distributed KKK literature in the lobby after they discovered that a black band was performing in the lounge. They stopped when directed to do so by the hotel manager. In January 1990 an individual or individuals broke into Woodfords Congregational Church in Portland and left KKK application forms inside forty-one hymnals. "This church is tremendously concerned with civil and human rights and we may have been targeted because of it," speculated Rev. Robert Middleton. In November 1991 three teenagers in Madison fashioned hoods from pillowcases and created their own crosses with which they approached the home of a biracial teenager before neighbors chased them away. The three hooded teens were arrested for disorderly conduct; one of them, the eighteen-year-old Jason Cyr, had a Franco-American surname. Two months after the Madison incident, two KKK recruiters distributed literature in the community.[36]

Although Catholics of French-Canadian descent had been the primary targets of the New England KKK during the 1920s, this ethnic population had largely become Americanized by the end of the twentieth century, with many members no longer exhibiting the traits that made them distinctive.[37] The modern Klan thus chose other targets. William Kontoes, a doghouse builder from Mechanic Falls and the Grand Dragon of Maine's Ku Klux

Klan, told an interviewer in 1992 that he opposed blacks, Jews, and homo-sexuals. When Mark Dion, a Portland police lieutenant who specialized in hate crimes, addressed a seminar at the University of Maine in March 1993 he told the students that both neo-Nazis and Ku Klux Klan members were present in the state, and he revealed that while gay men were their most frequent targets, blacks, Jews, and Asians were victims as well.[38]

Blacks were victimized in Augusta. In June 1996 the forty-four-year-old Vincent Hallowell and his accomplice, the eighteen-year-old Benjamin Newton, both of Augusta, burned a cross outside of an apartment building at Sand Hill where black and biracial families lived, "to put niggers in their place," Hallowell stated. Hallowell also told the press, "I'm purifying the streets," and that he was a KKK member, only to recant several days later his claim of ties to the Klan. Hallowell and Newton were charged with violations of civil rights laws for the cross burning. According to federal prosecutors, the pair had contemplated tarring and feathering a black person before deciding instead to burn a cross. Shortly after the cross burning three hundred people held a rally in Augusta to protest against racism. Both Hallowell and New-ton pleaded guilty to conspiracy charges for their role in intimidating black residents.[39]

A few days after the cross-burning incident at Sand Hill, two white men assaulted a black man in the same neighborhood, a neighborhood described by the reporter as "mainly Franco-American." Following the two racial incidents in Augusta, James Varner, the chair of the Bangor branch of the NAACP, commented that "racism, unfortunately, is still very much alive in this country."[40] The KKK's New England activities in recent decades illustrate this well.

As this chapter has demonstrated, the same spirit that motivated the Ku Klux Klan of the 1920s continued to persist to some degree in New England in the late twentieth century. The *Bangor Daily News* editor John Day suggested it had become an unfortunate part of the social fabric of Maine.[41] But the same could be said of the other northeastern states. Part of this nefarious spirit finds expression in a metamorphosed Klan, or in those who imitate it, including members of the religious and ethnic groups that were once the objects of the Klan's prejudice during the 1920s.

Conclusion

In 1925 Imperial Wizard Hiram W. Evans contended that the Ku Klux Klan had given disgruntled Americans a structure and a way to express themselves: "The Klan is blamed for stirring up trouble, but all we have done has been to give an outlet,—a voice and an organization,—to the bitter resentment of millions of Americans." From the Klan's origins, Evans asserted, it "spoke for the common people, voiced their instincts, gave them an outlet for their distress, and offered at least the beginnings of a means to resume control of their own country."[1] White Protestants had witnessed major changes in the ethnic and religious composition of New England as Catholics from Europe and Canada immigrated into the region in the nineteenth and twentieth centuries to supply the labor for its industries. To confront those changes New England Protestants joined two anti-Catholic, nativist movements in nineteenth century: the Know-Nothing movement in the 1850s and the American Protective Association in the 1880s and 1890s; in a third cycle of anti-Catholic nativism during the early twentieth century, Protestants joined the Ku Klux Klan in the 1920s to check the social and economic advances Catholics were making in New England. To expand its numbers and influence, the KKK refashioned itself in the northeastern borderlands region to enlist the support of foreign-born Protestants, such as Anglo-Canadians, as they confronted New England's Catholic population, much of it consisting of French-Canadian descendants. In short, the Ku Klux Klan provided New England Protestants a means by which to deal with the purported internal "enemy" of Catholics during the 1920s.

Much of the scholarship on the Klan published in recent decades has given credence to Evans's point of view that the movement attracted ordinary citizens who sought to reassert control over their rapidly changing communities in the 1920s.[2] This book has documented some of the ways in which the New England Klan functioned as a civic organization that advocated for such causes as municipal reform, public schools, Bible reading, English-language legislation, and prohibition. But this study has particularly demonstrated how the KKK's attacks on Franco-American and other Catholics in New England undermined its role in the polity. Nativism, religious prejudice, and class differences provide a more compelling explanation for the Klan's rise in New England in the 1920s. By exploding dynamite bombs, burning crosses, and confronting individuals verbally and physically, the Ku Klux Klan in the twenties functioned as a terrorist society that especially targeted the Catholic labor pool of the region.[3]

During the twenties ethnic Catholics in each of the six New England states countered the efforts of such proponents of Americanization as the Ku Klux Klan in order to preserve some of their traditional lifeways while making cultural adaptations to become Americans. Franco-Americans led the opposition throughout New England to the passage of English-only legislation in the period following World War I. They did not object to learning English, but they strenuously resisted attempts to eliminate French instruction from their parish schools, for they perceived an intimate connection between the French language and their Roman Catholic faith. Catholics of New England thus rejected the Klan's version of Americanism and insisted on exercising their constitutional rights as U.S. citizens. They worked against the nativism, religious prejudice, and class differences that motivated the Klan by exposing its hypocrisies and contradictions, by trying to secure the passage of anti-Klan legislation, and by their actions to circumscribe the Klan's activities and violence in their communities. Their efforts sometimes led to extralegal interventions, including physical confrontations, to counterattack the KKK. In the process Catholics in the Northeast helped to bring about the demise of this right-wing movement, one of the largest social movements the United States has ever experienced.

While the Klan of the twenties did not survive as a social movement, the issues it raised continued to fester well beyond the third decade of the twentieth century. Even more significant, the philosophies and the prejudices of the 1920s Klan have outlived it. Anti-Catholicism constitutes one of the most prominent examples. An intellectual anti-Catholicism thrived during the 1930s and 1940s. Nurtured by such Protestant ministers and writers as Paul Blanshard and Norman Vincent Peale, who both attracted large followings, anti-Catholicism also flourished in the middle of the twentieth century. The election of the Catholic presidential candidate John F. Kennedy in 1960 did not end anti-Catholicism in the United States. Reaction to Pope Paul VI's encyclical of 1968 against artificial means of contraception was, writes Philip Jenkins, reminiscent of "many long-familiar themes, above all a questioning of the legitimacy of foreign, Roman authority over American believers." This type of questioning had been a common refrain of the 1920s Klan. Today anti-Catholicism persists, Jenkins contends, because of its propensity to adapt to new circumstances in contemporary society.[4]

In addition to anti-Catholicism, many of the concerns the Ku Klux Klan raised in the 1920s continue to find expression in the contemporary period. Calls for immigration restrictions and advocacy of the English-only movement serve as but two examples in the policy arena. The KKK's complaints in the 1920s about the fecundity, unassimilability, and criminality of New England's French-Canadian immigrants are now heard against other groups entering the country, particularly Hispanics.

The Klan's racism has also persisted. As we have seen, the Ku Klux Klan reappeared in New England in the late twentieth century, albeit in a different form. In its new incarnation it integrated into its ranks Catholics who were resisting the social and economic advances that African Americans had made in their region as a result of affirmative action policies, court-ordered busing, and strikebreaking. The metamorphosed Klan of the 1970s, 1980s, and 1990s gave expression to the racial prejudices of a different era.

The influence of the 1920s Klan on New England—and, for that matter, on the rest of the United States—appears not yet to have run its course. Franco-Americans must still work to counter some of the effects of the Klan in their region, as can be seen in a recent debate over a proposed bill in Maine. In March 2009 Rhea Côté Robbins wrote an op-ed piece for the *Bangor Daily News* in support of LD 422, "An Act to Include the Study of Franco-American History in the System of Learning Results" (that is, in Maine's curricular guidelines for elementary and secondary schools.) Rep. Brian Bolduc, a Franco-American from Auburn, had introduced the legislation in a state where nearly one-fourth of the population claimed French or French-Canadian ancestry in the 2000 census. Robbins argued that Bolduc's bill sought "to undo the prejudices of the previous generations." Enactment of this legislation, she believed, would eventually result in the situation in which "the unspoken, hushed, unconscious, subconscious beliefs of prejudice against the French no longer will hold sway." Robbins maintained that those prejudices themselves were rooted in nativist groups such as the Ku Klux Klan. "Many have heard that the KKK marched against the French in Maine," she wrote. "I challenge the notion that the effect of that one element, the KKK, is not felt today in our present-day communities," Robbins argued, continuing: *"I believe strongly we all live out the legacy of the KKK in our modern-day policies—not as a conscious act, but as one that has become part of the social fabric of our communities."*[5]

Robbins reviewed some of the common veiled prejudices and affronts most senior Franco-Americans have encountered during their lives: "the rules—formal and informal—forbidding French to be spoken in many public places, the French jokes, the 'you must be French, you talk with your hands,' or 'you have an accent,' or the French in Maine is not a real French, a slang French, a patois, a dialect." The denigration of their French language is a sore point among many Franco-Americans, and it vexed Robbins. "Lies told about the language ad nauseam added up are all sly commentaries, which amounts to subtle ethnic cleansing," she charged. But that was not all: "Add to that the erasure of the French heritage culture and history from the archives of most towns in their historical societies, registers, etc.—the French contributions not seen fit to be collected over the years—and you have generations deep, entrenched, community-sanctioned prejudices." Robbins envisioned Bolduc's bill as a way to redress the long-standing prejudices against French-Canadian descendants and to encourage the development of a better-informed citizenry.[6]

Challenging Robbins, a Maine resident blogged against the proposed legislation to include the teaching of Franco-American history in the curriculum of the state's schools. Rogier van Bakel suggested the bill amounted to "ethnic pandering," and he dismissed Robbins's arguments in favor of Bolduc's bill "as tribal self-importance cloaked in secretly-cherished victimhood." Van Bakel especially took issue with some of Robbins's phrases, emphatically questioning and stating, "Really—*ethnic cleansing*? Such incendiary language is loaded for maximum effect, and seems designed to pre-emptively shut down the discussion. After all, no sane human being could possibly defend the Ku Klux Klan, right? Nor could a person of any moral standing condone 'ethnic cleansing,' a term whose conjoined twin is 'genocide.'" Van Bakel failed to understand the depth and the duration of the discrimination that Robbins's strong words meant to convey. He also debated Robbins about the role of Franco-Americans as targets of the Ku Klux Klan. "The KKK (which, as a political force in Maine, was at best a flash in the pan even in its 1920s heyday) didn't have it in for Franco-Americans per se. Instead," he asserted, "the hooded idiots were fiercely anti-Catholic; and since French-Acadian immigrants were overwhelmingly papists, they bore the brunt of the KKK's ire (in most places, the Klan was also rabidly anti-Irish, for instance)." Reflecting an inaccurate knowledge of the Ku Klux Klan's activities in Maine in the 1920s, van Bakel went on to state, "Judging by the historical record, the organization's Maine members engaged in ugly rhetoric, but rarely if ever in violence; in fact, they were more often on the receiving end of assaults and vandalism." Van Bakel disputed as well Robbins's claim about the longlasting effects of groups like the KKK on Franco-Americans: "Almost a century later, it's hard to square this slice of history with 'deep, entrenched, community-sanctioned prejudices' against French-Acadians, as perceived by Robbins and her ideological *copains* [friends]."[7]

Van Bakel failed to comprehend the insidious and persistent nature of the prejudice and discrimination endured by Maine's (and New England's) Franco-American population, not only during the 1920s but also over the course of the entire twentieth century. Particularly objectionable to Franco-Americans has been their denigration since World War I by Anglo-Protestant Yankees, who sometimes refer to them by the ethnic slur *frog*, a label as culturally and emotionally charged as the term *nigger* when used by a white person to designate an African American.[8] James Varner, the chair of the Bangor, Maine, branch of the National Association for the Advancement of Colored People, made the following comment in June 1996 about the persistence of racism after two incidents occurred in Augusta (see chapter 11): "All you have to do is look around at racial jokes in the workplace. You've got to be on your guard. If you're not part of the solution, you're part of the problem."[9] This has been an enduring reality for Franco-Americans, an ethnic group that continues to be the object of derisive commentary throughout the northeastern United States, as anecdotal evidence continues to attest.

Constance Backhouse's analysis of the Canadian Ku Klux Klan is applicable here. She argues that while the KKK in Canada was less violent than its U.S. counterpart, its effects were nonetheless damaging to the targeted individuals and groups. Downplaying the role of the Canadian KKK because it was less notorious than the American Klan "takes no notice of the jobs and businesses lost because the incumbents and candidates were of the wrong race, ethnicity, or religion. It sees no loss in the social relationships destroyed because the Klan would brook no 'sullying' of the white Protestant community," she contends. "Most of all, such analysis belies the insidious emotional turmoil suffered by all those who felt the impact of Klan threats, whether directed personally at them by name, or because of their membership in specific racial, ethnic, and religious communities."[10] Backhouse's arguments can be readily applied to the Ku Klux Klan of New England, which was less violent than the KKK of other regions of the United States, but whose intolerance was no less damaging. What Robbins tried to address in her op-ed piece was the lingering effect of cultural forces, that is, worldviews and belief systems, that rooted themselves in earlier historical periods and that have never been completely purged from the national consciousness, a phenomenon not unlike the persistence of racism in modern American society.

"To address the issue of racism in our time, Americans must acknowledge the importance of slavery in our past," writes the sociologist and best-selling author James Loewen.[11] We must similarly recognize the importance of the

Ku Klux Klan in earlier historical periods, particularly the 1920s, when so many ordinary Americans joined the organization to form one of the largest social movements the country has ever experienced. The Klan's presence in New England during that decade does not currently form part of the historical memory of most Americans, including those in New England. As the third cycle of anti-Catholic nativism, the Ku Klux Klan of the 1920s gave expression to cultural forces of the era. Whether overtly or not, the prejudices that ordinary Americans expressed through the KKK in that decade continue to find expression in contemporary society, even if refashioned and exploited by groups who were themselves previously targeted. Only by understanding and acknowledging the KKK's activities in New England (and in the rest of the country) during the twenties can we begin to confront the persistent cultural prejudices of modern society.

NOTES

Introduction

1. U.S. Congress, House Committee on Rules, *The Ku Klux Klan Hearings,* 67th Cong., 1st sess., 1921, in *Mass Violence in America* (New York: Arno Press and New York Times, 1969), 3–4, 12 October 1921, 74; "Peter Francis Tague," Biographical Directory of the United States Congress, 1774–Present, n.d., bioguide.congress.gov; *Washington Post,* 2 November 1930, 14. The *Washington Post*'s figures, which seem extraordinary, "came from an authoritative source," claimed the newspaper, which also indicated that the Klan had admitted nearly nine million members nationwide by 1925. Because national Ku Klux Klan records do not exist, membership figures necessarily represent estimates. Based on accounts in national newspapers and Klan reports, Kenneth Jackson has made the following personal estimates of the number of Klansmen and Klanswomen in New England for the period from 1915 to 1944: Vermont, two thousand; New Hampshire, two thousand; Rhode Island, five thousand; Massachusetts, twelve thousand; Maine, fifteen thousand; and Connecticut, twenty thousand. Given that Jackson's number of two million members nationwide is considerably less than the estimates of other scholars—such as Leonard Moore's, who has placed the society's strength at between three and six million members during the 1920s—Jackson's figures for individual New England states may similarly be low. *Washington Post,* 2 November 1930, 1; Kenneth T. Jackson, *The Ku Klux Klan in the City, 1915–1930* (New York: Oxford University Press, 1967), 235, 237, 288n; Leonard J. Moore, *Citizen Klansmen: The Ku Klux Klan in Indiana, 1921–1928* (Chapel Hill: University of North Carolina Press, 1991), 1, 44; Robert Moats Miller, "The Ku Klux Klan," in *Change and Continuity in Twentieth-Century America: The 1920's,* ed. John Braeman, Robert H. Bremner, and David Brody (Columbus: Ohio State University Press, 1968), 255.

2. François Weil, *Les Franco-Américains, 1860–1980* (Paris: Belin, 1989), 26; James S. Olson, *Catholic Immigrants in America* (Chicago: Nelson-Hall, 1987), 101; John Higham, *Strangers in the Land: Patterns of American Nativism, 1860–1925* (1955; repr., New Brunswick, N.J.: Rutgers University Press, 1992), 35–105, 264–99; Jackson, *The Ku Klux Klan in the City,* 21.

3. Higham, *Strangers in the Land,* 267–68, 289.

4. Moore, *Citizen Klansmen,* xii, 1, 2–3, 118, 188–90.

5. *New York Times,* 6 December 1922, 4, 23 December 1922, 1, 2; Constance Backhouse, *Colour-Coded: A Legal History of Racism in Canada, 1900–1950* (Toronto: Osgoode Society for Canadian Legal History by University of Toronto Press, 1999), 186; Julian Sher, *White Hoods: Canada's Ku Klux Klan* (Vancouver: New Star Books, 1983), 23–25, 30, 40, 48, 51; Martin Robin, *Shades of Right: Nativist and Fascist Politics in Canada, 1920–1940* (Toronto: University of Toronto Press, 1992), 11, 24, 25, 50, 54, 59; B. J. Grant, *When Rum Was King: The Story of the Prohibition Era in New Brunswick* (Fredericton, N.B.: Fiddlehead Poetry Books, 1984), 43–45;

James M. Pitsula, *Keeping Canada British: The Ku Klux Klan in 1920s Saskatchewan* (Vancouver: University of British Columbia Press, 2013), 11, 19, 243–44, 249; R. S. Pennefather, "A Roman Catholic View of the Orange Order in the 1920's," in *The Orange and the Black: Documents in the History of the Orange Order, Ontario and the West, 1890–1940* (Toronto: Orange and Black Publications, 1984), 42–43; J. B. McGeachy, "Immigration Issue in Western Canada," *New York Times,* 2 June 1929, sec. 3, 2.

6. R. Laurence Moore, *Religious Outsiders and the Making of Americans* (New York: Oxford University Press, 1986), xiii, 70. A history of U.S. Catholics that excludes French-Canadian immigrants and their Franco-American descendants is James M. O'Toole's *The Faithful: A History of Catholics in America* (Cambridge: Belknap Press of Harvard University Press, 2008.)

7. For overviews of the Klan, see David M. Chalmers, *Hooded Americanism: The History of the Ku Klux Klan,* 3rd ed. (1981; repr., Durham, N.C.: Duke University Press, 1987); Wyn Craig Wade, *The Fiery Cross: The Ku Klux Klan in America* (1987; repr., New York: Oxford University Press, 1998); and David J. Goldberg, "The Rapid Rise and the Swift Decline of the Ku Klux Klan," *Discontented America: The United States in the 1920s* (Baltimore: Johns Hopkins University Press, 1999), 117–39. C. Stewart Doty's history of discrimination against Franco-Americans contains a brief account of the Klan's activities in New England. See "How Many Frenchmen Does It Take to . . . ?" *Thought and Action* 11 (Fall 1995): 85–104.

8. Rory McVeigh, *The Rise of the Ku Klux Klan: Right-Wing Movements and National Politics* (Minneapolis: University of Minnesota Press, 2009), 10–11, 13–17. McVeigh's examination of the eighty issues of the *Imperial Night-Hawk* published in 1923 and 1924 found that only thirteen Klan events took place in Massachusetts, twelve in Maine, ten in Connecticut, two in New Hampshire, two in Rhode Island, and one in Vermont. McVeigh, *The Rise of the Ku Klux Klan,* 10–12, 17. The national Ku Klux Klan published the *Imperial Night-Hawk* from its Imperial Palace in Atlanta, from March 1923 to November 1924; it was followed by *Kourier Magazine* from December 1924 to February 1932, and then by *Kourier* from March 1932 to November 1936.

9. *Washington Post,* 2 November 1930, 14; U.S. Department of Commerce, Bureau of the Census, *Fourteenth Census of the United States Taken in the Year 1920* (Washington, D.C.: Government Printing Office, 1922), 2:39–40; Edward Bonner Whitney, "The Ku Klux Klan in Maine, 1922–1928: A Study with Particular Emphasis on the City of Portland" (honors thesis, Harvard College, 1966), ii. Although the term *Northeast* can also apply to the mid-Atlantic states of New York, Pennsylvania, and New Jersey, that designation in this book will refer specifically to the six New England states.

10. See, for example, the works by the former Klan members Henry P. Fry and Edgar I. Fuller: Fry, *The Modern Ku Klux Klan* (1922; repr., New York: Negro Universities Press, 1969), and Fuller, *The Visible of the Invisible Empire,* revised and edited by Geo. La Dura (Denver, Colo.: Maelstrom Publishing, 1925.) The traditional view is also espoused by such scholars as Emerson Hunsberger Loucks, *The Ku Klux Klan in Pennsylvania: A Study in Nativism* (New York: Telegraph Press, 1936); Seymour Martin Lipset and Earl Rabb, *The Politics of Unreason: Right-Wing Extremism in America, 1790–1970* (New York: Harper and Row, 1970); David H. Bennett, *The Party of Fear: From Nativist Movements to the New Right in American History* (Chapel Hill: University of North Carolina Press, 1988); and William D. Jenkins, *Steel Valley Klan: The Ku Klux Klan in Ohio's Mahoning Valley* (Kent, Ohio: Kent State University Press, 1990.) For a review of the historiography on the 1920s Klan, see Leonard J. Moore, "Historical Interpretations of the 1920's Klan: The Traditional View and the Populist Revision," *Journal of Social History* 24 (Winter 1990): 341–57.

11. Moore, "Historical Interpretations of the 1920's Klan," 342. See, for example, Robert Alan

Goldberg, *Hooded Empire: The Ku Klux Klan in Colorado* (Urbana: University of Illinois Press, 1981); Moore, *Citizen Klansmen;* Kathleen M. Blee, *Women of the Klan: Racism and Gender in the 1920s* (Berkeley: University of California Press, 1991); Shawn Lay, *Hooded Knights on the Niagara: The Ku Klux Klan in Buffalo, New York* (New York: New York University Press, 1995); see also the individual essays on the KKK in Texas, Colorado, California, and Oregon in *The Invisible Empire in the West: Toward a New Historical Appraisal of the Ku Klux Klan of the 1920s,* ed. Shawn Lay (Urbana: University of Illinois Press, 1992). A more recent study that downplays Klan violence—and negative portrayals of the Ku Klux Klan—and focuses on how members of the hooded society formed part of the prevailing culture during the early twentieth century can be found in Kelly J. Baker, *Gospel according to the Klan: The KKK's Appeal to Protestant America, 1915–1930* (Lawrence: University Press of Kansas, 2011). Two studies that do not follow the path of the above-cited monographs in their normative depictions of the 1920s Klan are those of Nancy MacLean, *Behind the Mask of Chivalry: The Making of the Second Ku Klux Klan* (New York: Oxford University Press, 1994), and Yvonne Brown, "Tolerance and Bigotry in Southwest Louisiana: The Ku Klux Klan, 1921–23," *Louisiana History* 47 (Spring 2006): 153–68. The most recent general history of the Ku Klux Klan in the twenties is Thomas R. Pegram's *One Hundred Percent American: The Rebirth and Decline of the Ku Klux Klan in the 1920s* (Chicago: Ivan R. Dee, 2011), which synthesizes the research of the past several decades and situates the KKK in the mainstream while also illustrating how the hooded society's extremism positioned it outside of mainstream culture.

12. *Portland (Maine) Press Herald,* 13 October 1923, 20, 1 January 1924, 24, 15 February 1924, 1, 11 March 1924, 11; *Portland (Maine) Evening Express,* 1 January 1924, B3; *Maine Klansman,* 10 January 1924, 2, 20 March 1924, 1; Harold B. Clifford, *Charlie York: Maine Coast Fisherman* (Camden, Maine: International Marine Publishing, 1974), 100–101; *The Ku Klux Klan Hearings,* 13 October 1921, 90.

13. Charles C. Alexander, *The Ku Klux Klan in the Southwest* (Lexington: University of Kentucky Press, 1965), 249; Chalmers, *Hooded Americanism,* 202; Goldberg, *Hooded Empire,* 78–83.

1. Arrival in New England

1. David M. Chalmers, *Hooded Americanism: The History of the Ku Klux Klan,* 3rd ed. (1981; repr., Durham, N.C.: Duke University Press, 1987), 8–9; David Chalmers, "Rule by Terror," Part I: "The History of the Ku Klux Klan," *American History Illustrated,* January 1980, 8; Wyn Craig Wade, *The Fiery Cross: The Ku Klux Klan in America* (New York: Simon and Schuster, 1987), 32–35.

2. Chalmers, *Hooded Americanism,* 425; Chalmers, "The History of the Ku Klux Klan," 9; Wade, *The Fiery Cross,* 40–41.

3. Chalmers, *Hooded Americanism,* 19; Chalmers, "The History of the Ku Klux Klan," 48.

4. Melvyn Stokes, *D. W. Griffith's The Birth of a Nation: A History of "The Most Controversial Motion Picture of All Time"* (New York: Oxford University Press, 2007), 3, 15, 43, 54; Chalmers, *Hooded Americanism,* 24–27; Wade, *The Fiery Cross,* 119–20, 138, 139; John Moffatt Mecklin, *The Ku Klux Klan: A Study of the American Mind* (New York: Harcourt, Brace, 1924), 71; David Chalmers, "Rule by Terror," Part II: "The Hooded Knights Revive in the 'Twenties," *American History Illustrated,* February 1980, 28.

5. Chalmers, *Hooded Americanism,* 29–30; Charles C. Alexander, *The Ku Klux Klan in the Southwest* (Lexington: University of Kentucky Press, 1965), 3; Wade, *The Fiery Cross,* 140–41, 144–45; William Peirce Randel, *The Ku Klux Klan: A Century of Infamy* (Philadelphia: Chilton, 1965), 182; Mecklin, *The Ku Klux Klan,* 4, 7–8.

6. Wade, *The Fiery Cross,* 153–55; Leonard J. Moore, *Citizen Klansmen: The Ku Klux Klan in Indiana, 1921–1928* (Chapel Hill: University of North Carolina Press, 1991), 15–16; Mecklin, *The Ku Klux Klan,* 7–8; Emerson Hunsberger Loucks, *The Ku Klux Klan in Pennsylvania: A Study in Nativism* (New York: Telegraph Press, 1936), 67–68; Chalmers, *Hooded Americanism,* 33–34; Charles C. Alexander, "Kleagles and Cash: The Ku Klux Klan as a Business Organization, 1915–1930," *Business History Review* 39 (1965): 359; Alexander, *The Ku Klux Klan in the Southwest,* 250; Randel, *The Ku Klux Klan,* 194; Edgar Fuller, *The Visible of the Invisible Empire,* revised and edited by Geo. La Dura (Denver, Colo.: Maelstrom Publishing, 1925), 17, 31.

7. Chalmers, *Hooded Americanism,* 38, 100–108; U.S. Congress, House Committee on Rules, *The Ku Klux Klan Hearings,* 67th Cong., 1st sess., 1921, in *Mass Violence in America* (New York: Arno Press and the New York Times, 1969), 8, 90; David H. Bennett, "Traditional Nativism's Last Stand: The Ku Klux Klan in the 1920s," *The Party of Fear: From Nativist Movements to the New Right in American History* (Chapel Hill: University of North Carolina Press, 1988), 211; Wade, *The Fiery Cross,* 162–66, 187–91, 192. In 1924 the KKK changed the distribution of fees, allotting $2.50 of the $10.00 initiation fee to the Grand Dragon and reducing accordingly the share remitted to the national office. Thomas R. Pegram, *One Hundred Percent American: The Rebirth and Decline of the Ku Klux Klan in the 1920s* (Chicago: Ivan R. Dee, 2011), 16.

8. David J. Goldberg, "The Rapid Rise and the Swift Decline of the Ku Klux Klan," *Discontented America: The United States in the 1920s* (Baltimore: Johns Hopkins University Press, 1999), 118; Mecklin, *The Ku Klux Klan,* 107; Wade, *The Fiery Cross,* 183; *Boston Daily Advertiser,* 16 January 1923, 2; Henry P. Fry, *The Modern Ku Klux Klan* (1922; repr., New York: Negro Universities Press, 1969), 45–46. Despite holding an academic appointment in New Hampshire, Mecklin appeared to be almost unaware of the Klan's presence in New England; although he made occasional reference to the fact that the KKK had permeated every section of the United States, he did not draw on its New England activities for the examples he used in his book, an omission that suggests he regarded the Klan of the 1920s primarily as a phenomenon of regions such as the South, Southwest, and West.

9. *Constitution and Laws of the Knights of the Ku Klux Klan Incorporated* (Atlanta, Ga.: Knights of the Ku Klux Klan, 1921), 32, 46, Vermont Historical Society Library, Vermont History Center, Barre, Vermont; Androscoggin County Ku Klux Klan Charter, Gerald E. Talbot Collection, African American Collection of Maine, Jean Byers Sampson Center for Diversity in Maine, University of Southern Maine Libraries; *Boston Sunday Herald,* 9 September 1923, 6.

10. A. J. Gordon, "Klan Dodgers Flood Maine," *Boston Sunday Herald,* 9 September 1923, 6; *Boston Daily Advertiser,* 9 January 1923, 2.

11. Wade, *The Fiery Cross,* 146, 185; Loucks, *The Ku Klux Klan in Pennsylvania,* 58–59; *Maine Klansman,* 20 March 1924, 7.

12. *New York Times,* 19 September 1921, 17; *Boston Daily Advertiser,* 8 January 1923, 2, 9 January 1923, 2, 10 January 1923, 2; Phil Goodstein, *In the Shadow of the Klan: When the KKK Ruled Denver, 1920–1926* (Denver, Colo.: New Social Publications, 2006), 22; Robert A. Goldberg, "Denver: Queen City of the Colorado Realm," in *The Invisible Empire in the West: Toward a New Historical Appraisal of the Ku Klux Klan of the 1920s,* ed. Shawn Lay (Urbana: University of Illinois Press, 1992), 41; Kenneth T. Jackson, *The Ku Klux Klan in the City, 1915–1930* (New York: Oxford University Press, 1967), 216, 287n; Pegram, *One Hundred Percent American,* 10.

13. *Boston Daily Advertiser,* 10 January 1923, 2; U.S. Department of Commerce, Bureau of the Census, *Fourteenth Census of the United States Taken in the Year 1920,* vol. 2 (Washington, D.C.: Government Printing Office, 1922), 38; Chalmers, "The Hooded Knights Revive in the 'Twenties," 31.

14. U.S. Department of Commerce, Bureau of the Census, *Religious Bodies, 1926* (Washing-

ton, D.C.: Government Printing Office, 1929), 2:44–45; *Fourteenth Census of the United States Taken in the Year 1920,* 2:39–40.

15. Rory McVeigh, *The Rise of the Ku Klux Klan: Right-Wing Movements and National Politics* (Minneapolis: University of Minnesota Press, 2009), 116, 118.

16. *Fourteenth Census of the United States Taken in the Year 1920,* 2:36, 707. Given their large Catholic and foreign-born populations, perhaps it is unsurprising that Massachusetts, Rhode Island, and Connecticut supplied 22.5 percent of the seventy-one members of the U.S. House of Representatives who cast votes against the National Origins Act of 1924, which restricted immigration in the United States. That legislation especially targeted Catholics and Jews. Raymond Tatalovich, *Nativism Reborn? The Official English Language Movement and the American States* (Lexington: University Press of Kentucky, 1995), 72, 74.

17. *Fourteenth Census of the United States Taken in the Year 1920,* 2:707; U.S. Department of Commerce, Bureau of the Census, *Fourteenth Census of the United States Taken in the Year 1920,* vol. 3 (Washington, D.C.: Government Printing Office, 1922), 155, 409, 437, 627, 913, 1049.

18. Yolande Lavoie, *L'émigration des Québécois aux États-Unis de 1840 à 1930* (Québec: Éditeur officiel du Québec, 1979), 45; Yves Roby, "L'évolution économique du Québec et l'émigrant (1850–1929)," in *L'émigrant québécois vers les États-Unis (1850–1920),* ed. Claire Quintal (Québec: Le Conseil de la Vie française en Amérique, 1982), 8, 12–13, 17; Yves Roby, *Les Franco-Américains de la Nouvelle-Angleterre (1776–1930)* (Sillery, Québec: Septentrion, 1990), 33–45, 227–32, 275–77; Paul-André Linteau, René Durocher, and Jean-Claude Robert, *Histoire du Québec contemporain: De la Confédération à la crise (1867–1929)* (Montréal: Boréal, 1989), 168, 405. The large majority of French-Canadian immigrants came to the United States from the Province of Québec. My examination of the records dating from 1790 to 1991 of all individuals of French-Canadian origin who became naturalized U.S. citizens while living in Lewiston, Maine, reveals that over 90 percent had been born in Québec—and probably as many as 95 percent—had been born in the province. Bruno Ramirez finds, however, that 23 percent of the French Canadians who emigrated to the United States in the period from 1906 to 1930 did so from provinces outside of Québec, including New Brunswick, Nova Scotia, Prince Edward Island, Ontario, the prairie provinces, and British Columbia; little scholarly attention has been devoted to these French-speaking Canadian emigrants. Mark Paul Richard, *Loyal but French: The Negotiation of Identity by French-Canadian Descendants in the United States* (East Lansing: Michigan State University Press, 2008), 261–62; Bruno Ramirez, with the assistance of Yves Otis, *Crossing the 49th Parallel: Migration from Canada to the United States, 1900–1930* (Ithaca, N.Y.: Cornell University Press, 2001), 68–69.

19. Yolande Lavoie, *L'émigration des Canadiens aux États-Unis avant 1930: Mesure du phénomène* (Montréal: Les Presses de l'Université de Montréal, 1972), 13; *U.S. Census, 1920.* For general accounts of French-Canadian immigrants and their descendants in the northeastern United States, see C. Stewart Doty, *The First Franco-Americans: New England Life Histories from the Federal Writers' Project, 1938–1939* (Orono: University of Maine Press, 1985); Gerard J. Brault, *The French-Canadian Heritage in New England* (Hanover, N.H.: University Press of New England, 1986); François Weil, *Les Franco-Américains, 1860–1980* (Paris: Belin, 1989); Armand Chartier, *The Franco-Americans of New England: A History,* trans. Robert J. Lemieux and Claire Quintal (Manchester, N.H.: ACA Assurance; Worcester, Mass.: Institut Français of Assumption College, 1999); Yves Roby, *The Franco-Americans of New England: Dreams and Realities,* trans. Mary Ricard (Sillery, Québec: Septentrion, 2004.)

20. *Boston Herald,* 25 January 1925, C7. On expressions of concern about national culture, see, for example, Jerome Dowd, "The Protection of National Culture as the Proper Basis of Immigration Restriction," *Scientific Monthly* 23 (September 1926): 206–9.

21. Robert Cloutman Dexter, "Fifty-Fifty Americans," *World's Work* 48 (August 1924): 366–71. Dexter was born in Nova Scotia of a Canadian father and American mother; he taught sociology at Skidmore College from 1923 to 1927 before becoming an ordained minister in the Unitarian Church and spending his career administering social service agencies. Lewis Anthony Dexter, introduction to *The Management of Purpose,* ed. Martin Sánchez-Jankowski and Alan J. Ware (New Brunswick, N.J.: Transaction Publishers, 2010), x.

2. Invasion of the Pine Tree State

1. *Sunday Press Herald* (Portland, Maine), 4 February 1923, 1–2; A. J. Gordon, "'King' Farnsworth of Maine Klan, Barber Once, Hypnotist Later," *Boston Herald,* 6 September 1923, 1; *Official Catholic Directory for the Year of Our Lord 1921* (New York: P. J. Kenedy and Sons, 1921), 527; U.S. Department of Commerce, Bureau of the Census, *Fourteenth Census of the United States Taken in the Year 1920* (Washington, D.C.: Government Printing Office, 1921), 1:20; James Paul Allen, "Catholics in Maine: A Social Geography" (Ph.D. diss., Syracuse University, 1970), 195, 209; U.S. Department of Commerce, Bureau of the Census, *Religious Bodies, 1926* (Washington, D.C.: Government Printing Office, 1929), 2:44.

2. Mark S. Massa, S.J., *Anti-Catholicism in America: The Last Acceptable Prejudice* (New York: Crossroad, 2003), 18–34; Philip Jenkins, *The New Anti-Catholicism: The Last Acceptable Prejudice* (New York: Oxford University Press, 2003), 27; Alexander Keyssar, *The Right to Vote: The Contested History of Democracy in the United States* (New York: Basic Books, 2000), 84, 86; Allan R. Whitmore, "'A Guard of Faithful Sentinels': The Know-Nothing Appeal in Maine, 1854–1855," *Maine Historical Society Quarterly* 20 (Winter 1981): 165, 170, 172–73, 183–84, 189–90; William Leo Lucey, S.J., *The Catholic Church in Maine* (Francestown, N.H.: Marshall Jones, 1957), 100, 124–25, 130–31, 134–35, 155; typescript notes of Rev. Philip Desjardins on Saint Joseph Parish, Lewiston, Maine, Chancery Archives, Roman Catholic Diocese of Portland, Maine; James H. Mundy, *Hard Times, Hard Men: Maine and the Irish, 1830–1860* (Scarborough, Maine: Harp Publications, 1990), 147; Diocese of Portland Centenary Year Edition, *Portland Sunday Telegram,* 6 November 1955, 6.

3. John Higham, *Strangers in the Land: Patterns of American Nativism, 1860–1925* (1955; repr. New Brunswick, N.J.: Rutgers University Press, 1992), 62, 84; *Lewiston Evening Journal,* 20 January 1896, 7; *Le Messager* (Lewiston), 4 February 1896.

4. *Maine Klansman,* 13 December 1923, 10.

5. Percival P. Baxter Scrapbooks, Maine State Library, Augusta, 17:71, 18:194; *New York Times,* 2 November 1922, 10; *Biddeford Daily Journal,* 16 January 1923, 1.

6. *Daily Kennebec Journal* (Augusta), 4 September 1923; *Portland Press Herald,* 5 January 1923, 10, 4 September 1923, 1, 13 February 1924, 1, 2; A. J. Gordon, "Ku Klux Klan Strikes First Blow in N.E. for Political Power," *Boston Herald,* 5 September 1923, 22; Edward Bonner Whitney, "The Ku Klux Klan in Maine, 1922–1928: A Study with Particular Emphasis on the City of Portland" (honors thesis, Harvard College, 1966), 31–32; Ernst Christian Helmreich, *Religion and the Maine Schools: An Historical Approach* (Brunswick: Bureau for Research in Municipal Government, 1960), 49; Robert H. Boone, "A Kleagle and His Klan: F. Eugene Farnsworth and the Ku Klux Klan in Maine" (paper, Wesleyan University, 1965), 33–34; Wyn Craig Wade, *The Fiery Cross: The Ku Klux Klan in America* (New York: Simon and Schuster, 1987), 197. Baxter later had a public falling out with Brewster, even going so far as to allege publicly prior to the Republican primary of 1928 that Brewster was a member of the Invisible Empire and that Brewster had told him that he could direct the Klan's vote to support his political allies.

Portland Press Herald, 14 June 1928, 1; *Boston Daily Advertiser,* 14 June 1928, 2; *New York Times,* 14 June 1928, 10. No "smoking gun" has ever been found that points to Brewster's membership in the KKK.

7. Pierre Vincent Bourassa, "The Catholic Church in the Franco-American Community" (honors thesis, Bowdoin College, 1978), 54; Boone, "A Kleagle and His Klan," 2–7; Gordon, " 'King' Farnsworth of Maine Klan," 22.

8. Boone, "A Kleagle and His Klan," 9, 10; *Boston Herald,* 24 January 1921, 1, 26 January 1921, 1, 5, 14 February 1921, 1, 4 April 1921, 1; *Boston Sunday Herald,* 6 March 1921, 1; *The Republic* (Boston), 19 March 1921, 2; Bourassa, "The Catholic Church in the Franco-American Community," 54; Gordon, "Ku Klux Klan Strikes First Blow in N.E. for Political Power," 1.

9. *Portland Sunday Press Herald,* 21 January 1923, 1, 5; *Maine Klansman,* 8 November 1923, 8.

10. *Lewiston Daily Sun,* 10 February 1923, 1, 17 February 1923, 1; *Portland Press Herald,* 10 March 1923, 1–2, 17 March 1923, 1–2; *Boston Daily Advertiser,* 24 March 1923, 2.

11. *Lewiston Daily Sun,* 19 April 1923, 5, 21 April 1923, 1, 4; Hiram Wesley Evans, "The Klan: Defender of Americanism," the Imperial Wizard of the Ku Klux Klan in an authorized interview with Stanley Frost, *Forum* 74 (December 1925): 812; *Maine Klansman,* 8 November 1923, 8.

12. *Lewiston Daily Sun,* 22 March 1923, 1, 10, 19 April 1923, 1, 5, 21 April 1923, 1, 4; Evans, "The Klan: Defender of Americanism," 811; *Maine Klansman,* 8 November 1923, 8.

13. *Maine Klansman,* 6 December 1923, 8; A. J. Gordon, "900 Join Klan in Portland as Throngs Watch," *Boston Herald,* 13 October 1923, 11; *Portland Press Herald,* 19 April 1924, 2; *Lewiston Daily Sun,* 1 November 1923, 5.

14. *Religious Bodies, 1926,* 2:44, 647; U.S. Department of Commerce, Bureau of the Census, *Fourteenth Census of the United States Taken in the Year 1920,* vol. 2 (Washington, D.C.: Government Printing Office, 1922), 39; *Sunday Press Herald,* 21 January 1923, 2; *Boston Daily Advertiser,* 8 February 1923, 2. Farnsworth's successor, E. L. Gayer, a doctor who was born in Indiana, would tend to denounce not only Catholics but also blacks and Jews in his KKK speeches in Maine. *New York Times,* 17 August 1934, 15; *Portland Press Herald,* 2 September 1924, 3, *Biddeford Weekly Journal,* 5 September 1924, 7.

15. *Portland Sunday Telegram,* 15 April 1923, 1; *Lewiston Daily Sun,* 16 April 1923, 2; *Maine Klansman,* 8 November 1923, 1; Cumberland County Registry of Deeds, Portland, Book 1135, p. 52, Book 1136, pp. 292–94. Born in Portland, W. H. Witham had practiced medicine in the city since 1910. Little is known about the other three men except that each was married and one was an insurance agent. Theodore Roosevelt Hodgkins, ed. and comp., *Brief Biographies, Maine: A Biographical Dictionary of Who's Who in Maine,* vol. 1, *1926–27* (Lewiston: Lewiston Journal, 1926), 280; *Directory of Portland,* vol. 64 (Portland: Portland Directory, 1923), 659, 762, 1015.

16. *Portland Press Herald,* 9 November 1923, 5, 10 January 1924, 1–2; *Lewiston Daily Sun,* 15 February 1924, 1; *La Justice de Biddeford,* 22 February 1924.

17. L. M., "A Reply to Bishop Walsh's Attack on the K.K.K.," *Maine Klansman,* 8 November 1923, 4–5.

18. *Sunday Press Herald,* 9 September 1923, 1; *Portland Press Herald,* 15 September 1923, 8, 13 October 1923, 1, 20; Gordon, "900 Join Klan in Portland as Throngs Watch," 1, 11; *Lewiston Daily Sun,* 13 October 1923, 1; *Maine Klansman,* 8 November 1923, 1.

19. Thomas R. Pegram, *One Hundred Percent American: The Rebirth and Decline of the Ku Klux Klan in the 1920s* (Chicago: Ivan R. Dee, 2011), 109–12; *Sunday Press Herald,* 4 February 1923, 2; *Portland Evening Express,* 1 December 1923, A3; *Lewiston Daily Sun,* 19 March 1924, 12; Helmreich, *Religion and the Maine Schools,* 50, 52, 54–55; *Lewiston Evening Journal,* 6 December

1920, 12, 3 January 1921, 1, 3, 8 February 1921, 14, 8 March 1921, 1; typescript notes of Rev. Philip Desjardins on Saint Joseph Parish and Saint Patrick Parish, Lewiston; Diary of Bishop Louis S. Walsh, Chancery Archives, Roman Catholic Diocese of Portland, 4 April 1921.

20. *Portland Press Herald,* 24 March 1923, 2; Bishop Walsh diary, 15 March 1923; Helmreich, *Religion and the Maine Schools,* 55–56; *Acts and Resolves as Passed by the Eighty-first Legislature of the State of Maine, 1923* (Augusta: Kennebec Journal Print Shop, 1923), chap. 166, "An Act to Provide for the Reading of the Bible in the Public Schools," 255.

21. Lane W. Lancaster, "The Democratic Party in Maine," *National Municipal Review* 18 (December 1929): 745; *Sunday Press Herald,* 16 December 1923, 1, 5; B. J. Grant, *When Rum Was King: The Story of the Prohibition Era in New Brunswick* (Fredericton, N.B.: Fiddlehead Poetry Books, 1984), 20–21; *Portland Press Herald,* 1 January 1924, 1; *Maine Klansman,* 10 January 1924, 7; *Rockland Courier-Gazette,* 27 July 1926, 3. In 1934, a year after national prohibition ended, the citizens of Maine voted to repeal the state's twenty-sixth amendment regarding prohibition. Lawrence Lee Pelletier, *The Initiative and Referendum in Maine* (Brunswick: Bowdoin College Bureau for Research in Municipal Government, 1951), 29.

22. Edward F. Dow and Orren C. Hormell, *City Manager Government in Portland, Maine,* University of Maine Studies, 2nd ser., no. 52 (Orono: University of Maine Press, 1940), 7, 21; *Boston Sunday Herald,* 9 September 1923, 8; Gordon, "Ku Klux Klan Strikes First Blow in N.E. for Political Power," 1; *Boston Herald,* 8 September 1923, 12; *Biddeford Daily Journal,* 10 September 1923, 1; *New York Times,* 10 September 1923, 19, 11 September 1923, 19.

23. Dow and Hormell, *City Manager Government in Portland, Maine,* 23–24, 26; *Portland Press Herald,* 7 September 1923, 8, 11 September 1923, 8; *Boston Herald,* 11 September 1923, 1, 8; Bishop Walsh diary, 10 September 1923; *New York Times,* 11 September 1923, 19; *New Republic: A Journal of Opinion,* vol. 36, no. 459, 19 September 1923, 87; *L'Etoile* (Lowell, Mass.), 11 September 1923, 1. In 2010, eighty-seven years after doing away with a popularly elected mayor, Portland citizens voted to begin electing their mayors again. Edward D. Murphy, "Portland Returns to Electing Its Mayor," *Portland Press Herald,* 3 November 2010, www.pressherald .com.

24. *New York Times,* 12 September 1923, 18; *Kloran of the Knights of the Great Forest K-TRIO* (Atlanta: Knights of the Ku Klux Klan, 1928), 46, Vermont Historical Society Library, Vermont History Center, Barre, Vermont; *L'Opinion Publique* (Worcester, Mass.), 13 September 1923, 4; *Boston Herald,* 12 September 1923, 20; *Lewiston Evening Journal,* 17 September 1923, 4.

25. *Fiery Cross* (Indianapolis, Ind.), 21 September 1923, 8.

26. *Portland Evening Express,* 1 December 1923, A3; Bishop Walsh diary, 4 December 1923; *Maine Klansman,* 13 December 1923, 1; G. S. Mertell to Bishop Louis S. Walsh, KKK clippings, Walsh file, Chancery archives.

27. *L'Opinion Publique,* 28 September 1923, 5; *Maine Klansman,* 15 November 1923; Stephen H. Goetz, "The Ku Klux Klan in New Hampshire, 1923–1927," *Historical New Hampshire* 43 (Winter 1988): 250–51; *Toronto Star,* 15 September 1923, cited in Julian Sher, *White Hoods: Canada's Ku Klux Klan* (Vancouver: New Star Books, 1983), 26.

28. A. J. Gordon, "Ku Klux Klan Will Add Hooded Women to Forces in Maine," *Boston Herald,* 12 September 1923, 1, 10; *Boston Daily Advertiser,* 18 February 1923, 9, 17 March 1923, 3; *Boston Herald,* 8 September 1923, 1; *Directory of Portland,* 1923, 1096; *Lewiston Daily Sun,* 24 January 1924, 11; *Portland Press Herald,* 13 October 1923, 20; *Sunday Press Herald,* 9 December 1923, 10. On the role of Klanswomen's activities as a means of normalizing and spreading racism, see Kathleen Blee, "Mothers in Race-Hate Movements," in *The Politics of Motherhood: Activist Voices from Left to Right,* ed. Alexis Jetter, Annelise Orleck, and Diana Taylor (Hanover, N.H.: University Press of New England, 1997), 247–56.

29. *Portland Press Herald,* 28 May 1924, 1; *Biddeford Daily Journal,* 28 May 1924, 1; *Portland Evening Express,* 13 May 1924, 1; *Jean McNair v. Gertrude M. Witham, et al.,* Ku Klux Women, Portland, Maine, Municipal Court, Civil Docket, no. 1110, 1924, Maine State Archives, Augusta (hereafter MSA); *Mary C. Wyman v. Gertrude M. Witham et al.,* Ku Klux Women, Portland, Maine, Municipal Court, Civil Docket, no. 1109, 1924, no. 1, 1925, no. 37, 1926, MSA.

30. *Portland Evening Express,* 8 April 1924, 1.

31. Kathleen M. Blee, *Women of the Klan: Racism and Gender in the 1920s* (Berkeley: University of California Press, 1991), 27–28; Charles C. Alexander, "Kleagles and Cash: The Ku Klux Klan as a Business Organization, 1915–1930," *Business History Review* 39 (1965): 364; Charles C. Alexander, *The Ku Klux Klan in the Southwest* (Lexington: University of Kentucky Press, 1965), 102–3; *Kloran or Ritual of the Women of the Ku Klux Klan* (Little Rock, Ark.: Parke-Harper, 1923), 37, Vermont Historical Society Library; WKKK citizenship application, Vermont Historical Society Library; pamphlet, "Ideals of the Women of the Ku Klux Klan" (n.p., n.d.), 2–3, 7, Vermont Historical Society Library; pamphlet, "Objects: Women of the Ku Klux Klan" (Little Rock, Ark.: Imperial Headquarters, n.d.), Women of the Ku Klux Klan (Maryland) records, Schlesinger Library, Radcliffe College, Cambridge, Mass.

32. Blee, *Women of the Klan: Racism and Gender in the 1920s,* 2, 180; Kathleen M. Blee, "Women in the 1920s' Ku Klux Klan Movement," *Feminist Studies* 17 (Spring 1991): 61; pamphlet, "Women of America! The Past! The Present! The Future! Outline of Principles and Teachings, Women of the Ku Klux Klan, Incorporated" (Little Rock, Ark.: Parke-Harper, 1923), 7, North Country Underground Railroad Historical Association, Au Sable Chasm, N.Y.; *Constitution and Laws of the Women of the Ku Klux Klan Adopted by [the] First Imperial Klonvocation at St. Louis, Missouri, on the Sixth Day of January, 1927* (Little Rock, Ark.: M. G. Pugh, 1927), 10, Schlesinger Library, Women of the Ku Klux Klan records.

33. *Portland Evening Express,* 27 March 1924, 1, 28 March 1924, 1, 8 April 1924, 1; undated, probably 1923, mimeographed letter in typescript from Gertrude M. Witham addressed "To the Klanswomen of Maine," Kennebec Historical Society, Augusta; *Portland Press Herald,* 27 March 1924, 1, 29 March 1924, 1, 11 April 1924, 1, 2, 25 April 1924, 1; receipt of Mrs. Elsie Madden, Women of the Ku Klux Klan, Maine Klan No. 17, 25 April 1924, Paul W. Bean Collection, Fogler Library Special Collections, University of Maine, Orono; Blee, *Women of the Klan,* 57–65; *Boston Herald,* 27 March 1924, 1, 9 April 1924, 17, 11 April 1924, 21; *Lewiston Daily Sun,* 9 April 1924, 12, 25 April 1924, 1; *La Justice de Biddeford,* 11 April 1924, 1.

34. *Boston Herald,* 16 March 1926, 5; *Lewiston Evening Journal,* 19 March 1926, 5; *Portland Press Herald,* 16 May 1924, 1, 4, 16 March 1926, 2; *Providence Journal,* 30 December 1924, 4. On the role of Anglo-Canadian immigrants in supporting the Ku Klux Klan movement in New England, see Mark Paul Richard, " 'Why Don't You Be a Klansman?' Anglo-Canadian Support for the Ku Klux Klan Movement in 1920s New England," *American Review of Canadian Studies* 40 (December 2010): 508–16.

35. Harrie B. Coe, ed., *Maine: Resources, Attractions, and Its People: A History* (New York: Lewis Historical Publishing, 1928), 4:60–61; Yolande Lavoie, *L'émigration des Québécois aux États-Unis de 1840 à 1930* (Québec: Éditeur officiel du Québec, 1979), 45; Yolande Lavoie, *L'émigration des Canadiens aux États-Unis avant 1930: Mesure du phénomène* (Montréal: Les Presses de l'Université de Montréal, 1972), 76; Randy William Widdis, *With Scarcely a Ripple: Anglo-Canadian Migration into the United States and Western Canada, 1880–1920* (Montreal: McGill-Queen's University Press, 1998), 42, 44–79, 179–289, 254, 350–51; Bruno Ramirez, with the assistance of Yves Otis, *Crossing the 49th Parallel: Migration from Canada to the United States, 1900–1930* (Ithaca, N.Y.: Cornell University Press, 2001), 105–13. On the emigration of English-speaking Canadians to the United States, see also Betsy Beattie, *Obligation and Oppor-*

tunity: Single Maritime Women in Boston, 1870–1930 (Montreal: McGill-Queen's University Press, 2000); and Nora Faires, "Leaving the 'Land of the Second Chance': Migration from Ontario to the Upper Midwest in the Nineteenth and Early Twentieth Centuries," in John J. Bukowczyk, Nora Faires, David R. Smith, and Randy William Widdis, *Permeable Border: The Great Lakes Basin as Transnational Region, 1650–1990* (Pittsburgh: University of Pittsburgh Press, 2005), 78–119.

36. *Rochester (N.H.) Courier,* 30 May 1924, 4; *Portland Press Herald,* 30 May 1924, 2, 27 June 1924, 2, 16 March 1926, 2; Boone, "A Kleagle and His Klan," 80.

37. Lawrence Wayne Moores Jr., "The History of the Ku Klux Klan in Maine, 1922–1931" (M.A. thesis, University of Maine, Orono, 1950), 33–34.

3. Confronting Franco-Americans in Maine

1. *Bangor Daily Commercial,* 5 February 1924, 3; *Le Messager* (Lewiston), 11 August 1924, 8, 21 November 1924, 8; *Lewiston Daily Sun,* 11 August 1924, 1, 12, 23 October 1924, 1, 8, 23 November 1924, 12; *Portland Press Herald,* 30 August 1924, 1; *Portland Evening Express,* 30 August 1924, 2; *Washington Post,* 2 November 1930, 14; Edward Bonner Whitney, "The Ku Klux Klan in Maine, 1922–1928: A Study with Particular Emphasis on the City of Portland" (honors thesis, Harvard College, 1966); Lawrence Wayne Moores Jr., "The History of the Ku Klux Klan in Maine, 1922–1931" (M.A. thesis, University of Maine, Orono, 1950), 99–100. For a summary of major episodes of Klan violence in different regions of the United States from the early to the middle 1920s, see Thomas R. Pegram, "The Problem of Hooded Violence: Moral Vigilantism, Enemies, and Provocation," in *One Hundred Percent American: The Rebirth and Decline of the Ku Klux Klan in the 1920s* (Chicago: Ivan R. Dee, 2011), 157–83; for a condensed version of the KKK's interactions with Maine Franco-Americans, see Mark Paul Richard, " 'This Is Not a Catholic Nation': The Ku Klux Klan Confronts Franco-Americans in Maine," *New England Quarterly* 82:2 (June 2009): 285–303.

2. U.S. Department of Commerce, Bureau of the Census, *Fourteenth Census of the United States Taken in the Year 1920,* vol. 2 (Washington, D.C.: Government Printing Office, 1922), 710; U.S. Department of Commerce, Bureau of the Census, *Fourteenth Census of the United States Taken in the Year 1920,* vol. 3 (Washington, D.C.: Government Printing Office, 1922), 409.

3. *Fellowship Forum* (Washington, D.C.), 29 January 1927, 1–2.

4. *New York Times,* 31 August 1924, sec. 2, 2; *Portland Press Herald,* 22 November 1921, 17; Frederick L. Collins, "Way Down East with the K.K.K." *Collier's,* 15 December 1923, 29.

5. *Maine Klansman,* 6 December 1923, 3; *New York World,* 16 December 1923, 1S, 2S.

6. *New York World,* 16 December 1923, 1S.

7. Ku Klux Klan Charter, Dexter Historical Society, Dexter, Maine; Meeting Minutes of the Dexter KKK, January 1924-January 1925, Dexter Historical Society; *Dexter Maine Directory, 1927* (n.p.: D. C. Rollins, 1927). The Dexter directory for 1927 is the only one that exists for the midtwenties. No rosters of the Dexter (or of any other Maine) klavern have been found, making it necessary to rely on the meeting minutes and charter of the Dexter Klan to reconstruct its membership. Dexter Klan members not found in the directory may have come from surrounding communities, such as Ripley, Cambridge, Corinna, Garland, and St. Albans, or they may simply have been visiting from other klaverns in Brewer or Waterville or from the communities of Monson and Pittsfield, as some meeting minutes (e.g., 26 June 1924, 31 July 1924) suggested.

8. See, for example, Leonard J. Moore, *Citizen Klansmen: The Ku Klux Klan in Indiana, 1921–1928* (Chapel Hill: University of North Carolina Press, 1991), 45, 63–65; Robert A. Goldberg, *Grassroots Resistance: Social Movements in Twentieth Century America* (Belmont, Calif.: Wadsworth, 1991), 81–82, 174; Shawn Lay, *Hooded Knights on the Niagara: The Ku Klux Klan in Buffalo, New York* (New York: New York University Press, 1995), 114; Eckard V. Toy, "Robe and Gown: The Ku Klux Klan in Eugene, Oregon, during the 1920s," in *The Invisible Empire in the West: Toward a New Historical Appraisal of the Ku Klux Klan of the 1920s,* ed. Shawn Lay (Urbana: University of Illinois Press, 1992), 166; William D. Jenkins, *Steel Valley Klan: The Ku Klux Klan in Ohio's Mahoning Valley* (Kent, Ohio: Kent State University Press, 1990), 83.

9. *New York World,* 16 December 1923, 1S, 2S; *Daily Kennebec Journal* (Augusta), 18 March 1924, 1; Dorothy A. Blanchard, "Into the Heart of Maine: A Look at Dexter's Franco-American Community," *Maine Historical Society Quarterly* 33 (Summer 1993): 30.

10. Dexter Klan Meeting Minutes, Dexter Historical Society, 28 February 1924, 6 March 1924, 11 March 1924, 24 April 1924, 21 August 1924. There is no indication in the Dexter Klan meeting minutes whether Brewster accepted or declined the invitation, but a Portland newspaper reported that he spoke at Dexter's Library Square to a group of about nine hundred people in August. *Portland Press Herald,* 26 August 1924, 1.

11. *Portland Press Herald,* 27 November 1923, 13; *Lewiston Evening Journal,* 20 June 1924, 1; Ernst Christian Helmreich, *Religion and the Maine Schools: An Historical Approach* (Brunswick, Maine: Bureau for Research in Municipal Government, 1960), 46. Béatrice C. Craig argues that French Canadians from the lower Saint Lawrence had colonized northern Maine's Saint John Valley along with Acadians from southern New Brunswick beginning in 1785. See Craig, "Early French Migrations to Northern Maine, 1785–1850," *Maine Historical Society Quarterly* 25 (Spring 1986): 230–47; and Craig, "Immigrants in a Frontier Community: Madawaska, 1785–1850," *Histoire sociale/Social History* 19 (novembre-November 1986): 277–97. On Brewster's gubernatorial bid in 1924, see John Syrett, "Principle and Expediency: The Ku Klux Klan and Ralph Owen Brewster in 1924," *Maine History* 39 (Winter 2000–2001): 215–39.

12. *Report of the State Commissioner of Education of the State of Maine for the School Biennium Ending June 30, 1924* (Augusta: Maine Department of Education, 1924), 40; Ralph O. Brewster to Rev. A. C. Goddard, Chestnut St. Methodist Church, Portland, Maine, 20 March 1924, Ralph Owen Brewster Papers, George J. Mitchell Department of Special Collections and Archives, Bowdoin College Library, Brunswick (hereafter ROBP); Ku Klux Klan Kreed, n.d., Ku Klux Klan folder, Kennebec Historical Society, Augusta; *Maine Klansman,* 20 March 1924, 3; Kenneth T. Jackson, *The Ku Klux Klan in the City, 1915–1930* (New York: Oxford University Press, 1967), 186, 205, 285n; David M. Chalmers, *Hooded Americanism: The History of the Ku Klux Klan,* 3rd ed. (1981; repr., Durham, N.C.: Duke University Press, 1987), 88–89, 199; Rory McVeigh, *The Rise of the Ku Klux Klan: Right-Wing Movements and National Politics* (Minneapolis: University of Minnesota Press, 2009), 115. On the practice of women religious teaching in the public schools of Maine's St. John Valley, see Helmreich, *Religion and the Maine Schools.*

13. John Higham, *Strangers in the Land: Patterns of American Nativism, 1860–1925* (1955; repr., New Brunswick, N.J.: Rutgers University Press, 1992), 61; leaflet, "Loyal Orange Institution, United States of America," n.d., ROBP; Resolutions of the State Grand Lodge of Maine, Loyal Orange Institution of the U.S.A., 5–6 June 1923, ROBP; application form of Orange Order of USA, [1923?], ROBP.

14. *Bangor Daily Commercial,* 1 April 1924, 4; *Bangor Daily News,* 2 September 1924, 5; flyer, "Roman Catholicism under the Searchlight," 1920s scrapbook, Benjamin C. Bubar Papers, Fogler Library Special Collections, University of Maine, Orono; Moses King Jr., Lewiston,

to Ralph O. Brewster, 25 October 1923, 4 March 1925, 13 May 1925, ROBP; pamphlet, Moses King Jr., "Why I Am an Orangeman" [1925], ROBP; Robert Alan Goldberg, *Hooded Empire: The Ku Klux Klan in Colorado* (Urbana: University of Illinois Press, 1981), 23.

15. Thomas Germon, Waterville, Maine, to Hon. Ralph O. Brewster, 12 December 1923, 4 January 1924, ROBP; *Lewiston Evening Journal,* 20 June 1924, 1.

16. *Lewiston Evening Journal,* 14 June 1924, 1, 1 July 1924, 2. Maine lawmakers had introduced bills as early as 1921 to amend the state's constitution to disallow the use of public funds for sectarian institutions, but they never garnered the necessary two-thirds majority of the House of Representatives and Senate to pass a proposed amendment; the issue went to a statewide referendum in 1926, but perhaps partly because of the KKK's decline in the state, voters soundly rejected the measure. Helmreich, *Religion and the Maine Schools,* 39, 41–43; *Biddeford Daily Journal,* 24 March 1925, 1; Rita Mae Breton, "Red Scare: A Study in Maine Nativism, 1919–1925" (M.A. thesis, University of Maine, Orono, 1972), 199; Lawrence Lee Pelletier, *The Initiative and Referendum in Maine* (Brunswick: Bowdoin College Bureau for Research in Municipal Government, 1951), 29.

17. *New York Times,* 3 July 1924, 6; *Lewiston Evening Journal,* 15 July 1924, 1; *Portland Press Herald,* 25 June 1924, 1, 15 July 1924, 1, 2; Ku Klux Klan Kreed, n.d., Kennebec Historical Society.

18. *Lewiston Evening Journal,* 1 August 1924, 1, 2, 7 August 1924, 1; *New York Times,* 3 August 1924, sec. 2, 1; *Portland Press Herald,* 8 August 1924, 14.

19. Part of the Klan Kreed reads as follows: "I do not believe in mob violence, but I do believe that laws should be enacted to prevent the causes of mob violence." *Maine Klansman,* 8 November 1923, 8.

20. Charles A. Scontras, *Organized Labor in Maine: War, Reaction, Depression, and the Rise of the CIO, 1914–1943* (Orono: Bureau of Labor Education, University of Maine, 2002), 171, 176; *Bangor Daily Commercial,* 4 February 1924, 3, 5 February 1924, 3; *Maine Klansman,* 6 December 1923, 7; *Portland Press Herald,* 21 September 1923, 24, 5 February 1924, 1; *Biddeford Daily Journal,* 5 February 1924, 1; George Crocker, Greenville Junction, Maine, to "Fellow Worker" [at American Civil Liberties Union, New York, N.Y.], 27 March 1924, vol. 259, American Civil Liberties Union Archives, Harvard Law School Library, Cambridge (hereafter ACLU Archives).

21. *Biddeford Daily Journal,* 5 February 1924, 1; *Bangor Daily Commercial,* 5 February 1924, 3, 26 February 1924, 10, 4 March 1924, 5, 15 March 1924, 1, 20 March 1924, 5; *Portland Press Herald,* 5 February 1924, 1, 6 February 1924, 1, 22 March 1924, 1, 3; Scontras, *Organized Labor in Maine,* 178; *Daily Kennebec Journal,* 21 March 1924, 1, 22 March 1924, 1; Piscataquis County Supreme Judicial Court, March Term 1924, *State of Maine v. Robert Pease, John Lucell, [sic] and Willard Parent,* Maine State Archives, Augusta; Bob Pease, State Prison, Thomaston, Maine, to the American Civil Liberties Union [New York, N.Y.], 19 April 1925, vol. 286, ACLU Archives. Although John Lucelle had a French-sounding surname, he was not of French-Canadian descent: born George Pazley, he had changed his name after a falling out with his father. The IWW hired an attorney to appeal the convictions of Lucelle and the other two men, but the attorney disappeared; by the time the IWW realized what had happened, its Maine organizers had nearly completed their sentences. In contrast to the Maine experience, the Ku Klux Klan of Colorado went against its principles of opposition to Catholics, the foreign-born, and the IWW in the hopes of gaining political power, for in 1927 Fremont County Klan members joined the IWW, the union organizing miners, and some of them promoted the IWW-led strike designed to push mine owners to increase wages; in addition, some KKK businessmen provided shelter, food, and clothing to strikers. Klan members engaged in these activities in

order to attract electoral support from Catholics and immigrants, and some gained office in 1928 as a result. *Portland Press Herald,* 22 March 1924, 3; Carl Keller, Acting Secretary [IWW], General Defense Committee, Chicago, Illinois, to Lucille B. Milner [ACLU], New York City, 16 March 1925, vol. 286, ACLU Archives; Goldberg, *Hooded Empire,* 146–47.

22. *Sanford Tribune and Advocate,* 14 August 1924, 1; *Biddeford Daily Journal,* 11 August 1924, 8; *Biddeford Weekly Journal,* 15 August 1924, 3; *La Justice de Biddeford,* 22 August 1924.

23. *Sanford Tribune and Advocate,* 10 July 1924, 1, 28 August 1924, 1, 4 September 1924, 1, 11 September 1924, 1.

24. *La Justice de Biddeford,* 14 March 1922, 1, 16 March 1923, 1; *Portland Press Herald,* 28 April 1923, 5, 3 March 1924, 1; *Biddeford Daily Journal,* 28 April 1923, 5, 4 March 1924, 2, 11 March 1924, 1; *Portland Evening Express,* 4 March 1924, 9.

25. *Biddeford Daily Journal,* 29 August 1924, 1, 30 August 1924, 1; *Portland Press Herald,* 30 August 1924, 1; *Portland Evening Express,* 30 August 1924, 2.

26. *Biddeford Daily Journal,* 30 August 1924, 1.

27. *Portland Press Herald,* 1 September 1924, 16, 2 September 1924, 3; *Biddeford Daily Journal,* 2 September 1924, 8; *Biddeford Weekly Journal,* 5 September 1924, 7.

28. *Maine Klansman,* 10 January 1924, 7, 20 March 1924, 3; *Lewiston Daily Sun,* 28 February 1924, 14, 19 March 1924, 1, 12, 3 May 1924, 16; *Le Messager,* 19 March 1924, 6. Class differences between Lewiston's "American" and Franco-American populations were fairly dramatic in 1920. Whereas 65.9 percent of the "American" men held blue-collar jobs, 84 percent of Franco-Americans did; in addition, whereas 34 percent of the working "American" men held white-collar positions, only 15.9 percent of the Franco-American men did. Given that Klansmen would have come from the "American" population, one can infer that socioeconomic differences distinguished Klan members from French speakers in Lewiston and quite likely in other cities and towns of Maine as well. No rosters of the Androscoggin Klan No. 46, chartered in 1925, have been found. Most members may have lived in Auburn, however, if the residence of KKK officers is any indication: ten of the twelve Klan officers listed on the charter made their home in Auburn, and the other two could not be found in the Androscoggin directories. The directories provide limited information on the occupations of nine Androscoggin Klan officers: five were shoeworkers, and one each was an auto mechanic, farmer, salesman, and clerk. Mark Paul Richard, *Loyal but French: The Negotiation of Identity by French-Canadian Descendants in the United States* (East Lansing: Michigan State University Press, 2008), 111; Androscoggin County Ku Klux Klan Charter, Gerald E. Talbot Collection, African American Collection of Maine, Jean Byers Sampson Center for Diversity in Maine, University of Southern Maine Libraries; *Directory of Androscoggin County, Maine, 1924–1925* (Portland: Portland Directory, 1924), 162, 185, 200, 215, 221, 246, 268, 307, 634; *Directory of Androscoggin County, Maine, 1926* (Portland: Portland Directory, 1926), 116.

29. *Lewiston Daily Sun,* 25 April 1924, 1, 11, 11 August 1924, 1, 12; *Le Messager,* 11 August 1924, 8; *Lewiston Evening Journal,* 11 August 1924, 10.

30. Duane Lockard, *New England State Politics* (Princeton, N.J.: Princeton University Press, 1959), 80; Lane W. Lancaster, "The Democratic Party in Maine," *National Municipal Review* 18 (December 1929): 744.

31. Theodore Roosevelt Hodgkins, ed. and comp., *Brief Biographies, Maine: A Biographical Dictionary of Who's Who in Maine,* vol. 1, *1926–27* (Lewiston: Lewiston Journal, 1926), 198; *Maine Register: State Year-Book and Legislative Manual,* no. 53 (Portland: Portland Directory, 1922), 256, 277; foreword to William Robinson Pattangall, "Is the Ku Klux Klan Un-American?" An authorized interview by Stanley Frost, *Forum* 74 (September 1925): 322.

32. *Boston Herald,* 13 March 1924, 14; Arnold S. Rice, *The Ku Klux Klan in American Politics*

(1962; repr., New York: Haskell House, 1972), 76–77, 79–80; Chalmers, *Hooded Americanism,* 207–8; J. Joseph Huthmacher, "Ku Klux Years," in *Massachusetts People and Politics, 1919–1933* (Cambridge: Belknap Press of Harvard University Press, 1959), 98; Associated Press article in *Portland Press Herald,* June 26, 1924, 1; David Chalmers, "Rule by Terror," Part II: "The Hooded Knights Revive in the 'Twenties," *American History Illustrated,* February 1980, 35; Wyn Craig Wade, *The Fiery Cross: The Ku Klux Klan in America* (New York: Simon and Schuster, 1987), 198–99; Kenneth T. Jackson, *The Ku Klux Klan in the City, 1915–1930* (New York: Oxford University Press, 1967), 248; *Portland Press Herald,* 30 June 1924, 1.

33. *Portland Press Herald,* 8 August 1924, 1, 14 August 1924, 2, 19 August 1924, 8; *New York Times,* 3 September 1924, 2.

34. Rice, *The Ku Klux Klan in American Politics,* 74–75.

35. Thomas Carens, "Dawes Opens Maine Fight, Opposing Klan; Gives Issue Impetus," *Boston Sunday Herald,* 24 August 1924, 1; Charles G. Dawes, *Notes as Vice President, 1928–1929* (Boston: Little, Brown, 1935), 23–25, 27–28; Moore, *Citizen Klansmen,* 162; Chalmers, *Hooded Americanism,* 213–14; Rice, *The Ku Klux Klan in American Politics,* 82. The Progressive Party presidential candidate Sen. Robert M. LaFollette of Wisconsin spoke out against the Klan in August 1924, leaving Calvin Coolidge as the only presidential contender not to denounce the group during the 1924 campaign. Rice, *The Ku Klux Klan in American Politics,* 82–83.

36. Carens, "Dawes Opens Maine Fight, Opposing Klan"; Chalmers, *Hooded Americanism,* 213–14.

37. *New York Times,* 3 September 1924, 2.

38. John D. Anderson, "Nation's Eyes Now on Maine," *Detroit Free Press,* 7 September 1924, part 1, 19; *New York Times,* 8 September 1924, 1; *New York World,* 6 September 1924, 10.

39. *Lewiston Daily Sun,* 10 September 1924, 1, 15 September 1924, 4, 14; *Le Messager,* 10 September 1924, 1.

40. Chalmers, *Hooded Americanism,* 200, 256, 259; *New York Times,* 10 September 1924, 20. The KKK also helped to elect governors in Colorado, Ohio, Louisiana, Indiana, Kansas, Tennessee, Oregon, and Wisconsin in the 1920s. Charles C. Alexander, *The Ku Klux Klan in the Southwest* (Lexington: University of Kentucky Press, 1965), 159; Chalmers, "The Hooded Knights Revive in the 'Twenties," 34.

41. Pattangall, "Is the Ku Klux Klan Un-American?," 323, 325–26, 328; Harold B. Clifford, *Charlie York: Maine Coast Fisherman* (Camden, Maine: International Marine,1974), 101.

42. *La Justice de Biddeford,* 2 November 1923; Moores, "The History of the Ku Klux Klan in Maine," 33–34; *Portland Press Herald,* 2 September 1924, 3; *Biddeford Daily Journal,* 2 September 1924, 8.

43. *Lewiston Evening Journal,* 20 October 1924, 12, 23 October 1924, 1, 12; *Lewiston Daily Sun,* 20 October 1924, 1, 4, 23 October 1924, 1, 3 November 1924, 12; *Portland Evening Express,* 20 October 1924, 10.

44. Bill of Complaint filed 6 May 1924 and dismissed on 14 July 1924, Supreme Judicial Court in Equity, Cumberland County, April Term 1924, no. 3735, MSA; Bill of Complaint filed 6 May 1924 and dismissed on 8 August 1924, Supreme Judicial Court in Equity, Cumberland County, April Term 1924, no. 3731, MSA; *Portland Press Herald,* 8 May 1924, 1.

45. *Lewiston Daily Sun,* 13 May 1924, 1, 30 May 1924, 1; Bill of Complaint filed 12 May 1924, Supreme Judicial Court in Equity, Cumberland County, April Term 1924, file #3749, MSA; *Portland Press Herald,* 13 May 1924, 1, 27 May 1924, 1; Gerry L. Brooks and Frank H. Haskell to Hon. Guy H. Sturgis, Justice, Supreme Judicial Court, 15 May 1924, Supreme Judicial Court in Equity, Cumberland County, April Term 1924, file #3749, MSA; dismissal of Moses W. Lucas

in *Equity v. Loyal Realty Company et al.,* dated 28 May 1924, Supreme Judicial Court in Equity, Cumberland County, April Term 1924, file #3749, MSA.

46. *Biddeford Daily Journal,* 23 May 1925, 1; *Milton C. Bennett, Plaintiff of Portland, v. F. Herbert Hathorn and D. D. Terrill, both of Bangor, defendants,* Penobscot County Superior Court, January Term 1926, no. 103, MSA; Milton Charles Bennett, "The Klansmen's Rally Song," 1924, Sheet Music Collection, Maine Historical Society, Portland; *Bangor Daily Commercial,* 21 May 1925, 5.

47. *Boston Herald,* 17 December 1924, 9; *Portland Press Herald,* 18 December 1924, 15; *Lewiston Daily Sun,* 27 April 1925, 2, 14 November 1925, 1; *Bill of Complaint of J. Carleton Bicknell, J. Wilder Haggett, Stephen Morrill, and John F. Davis v. Loyal Realty Company,* dated 10 November 1925, Cumberland County Supreme Judicial Court in Equity, January Term 1926, file #4106, MSA. Maine Savings Bank was not named as a defendant in this suit, for it had discharged its mortgage to the Loyal Realty Company on 12 February 1925. Cumberland County Registry of Deeds, Book 1135, p. 52.

48. Plaintiffs' Specifications to *Bill of Complaint of J. Carleton Bicknell, J. Wilder Haggett, Stephen Morrill, and John F. Davis v. Loyal Realty Company,* dated 29 December 1925, Cumberland County Supreme Judicial Court in Equity, January Term 1926, file #4106, MSA; Cumberland County Supreme Judicial Court in Equity, January Term 1926, 2 January 1926, file #4106, MSA; *Portland Sunday Telegram,* 9 August 1936, 1A, 3A. DeForest Perkins was born in Maine in 1873 and was an educator by profession: from 1893 to 1918 he served as a teacher, principal, and superintendent of schools in various Maine communities, including Portland. Hodgkins, *Brief Biographies, Maine,* 202.

49. *Lewiston Daily Sun,* 18 February 1926, 1, 11 June 1926, 1; Consent decree, dated 30 March 1926, Cumberland County, Supreme Judicial Court in Equity, January Term 1926, file #4106, MSA; Cumberland County Registry of Deeds, Book 1228, pp. 282–83, Book 1239, p. 320.

50. *Boston Herald,* 29 August 1926, 7; Portland, Maine, K.K.K. ticket, American Radicalism Collection, Special Collections, Michigan State University Library, East Lansing.

51. *New York Times,* 31 October 1926, sec. 2, 2, 3 November 1926, 12, 27 November 1926, 1, 4, 29 November 1926, 1, 30 November 1926, 1; *Portland Press Herald,* 25 November 1926, 1, 30 November 1926, 1; *Lewiston Evening Journal,* 30 November 1926, 1; *La Justice de Sanford (Maine),* 2 December 1926, 1. The French-language newspaper of Sanford noted after Gould's election that his supporters had accused Brewster of trying to curry Klan favor for a Senate bid in 1928. While Brewster won reelection as governor in September 1926, he lost his bids for the U.S. Senate in 1928 and 1930 and then lost the race for a seat in the U.S. House of Representatives in 1932. Those defeats did not end his political career, however. In 1934, he won his first election to the U.S. House, where he served for three terms, and in 1940 he won a seat in the U.S. Senate, where he served for two terms until his defeat in 1952. Incidentally, from 1943 Ralph O. Brewster slightly modified his identity by using Owen as his common name. *La Justice de Sanford,* 2 December 1926, 1; *New York Times,* 14 September 1926, 1, 26 December 1961, 25; *Portland Press Herald,* 19 June 1928, 1; *Washington Post,* 26 December 1961, B3.

52. *New York Times,* 21 February 1926, sec. 8, 1; *Biddeford Daily Journal,* 17 February 1923, 8; A. J. Gordon, "Opposition to Klan in Maine Growing Daily," *Boston Herald,* 10 September 1923, 1.

53. *Bates Student* (Lewiston), 16 November 1923, 1; *Boston Herald,* 12 November 1923, 14; *Bangor Daily News,* 28 February 1923, 2; *Portland Press Herald,* 18 January 1923, 1, 6 March 1923, 15; *Lewiston Daily Sun,* 18 January 1923, 9, 26 March 1923, 12, 18 November 1925, 1, 25 May 1926, 1, 26 May 1926, 1; Hodgkins, *Brief Biographies, Maine,* 238; *Boston Daily Advertiser,*

18 January 1923, 2; *Legislative Record of the Eighty-First Legislature of the State of Maine, 1923* (Augusta: Kennebec Journal, 1923), 780; *Waterville (Maine) Morning Sentinel,* 26 May 1926, 1, 5; *Maine Register: State Year-Book and Legislative Manual,* no. 57 (Portland: Portland Directory, 1926), 263, 284; *Lewiston Evening Journal,* 5 June 1926, 2.

54. *Washington Post,* 2 November 1930, 14; *Boston Herald,* 18 February 1927, 1; Peggy Pascoe, *What Comes Naturally: Miscegenation Law and the Making of Race in America* (New York: Oxford University Press, 2009), 181–82.

55. *La Justice de Biddeford,* 22 March 1929, 1; *New York Times,* 19 March 1929, 12; *Portland Press Herald,* 28 March 1929, 1, 29 March 1929, 1, 30 March 1929, 1, 17; Hugh S. Kelley, Realm Office, Scarboro, Maine, to Howard C. Hatch, Wells, Maine, 9 September 1935, Ku Klux Klan file, Maine History Collection, Dyer Library, Saco, Maine; *The Kourier* (Atlanta, Ga.), vol. 12, no. 10 (September 1936): cover; Chalmers, *Hooded Americanism,* 5. Not until Imperial Wizard Hiram W. Evans confirmed in 1937 that Sen. J. Thomas Heflin had joined the KKK in the late 1920s did it become public knowledge that Heflin was a Klan member and not simply a supporter of the organization. Rice, *The Ku Klux Klan in American Politics,* 89–90.

56. C. Stewart Doty, "How Many Frenchmen Does It Take to . . . ?" *Thought and Action* 11 (Fall 1995): 93; *L'Etoile* (Lowell, Mass.), 31 July 1924, 1; *Boston Herald,* 31 July 1924, 1, 2 August 1924, 2, 3 August 1924, 8.

57. On the ethnic conflicts between Bishop Louis S. Walsh and Maine's Franco-American population, see Michael Guignard, "The Case of Sacred Heart Parish," *Maine Historical Society Quarterly* 22 (Summer 1982): 21–36; Michael Guignard, "Maine's Corporation Sole Controversy," *Maine Historical Society Newsletter* 12 (Winter 1973): 111–30; and Richard, *Loyal but French,* 103–4, 139–44.

58. James S. Olson, *Catholic Immigrants in America* (Chicago: Nelson-Hall, 1987), 15, 33–46, 197–202; Mémorial du Monastère du Sacré-Coeur, Lewiston, Archives of the Dominican Sisters, Sabattus, Maine, 14 May 1922, 2:310; diary of Bishop Louis S. Walsh, Chancery Archives, Roman Catholic Diocese of Portland, Maine, 24 October 1923, 31 December 1923; *Acts and Resolves as Passed by the Seventy-Ninth Legislature of the State of Maine, 1919* (Augusta: Kennebec Journal, 1919), chap. 146.

59. Celeste P. DeRoche, " 'These Lines of My Life': Franco-American Women in Westbrook, Maine: The Intersection of Ethnicity and Gender, 1884–1984" (M.A. thesis, University of Maine, 1994), 98; Celeste DeRoche, "How Wide the Circle of We: Cultural Pluralism and American Identity, 1910–1954" (Ph.D. diss., University of Maine, 2000), 25; circular newsletter, "Le Pain de Chez-Nous," 8 January 1923, 1, Ursuline Sisters, Mount Merici Convent, Waterville, Maine; interview with Candide Desrosiers by Marc Chasse, Sainte-Agathe, Maine, 19 March 2001, VHS video, Sainte-Agathe Historical Society, St. Agatha, Maine.

60. Pierre Vincent Bourassa, "The Catholic Church in the Franco-American Community" (honors thesis, Bowdoin College, 1978), 58–59.

61. *New York Times,* 5 September 1924, 3; *La Justice de Biddeford,* 29 August 1924, 1.

62. Walter D. Kamphoefner, "The Handwriting on the Wall: The Klan, Language Issues, and Prohibition in the German Settlements of Eastern Texas," *Southwestern Historical Quarterly* 112 (July 2008): 52–66.

63. *Le Messager,* 23 April 1923, 1; *La Justice de Biddeford,* 28 March 1924. For an extensive treatment of how Franco-Americans negotiated their identity in the host society in the nineteenth and twentieth centuries, see Richard, *Loyal but French.*

64. Arthur G. Staples, Editor, Lewiston Evening Journal, to Ralph O. Brewster, 20 December [1924], ROBP; Ralph O. Brewster to Louis Lachance Jr., Lewiston, 24 December 1924,

ROBP; Ralph O. Brewster to Arthur G. Staples, 24 December 1924, ROBP; *Le Messager,* 9 February 1925, 24 June 1927, 2 April 1930; *La Justice de Biddeford,* 13 June 1930.

65. Moore, *Citizen Klansmen;* Kathleen M. Blee, *Women of the Klan: Racism and Gender in the 1920s* (Berkeley: University of California Press, 1991); Lay, *Hooded Knights on the Niagara;* Lay, ed., *The Invisible Empire in the West.*

66. See, for example, William MacDonald, "The French Canadians in New England," *Quarterly Journal of Economics* 12 (April 1898): 265; Alexandre-Louis Mothon, cited in J. Antonin Plourde, *Dominicains au Canada: Livre des documents,* vol. 2: *Les cinq fondations avant l'autonomie (1881–1911)* (n.p., 1975), 48; Robert Cloutman Dexter, "Fifty-Fifty Americans," *World's Work* 48 (August 1924): 369–70.

67. Charles C. Alexander suggests that the opposition of southern Louisiana's French Catholic Cajun population to the Ku Klux Klan prevented it from growing rapidly in the state during the 1920s but, like Yvonne Brown, he does not discuss any specific confrontations between Louisiana's French speakers and the KKK. Alexander, *The Ku Klux Klan in the Southwest,* 47; Brown, "Tolerance and Bigotry in Southwest Louisiana: The Ku Klux Klan, 1921–1923," *Louisiana History* 47 (Spring 2006): 153–68.

4. Expansion in the Granite State

1. Hobart Pillsbury, "Ku Klux Klan Circles Country by Forming New Hampshire Order," *Boston Sunday Herald,* 4 December 1921, 12. *The Republic* (Boston, 10 December 1921, 2) itself questioned sardonically, "Can anything be more absurd than such an organization for such a purpose in a State in which the Negroes constitute less than one per cent. of the white population?"

2. *Manchester Leader and Evening Union,* 30 November 1921, 5; *Manchester Daily Mirror,* 20 January 1923, 1; *L'Impartial* (Nashua, N.H.), 20 January 1923, 1.

3. *Boston Sunday Advertiser,* 21 January 1923, 1; *Boston Daily Advertiser,* 23 January 1923, 2.

4. *L'Avenir National* (Manchester), 20 January 1923, 1; *L'Impartial,* 23 January 1923; Herrick Aiken Scrapbook, 1908–1925, New Hampshire Historical Society, Concord (hereafter NHHS); *Manchester Leader and Evening Union,* 20 January 1923, 1, 6 February 1923, 1.

5. *Manchester Leader and Evening Union,* 23 January 1923, 2, 6 February 1923, 1; *L'Avenir National,* 6 February 1923, 1; House Bill 185, New Hampshire Senate and House Bills (1923), vol. 2, New Hampshire State Library, Concord (hereafter NHSL); *Manchester Daily Mirror,* 23 January 1923, 1; Journal of the New Hampshire House of Representatives, January Session, 1923, 132, 193, NHHS.

6. House Bill 265, New Hampshire Senate and House Bills (1923), vol. 2, NHSL; *Granite Monthly* 55, no. 2 (February 1923): 46; *Concord Daily Monitor and New Hampshire Patriot,* 21 March 1923, 1; Journal of the New Hampshire House of Representatives, January Session, 1923, 140, 360, 706. The ten states that succeeded in enacting anti-masking and anti-Klan legislation in the 1920s were as follows: Arizona (1923), Illinois (1923), Iowa (1924), Louisiana (1924), Michigan (1929), Minnesota (1923), New Mexico (1923), North Dakota (1923), Oklahoma (1923), and Texas (1925.) Jack Swertfeger Jr., "Anti-Mask and Anti-Klan Laws," *Journal of Public Law* 1 (Spring 1952): 195–96.

7. *L'Impartial,* 1 November 1923, 1; *Boston Herald,* 1 November 1923, 4; *Rochester (N.H.) Courier,* 2 November 1923, 8; U.S. Department of Commerce, Bureau of the Census, *Religious Bodies, 1926,* vol. 2 (Washington, D.C.: Government Printing Office, 1929), 44, 647; U.S. Department of Commerce, Bureau of the Census, *Fourteenth Census of the United States Taken*

in the Year 1920, vol. 2 (Washington, D.C.: Government Printing Office, 1922), 39; *Maine Klansman,* 15 November 1923; *L'Avenir National,* 9 November 1923, 6.

8. *Boston Herald,* 17 November 1923, 13, 18 November 1923, 11; *Boston Daily Advertiser,* 17 November 1923, 3; Thomas R. Pegram, *One Hundred Percent American: The Rebirth and Decline of the Ku Klux Klan in the 1920s* (Chicago: Ivan R. Dee, 2011), 16.

9. *Boston Sunday Herald,* 2 December 1923, 4; Wilfrid H. Paradis, *Upon this Granite: Catholicism in New Hampshire, 1647–1997* (Portsmouth, N.H.: Peter E. Randall,1998), 148. Little information exists on the women's Klan organizations of New Hampshire, but a surviving embossed seal reveals that the Rochester Women of the Ku Klux Klan represented the third such organization in the Granite State. Embossed seal, Women of the Ku Klux Klan No. 3, Rochester, N.H., Rochester Historical Society, Rochester.

10. *Boston Sunday Advertiser,* 18 November 1923, 2; *Rochester Courier,* 8 December 1922, 1, 23 November 1923, 1, 7 December 1923, 1; *Le Courier de Lawrence (Mass.),* 23 November 1923, 4; *Boston Herald,* 5 December 1923, 12; *L'Impartial,* 6 December 1923, 1. New Hampshire Franco-Americans like Lanoix tended to be Democratic partisans. Duane Lockard, *New England State Politics* (Princeton, N.J.: Princeton University Press, 1959), 66.

11. *Maine Klansman,* 13 December 1923, 1; Stephen H. Goetz, "The Ku Klux Klan in New Hampshire, 1923–1927," *Historical New Hampshire* 43 (Winter 1988): 253–56.

12. Goetz, "The Ku Klux Klan in New Hampshire," 250–51; *L'Etoile* (Lowell, Mass.), 8 February 1924, 8; *Concord Daily Monitor and New Hampshire Patriot,* 3 January 1924, 1; A. J. Gordon, "Klan Opens Its Campaign in N.H. on 'Dismal' Day," *Boston Herald,* 3 January 1924, 1, 3; *L'Avenir National,* 3 January 1924, 1; *Portsmouth Herald,* 3 January 1924, 4; *Maine Klansman,* 10 January 1924, 5, 8.

13. *Maine Klansman,* 20 March 1924, 7.

14. *Maine Klansman,* 10 January 1924, 5; Goetz, "The Ku Klux Klan in New Hampshire," 250–51; *Concord Daily Monitor and New Hampshire Patriot,* 30 January 1924, 10.

15. *Concord Daily Monitor and New Hampshire Patriot,* 29 January 1924, 1, 3.

16. *Concord Daily Monitor and New Hampshire Patriot,* 4 February 1924, 1, 5; *Boston Daily Advertiser,* 5 February 1924, 7.

17. *Rochester Courier,* 22 February 1924, 1; *Foster's Daily Democrat* (Dover, N.H.), 19 February 1924, 5; *Concord Daily Monitor and New Hampshire Patriot,* 19 February 1924, 3.

18. *Rochester Courier,* 22 February 1924, 1; *Foster's Daily Democrat,* 20 February 1924, 3; *Fourteenth Census of the United States Taken in the Year 1920,* 2:710.

19. *L'Impartial,* 9 January 1923, 28 June 1923, 3 July 1926; *L'Avenir National,* 24 January 1923, 4, 23 April 1923, 4, 20 September 1923, 6, 20 October 1923, 6, 31 January 1924, 4, 1 July 1924, 6, 24 February 1926, 6.

20. Paradis, *Upon this Granite,* 130, 150–51; Gerard J. Brault, *The French-Canadian Heritage in New England* (Hanover, N.H.: University Press of New England, 1986), 73. New England Franco-Americans have claimed Guertin as the region's first Franco-American bishop. Although John Stephen Michaud became the bishop of Burlington in the 1890s, only on his father's side did he have French-Canadian ancestry, but perhaps more important, he "did not readily identify with Franco-Americans," notes Gerard Brault in *The French-Canadian Heritage in New England,* 73.

21. Edward George Hartmann, "The Post-War Americanization Drive," in *The Movement to Americanize the Immigrant* (New York: Columbia University Press, 1948), 242; House Bill 262, New Hampshire Senate and House Bills (1919), 2:12–13, 23–24, 27–46, NHSL; *Le Canado-Américain* (Manchester), 25 February 1919, 1; Records of the Committee on Education, New Hampshire House of Representatives, 1913–33, 11 February 1919, 31, New Hampshire State

Archives, Concord; chapter 106, *Laws of the State of New Hampshire Passed in 1919* (Concord: Evans, 1919), 155, 161; *L'Avenir National,* 23 April 1920, 6.

22. *Boston Herald,* 30 January 1924, 6, 7 May 1924, 15; *Lewiston Daily Sun,* 8 May 1924, 11; *Dover, Somersworth, Rochester, Farmington, Durham (New Hampshire), Berwick (Maine) Directory, 1924* (Springfield, Mass.: H. A. Manning, 1924), 26:486; Strafford County Registry of Deeds, Dover, N.H., Book 409, pp. 474–77, Book 411, pp. 64, 70, Book 412, p. 54; *Boston Daily Advertiser,* 12 November 1925, 10; *Foster's Daily Democrat,* 29 January 1924, 3; *Rochester Courier,* 1 February 1924, 1, 8 February 1924, 1. The Klan estate also served as the site of social gatherings, including Gayer's wedding to Prudence W. Babb, his second wife, in August 1924; the Klan even held a public dance at its Rochester estate to raise money to support its headquarters. *Portland Press Herald,* 27 August 1924, 4; *Boston Sunday Herald,* 7 September 1924, 10.

23. *Foster's Daily Democrat,* 2 June 1924, 8; *New York Times,* 2 June 1924, 2; *Boston Herald,* 2 June 1924, 1; *Portland Press Herald,* 2 June 1924, 1; *Brattleboro (Vt.) Daily Reformer,* 2 June 1924, 3; *Boston Daily Advertiser,* 2 June 1924, 2.

24. *Boston Herald,* 1 July 1924, 1, 4, 12 July 1924, 1; *Burlington (Vt.) Free Press and Times,* 2 July 1924, 1; *La Justice de Biddeford,* 11 July 1924; *Concord Daily Monitor and New Hampshire Patriot,* 12 July 1924, 1; *New York Times,* 14 July 1924, 5; *Boston Sunday Herald,* 13 July 1924, 7.

25. *New York World,* 27 September 1924, 4; *New York Times,* 27 September 1924, 3; *Boston Herald,* 27 September 1924, 3.

26. *Concord Daily Monitor and New Hampshire Patriot,* 7 November 1924, 1; *Biddeford Daily Journal,* 7 November 1924, 1; Charles Drury, "Klan and Foes near Clash; Feeling Higher in K.C. Man's Death," *Boston Herald,* 8 November 1924, 1, 2; *Biddeford Daily Journal,* 7 November 1924, 1. The *Boston Herald* subsequently reported the arrest of an individual charged with Travis's murder but did not mention any Klan affiliation. Charles Drury, "Arrest Made in Travers Case," *Boston Herald,* 10 November 1924, 1. Newspaper accounts differ on the last name of the murdered man: the Concord and Biddeford newspapers identified his surname as "Travis," and the Boston newspaper as "Travers."

27. *L'Impartial,* 9 August 1924, 1; *L'Avenir National,* 13 August 1926, 1; *Fellowship Forum* (Washington, D.C.), 2 April 1927, 3.

28. Goetz, "The Ku Klux Klan in New Hampshire," 247; *Washington Post,* 2 November 1930, 14; *Manchester Leader and Evening Union,* 24 March 1924, 1, 25 April 1924, 1; *Boston Sunday Herald,* 24 August 1924, 2.

29. Strafford County Registry of Deeds, Book 409, pp. 474–75, Book 421, p. 325; *Boston Herald,* 22 March 1925, 12A, 17 May 1925, 4A; *Rochester Courier,* 27 March 1925, 7; Goetz, "The Ku Klux Klan in New Hampshire," 262; Leonard J. Moore, *Citizen Klansmen: The Ku Klux Klan in Indiana, 1921–1928* (Chapel Hill: University of North Carolina Press, 1991), xii; *Biddeford Daily Journal,* 11 October 1926, 2; *L'Avenir National,* 24 August 1926, 3.

30. *Washington Post,* 2 November 1930, 14; *Kourier Magazine* (Atlanta, Ga.), January 1931, 47, December 1931, 39; *The Kourier* (Atlanta, Ga.), May 1935, 45.

31. *L'Avenir National,* 27 November 1925, 3, 24 February 1926, 2, 18 March 1926, 1, 26 April 1926, 1; *Nashua Telegraph,* 23 February 1926, 1; *L'Impartial,* 25 February 1926, n.p.

32. Goetz, "The Ku Klux Klan in New Hampshire," 263.

5. Rebuff in the Green Mountain State

1. *Montpelier Evening Argus,* 9 December 1922, 7; *Boston Daily Advertiser,* 1 February 1923, 4.

2. *Washington Post,* 2 November 1930, 14. As noted in the introduction, assessing Klan strength is problematic. Other estimates of Klan numbers in the Green Mountain State have

ranged from as low as two thousand to somewhere between ten thousand and fourteen thousand persons. Michael Sherman, Gene Sessions, and P. Jeffrey Potash, "'Behind the Times,' 1900–1927," in *Freedom and Unity: A History of Vermont* (Barre: Vermont Historical Society, 2004), 405. Once again, the *Washington Post*'s higher figures give us a sense of the Klan's probable influence in Vermont.

3. Nancy L Gallagher, *Breeding Better Vermonters: The Eugenics Project in the Green Mountain State* (Hanover, N.H.: University Press of New England, 1999), 6, 40, 44, 95–97, 185–86; Deborah Pickman Clifford and Nicholas R. Clifford, "'Her Great Product Is Character': Vermont in 1927," in *"The Troubled Roar of the Waters": Vermont in Flood and Recovery, 1927–1931* (Hanover, N.H.: University Press of New England, 2007), 52–54. No direct connection has been established between the Ku Klux Klan and the eugenics project in Vermont, likely in part because the KKK was waning as the eugenics movement gained ground.

4. *Boston Daily Advertiser,* 3 February 1923, 4; *Rutland Daily Herald,* 3 September 1924, 1, 5 September 1924, 2, 6 September 1924, 2; Thomas R. Pegram, *One Hundred Percent American: The Rebirth and Decline of the Ku Klux Klan in the 1920s* (Chicago: Ivan R. Dee, 2011), 119–56.

5. U.S. Department of Commerce, Bureau of the Census, *Fourteenth Census of the United States Taken in the Year 1920,* vol. 2 (Washington, D.C.: Government Printing Office, 1922), 710. A useful listing of Vermont newspaper articles on the KKK of the 1920s can be found in Steve Hight, "Ku Klux Klues: An Introduction to and a Bibliography for the Study of a Century of the Ku Klux Klan, with Special Emphasis on the 1920's, Particularly in Vermont" (typescript, University of Vermont, 1974.)

6. *Bethel (Vt.) Courier,* 5 June 1924, 2; U.S. Department of Commerce, Bureau of the Census, *Religious Bodies, 1926,* vol. 2 (Washington, D.C.: Government Printing Office, 1929), 44, 647; *Fourteenth Census of the United States Taken in the Year 1920,* 2:39.

7. *Bethel Courier,* 23 October 1924, 2.

8. *Journal of the Senate of the State of Vermont,* biennial session, 1919 (Montpelier: Capital City Press, 1919), 302, 351, 538, 619, 632; *Vermont Legislative Directory, Biennial Session, 1919* (n.p.: Secretary of State, 1919), 518, 541; *Vermont Legislative Directory, Biennial Session, 1921* (n.p.: Secretary of State, 1921), 561; *New York Times,* 5 March 1945, 19; *U.S. Census, 1920; Journal of the House of the State of Vermont,* biennial session, 1919 (Montpelier: Capital City Press, 1919), 488, 510–11.

9. *Journal of the House of the State of Vermont,* biennial session, 1921 (Montpelier: Capital City Press), 212; *Vermont Legislative Directory, 1921;* House Bills, General Assembly of the State of Vermont, Session of 1921, 623, Vermont Department of Libraries, Montpelier.

10. Chroniques du Couvent St. Louis, 1862–1935, Sisters of Providence, Winooski, Vermont (hereafter Chroniques of the Sisters of Providence), 3 September 1917, 192, 20 February 1921, 245.

11. Chroniques of the Sisters of Providence, 20 February 1921, 245, 246; *Burlington Daily Free Press,* 23 February 1921, 1. For a fuller treatment of the concept of an intertwined American and French-Canadian identity in the northeastern United States, see Mark Paul Richard, *Loyal but French: The Negotiation of Identity by French-Canadian Descendants in the United States* (East Lansing: Michigan State University Press, 2008.)

12. *Burlington and Winooski (Vermont) Directory, 1921,* vol. 32 (Springfield, Mass.: H. A. Manning, 1921), 520, 521, 574, 576; *Burlington Daily Free Press,* 2 December 1913, 7, 23 February 1921, 1; *Vermont Legislative Directory, 1921,* 551.

13. Joseph N. Couture, S.S.E., vitae of Vermont clergy, vol. 4, sec. 3, Priests Ordained or Admitted into the Diocese since 1910, 430, 432, Roman Catholic Archives, Diocese of Burlington, Burlington, Vermont; Robert Rumilly, *Histoire des Franco-Américains* (Montréal:

By the author, 1958), 319; *The Holy Cross Purple* 13, no. 2 (October 1901): 68; *Burlington Free Press,* 2 April 1938, 11; receipt book of Artisans, Papers of Most Reverend Joseph John Rice, D.D., 1929–38, Diocese of Burlington; Certificat de Dotation, Société des Artisans Canadiens-Français, Bishop Rice Papers, 1929–38; L. Albert Vezina, Rector [Sacred Heart of Mary Parish, Rutland] to Rt. Rev. J. J. Rice, D.D., Burlington, 17 February 1921, Rutland, Sacred Heart of Mary file, Diocese of Burlington; personnel card file, Diocese of Burlington; Joseph J. Rice, Bishop of Burlington, to Rev. L. A. Vezina, Pastor of the Sacred Heart of Mary Parish, Rutland, 11 June 1921, Rutland, Sacred Heart of Mary file, Diocese of Burlington; J. E. Pariseau, St. Joseph's Rectory, Burlington, to His Excellency, J. J. Rice, D.D., 24 March 1934, St. Joseph, Burlington, file, Diocese of Burlington; J. J. Rice, Bishop of Burlington to Reverend J. E. Pariseau, P.R., Saint Joseph's Church, Burlington, 21 July 1934, St. Joseph, Burlington, file, Diocese of Burlington.

14. Chroniques of the Sisters of Providence, 20 February 1921, 246; *Journal of the House of the State of Vermont,* 1921, 451, 458, 461; Vermont House Bills, 1921, 1057–58; *Burlington Daily Free Press,* 9 March 1921, 1; *Vermont Legislative Directory, 1921,* 522 and unnumbered pages.

15. Wyn Craig Wade, *The Fiery Cross: The Ku Klux Klan in America* (New York: Simon and Schuster, 1987), 170–75; *Fiery Cross* (Indianapolis, Ind.), 9 November 1923, 9; *Imperial Night-Hawk* (Atlanta, Ga.), 17 October 1923, 1.

16. *Rutland Daily Herald,* 8 May 1924, 1; *Springfield (Vt.) Reporter,* 8 May 1924, 1; *Bellows Falls Times,* 8 May 1924, 2, 15 May 1924, 7.

17. *St. Albans Daily Messenger,* 18 August 1924, 3; P. M. McKenna, St. Monica Rectory, Barre, Vermont, to Right Reverend Bishop [J. J. Rice], 31 July [1925], Barre, Vermont, file, Diocese of Burlington; *Barre Daily Times,* 29 July 1925, 1, 3 August 1925, 1; *Barre and Montpelier (Vermont) Directory,* vol. 32 (Springfield, Mass.: H. A. Manning, 1927), 158, 257; [Rev.] E. F. Cray, St. Monica's Rectory, Barre, to Rt. Rev. J. J. Rice, D.D., Bishop of Burlington, 11 February 1927, Barre, Vermont, file, Diocese of Burlington; land records, City Clerk's Office, Barre, Book 35, pp. 413–17; *St. Monica Parish, Barre, Vermont, 2003* (n.p.: n.p., 2003), 3.

18. [Rev. W. P. Crosby], St. Augustine's Rectory, Montpelier, to Rt. Rev. J. J. Rice, D.D., 7 January 192[5].

19. *Montpelier Evening Argus,* 21 July 1924, 1; *The Church of St. Augustine at Montpelier, Vermont: 1892–1992, A Century of Blessings* [n.p., 1992], 21; *Bethel Courier,* 24 July 1924, 2.

20. (Mrs.) Robert Carver, Montpelier, to Governor [Richard] Snelling, 3 May 1982, Ku Klux Klan files, Vermont State Archives, Office of the Secretary of State, Montpelier; *Manning's Barre and Montpelier Directory, 1983,* vol. 73 (Bellows Falls: H. A. Manning, 1983), 148. Born in Montpelier in 1917, Carver was raised Catholic but converted to Judaism later in life. There are some small discrepancies in ages and dates in her account. It is possible that she recalled the cross burning at St. Augustine's cemetery in 1924, when she would have been seven years old, or she may have recalled seeing Klan members celebrating the Fourth of July at Montpelier in 1927, an event described later in this chapter that drew thousands of white-robed individuals to the state capital. Frances Emmons Carver interview by Rebecca Sherlock, Montpelier, 25 June 1989, Vermont Historical Society Library, Vermont History Center, Barre; *Brattleboro Daily Reformer,* 5 July 1927, 1; *Rutland Daily Herald,* 5 July 1927, 8. Despite any factual errors, Carver's account is authentic.

21. Carver interview; Steve Hight, "White Robes among the Green Mountains: Reflections on Research of the Ku Klux Klan in Vermont, 1922–1927" (honors thesis, University of Vermont, 1976), 209, 217.

22. *Brattleboro Daily Reformer,* 23 November 1925, 3; *Barre and Montpelier (Vermont) Directory,* vol. 31 (Springfield, Mass.: H. A. Manning, 1926), 357, 395; *Burlington Free Press and*

Times, 20 February 1926, 1, 22 February 1926, 2; *The Church of St. Augustine at Montpelier, Vermont,* 21. Davis did not discuss his work in defending the KKK in his autobiography, Deane C. Davis with Nancy Price Graff, *Deane C. Davis: An Autobiography* (Shelburne, Vt.: New England Press, 1991.)

23. *Vermont Legislative Directory, Biennial Session, 1923* (Montpelier: Secretary of State, 1923), 404; *Journal of the Senate of the State of Vermont,* biennial session, 1923 (Montpelier: Capital City Press, 1923), 3, 133, 167; Senate Bills, Vermont, session of 1923, 224, 225, Vermont Department of Libraries; *Burlington Free Press and Times,* 9 February 1923, 1, 16 February 1923, 2; *Montpelier Evening Argus,* 15 February 1923, 7; *Rutland Daily Herald,* 16 February 1923, 1.

24. *Rutland Daily Herald,* 26 February 1925, 1; *Vermont Legislative Directory, Biennial Session, 1925* (Montpelier: Secretary of State, 1925), 431; *Journal of the Senate of the State of Vermont,* biennial session, 1925 (Montpelier: Capital City Press, 1925), 1, 239; Senate Bills, Vermont, session of 1925, 201–4, Vermont Department of Libraries; Jack Swertfeger Jr., "Anti-Mask and Anti-Klan Laws," *Journal of Public Law* 1 (Spring 1952): 195–96.

25. *Caledonian-Record* (St. Johnsbury, Vt.), 1 May 1924, 1, 6 May 1924, 1, 8 May 1924, 1, 5; *Brattleboro Daily Reformer,* 2 May 1924, 2.

26. *Bellows Falls Times,* 29 May 1924, 2.

27. *Caledonian-Record,* 27 August 1924, 1, 4.

28. *St. Albans Weekly Messenger,* 2 October 1924, 1.

29. *Waterbury Record,* reproduced in the *Burlington Daily News,* 5 May 1924, 4.

30. *Burlington Free Press and Times,* 1 May 1924, 2; *Springfield (Vt.) Reporter,* 24 April 1924, 8; *Rutland Daily Herald,* 3 May 1924, 4.

31. *Bennington Evening Banner,* 3 September 1924, 1; *St. Albans Daily Messenger,* 5 September 1924, 4.

32. *Bennington Evening Banner,* 25 September 1924, 1, 1 October 1924, 1.

33. *Vermont Journal* (Windsor), 24 October 1924, 1.

34. *Rutland News,* 17 October 1924, 1, 24 October 1924, 10; *Rutland Daily Herald,* 18 October 1924, 3, 4, 22 October 1924, 3, 24 October 1924, 1; *Burlington Free Press and Times,* 18 October 1924, 2.

35. *Rutland Daily Herald,* 3 November 1924, 1, 7.

36. *Rutland Daily Herald,* 18 November 1924, 1; *Rutland News,* 18 November 1924, 6, 19 November 1924, 2; *Burlington Free Press and Times,* 3 February 1925, 9.

37. *Brattleboro Daily Reformer,* 24 December 1924, 1; *Caledonian-Record,* 24 December 1924, 1; *New York Times,* 25 December 1924, 12. For a fictional account of the Vermont Klan that incorporates some historically accurate events that took place in the Green Mountain State, such as the secretary of state's refusal to approve the KKK's application to do business in Vermont, see Karen Hesse, *Witness* (New York: Scholastic Press, 2001.)

38. Charles Drury, "Accuses Kleagle, Now in Flight, of Robbery of Vermont Church," *Boston Herald,* 15 August 1924, 1, 2; *Burlington Free Press and Times,* 10 November 1924, 6, 25 August 1924, 1; *U.S. Census, 1920;* Charles Drury, "Wants Klan to Catch Kleagle," *Boston Herald,* 16 August 1924, 16; *Boston Herald,* 20 August 1924, 1, 5 November 1924, 24; *New York Times,* 7 November 1924, 14.

39. Drury, "Accuses Kleagle, Now in Flight," 1, 2; *Burlington Free Press and Times,* 11 November 1924, 8.

40. *Burlington Free Press and Times,* 16 August 1924, 4; *News and Citizen* (Hyde Park, Vt.), 20 August 1924, 4.

41. *Biddeford Daily Journal,* 7 November 1924, 8; *Burlington Free Press and Times,* 7 November 1924, 7, 8 November 1924, 6, 10 November 1924, 6; *New York Times,* 7 November 1924, 14.

42. *New York Times,* 19 November 1924, 18; *Burlington Free Press and Times,* 19 November 1924, 8, 7 January 1925, 2, 3 September 1925, 1; *Vermont Legislative Directory, Biennial Session, 1923* (n.p.: Secretary of State, 1923), 519; *Vermont Legislative Directory, Biennial Session, 1925* (n.p.: Secretary of State, 1925), 547.

43. *Brattleboro Daily Reformer,* 20 August 1924, 3–4; Charles Drury, "War Within N.E. Klan," *Boston Herald,* August 20, 1924, 1, 2; A. J. Massi of Barton, Vt., to the *Barton Monitor,* reproduced in the *Bethel Courier,* 23 October 1924, 8; David M. Chalmers, *Hooded American-ism: The History of the Ku Klux Klan,* 3rd ed. (1981; repr., Durham, N.C.: Duke University Press, 1987), 51–52.

44. Maudean Neill, *Fiery Crosses in the Green Mountains: The Story of the Ku Klux Klan in Vermont* (Randolph Center, Vt.: Greenhills Books, 1989), 59–60; John Higham, *Strangers in the Land: Patterns of American Nativism, 1860–1925* (1955; repr., New Brunswick, N.J.: Rutgers University Press, 1992), 327–29; William D. Jenkins, *Steel Valley Klan: The Ku Klux Klan in Ohio's Mahoning Valley* (Kent, Ohio: Kent State University Press, 1990), 153.

45. *Washington Post,* 2 November 1930, 14.

46. *News and Citizen,* 6 May 1925, 1; *Rutland Daily Herald,* 3 August 1925, 2, 5 July 1927, 8; *Montpelier Evening Argus,* 3 August 1925, 8; *Brattleboro Daily Reformer,* 5 July 1927, 1.

47. *Kourier Magazine* (Atlanta, Ga.) 7, no. 1 (December 1930): 28; 7, no. 2 (January 1931): 38; 7, no. 9 (August 1931): 35.

48. *Burlington Free Press and Times,* 12 November 1924, 9.

49. W. R. Cameron, "A Call to Colors," and "A Klansman's Prayer," Vermont Historical Society Library, Vermont History Center; *U.S. Census, 1920; Times-Argus* (Barre-Montpelier), 25 June 1960, 6; typescript by William Roderick Cameron, addressed "To Whom It May Concern," William R. Cameron Papers, Aldrich Public Library, Barre; *Barre and Montpelier (Vermont) Directory,* vol. 33 (Springfield, Mass.: H. A. Manning, 1928), 80. Cameron also became a promoter of the Boy Scout movement, for which he wrote the marching song, "Little Men." *Times-Argus,* 25 June 1960, 6. On the granite industry in Barre, see C. Stewart Doty, *The First Franco-Americans: New England Life Histories from the Federal Writers' Project, 1938–1939* (Orono: University of Maine Press, 1985), 102–18.

50. *New York Times,* 4 May 1924, sec. 2, 7; *Fellowship Forum* (Washington, D.C.), 19 November 1927, 7; V. M. Kipp, "Canadian Province Turns to the Klan," *New York Times,* 8 July 1928, sec. 3, 7; Pegram, *One Hundred Percent American,* 22, 128.

51. Chalmers, *Hooded Americanism,* 279; Phil Goodstein, *In the Shadow of the Klan: When the KKK Ruled Denver, 1920–1926* (Denver, Colo.: New Social Publications, 2006), 226; Robert Alan Goldberg, *Hooded Empire: The Ku Klux Klan in Colorado* (Urbana: University of Illinois Press, 1981), 28; Kenneth T. Jackson, *The Ku Klux Klan in the City, 1915–1930* (New York: Oxford University Press, 1967), 120, 166, 195; Christine K. Erickson, "The Boys in Butte: The Ku Klux Klan Confronts the Catholics, 1923–1929" (M.A. thesis, University of Montana, 1991), 84–85, 102n16.

52. *St. Albans Weekly Messenger,* 17 April 1924, 1; *Burlington Free Press and Times,* 12 June 1924, 4.

53. U.S. Department of Commerce, Bureau of the Census, *Fourteenth Census of the United States Taken in the Year 1920,* vol. 1 (Washington, D.C.: Government Printing Office, 1921), 20, and vol. 2, 1252.

54. Impressions of Vermont as a tolerant state cannot be carried too far, however. Lest one become enamored with notions of Vermont exceptionalism, which date back to the colonial period when Vermont was an independent republic prior to joining the United States in 1791, one need only recall that sizable numbers of women and men from the Green Mountain State

joined the KKK in the 1920s. In addition, as highlighted in the opening paragraphs of this chapter, one of Vermont's U.S. senators became a leading national advocate of stricter immigration laws during the decade, native son Calvin Coolidge signed into law the Immigration Restriction Act of 1924, and the Vermont eugenics movement took root in the mid-1920s. Gallagher, *Breeding Better Vermonters*, 6, 44; Clifford and Clifford, "'Her Great Product Is Character': Vermont in 1927," 43–44.

6. Confronting Irish Catholic Politicians in the Bay State

1. *Boston Herald*, 17 November 1923, 13; *Boston Sunday Advertiser*, 18 November 1923, 2.

2. U.S. Department of Commerce, Bureau of the Census, *Fourteenth Census of the United States Taken in the Year 1920*, vol. 1 (Washington, D.C.: Government Printing Office, 1921), 20, and vol. 2 (1922), 34, 39, 711; U.S. Department of Commerce, Bureau of the Census, *Religious Bodies, 1926*, vol. 2 (Washington, D.C.: Government Printing Office, 1929), 44, 647. Among the foreign-born in Massachusetts in 1920, 14.2 percent were Anglo-Canadians and 10.0 percent were French Canadians. *Fourteenth Census*, 2:711.

3. *General Acts Passed by the General Court of Massachusetts, in the Year 1917* (Boston: Wright and Potter Printing, 1917), chap. 321, pp. 328–29; *General Acts Passed by the General Court of Massachusetts, in the Year 1919* (Boston: Wright and Potter Printing, 1919), chap. 295, pp. 273–74; Edward George Hartmann, *The Movement to Americanize the Immigrant* (New York: Columbia University Press, 1948), 241.

4. *New York Times*, 19 September 1921, 17, 8 February 1923, 16.

5. KKK pamphlet, "A Mobilization of Americans!," Boston Athenaeum Special Collections, Boston; letter of T. A. Jackson, Propagation Department, Northern New England [1920s], originating from Boston but written on national Ku Klux Klan (Atlanta, Ga.) stationery, Boston Athenaeum Special Collections; KKK questionnaire, 192–, Boston Athenaeum Special Collections.

6. *Boston Herald*, 1 June 1922, 8, 27 September 1923, 1, 28 September 1923, 1; *L'Opinion Publique* (Worcester, Mass.), 10 July 1922, 5, 22 September 1923, 5; Charles W. Estus Sr. and John F. McClymer, "The Tribal Twenties," *gå till Amerika: The Swedish Creation of an Ethnic Identity for Worcester, Massachusetts*, ed. Caroline F. Sloat (Worcester: Worcester Historical Museum, 1994), 126; *L'Etoile* (Lowell, Mass.), 24 September 1923, 1; *Boston Daily Advertiser*, 28 September 1923, 2, 6; Albert B. Southwick, "Worcester's Klans and Kleagles," *Once-Told Tales of Worcester County* (Worcester: Worcester Telegram and Gazette, 1985), 137; *Boston Evening Transcript*, 28 September 1923, 2.

7. *Boston Herald*, 27 September 1923, 1, 28 September 1923, 1, 3; *Worcester Evening Post*, 20 October 1924, 1; *L'Etoile*, 25 October 1923. No evidence exists that Farnsworth and other Klan members perceived differences in skin color among Lebanese, Syrian, southern Italian, or other Catholics in New England.

8. Estus and McClymer, "The Tribal Twenties," 125, 126, 130; Kevin L. Hickey, "The Immigrant Klan: A Socio-Economic Profile of the KKK Membership in Worcester, Massachusetts, 1922–25," 6, 8–10, table E, paper presented at the meeting of the American Association of Geographers, Los Angeles, 1981, and shared with the author; Shawn Lay, *Hooded Knights on the Niagara: The Ku Klux Klan in Buffalo, New York* (New York: New York University Press, 1995), 106.

9. *The Fiery Cross* (Indianapolis, Ind.), 1 June 1923, 1; *Boston Herald*, 23 October 1923, 1; *Boston Daily Advertiser*, 24 October 1923, 4; *The Dawn* (Chicago), 27 October 1923, 8; *The Republic* (Boston), 20 January 1923, 1; *California Eagle* (Los Angeles), 27 January 1923, 1. The Ku Klux

Klan also established chapters at universities outside of New England, including Princeton University, in the 1920s. David H. Bennett, "Traditional Nativism's Last Stand: The Ku Klux Klan in the 1920s," in *The Party of Fear: From Nativist Movements to the New Right in American History* (Chapel Hill: University of North Carolina Press, 1988), 229.

10. Lothrop Stoddard, *The Rising Tide of Color Against White World-Supremacy* (New York: Charles Scribner's Sons, 1922), title page, 221, 308; *Boston Sunday Advertiser,* 7 January 1923, 1. Not all of those affiliated with the Klan at Harvard were students, former students, or administrators: a Harvard library janitor who used to speak disparagingly about Irish Catholics approached Clarence Gohdes, a Harvard graduate student, to join the KKK in 1925. See Clarence Gohdes, "The Ku Klux Klan and the Classics," *Georgia Review* 6 (Spring 1953): 18–24.

11. *Boston Sunday Advertiser,* 14 January 1923, 1, 2.

12. *New York Times,* 19 September 1921, 17.

13. *Boston Daily Advertiser,* 16 January 1923, 2; Bruce Bliven, "Boston: The Racial Moralities," *New Republic* 31 (31 May 1922): 15; *The Crusader,* the "Official Organ of Detroit Council, No. 305, K. of C.," 27 April 1922, 1; *Boston Herald,* 26 March 1924, 1.

14. *Boston Daily Advertiser,* 10 January 1923, 2.

15. *Journal of the House of Representatives of the Commonwealth of Massachusetts, 1923* (Boston: Wright and Potter Printing, 1923), 4 January 1923, 30, 8 January 1923, 36; *Montpelier Evening Argus,* 4 December 1922, 1; *Brattleboro Daily Reformer,* 4 December 1922, 1; *Providence Evening Bulletin,* 29 November 1922, 2; Commonwealth of Massachusetts, *A Manual for the Use of the General Court for 1923–1924* (Boston: Wright and Potter, 1923), 484; Massachusetts Legislative Documents, House (1923), No. 219, Boston Public Library, Boston; *Boston Sunday Advertiser,* 14 January 1923, 3.

16. *A Manual for the Use of the General Court for 1923–1924,* 483; Massachusetts Legislative Documents, House (1923), No. 189, No. 190, No. 265, No. 566; *Journal of the House of Representatives, 1923,* 4 January 1923, 30, 8 January 1923, 39, 15 January 1923, 82 and 1024; *Boston Daily Advertiser,* 4 February 1923, 4.

17. *Journal of the House of Representatives, 1923,* 1 February 1923, 208, 219, 249–50, 259–60; *Boston Herald,* 8 February 1923, 13; *Republic,* 17 February 1923, 2.

18. Massachusetts Legislative Documents, House (1923), No. 803; *Boston Herald,* 16 January 1923, 24; *New York Times,* 16 January 1923, 13, 17 January 1923, 8; *Journal of the House of Representatives, 1923,* 16 January 1923, 111–13; *Boston Daily Advertiser,* 17 January 1923, 3; *A Manual for the Use of the General Court for 1923–1924,* 473; *La Tribune* (Woonsocket, R.I.), 17 January 1923, 1.

19. *The Commonwealth of Massachusetts Journal of the Senate for the Year 1923* (Boston: Wright and Potter, 1923), 19 January 1923, 88, 23 January 1923, 106–7, 815; *A Manual for the Use of the General Court for 1923–1924,* 464; Massachusetts Legislative Documents, Senate (1923), Boston Public Library, No. 219; *L'Avenir National* (Manchester, N.H.), 24 January 1923, 1; *Boston Daily Advertiser,* 24 January 1923, 2.

20. Commonwealth of Massachusetts, *A Manual for the Use of the General Court for 1925–1926* (Boston: Wright and Potter, 1925), 485; *Journal of the House of Representatives of the Commonwealth of Massachusetts, 1924* (Boston: n.p., 1924), 2 January 1924, 26, 22 January 1924, 187, 23 January 1924, 192; Massachusetts Legislative Documents, House (1924), Boston Public Library, No. 22, No. 54; *Boston Herald,* 2 August 1924, 2. The Massachusetts House held its last session in 1924 on June 5, and Kelly was not a member of the legislature in 1925, which possibly explains why the body did not take up his proposed bill.

21. *Journal of the House of Representatives of the Commonwealth of Massachusetts, 1925* (Boston: Wright and Potter, 1925), 7 January 1925, 29, 22 January 1925, 146, 24 February 1925, 379–80,

25 February 1925, 396, 397; Massachusetts Legislative Documents, House (1925), Boston Public Library, No. 154, No. 962. In 1927 Rep. John Holmes, a Republican from Brockton, introduced House Bill No. 709, the petition of one Ralph A. Bird, "An Act making it a Felony for any Person to Organize or hold membership in any Secret, Oath-Bound Corporation, Association, Society or Fraternal Benefit Society." While the bill's title might lead one to consider it an anti-Klan measure, the legislation would have prohibited Massachusetts residents from joining societies "whose center of government is in a foreign country or whose chief executive officer is not a citizen of the United States," the very kind of measure the KKK would have supported. The Legal Affairs Committee reported adversely on the bill, and the House accepted its report. Commonwealth of Massachusetts, *A Manual for the Use of the General Court for 1927–1928* (Boston: Wright and Potter, 1927), 489; Massachusetts House documents (1927), Boston Public Library, No. 709; *Journal of the House of Representatives of the Commonwealth of Massachusetts, 1927* (Boston: Wright and Potter, 1927), 18 January 1927, 188, 2 March 1927, 400, 3 March 1927, 419.

22. Commonwealth of Massachusetts, *A Manual for the Use of the General Court for 1929–1930* (Boston: Wright and Potter, 1929), 494; Massachusetts House documents (1929), Boston Public Library, No. 895; *Journal of the House of Representatives of the Commonwealth of Massachusetts, 1929* (Boston: Wright and Potter, 1929), 18 January 1929, 160, 21 February 1929, 371, 385; *New York Times,* 25 May 1919, 19 September 1920.

23. *Fiery Cross,* 9 November 1923, 9; Emerson Hunsberger Loucks, *The Ku Klux Klan in Pennsylvania: A Study in Nativism* (New York: Telegraph Press, 1936), 201–2; *Boston Daily Advertiser,* 16 January 1923, 2; James Michael Curley, *I'd Do It Again: A Record of All My Uproarious Years* (1957; repr., New York: Arno Press, 1976), 147, 158, 364.

24. *Boston Herald,* 18 January 1923, 12, 14 February 1921, 1.

25. *The Dawn,* 10 February 1923, 15; *New York Times,* 29 January 1923, 17; American Civil Liberties Union (ACLU) Archives, Harvard Law School Library, Cambridge, Massachusetts, vol. 229, "Report on Civil Liberty Situation for Week Ending February 3, 1923."

26. *Daily Kennebec Journal* (Augusta), 10 September 1923, 2; *Boston Sunday Herald,* 9 September 1923, 6.

27. *New York Times,* 7 October 1922, 15; *The Dawn,* 21 October 1922, 10; *L'Etoile,* 12 January 1923, 4; *Boston Daily Advertiser,* 17 January 1923, 3.

28. *Boston Evening Transcript,* 29 September 1923, 9; *Boston Herald,* 29 September 1923, 1, 3.

29. *Boston Telegram,* 22 October 1923, 14.

30. *Boston Herald,* 6 October 1923, 22, 23 October 1923, 2; ACLU Archives, vol. 229, "Report on Civil Liberty Situation for Week Ending October 13, 1923"; *New York Times,* 22 October 1923, 25; *Boston Globe,* 31 October 1923, 24.

31. *Boston Herald,* 1 October 1923, 1, 3, 3 October 1923, 2, 7 October 1923, 9.

32. *Nation* 118 (12 March 1924): 270.

33. *Maine Klansman,* 20 March 1924, 3.

34. *Boston Herald,* 27 September 1924, 20.

35. *Boston Daily Advertiser,* 30 September 1924, 2; *L'Etoile,* 8 October 1924; *Boston Sunday Herald,* 19 October 1924, 10.

36. *L'Etoile,* 23 October 1924; J. Joseph Huthmacher, "Ku Klux Years," in *Massachusetts People and Politics, 1919–1933* (Cambridge: Belknap Press of Harvard University Press, 1959), 104–5.

37. *Boston Herald,* 20 April 1924, 1; *La Tribune,* 22 April 1924; *L'Opinion Publique,* 21 April 1924, 1; Huthmacher, "Ku Klux Years," 104–5; Joseph F. Dinneen, "The Kingfish of Massachusetts," *Harpers Magazine* 173 (September 1936): 345.

38. Curley, *I'd Do It Again*, 181–83.

39. *Boston Evening Transcript*, 25 October 1924, 1, 11; *New York Times*, 26 October 1924, 6.

40. *Boston Evening Transcript*, 25 October 1924, 11; *New Bedford (Mass.) Times*, 24 October 1928, 4.

41. *Boston Herald*, 11 June 1925, 1, 4.

42. *Boston Herald*, 12 June 1925, 3, 26 June 1925, 2.

43. *Boston Herald*, 7 July 1925, 16.

44. *Boston Herald*, 10 July 1926, 2; *Boston Daily Advertiser*, 10 July 1926, 6.

45. Curley, *I'd Do It Again*, 188; *Boston Herald*, 3 August 1925, 1.

7. Counterattack by Commonwealth Catholics

1. *Boston Herald*, 16 June 1922, 24.

2. *Boston Sunday Advertiser*, 21 January 1923, 2; *Boston Herald*, 24 January 1923, 1, 6; *Portland (Maine) Press Herald*, 24 January 1923, 2; Hamilton, 22 January 1923, cited in *Sanford (Maine) Tribune and Advocate*, 22 May 1924, 1.

3. *Boston Herald*, 16 December 1922, 18.

4. *Boston Herald*, 27 November 1922, 1, 29 November 1922, 1, 7; *Republic* (Boston), 2 December 1922, 1.

5. *Boston Herald*, 5 December 1922, 18, 21 October 1922, 4; E. M. McNulty, "John Francis Hylan," *New Catholic Encyclopedia* (New York: McGraw-Hill, 1967), 7:284.

6. *Boston Daily Advertiser*, 12 November 1923, 4. Among the Massachusetts members of the National Vigilance Association were the president of Williams College, H. A. Garfield, the president of Wellesley College, Ellen F. Pendleton, and the speaker of the Massachusetts House of Representatives, B. Loring Young. *Boston Daily Advertiser*, 12 November 1923, 4.

7. *Boston Daily Advertiser*, 18 August 1924, 6.

8. *New York Times*, 21 September 1924, 25.

9. Thomas Carens, "Convention Has Klan Problem: Make-up of State G.O.P. Platform Committee Points to Action," *Boston Herald*, 12 September 1924, 8; *New York Times*, 21 September 1924, 25.

10. Melvyn Stokes, *D. W. Griffith's The Birth of a Nation: A History of "The Most Controversial Motion Picture of All Time"* (New York: Oxford University Press, 2007), 146; *Biddeford (Maine) Daily Journal*, 8 September 1924, 5.

11. *La Tribune* (Woonsocket, R.I.), 17 January 1923, 1; *L'Etoile* (Lowell, Mass.), 16 January 1923, 1; *L'Impartial* (Nashua, N.H.), 18 January 1923; *Boston Daily Advertiser*, 16 January 1923, 3, 17 January 1923, 2, 18 January 1923, 13; *Le Citoyen* (Haverhill, Mass.), 18 January 1923, 1; Susan Mann Trofimenkoff, *Action Française: French Canadian Nationalism in the Twenties* (Toronto: University of Toronto Press, 1975), 76–79; *Imperial Night-Hawk* (Atlanta, Ga.), 4 April 1923, 8.

12. *Boston Herald*, 21 October 1922, 4, 25 September 1924, 10; *Boston Daily Advertiser*, 24 January 1923, 2; *L'Etoile*, 25 September 1924, 1.

13. *Boston Sunday Advertiser*, 7 January 1923, 3, 14 January 1923, 2; *L'Avenir National* (Manchester, N.H.), 6 January 1923, 8, 24 November 1924, 1; William Wolkovich-Valkavicius, "The Ku Klux Klan in the Nashoba Valley," *Historical Journal of Massachusetts* 18 (Winter 1990): 71–72; Charles H. Smith, Manager, Smithsonian Bureau of Investigation, Boston, to William Cardinal O'Connell, Boston, 10 January 1923, Ku Klux Klan file, Archdiocese of Boston Archives, Brighton, Massachusetts; *Boston Daily Advertiser*, 19 January 1923, 2, 3.

14. *Boston Daily Advertiser*, 24 January 1923, 4.

15. *Le Citoyen,* 7 September 1923; *L'Etoile,* 15 August 1923, 1, 5.

16. *L'Opinion Publique* (Worcester, Mass.), 15 May 1924, 1; *Boston Daily Advertiser,* 14 July 1924, 2.

17. *Boston Herald,* 21 July 1924, 1.

18. *L'Etoile,* 25 July 1924, 1, 6; *L'Opinion Publique,* 26 July 1924, 5; *Le Citoyen,* 1 August 1924, 1.

19. *Boston Sunday Herald,* 27 July 1924, 1, 4.

20. *New York Times,* 31 July 1924, 1; *Boston Herald,* 31 July 1924, 1, 1 August 1924, 1; *L'Etoile,* 31 July 1924, 1, 3; *Biddeford Daily Journal,* 31 July 1924, 1; *L'Opinion Publique,* 31 July 1924, 6; *Boston Sunday Herald,* 3 August 1924, 8.

21. *Le Courier de Lawrence (Mass.),* 8 August 1924, 4; *L'Etoile,* 1 August 1924, 6; *Boston Herald,* 1 August 1924, 1.

22. *Boston Herald,* 1 August 1924, 1; *New York Times,* 1 August 1924, 13, 19 August 1924, 36; *L'Etoile,* 1 August 1924, 6.

23. *Boston Daily Advertiser,* 4 October 1924, 8; *L'Opinion Publique,* 6 August 1924, 1.

24. *L'Opinion Publique,* 24 May 1924, 1, 30 July 1924, 1; *Boston Herald,* 30 July 1924, 1, 31 July 1924, 2; *New York Times,* 30 July 1924, 1, 31 July 1924, 1; *L'Etoile,* 31 July 1924, 1.

25. *Washington Post,* 30 July 1924, 1; *L'Etoile,* 31 July 1924, 1, 4; *L'Opinion Publique,* 30 July 1924, 4, 31 July 1924, 1; *Boston Globe,* 30 July 1924, 7.

26. *New York Times,* 2 August 1924, 10; *Boston Herald,* 2 August 1924, 2; *Portland Press Herald,* 2 August 1924, 2.

27. *L'Etoile,* 1 August 1924, 1, 6; Commonwealth of Massachusetts, *A Manual for the Use of the General Court for 1923–1924* (Boston: Wright and Potter, 1923), 478; Commonwealth of Massachusetts, *Journal of the Senate for the Year 1925* (Boston: Wright and Potter, 1925), 45, 817; Chapter 284, *Acts and Resolves Passed by the General Court of Massachusetts in the Year 1925* (Boston: Wright and Potter, 1925), 323–25.

28. *New York Times,* 2 August 1924, 10; *Boston Herald,* 2 August 1924, 2; *Boston Daily Advertiser,* 2 August 1924, 19.

29. *Boston Herald,* 2 August 1924, 1; *Biddeford Daily Journal,* 2 August 1924, 1; *New York Times,* 2 August 1924, 10. It is unclear why the French-language press reported far fewer numbers, with *L'Etoile* (2 August 1924, 1) indicating that there were 100 Klan members and *L'Opinion Publique* (2 August 1924, 1) about 350.

30. *Boston Herald,* 2 August 1924, 1; *New York Times,* 2 August 1924, 10; *Biddeford Daily Journal,* 2 August 1924, 1.

31. *L'Opinion Publique,* 20 September 1924, 1; *L'Impartial,* 23 September 1924, 1.

32. *L'Opinion Publique,* 18 October 1924, 1; *Boston Sunday Herald,* 19 October 1924, 1, 10; *New York Times,* 19 October 1924, 1; *Boston Herald,* 20 October 1924, 1; *Worcester (Mass.) Sunday Telegram,* 19 October 1924, 1A, 11B; *Worcester (Mass.) Evening Post,* 21 October 1924, 1; "Klan Plane Crippled by Shot From Crowd," *Richmond-Times Dispatch* (Richmond, Va.), 19 October 1924, 1.

33. *New York Times,* 19 October 1924, 1, 20 October 1924, 18; *Boston Sunday Herald,* 19 October 1924, 1; *L'Etoile,* 20 October 1924, 1; *Boston Daily Advertiser,* 20 October 1924, 2; *Biddeford Daily Journal,* 20 October 1924, 2.

34. *L'Opinion Publique,* 11 October 1924, 2; *Boston Daily Advertiser,* 19 December 1924, 6.

35. *L'Opinion Publique,* 29 October 1924, 1, 30 October 1924, 1.

36. *La Tribune,* 15 April 1925; *New York Times,* 29 April 1925, 23; *Boston Herald,* 29 April 1925, 1, 30 April 1925, 7; *L'Opinion Publique,* 29 April 1925, 1; *New York World,* 30 April 1925, 2. One month later, when the Ku Klux Klan returned to Northbridge, there were six hundred of them,

and they took the offensive: during another clash with their foes, Klan members severely beat two anti-Klan sympathizers and turned over the vehicles of two of them. *New York Times,* 20 May 1925, 10.

37. *La Tribune,* 1 May 1925; *L'Opinion Publique,* 1 May 1925, 1; *Gardner (Mass.) News,* 1 May 1925, 1.

38. *Boston Herald,* 2 May 1925, 1; *La Justice de Sanford (Maine),* 7 May 1925, 1; *L'Opinion Publique,* 2 May 1925, 1.

39. *L'Opinion Publique,* 4 May 1925, 1, 6 May 1925, 1, 8 May 1925, 1; *New York Times,* 4 May 1925, 14; *Boston Herald,* 4 May 1925, 1; *Boston Daily Advertiser,* 4 May 1925, 8.

40. *Boston Herald,* 8 June 1925, 1; *L'Etoile,* 9 June 1925; *Kloran of the Knights of the Great Forest K-TRIO* (Atlanta: Knights of the Ku Klux Klan, 1928), 45, Vermont Historical Society Library, Vermont History Center, Barre; *The Republic* (Boston), 13 June 1925, 2.

41. *Boston Herald,* 11 June 1925, 4; *L'Opinion Publique,* 10 June 1925, 1, 11 June 1925, 1, 8; *Biddeford Daily Journal,* 10 June 1925, 1; *New York Times,* 21 June 1925, 15; *Boston Sunday Advertiser,* 21 June 1925, 2; *L'Etoile,* 11 June 1925.

42. *L'Opinion Publique,* 12 June 1925, 1, 6; *Boston Herald,* 12 June 1925, 3, 13 June 1925, 3.

43. *L'Etoile,* 16 July 1925; *L'Opinion Publique,* 15 July 1925, 1.

44. *New York Times,* 3 August 1925, 1, 13 August 1925, 21; *L'Opinion Publique,* 3 August 1925, 1; *Boston Herald,* 3 August 1925, 1, 2; *La Tribune,* 3 August 1925, 1; *L'Avenir National,* 12 August 1925, 8; *Boston Globe,* 24 September 1925, 10.

45. *La Tribune,* 11 August 1925, 1; *Boston Herald,* 12 August 1925, 4.

46. *La Tribune,* 11 August 1925, 1; *Boston Herald,* 12 August 1925, 4; *New York Times,* 12 August 1925, 23; *Boston Globe,* 11 August 1925, 1, 19 August 1925, 17.

47. *La Tribune,* 12 August 1925, 1; *Providence (R.I.) Journal,* 21 June 1927, 1.

48. *Boston Herald,* 28 May 1925, 1, 4, 18 June 1925, 12, 13 August 1925, 1, 14 August 1925, 13; *New York Times,* 13 August 1925, 21; *Boston Globe,* 13 August 1925, 2.

49. *Boston Post,* 15 August 1925, 10.

50. John S. Codman, Boston, Massachusetts, American Civil Liberties Union, to His Excellency, [Alvan T. Fuller], The Governor, 14 August 1925, American Civil Liberties Union Archives, vol. 286, Harvard Law School Library, Cambridge, Massachusetts; *Boston Evening Transcript,* 1 August 1924, 5; *Boston Post,* 15 August 1925, 3; James Michael Curley, *I'd Do It Again: A Record of All My Uproarious Years* (1957; repr., New York: Arno Press, 1976), 188; *Boston Herald,* 3 August 1925, 1.

51. *New York Times,* 19 September 1925, 9; *Boston Herald,* 19 September 1925, 1, 6; *Biddeford Daily Journal,* 19 September 1925, 1; *L'Opinion Publique,* 19 September 1925, 1; *New York World,* 20 September 1925, 10; *Providence Evening Bulletin,* 19 September 1925, 4; *L'Etoile,* 19 September 1925, 1; *Boston Evening Globe,* 19 September 1925, 1.

52. *Boston Herald,* 9 September 1925, 36; *Boston Globe,* 9 September 1925, 2.

53. *Washington Post,* 2 November 1930, 14; *New York Times,* 21 February 1926, sec. 8, 1.

54. *L'Etoile,* 30 March 1926; *L'Opinion Publique,* 27 March 1926, 1.

55. *Fellowship Forum* (Washington, D.C.), 17 July 1926, 6; Kathleen M. Blee, *Women of the Klan: Racism and Gender in the 1920s* (Berkeley: University of California Press, 1991), 27–28; *New York Times,* 6 September 1926, 30; *Boston Herald,* 7 September 1926, 13.

56. *Biddeford Daily Journal,* 2 October 1926, 1.

57. *Boston Daily Advertiser,* 16 February 1927, 3; *Boston Herald,* 16 February 1927, 1.

58. *New York Times,* 13 June 1927, 21; Duane Lockard, *New England State Politics* (Princeton, N.J.: Princeton University Press, 1959), 123; David M. Chalmers, *Hooded Americanism: The History of the Ku Klux Klan,* 3rd ed. (1981; repr., Durham, N.C.: Duke University Press, 1987),

206. Walsh served as governor of Massachusetts from 1916 to 1919 and as a U.S. senator from 1919 to 1947. Lockard, *New England State Politics,* 128.

59. *Kourier Magazine* (Atlanta, Ga.) 3, no. 3 (February 1927): 8–11.

60. *Washington Post,* 18 March 1929, 1; *New York Times,* 18 March 1929, 8, 19 March 1929, 12; John Temple Graves II, "Blow to Klan Seen In Heflin's Defeat," *New York Times,* 9 January 1938, sec. 4, 7.

61. *New York Times,* 25 April 1929, 1. After the Senate debate on Heflin's resolution, the *New York Times* (25 April 1929, 6) reported it had learned that the bottle-throwing incident, upon which Heflin based his resolution, had taken place when local youths tried to avenge a grudge against the police sergeant for his aggressive policing and was not directed at Heflin.

62. *New York Times,* 25 April 1929, 1, 6; 2 May 1929, 1.

63. *Kourier Magazine* 7, no. 1 (December 1930): 28; 7, no. 2 (January 1931): 47–48; 7, no. 7 (June 1931): 35; 7, no. 8 (July 1931): 38.

64. *Kourier Magazine,* 7, no. 2 (January 1931): 19–20; 7, no. 12 (November 1931): 14, 33; *The Kourier* (Atlanta, Ga.) 9, no. 5 (April 1933): 42; 9, no. 6 (May 1933): 32; George K. Gardner and Charles D. Post, "The Constitutional Questions Raised by the Flag Salute and Teachers' Oath Acts in Massachusetts," *Boston University Law Review* 16 (November 1936): 805; Chapter 370, *Acts and Resolves Passed by the General Court of Massachusetts in the Year 1935* (Boston: Jordan and More, 1935), 412.

65. Ronald A. Petrin, *French Canadians in Massachusetts Politics, 1885–1915: Ethnicity and Political Pragmatism* (Philadelphia: Balch Institute Press, 1990), 164, 168.

66. O'Connell's biography provides no information to suggest that the prelate intervened with the KKK in Massachusetts. Archdiocesan files contain a small amount of correspondence on the Ku Klux Klan from individuals such as Curley, who passed along KKK literature, and Detective Charles Smith, who informed O'Connell of anti-Catholic activities the KKK had pursued in Louisiana that they might attempt in Massachusetts. While the files do not offer evidence of any anti-Klan activities on O'Connell's part, they do underscore his interest in Americanization. In May 1926 O'Connell joined as a life associate member the Loyal Legion of America, a nonsectarian society that supported the post–World War I Americanization movement; as a fraternal benefit society that advocated "AMERICANISM, PATRIOTISM, LOYALTY," in the pursuit of the constitutional principles of "freedom of individual action, speech and religious liberty," the Loyal Legion had the following requirement for membership: "Belief in supreme being, an American, white citizen of good character or one who has first papers." As the bishop of Portland (1901–6), O'Connell had come into conflict with Franco-Americans in Maine who feared he was trying to anglicize the state's French-speaking parishes. Through their French-language press, Franco-Americans in Massachusetts would have known of this tension with the Irish prelate. James M. O'Toole, *Militant and Triumphant: William Henry O'Connell and the Catholic Church in Boston, 1859–1944* (Notre Dame, Ind.: University of Notre Dame Press, 1992; James M. Curley, Mayor of Boston, to Monsignor Richard J. Haberlin [secretary, Archdiocese of Boston], Boston, 22 July 1924, KKK file, Archdiocese of Boston; Charles H. Smith, Manager, Smithsonian Bureau of Investigation, Boston, to William Cardinal O'Connell, Boston, 10 January 1923, KKK file, Archdiocese of Boston; Charles H. Smith, Manager, Smith Detective and Research Bureau, Boston, to William Cardinal O'Connell, Boston, 16 August 1924, KKK file, Archdiocese of Boston; pamphlet on Loyal Legion of America, Inc., Loyal Legion of America file, Archdiocese of Boston; typescript flyer on Loyal Legion of America, Loyal Legion of America file, Archdiocese of Boston; B. J. Boshier, Grand Supreme Organizer, Loyal Legion of America to Cardinal McConnell [*sic*], Boston, 15 May 1926, Loyal Legion of America file, Archdiocese of Boston; R. J. Haberlin, Secretary, to Brian J.

Boshier, Loyal Legion of America, New York City, 25 May 1926, Loyal Legion of America file, Archdiocese of Boston; certificate of enrollment of Cardinal O'Connell in the Loyal Legion of America, Loyal Legion of America file, Archdiocese of Boston; Mark Paul Richard, *Loyal but French: The Negotiation of Identity by French-Canadian Descendants in the United States* (East Lansing: Michigan State University Press, 2008), 94–96.

67. On these ethnic conflicts, see C. Stewart Doty, *The First Franco-Americans: New England Life Histories from the Federal Writers' Project, 1938–1939* (Orono: University of Maine Press, 1985), 154; Yves Roby, *Les Franco-Américains de la Nouvelle-Angleterre (1776–1930)* (Sillery, Québec: Septentrion, 1990), 162–69, 176–78.

68. David M. Chalmers, *Hooded Americanism*, 298; Todd Tucker, *Notre Dame vs. the Klan: How the Fighting Irish Defeated the Ku Klux Klan* (Chicago: Loyola Press, 2004); David J. Goldberg, "Unmasking the Ku Klux Klan: The Northern Movement against the KKK, 1920–1925," *Journal of American Ethnic History* 15 (Summer 1996): 42–43; William D. Jenkins, *Steel Valley Klan: The Ku Klux Klan in Ohio's Mahoning Valley* (Kent, Ohio: Kent State University Press, 1990), 137–39. See Nancy MacLean, *Behind the Mask of Chivalry: The Making of the Second Ku Klux Klan* (New York: Oxford University Press, 1994), 181–88, for an exploration of the similarities and differences between the Ku Klux Klan and fascists in Europe during the 1930s, as well as her intriguing conclusion about the role minorities in the United States played in preserving democracy during this volatile period in world history. MacLean argues, for example, that the KKK, German National Socialism, and Italian Fascism were all postwar movements that capitalized on economic distress and class conflicts, all had elite support as well as police and armed forces assistance to cover their acts of terror, and each movement maintained its own ritualized demonstrations of power. See also Rory McVeigh, *The Rise of the Ku Klux Klan: Right-Wing Movements and National Politics* (Minneapolis: University of Minnesota Press, 2009), 62–63, 87.

8. Attempt to Americanize the Ocean State

1. *La Tribune* (Woonsocket), 5 August 1924; C. Stewart Doty, *The First Franco-Americans: New England Life Histories from the Federal Writers' Project, 1938–1939* (Orono: University of Maine at Orono Press, 1985), 156; Norman W. Smith, "The Ku Klux Klan in Rhode Island," *Rhode Island History* 37 (May 1978): 44; *Rhode Island Klansman* 1, no. 1, cited in *Providence News*, 16 July 1924, 1–2; U.S. Department of Commerce, Bureau of the Census, *Religious Bodies, 1926*, vol. 2 (Washington, D.C.: Government Printing Office, 1929), 44, 647; U.S. Department of Commerce, Bureau of the Census, *Fourteenth Census of the United States Taken in the Year 1920*, vol. 2 (Washington, D.C.: Government Printing Office, 1922), 40.

2. Edward George Hartman, "The Post-War Americanization Drive," in *The Movement to Americanize the Immigrant* (New York: Columbia University Press, 1948), 242; *Acts and Resolves Passed by the General Assembly of the State of Rhode Island and Providence Plantations at the January Session, A.D. 1919* (Pawtucket: Pawtucket Linotyping, 1919), 212–15.

3. Annals of Our Lady of Lourdes, Providence, 25 September 1920, Historical Archives of the Religious of Jesus and Mary, Institut Français, Assumption College, Worcester, Mass.

4. *Manual with Rules and Orders for the Use of the General Assembly of the State of Rhode Island* (hereafter *Rhode Island Manual*), *1921–1922* (Providence: Secretary of State, 1922), 416; House Bills, 1922, Rhode Island State Archives, Providence (hereafter RISA); *Acts and Resolves Passed by the General Assembly of the State of Rhode Island and Providence Plantations at its January Session, A.D. 1922* (Providence: E. L. Freeman, 1922), 164–65; Ephémérides, vol. 20, 4, L'Union Saint-Jean-Baptiste d'Amérique Archives, Assumption College Special Collections, Worcester,

Mass.; Evelyn Savidge Sterne, *Ballots & Bibles: Ethnic Politics and the Catholic Church in Providence* (Ithaca, N.Y.: Cornell University Press, 2004), 221; Elie Vézina [general secretary, L'Union Saint-Jean-Baptiste d'Amérique, Woonsocket] to Hon. Emery J. SanSouci [governor of Rhode Island], Providence, 24 April 1922, in Ephémérides, vol. 20, 8. Eighteen mutual-benefit societies from throughout New England had merged to form l'Union Saint-Jean-Baptiste in 1900. Gerard J. Brault, *The French-Canadian Heritage in New England* (Hanover, N.H.: University Press of New England, 1986), 77.

    5. *Rhode Island Manual, 1921–1922,* 394; Doty, *The First Franco-Americans,* 156; Duane Lockard, *New England State Politics* (Princeton, N.J.: Princeton University Press, 1959), 177, 177n, 197; *Manual with Rules and Orders for the Use of the General Assembly of the State of Rhode Island, 1925–1926* (Providence: Secretary of State, 1926), 411; Brault, *The French-Canadian Heritage in New England,* 67. A banker, Aram Pothier served in the Rhode Island legislature in 1887 and 1888 and became the first Franco-American mayor of Woonsocket (and in all of New England) in 1894 and 1895; Pothier served as lieutenant governor in 1897 and 1898 and as a member of the state board of education from 1907 to 1909; he won eight terms as governor of Rhode Island, serving from 1909 to 1915 and again from 1925 until his death in 1928. Born in Maine, Emery SanSouci, a merchant, served on the common council of Providence from 1901 to 1906, as Pothier's aide-de-camp from 1909 to 1914, and as lieutenant governor from 1915 to 1921, before becoming a one-term governor from 1921 to 1923. *Guide Officiel des Franco-Américains, 1922,* 4th ed. (Fall River, Mass.: Albert A. Bélanger, 1922), 225, 233; *Manual with Rules and Orders for the Use of the General Assembly of the State of Rhode Island, 1925–1926* (Providence: Secretary of State, 1926), 411; Richard Sherman Sorrell, "The Sentinelle Affair (1924–1929) and Militant *Survivance:* The Franco-American Experience in Woonsocket, Rhode Island" (Ph.D. diss., State University of New York at Buffalo, 1976), 123, 124; Brault, *The French-Canadian Heritage in New England,* 67, 158; *Rhode Island Manual, 1921–1922,* 394; *L'Union* (Woonsocket), January 1921, 1.

    6. Emery J. SanSouci, Governor, To the Honorable Secretary of State, Providence, Rhode Island, 3 May 1922, in Ephémérides, vol. 20, 19; Elie Vézina, Secretary General, [l'Union Saint-Jean-Baptiste d'Amérique], Woonsocket, to His Excellency Emery J. Sansouci [governor of Rhode Island], Providence, 3 May 1922, in Ephémérides, vol. 20, 20–21; Sterne, *Ballots & Bibles,* 222; newspaper articles in English and French inserted into the Ephémérides, vol. 20, 23–41; Sorrell, "The Sentinelle Affair (1924–1929) and Militant *Survivance,*" 166, 247.

    7. *Providence Evening Bulletin,* 12 December 1922, 4; *Providence Journal,* 28 December 1922, 4; *L'Etoile* (Lowell, Mass.), 18 January 1923, 1.

    8. *Providence News,* 13 January 1923, 1; *Providence Evening Bulletin,* 13 January 1923, 5; *Boston Sunday Advertiser,* 14 January 1923, 2; *Manual with Rules and Orders for the Use of the General Assembly of the State of Rhode Island, 1923–1924* (Providence: Secretary of State, 1924), 398.

    9. *Boston Daily Advertiser,* 18 January 1923, 3, 19 January 1923, 3; *Providence Evening Bulletin,* 17 January 1923, 3, 18 January 1923, 4, 19 January 1923, sec. 2, 5; *L'Etoile,* 18 January 1923, 1; *Providence Journal,* 18 January 1923, 9; David J. Goldberg, "The Rapid Rise and the Swift Decline of the Ku Klux Klan," in *Discontented America: The United States in the 1920s* (Baltimore: Johns Hopkins University Press, 1999), 123. Thomas R. Pegram reveals that, while the KKK opposed certain films that went against its sensibilities of white supremacy and Protestantism, Klan production companies emerged in the Midwest to develop films to promote white Protestant community. Pegram, *One Hundred Percent American: The Rebirth and Decline of the Ku Klux Klan in the 1920s* (Chicago: Ivan R. Dee, 2011), 29–31.

    10. *Boston Daily Advertiser,* 20 January 1923, 3.

11. *Providence Journal,* 5 February 1923, 2.

12. *Boston Daily Advertiser,* 15 January 1923, 4.

13. *Rhode Island Manual, 1923–1924,* 405, 414; House Bills, 1923–24, RISA. Lamarre and Belhumeur drafted the legislation with the assistance of Lt. Gov. Felix A. Toupin, a Democrat from Lincoln, and Eugene L. Jalbert, president of the Woonsocket-based American Federation of French Catholic Societies. The Lamarre-Belhumeur bill garnered the endorsements of fourteen Democratic members of the Rhode Island House of Representatives, all with Franco-American surnames and representing the communities of Woonsocket, Central Falls, Warren, Lincoln, Burrillville, and Pawtucket; the bill also gained the endorsement of a Franco-American state senator from Pawtucket. *Providence Journal,* 7 February 1923, 2; *Rhode Island Manual, 1923–1924,* 396.

14. English-language newspaper clipping dated 23 February 1923, inserted into Ephémérides, vol. 20, 42; Elie Vézina, Secrétaire général, l'Union St. Jean-Baptiste d'Amérique, Woonsocket, aux Présidents et Presidentes des Conseils du Rhode Island, 15 March 1923, in Ephémérides, vol. 20, 49.

15. *Providence News,* 21 April 1923, 1; *Providence Journal,* 8 June 1923, 3; *Rhode Island Manual, 1923–1924,* 309, 398; Senate bills, RISA, 1923.

16. *Providence News,* 21 April 1923, 1.

17. *Providence Evening Bulletin,* 3 January 1923, 3, 17 January 1923, 2; House bills, 1923, RISA; *Providence Journal,* 4 January 1923, 2, 18 January 1923, 22, 14 December 1923, 15; *Boston Daily Advertiser,* 18 January 1923, 3.

18. *Rhode Island Manual, 1923–1924,* 396; *Providence Journal,* 16 January 1923, 2, 21 January 1923, 6, 22 January 1923, 2; *La Tribune,* 16 January 1923, 1; *Providence Evening Bulletin,* 1 February 1923, sec. 3, 6.

19. *Providence Journal,* 18 September 1923, 12; *Providence Evening Bulletin,* 4 December 1923, 4.

20. *Providence Journal,* 20 October 1923, 22; *Providence Evening Bulletin,* 19 October 1923, 1.

21. *Providence Journal,* 25 November 1923, sec. 3, 2.

22. *Providence Journal,* 8 December 1923, 1, 9 December 1923, 1, 4, 11 December 1923, 1; *New York Times,* 8 December 1923, 11; *Providence Sunday Journal,* 9 December 1923, sec. 3, 2; Sterne, *Ballots & Bibles,* 97, 116, 138; "Mayors of the City of Providence," online at http://cityof. providenceri.com/CityHall/tableofcontents.html; *Providence Evening Bulletin,* 10 December 1923, 3, 11 December 1923, 3.

23. *Providence News,* 10 December 1923, 1.

24. *Rhode Island Manual, 1923–1924,* 413; House bills, 1924, RISA; *Acts and Resolves Passed by the General Assembly of the State of Rhode Island and Providence Plantations at the January Session, A.D. 1924* (Providence: E. L. Freeman, 1925 [*sic*]), 40, 41; *Providence Journal,* 2 February 1924, 13; *Providence Evening Bulletin,* 7 February 1924, 1.

25. *Rhode Island Manual, 1923–1924,* 407, 420; House bills, 1924, RISA.

26. *Providence Journal,* 18 February 1924, 4, 27 February 1924, 17; Smith, "The Ku Klux Klan in Rhode Island," 36; *Providence Visitor,* 21 February 1924, 6; *Providence Evening Bulletin,* 29 February 1924, 8.

27. *Providence News,* 13 February 1924, 1, 2, 25 February 1924, 1; *Fourteenth Census of the United States Taken in the Year 1920,* vol. 2, 40. The Rhode Island Klan counted among its members at least one lawmaker, the state senator Charles S. Weaver, who in 1927 introduced a bill against miscegenation. Although Maine and Connecticut also introduced miscegenation bills likely inspired by the KKK in 1927, no measure passed. Joseph W. Sullivan, "Rhode

Island's Invisible Empire: A Demographic Glimpse into the Ku Klux Klan," *Rhode Island History* 47, no. 2 (1989): 76; Peggy Pascoe, *What Comes Naturally: Miscegenation Law and the Making of Race in America* (New York: Oxford University Press, 2009), 181–82.

28. *Providence News,* 15 February 1924, 1, 1 March 1924, 1; *Rhode Island Pendulum,* 6 March 1924, 1; *New York World,* 7 June 1924, 4; *Providence Evening Bulletin,* 16 August 1924, 1; *Providence Journal,* 21 June 1927, 1.

29. *Providence News,* 26 February 1924, 1, 1 March 1924, 1.

30. *Providence Sunday Journal,* 2 March 1924, 6.

31. *Providence Journal,* 24 March 1924, 2.

32. *East Greenwich, North Kingstown, and Warwick, Rhode Island, Directory, 1922* (Salem, Mass.: Charles H. Dunham, 1922), 68; *Dunham's East Greenwich, North Kingstown, and Warwick, Rhode Island, Directory, 1925* (Salem, Mass.: Charles H. Dunham, 1925), 58; *Rhode Island Pendulum,* 10 April 1924, 1, n.p.

33. *Providence Journal,* 11 April 1924, 1–2; *La Tribune,* 11 April 1924.

34. *Providence Evening Bulletin,* 7 April 1924, 8; *Providence Journal,* 8 April 1924, 5.

35. *Providence Journal,* 9 April 1924, 5.

36. *Providence Journal,* 26 June 1924, 1, 29 June 1924, 1, 2; *Providence News,* 25 June 1924, 3; Harvey [Almy Baker] to Marion [Baker], [June 27, 1924], Harvey Almy Baker Papers, Rhode Island Historical Society (hereafter RIHS), Providence, Rhode Island; William G. McAdoo, Los Angeles, California, to Harvey A. Baker, Providence, Rhode Island, 2 June 1924, Harvey Almy Baker Papers, RIHS; "Harvey Almy Baker," typescript, Harvey Almy Baker Papers, RIHS; *Providence Evening Bulletin,* 1 July 1924, sec. 3, 2.

37. *Providence Sunday Journal,* 22 June 1924, 7; *Providence News,* 23 June 1924, 1; *Providence Evening Bulletin,* 23 June 1924, sec. 2, 6.

38. *Providence News,* 27 June 1924, 5, 30 June 1924, 2; U.S. Department of Commerce, Bureau of the Census, *Fourteenth Census of the United States Taken in the Year 1920,* vol. 1 (Washington, D.C.: Government Printing Office, 1921), 46–47. Here I differ slightly with Norman W. Smith, who argues that the Rhode Island Klan was a rural movement. In 1920 the Bureau of the Census classified towns or cities with a population of twenty-five hundred or more people as urban. The urbanization of the other New England states in 1920 was as follows: Vermont, 31.2 percent; Maine, 39.0 percent; New Hampshire, 63.1 percent; Connecticut, 67.8 percent; and Massachusetts, 94.8 percent. Smith, "The Ku Klux Klan in Rhode Island," 43; *Fourteenth Census of the United States Taken in the Year 1920,* vol. 1, 43, 46–47.

39. *Providence News,* 27 June 1924, 5; *Fourteenth Census,* vol. 2, 711.

40. *Providence News,* 25 June 1924, 1, 20; *La Sentinelle* (Woonsocket), 28 June 1924, 1; Ku Klux Klan membership card, Ernest M. Verry Papers, RIHS; *Providence Journal,* 25 June 1924, 3.

41. *Providence News,* 26 June 1924, 4; Rhode Island Visitors Network, "Washington County, Rhode Island," n.d., www.rhodeislandvisitorsnetwork.com; Richard Sherman Sorrell, "The Sentinelle Affair (1924–1929) and Militant *Survivance,*" 108; Richard S. Sorrell, "Sentinelle Affair (1924–1929)—Religion and Militant Survivance in Woonsocket, Rhode Island," *Rhode Island History* 36 (1977): 76; *Woonsocket Call and Evening Reporter,* 28 July 1924, 1; *La Tribune,* 1 August 1924.

42. *Providence Evening Bulletin,* 28 July 1924, 7; *Woonsocket Call and Evening Reporter,* 28 July 1924, 1; *Providence Sunday Journal,* 27 July 1924, 2.

43. *La Tribune,* 5 August 1924, 6 August 1924; *Woonsocket Call and Evening Reporter,* 5 August 1924, 2; *Providence Journal,* 7 August 1924, 2.

44. *Boston Daily Advertiser,* 6 August 1924, 6; *Woonsocket Call and Evening Reporter,* 5 August

1924, 1; *L'Etoile,* 6 August 1924, 1; *New York Times,* 6 August 1924, 17; *L'Opinion Publique* (Worcester, Mass.), 6 August 1924, 1; *La Tribune,* 5 August 1924; *Providence Journal,* 6 August 1924, 2, 7 August 1924, 2; *Providence Evening Bulletin,* 6 August 1924, 6; *L'Avenir National* (Manchester, N.H.), 6 August 1924, 1.

45. Lucille B. Milner, Field Secretary, American Civil Liberties Union, New York, to Lucien C. Sansouci, Woonsocket, 20 August 1924, ACLU Archives, vol. 266, Harvard Law School Library, Cambridge; Lucien C. Sansouci, Woonsocket, to Lucille B. Milner, Field Secretary, ACLU, New York, 4 September 1924, ACLU Archives, vol. 266; [Lucille B. Milner], Field Secretary, ACLU, New York, to Thomas Curran, Providence, 9 September 1924, ACLU Archives, vol. 266.

46. *La Sentinelle,* 6 August 1924, 8.

47. *New York World,* 28 August 1924, 13.

48. John Higham, *Strangers in the Land: Patterns of American Nativism, 1860–1925* (1955; repr., New Brunswick, N.J.: Rutgers University Press, 1992), 294–95; Kathleen M. Blee, *Women of the Klan: Racism and Gender in the 1920s* (Berkeley: University of California Press, 1991), 93–98.

49. *Providence News,* 8 September 1924, 1; *Rhode Island Pendulum,* 27 November 1924; Nancy MacLean, *Behind the Mask of Chivalry: The Making of the Second Ku Klux Klan* (New York: Oxford University Press, 1994), xiii.

50. *Providence News,* 8 September 1924, 1, 9 September 1924, 1; *Providence Evening Bulletin,* 16 August 1924, 1; *Providence Journal,* 20 August 1924, 1. After Westervelt's departure as the leader of the Rhode Island Klan, Harry T. Lutterman of Darien, Conn., headed the organization of both states. *Providence Journal,* 21 June 1927, 1; *New York Times,* 6 December 1924, 11.

51. *Rhode Island Pendulum,* 18 September 1924, 1; *Providence News,* 9 September 1924, 1; *Providence Journal,* 30 December 1924, 4.

52. *Providence Journal,* 14 July 1924, 3; *Providence News,* 9 September 1924, 2, 27 October 1924, 1, 2; *Rhode Island Pendulum,* 18 September 1924, 1; "Jesse Houghton Metcalf," Biographical Directory of the United States Congress, 1774–Present, bioguide.congress.gov. Founded by the former Imperial Wizard William J. Simmons, the Kamelia rivaled the organization of the Women of the Ku Ku Klan. Incidentally, Jesse Metcalf won both elections on November 4, 1924, one to complete the unexpired term of his predecessor, who died in office, and the other to a full term of his own, beginning in March 1925. Metcalf served Rhode Island in the U.S. Senate from 1924 to 1937. Pegram, *One Hundred Percent American,* 26; "Jesse Houghton Metcalf," bioguide.congress.gov.

53. *Providence News,* 31 October 1924, 16.

9. Infiltrating the Rhode Island Militia and Implication in the Sentinelle Affair

1. *Providence Journal,* 17 March 1928, 1.

2. Richard Sherman Sorrell, "The Sentinelle Affair (1924–1929) and Militant *Survivance:* The Franco-American Experience in Woonsocket, Rhode Island" (Ph.D. diss., State University of New York at Buffalo, 1976), 167; *Manual with Rules and Orders for the Use of the General Assembly of the State of Rhode Island* (hereafter *Rhode Island Manual*), *1925–1926* (Providence: Secretary of State, 1926), 434; House Bills, 1925, Rhode Island State Archives, Providence (hereafter RISA). Edouard Belhumeur was born in St. Felix de Valois, Québec, but was educated in Massachusetts. Henri Nesbitt was born in Bathurst, New Brunswick, and was educated in the grammar schools of Québec City; a compositor, he "has been employed on the leading French and English newspapers of the Province of Quebec, as well as many of the leading dailies in this

country," noted the *Rhode Island Manual.* Their backgrounds suggest the important position the French language held in their lives. Nesbitt joined the General Assembly in January 1925, at which point Albert J. Lamarre no longer served. *Rhode Island Manual, 1925–1926,* 364, 366, 421, 434.

3. *Acts and Resolves Passed by the General Assembly of the State of Rhode Island and Providence Plantations at the January Session, A.D. 1925* (Pawtucket: Auto Press, 1925), 231, 233–34; Sorrell, "The Sentinelle Affair (1924–1929) and Militant *Survivance,*" 167; *L'Union* (Woonsocket), May 1925. Interestingly enough, Rhode Island acted similarly in 1992 by becoming an English Plus state, thus supporting the counteroffensive against the movement to establish English as the official language; the Ocean State's legislation stipulates that "it shall be the policy of the state of Rhode Island to welcome and encourage the presence of diverse cultures and the use of diverse languages in business, government, and private affairs in this state." Raymond Tatalovich, *Nativism Reborn? The Official English Language Movement and the American States* (Lexington: University Press of Kentucky, 1995), 21.

4. *Providence Evening Bulletin,* 9 June 1924, 1; *Rhode Island Manual, 1925–1926,* 435; House Bills, 1925, RISA; *Acts and Resolves,* 1925, 10; H 792, House bills 1927, RISA; *Acts and Resolves Passed by the General Assembly of the State of Rhode Island and Providence Plantations at the January Session, A.D. 1927* (Pawtucket, R.I.: Auto Press, 1927), 518–19; H 511A, *Acts and Resolves Passed by the General Assembly of the State of Rhode Island and Providence Plantations at the January Session, A.D. 1928* (Providence: Oxford Press, 1928), 546–48; S 81, Senate Bills, 1930, RISA; *Acts and Resolves Passed by the General Assembly of the State of Rhode Island and Providence Plantations at the January Session, A.D. 1930* (Providence: Oxford Press, 1930), 233–35.

5. *L'Union,* May 1925, 4, June 1925, 3.

6. *Providence Journal,* 18 August 1925, 3; *Boston Globe,* 18 August 1925, 8.

7. *Washington Post,* 2 November 1930, 14; T. W. Stevens, Grand Dragon of Connecticut-Rhode Island, Bridgeport, Connecticut, to "Esteemed Klansman," 9 August 1927, Ernest M. Verry Papers, Rhode Island Historical Society, Providence (hereafter RIHS); undated, mimeographed letter of H. W. Evans, Imperial Wizard, Knights of the Ku Klux Klan, Washington, D.C., to "Faithful and Esteemed Klansman," Ernest M. Verry Papers, RIHS. Ernest M. Verry of East Greenwich was a teamster and a member of the Klan-dominated First Light Infantry of Rhode Island. World War I draft registration card of Ernest Verry, www.ancestrylibrary.com; *U.S. Census, 1920; U.S. Census, 1930;* Joseph W. Sullivan, comp., "Rhode Islanders identified as members of the Ku Klux Klan during the General Assembly's investigation, March–April, 1928," 1987, 4, Ku Klux Klan in Rhode Island, vertical file, RIHS.

8. *Providence Evening Bulletin,* 2 February 1925, 5; *Rhode Island Pendulum* (East Greenwich), 10 December 1925, 22 July 1926, 1.

9. *Providence Evening Bulletin,* 27 June 1927, 1, 7.

10. *Providence Evening Bulletin,* 2 February 1927, 4; *Providence Journal,* 3 February 1927, 22; S 55, Senate bills, 1927, RISA.

11. Sorrell, "The Sentinelle Affair (1924–1929) and Militant *Survivance,*" 321; Gerard J. Brault, *The French-Canadian Heritage in New England* (Hanover, N.H.: University Press of New England, 1986), 87, 88. Born in Woonsocket, Daignault attended Collège Sainte-Marie in Sherbrooke, Québec, earned his bachelor's degree at Boston College, and studied law at Columbia University; prior to the Sentinelle affair, he served in the Rhode Island legislature and as Woonsocket city attorney. *Guide Officiel des Franco-Américains, 1922,* 4th ed. (Fall River, Mass.: Albert A. Bélanger, 1922), 234.

12. Richard S. Sorrell, "Sentinelle Affair (1924–1929)—Religion and Militant Survivance in Woonsocket, Rhode Island," *Rhode Island History* 36 (1977): 67, 68; Brault, *The French-*

Canadian Heritage in New England, 87–88. *La Sentinelle's* circulation may have reached as high as twenty thousand, according to its editors, but at least one moderate questioned whether its circulation ever exceeded eight thousand. Sorrell, "The Sentinelle Affair (1924–1929) and Militant *Survivance,*" 294–95.

13. Brault, *The French-Canadian Heritage in New England,* 87–88; Richard S. Sorrell, "*La Sentinelle* and *La Tribune:* The Role of Woonsocket's French-Language Newspapers in the Sentinelle Affair of the 1920s," in *Steeples and Smokestacks: A Collection of Essays on the Franco-American Experience in New England,* ed. Claire Quintal (Worcester, Mass.: Éditions de l'Institut français, Assumption College, 2003), 342, 344; Sorrell, "Sentinelle Affair (1924–1929)—Religion and Militant Survivance in Woonsocket, Rhode Island," 73; C. Stewart Doty, "'Monsieur Maurras est ici': French Fascism in Franco-American New England," *Journal of Contemporary History* 32, no. 4 (1997): 535; Sorrell, "The Sentinelle Affair (1924–1929) and Militant *Survivance,*" 318.

14. Doty, "'Monsieur Maurras est ici,'" 534; Sorrell, "Sentinelle Affair (1924–1929)—Religion and Militant Survivance in Woonsocket, Rhode Island," 68, 69; Brault, *The French-Canadian Heritage in New England,* 87–88; Sorrell, "The Sentinelle Affair (1924–1929) and Militant *Survivance,*" 240, 242; Sorrell, "*La Sentinelle* and *La Tribune,*" 351–52.

15. Doty, "'Monsieur Maurras est ici,'" 535; *La Justice* (Holyoke, Mass.), 2 July 1925; Sorrell, "*La Sentinelle* and *La Tribune,*" 348–49.

16. *Fellowship Forum* (Washington, D.C.), 26 February 1927, 6.

17. *Fellowship Forum,* 30 April 1927, 3.

18. Brault, *The French-Canadian Heritage in New England,* 88; *La Tribune* (Woonsocket), 28 July 1927; Sorrell, "The Sentinelle Affair (1924–1929) and Militant *Survivance,*" 145. The parade was not the only Klan action in the mid-1920s to intimidate those who opposed the hooded society. The *Providence Evening Bulletin* observed in 1925, for example, that crosses burned "on all the hills surrounding Woonsocket on Christmas Eve." *Providence Evening Bulletin,* 28 December 1925, sec. 2, 2.

19. *La Tribune,* 3 September 1927, 1.

20. *Providence Sunday Journal,* 8 April 1928, 1; U.S. Congress, *Congressional Record,* 70th Cong., 1st sess., vol. 69, no. 98 (13 April 1928), 6619–20.

21. *La Tribune,* 9 May 1928.

22. *La Tribune,* 7 May 1928.

23. *Providence Sunday Journal,* 24 June 1928, 1; *Providence Journal,* 2 July 1928, 1, 2.

24. *La Tribune,* 29 October 1928, 1 November 1928. In the KKK hierarchy a Grand Titan oversaw the provinces of a Dominion and reported to the Grand Dragon, leader of the realm. Annie Cooper Burton, *The Ku Klux Klan* (Los Angeles: Warren T. Potter, 1916), www.books. google.com; *Kloran of the Knights of the Great Forest K-TRIO* (Atlanta, Ga.: Knights of the Ku Klux Klan, 1928), 45–46, Vermont Historical Society Library, Vermont History Center, Barre.

25. *New Bedford Times,* 5 November 1928, 8.

26. *Fellowship Forum,* 8 December 1928.

27. *Rhode Islander* (Providence), 14 December 1928, 1, 4.

28. Doty, "'Monsieur Maurras est ici,'" 527–28.

29. *New York Times,* 18 March 1928, 2; Joseph W. Sullivan, "Rhode Island's Invisible Empire: A Demographic Glimpse into the Ku Klux Klan," *Rhode Island History* 47, no. 2 (1989): 75; *Providence Journal,* 17 March 1928, 1.

30. *Providence Journal,* 26 February 1924, 17, 7 June 1924, 1; *Providence News,* 21 May 1924, 1; *New York Times,* 7 June 1924, 3.

31. *Providence Evening Bulletin,* 17 March 1928, 1, 5, 19 March 1928, 4, 20 March 1928, 2;

Sullivan, "Rhode Island's Invisible Empire," 75; *Manual with Rules and Orders for the Use of the General Assembly of the State of Rhode Island, 1927–1928* (Providence: E. L. Freeman, 1928), 448; State of Rhode Island and Providence Plantations, *Annual Report of the Adjutant General and Quartermaster General of the State of Rhode Island for the Year 1928* (Providence: Snow and Farnham, 1929), 31 December 1928, 19; H 832, House Bills, 1928, RISA; *Providence Sunday Journal,* 18 March 1928, 1; *La Tribune,* 20 March 1928, 1; *New York Times,* 20 March 1928, 45; *Providence Journal,* 20 March 1928, 1.

32. H 952, H 952 Substitute A, House Bills, 1928, RISA; *Rhode Island Manual, 1927–1928,* 440–41; *Providence Evening Bulletin,* 24 March 1928, 1; *New York Times,* 24 March 1928, 30.

33. H 953, House Bills, 1928, RISA; *Providence Evening Bulletin,* 20 March 1928, 22 March 1928; *Rhode Island Manual, 1927–1928,* 412–13, 432. Herbert Bliss had extensive military experience: he served as captain of Company F, First Rhode Island U.S. Volunteer Infantry, during the Spanish-American War in 1898; he also served as a colonel commanding the Rhode Island State Guard from 1914 to 1920 and was a retired brigadier general of the Rhode Island militia. *Rhode Island Manual, 1927–1928,* 432.

34. *Providence Evening Bulletin,* 24 March 1928, 1; *Providence Sunday Journal,* 25 March 1928, 1.

35. Transcript of Hearing, Adjutant General / Ku Klux Klan, January Session 1928, 1, 3–4, 9–10, RISA.

36. Hearing, Adjutant General / Klu Klux Klan, 14–17, 21–22.

37. State of Rhode Island and Providence Plantations, Report of [the] Adjutant General, Providence, R.I., 20 March 1928, 1–3.

38. Arthur C. Cole, Adjutant General, Providence, to His Excellency, the Governor and Commander-in-Chief, State of Rhode Island, 3 January 1928, 4–5, appended to Adjutant General's Report of 20 March 1928; *Providence Journal,* 22 March 1928.

39. Hearing, Adjutant General / Ku Klux Klan, 26–28, 43.

40. Charles P. Sisson, Attorney General, State of Rhode Island, to Arthur C. Cole, Adjutant-General, Providence, 20 March 1928, 6–8, appended to Adjutant General's Report of 20 March 1928.

41. Hearing, Adjutant General / Ku Klux Klan, 78–80.

42. Hearing, Adjutant General / Ku Klux Klan, 142–45, 149–52, 154, 156–60, 162–63, 174; *Providence Journal,* 29 March 1928, 11, 30 March 1928, 4.

43. *Providence Evening Bulletin,* 29 March 1928, 3.

44. *Providence Evening Bulletin,* 30 March 1928, 1; *Providence Journal,* 31 March 1928, 1.

45. *Providence Evening Bulletin,* 30 March 1928, 3, 3 April 1928, 2. Because only portions of the House Militia Committee hearing transcripts have survived, it is necessary to use accounts reported in the press to fill gaps in the testimony. RISA has the transcripts of pp. 1–175 and 889–1025; RIHS has pp. 721–825.

46. *Providence Journal,* 4 April 1928, 1, 5 April 1928, 8, 12 April 1928, 1; *Providence Evening Bulletin,* 4 April 1928, 1–2.

47. *Rhode Islander,* 6 April 1928, 1–2.

48. Testimony of John E. Schlemmer, of Greenville, R.I., et al., 10 April 1928, 721, 730–31, 745, 747, RIHS.

49. Testimony of Schlemmer et al., 756–77; *Providence Evening Bulletin,* 24 March 1928; *New York Times,* 24 March 1928, 30.

50. Hearing, Adjutant General / Ku Klux Klan, 914–15, 917–22, 933–35, 947, 976, 983; *Providence Evening Bulletin,* 12 April 1928, 1; *Providence Journal,* 13 April 1928, 5; *New York Times,* 13 April 1928. 27.

51. *Providence Evening Bulletin,* 12 April 1928, 1, 13 April 1928, 4; Hearing, Adjutant General / Ku Klux Klan, 935; *Providence Journal,* 14 April 1928, 5.

52. *Providence Evening Bulletin,* 13 April 1928, 4; *Boston Daily Advertiser,* 14 April 1928, 2; *Providence Journal,* 14 April 1928, 5; Sullivan, "Rhode Island's Invisible Empire," 78, 81, 82.

53. *Rhode Islander,* 27 April 1928, 1, 4; *Boston Daily Advertiser,* 14 April 1928, 2; *New York Times,* 9 February 1952, 8.

54. *Providence Journal,* 14 April 1928, 5; *Providence Evening Bulletin,* 18 April 1928, 1–2.

55. *Providence Evening Bulletin,* 19 April 1928, 1–2; *Providence Journal,* 20 April 1928, 4.

56. *Boston Daily Advertiser,* 17 April 1928, 8; *Providence Journal,* 20 April 1928, 4, 25 April 1928, 3, 1 May 1928, 24; *Annual Report of the Adjutant General . . . for the Year 1928,* 9.

57. H 985, House Bills, 1928, RISA; *Providence Journal,* 21 April 1928, 1, 7; *Providence News,* 21 April 1928, 1.

58. *Providence News,* 21 April 1928, 1; *Providence Journal,* 21 April 1928, 5.

59. *Providence News,* 22 June 1928, 1, 23 June 1928, 7; *Providence Journal,* 10 January 1929, 1; *New York Times,* 10 January 1929, 5; *La Tribune,* 10 January 1929, 1.

60. *Providence Journal,* 17 June 1929, 1, 3, 14 October 1932, 3; mimeographed meeting notice from J. W. Perry, Grand Dragon, Ku Klux Klan Realm of Connecticut–Rhode Island [May 1930], Ernest M. Verry Papers, RIHS; mimeographed meeting notice from J. W. Perry, Grand Dragon, Connecticut–Rhode Island to all Loyal Patriots of Province No. 2, Realm of Connecticut–Rhode Island, [October 1932], Ernest M. Verry Papers, RIHS; *Kourier Magazine,* 7, no. 10 (September 1931): 45; letter, reproduced in Sullivan, "Rhode Island's Invisible Empire," 79.

61. David Patten, "The Goofy Years—No. 7," typescript, 4, David Patten papers, RIHS.

62. Evelyn Savidge Sterne, *Ballots & Bibles: Ethnic Politics and the Catholic Church in Providence* (Ithaca, N.Y.: Cornell University Press, 2004), 221, 232–34; History Central, "Presidential Election 1928: States Carried," www.historycentral.com.

10. Encountering Secession in the Constitution State

1. U.S. Department of Commerce, Bureau of the Census, *Religious Bodies, 1926,* vol. 2 (Washington, D.C.: Government Printing Office, 1929), 44, 647; U.S. Department of Commerce, Bureau of the Census, *Fourteenth Census of the United States Taken in the Year 1920,* vol. 2 (Washington, D.C.: Government Printing Office, 1922), 40; *New York Times,* 21 February 1926, sec. 8, 1; *New Haven Journal-Courier,* 5 January 1926, 3; Kenneth T. Jackson, *The Ku Klux Klan in the City, 1915–1930* (New York: Oxford University Press, 1967), 254.

2. *Fourteenth Census,* vol. 2, 36, 711; *Religious Bodies, 1926,* vol. 2, 44; *Fourteenth Census,* vol. 3 (1923), 155, 409, 437, 627, 913, 1049.

3. Yves Roby, *Les Franco-Américains de la Nouvelle-Angleterre (1776–1930)* (Sillery, Québec: Septentrion, 1990), 291–92; Connecticut State Library, "Marcus Hensey Holcomb," 2011, www.cslib.org/gov.

4. Edward George Hartmann, "The Post-War Americanization Drive," in *The Movement to Americanize the Immigrant* (New York: Columbia University Press, 1948), 237–38.

5. State of Connecticut, *Register and Manual, 1923* (Hartford: Published by the State, 1923), 466; *Journal of the Senate of the State of Connecticut, January Session 1923* (Hartford: Published by the State, 1923), 76, 170; Connecticut General Assembly Rejected Bills 1923, Record Group 2, Connecticut State Library Archives, Hartford; H. B. 381, State of Connecticut General Assembly (January Session, 1923), Connecticut State Library, Hartford; *Hartford Courant,* 21 March 1923, 14; *L'Avenir National* (Manchester, N.H.), 26 March 1923, 1; Alma Forcier,

Secrétaire, L'Union St-Jean-Baptiste d'Amérique Conseil Gagnon No. 178, Killingly, Conn., to Elie Vézina, Secrétaire Général, L'Union St-Jean-Baptiste d'Amérique Bureau Général, Woonsocket, R.I., 21 March 1921 [*sic*], Ephémérides, vol. 18, Union Saint-Jean-Baptiste Archives, Assumption College, Worcester, Mass.

6. *L'Avenir National,* 26 March 1923, 1, 5; Fred W. Hurley, comp., *Roll, Committees and Rules of the General Assembly of Connecticut* (Hartford: n.p., 1923); Stenographer's Notes of Public Hearings before the Joint Standing Committee on Education, General Assembly, State of Connecticut (January Session, 1923), 20 March 1923, 207, Connecticut State Library; *Public Acts Passed by the General Assembly of the State of Connecticut in the Year 1923* (Hartford: Published by the State, 1923), chap. 166.

7. *New York Times,* 4 September 1921, 11, 18 June 1922, sec. 7, 6, 1 August 1922, 21; *Boston Sunday Herald,* 21 May 1922, 12; *Boston Daily Advertiser,* 29 January 1923, 2; Connecticut State Library, "Roster of Connecticut Governors," 2011 www.cslib.org/gov; *Dawn* (Chicago, Ill.), 11 November 1922.

8. *New York World,* 23 December 1922, 2; *New York Times,* 25 December 1922, 1, 26 December 1922, 3, 8 January 1923, 4, 27 November 1922, 1; *Boston Sunday Advertiser,* 7 January 1923, 2.

9. Jack Swertfeger Jr., "Anti-Mask and Anti-Klan Laws," *Journal of Public Law* 1 (Spring 1952): 195–96; State of Connecticut, *Register and Manual, 1923,* 468; *New York Times,* 24 January 1923; *Journal of the Senate of the State of Connecticut, January Session 1923,* 113, 254; *Hartford Courant,* ProQuest Historical Newspapers, 19 February 1923, 1; card catalog of legislation, Law and Legislative Reference, Connecticut State Library.

10. *New York Times,* 9 August 1924, 2, 13 May 1925, 15; *La Sentinelle* (Woonsocket), 26 April 19[2]4, 4, 8 May 1924, 1; *L'Etoile* (Lowell, Mass.), 5 May 1924, 1; *La Justice de Biddeford (Maine),* 9 May 1924, 1; *L'Opinion Publique* (Worcester, Mass.), 26 July 1924, 6; *L'Impartial* (Nashua, N.H.), 29 July 1924.

11. *Boston Daily Advertiser,* 29 January 1923, 2; Ku Klux Klan, 1915–, Pamphlets, Connecticut Historical Society, Hartford.

12. *Providence News,* 18 June 1924, 1, 2.

13. Duane Lockard, *New England State Politics* (Princeton, N.J.: Princeton University Press, 1959), 240–41; *Boston Daily Advertiser,* 30 January 1923, 4; *Providence News,* 27 June 1924, 5.

14. *New York Times,* 11 September 1924, 6; *Hartford Courant,* 11 September 1924, 12.

15. *New York Times,* 18 September 1924, 6; *Hartford Courant,* 18 September 1924, 11.

16. *New York Times,* 18 September 1924, 6, 19 September 1924, 5; *Hartford Courant,* 19 September 1924, 2; *Boston Herald,* 19 September 1924, 2.

17. *Hartford Courant,* cited in *The Dawn,* 6 January 1923, 6; *Hartford Courant,* ProQuest Historical Newspapers, 5 February 1923, 1; *New York Times,* 19 August 1923, 2, 6 December 1924, 11; *Providence Journal,* 20 August 1924, 1; *Providence News,* 9 September 1924, 1.

18. *Boston Herald,* 4 October 1925, 6; *New York Times,* 5 January 1926, 13; *Rutland (Vt.) Daily Herald,* 5 January 1926, 1; *New Haven Journal-Courier,* 5 January 1926, 3.

19. *New York Times,* 21 February 1926, sec. 8, 1; Jackson, *The Ku Klux Klan in the City,* 254.

20. *New Haven Directory, 1926* (New Haven: Price and Lee, 1926), 259, 741; *New York Times,* 5 January 1926, 13; *New Haven Journal-Courier,* 5 January 1926, 3, 6 January 1926, 2; *Constitution and Laws of the Knights of the Ku Klux Klan Incorporated* (Atlanta: Knights of the Ku Klux Klan, 1921), 32, Vermont Historical Society Library, Vermont History Center, Barre; *Pittsburgh Courier,* 9 January 1926, 1.

21. *Pittsburgh Courier,* 9 January 1926, 1; *New York Times,* 6 January 1926, 20; *New Haven Journal-Courier,* 6 January 1926, 6.

22. *L'Opinion Publique,* 24 August 1926, 5; *La Tribune* (Woonsocket), 6 October 1926, 1;

Hartford Courant, ProQuest Historical Newspapers, 22 August 1926, B8, 24 September 1926, 2, 6 October 1926, 7; *L'Avenir National,* 24 September 1926, 1.

23. *Washington Post,* 2 November 1930, 14.

24. *Boston Sunday Advertiser,* 2 January 1927, 4; *New York Times,* 12 August 1928, 22.

25. State of Connecticut, *Register and Manual, 1927* (Hartford: Published by the State, 1927), 513, 517; *Journal of the House of Representatives of the State of Connecticut, January Session, 1927* (Hartford: Published by the State, 1927), 120, 135, 464; *Hartford Courant,* ProQuest Historical Newspapers, 21 January 1927, 1; H. B. 65, Connecticut General Assembly Rejected Bills 1927, Record Group 2, Connecticut State Archives.

26. *Lewiston (Maine) Daily Sun,* 7 February 1928, 1; *Pittsburgh Courier,* 26 January 1929, 4.

27. *Hartford Courant,* ProQuest Historical Newspapers, 17 May 1927, 2, 27 June 1927, 16; *Boston Daily Advertiser,* 27 June 1927, 3; *La Justice de Sanford (Maine),* 8 July 1927, 1. T. W. Stevens became Grand Dragon of Connecticut and Rhode Island by August 1927. T. W. Stevens, Grand Dragon of Connecticut-Rhode Island, Bridgeport, Conn., to "Esteemed Klansman," 9 August 1927, Ernest M. Verry Papers, Rhode Island Historical Society, Providence.

28. "Women of the Ku Klux Klan Song Sheet," KKK pamphlets, Connecticut Historical Society.

29. *New York Times,* 10 June 1929, 27; *Norwich (Conn.) Bulletin,* 10 June 1929, 1; Jack Elliott, "Heflin Hits at Bingham and Church," *Hartford Courant,* ProQuest Historical Newspapers, 10 June 1929, 1.

30. *Hartford Courant,* ProQuest Historical Newspapers, 24 December 1931, 6; *Kourier Magazine* 7, no. 2 (January 1931): 47, 7, no. 4 (March 1931): 34, 7, no. 10 (September 1931): 45; *Kourier* 8, no. 5 (April 1932): 32, (July 1932): 36. The fire that destroyed the United Protestant Church apparently originated in the cellar beneath the kitchen. *Hartford Courant,* ProQuest Historical Newspapers, 24 December 1931, 6.

31. Typescript Christmas message from J. W. Perry, Grand Dragon, Realm of Connecticut–Rhode Island, 10 December 1932 to All Loyal Klansmen of the Realm of Connecticut–Rhode Island, KKK pamphlets, Connecticut Historical Society.

32. State of Connecticut, *Register and Manual, 1933* (Hartford: Published by the State, 1933), 459; *Journal of the House of Representatives of the State of Connecticut, January Session 1933* (Hartford: Published by the State, 1933), 300, 850–51; *Kourier* 9, no. 4 (March 1933): 10; *Hartford Courant,* ProQuest Historical Newspapers, 11 March 1933, 7.

11. Reappearance in the Late Twentieth Century

1. David M. Chalmers, *Hooded Americanism: The History of the Ku Klux Klan,* 3rd ed. (1981; repr., Durham, N.C.: Duke University Press, 1987), 424; Kathleen M. Blee, *Women of the Klan: Racism and Gender in the 1920s* (Berkeley: University of California Press, 1991), 175–76; Wyn Craig Wade, *The Fiery Cross: The Ku Klux Klan in America* (New York: Simon and Schuster, 1987), 254, 258, 276–306, 401–2; Kenneth T. Jackson, *The Ku Klux Klan in the City, 1915–1930* (New York: Oxford University Press, 1967), 253; Richard T. Schaefer, "The Ku Klux Klan: Continuity and Change," *Phylon* 32, no. 2 (1971): 153.

2. *Portland Evening Express,* 3 February 1977, 3; John Lovell, "Maine Klansman: 'I've Ruffled a Few Feathers,'" *Maine Sunday Telegram* (Portland), 6 February 1977, 1, 18A; Maureen Connolly, "Longley Orders Watch on Maine Klan Actions," *Lewiston Daily Sun,* 8 February 1977, 1. Newspaper reporters used both Porter and Peter as Bodine's first name, and it was impossible to verify which was accurate.

3. John Lovell, "Maine's Klan Chief Gets Transferred," *Portland Evening Express,* 7 Febru-

ary 1977, 12; Southern Poverty Law Center, 2011, "David Duke" www.splcenter.org; Connolly, "Longley Orders Watch on Maine Klan Actions," 1, 12; John S. Day, "Longley Orders State Police to Eyeball Klan," *Bangor Daily News,* 8 February 1977, 17.

4. Bonny Rodden, "KKK, Bike Gangs Lend Support to Nuclear Plant," *New Orleans Times Picayune,* 15 October 1978, 3. By the late twentieth century, the Ku Klux Klan consisted of separate organizations, such as Wilkinson's Invisible Empire of the Knights of the Ku Klux Klan and David Duke's Knights of the Ku Klux Klan. By 1997, notes Kathleen Blee, the Klan comprised twelve competing organizations and about seventy-five factions, with women making up an estimated one-fourth of the total membership. Under Duke's leadership in the 1970s the Klan allowed women and Catholics to join the organization as regular, not as auxiliary, members. Blee, *Women of the Klan,* 248–49; Chalmers, *Hooded Americanism,* 414.

5. Rodden, "KKK, Bike Gangs Lend Support to Nuclear Plant," 3; *Houston Post,* 15 October 1978, 17A.

6. Steve Wilson, *New York Times,* 16 October 1978, 30; *New Orleans Times-Picayune,* 18 September 1974, 12; *Washington Post,* 16 October 1978, A5.

7. *New York Times,* 8 December 1979, 26; Jack Jackson, " 'Get out, KKK' was this week-end's chant in Boston," *Chicago Defender,* 10 December 1979, 5; *Chicago Defender,* 10 December 1979, 5; Southern Poverty Law Center, "David Duke"; Memorandum on Strategies to Combat Hatred and Violence, from Jacob Schlitt, Regional Director, New England Regional Office, United States Commission on Civil Rights, Boston, to John I. Binkley, Acting Deputy Staff Director for Regional Programs, 13 November 1981, 8, Ku Klux Klan files, Vermont State Archives, Office of the Secretary of State, Montpelier. Duke ran for the office of president of the United States in 1980, 1988, and again in 1992. Southern Poverty Law Center, "David Duke."

8. *Chicago Defender,* 10 December 1979, 5; *New York Times,* 22 October 1979, B2, 8 December 1979, 26.

9. *New York Times,* 14 September 1980, 46, 15 September 1980, B9; *Washington Post,* 14 September 1980, A15.

10. *Washington Post,* 15 September 1980, A14; *Jet* (Chicago) 59 (2 October 1980): 7; *New York Times,* 15 September 1980, B9; Matthew L. Wald, *New York Times,* 21 September 1980, sec. 23, 3.

11. *New York Times,* 22 March 1981, 38, 16 March 1981, B2, 24 March 1981, B2; *Washington Star,* 22 March 1981, A7; *Washington Post,* 22 March 1981, A7; *Los Angeles Times,* 22 March 1981, 4; *Christian Science Monitor,* 23 March 1981, 2.

12. *New York Times,* 29 March 1981, E5; Matthew L. Wald, "Meriden Resents Image Caused by Klan Clashes," *New York Times,* 18 July 1981, 26.

13. *New York Times,* 12 July 1981, 25, 11 October 1981, 41; *Bilalian News* (Chicago), 31 July 1981, 7; *Atlanta Daily World,* 14 July 1981, 6.

14. State of Connecticut, *Public and Special Acts Passed by the General Assembly, October, 1979, Special Session, February, 1980, Regular Session* (Hartford: State of Connecticut, 1980), 41; Memorandum from Jacob Schlitt to John I. Binkley, 6–7; State of Connecticut, *Public and Special Acts Passed by the General Assembly, January, 1981, Regular Session, July, 1981, Special Session* (Hartford: State of Connecticut, 1981), 338; *Atlanta Voice,* 13 June 1981, 2.

15. *New York Times,* 18 March 1982, B2, 20 March 1982, 30; Matthew L. Wald, "Klan Is Jeered at 2d Meriden Rally," *New York Times,* 21 March 1982, 39B.

16. *New York Times,* 1 May 1983, sec. 1, 37, 26 June 1983, sec. 1, 29, 31 August 1986, sec. 1, 45.

17. Michael Winerip, "Our Towns: Catholic Connecticut Yankee Who Heads the Klan," *New York Times,* 16 September 1986, B2; *Providence Journal Bulletin,* 2 September 1986, A4.

18. *Providence Journal,* 1 September 1981, D4; Memorandum from Jacob Schlitt to John I. Binkley, 8; Karen Lee Ziner, "The Klan among Us," *Providence Journal,* 21 February 1982, M6, M12; Karen Ellsworth, "Sickles Sentenced to 9-Month Term," *Evening Bulletin* (Providence), 14 September 1982, A2; Tracy Breton, "KKK Case Overturned; Court Erred, *Providence Journal,* 18 January 1984, A14.

19. *Burlington Free Press,* 16 May 1982, 1, 6A; Allan Abbey, "Klan Labels Vermont Rally A Success, Vows to Return," *Burlington Free Press,* 17 May 1982, 1, 7A; *Town of Wilmington v. John Doe and Jane Doe,* Windham Superior Court, Ku Klux Klan files, Vermont State Archives.

20. Flyer, "Stop the racist KKK in Wilmington, Vt.," by the International Committee Against Racism, submitted as Exhibit A, *Town of Wilmington v. John Doe and Jane Doe.*

21. *Burlington Free Press,* 16 May 1982, 1, 6A; Memorandum of Mike Sinclair, Secretary of Civil and Military Affairs, to Governor [Richard] Snelling on Klan Demonstration, Wilmington, 15 May 1982, dated 17 May 1982, Ku Klux Klan files, Vermont State Archives; *New York Times,* 16 May 1982, 26.

22. *Burlington Free Press,* 16 May 1982, 1; *Rutland Daily Herald,* 17 July 1984, 6; Vermont Advisory Committee to the U.S. Commission on Civil Rights, "Civil Rights Developments in Vermont, 1982" (February 1983), 5, Ku Klux Klan files, Vermont State Archives.

23. *New York Times,* 31 May 1982, A9; Memorandum of Mike Sinclair [Vermont Secretary of Civil and Military Affairs,] to Governor [Richard] Snelling on the Klu [*sic*] Klux Klan Demonstration, Brattleboro Common, 29 May 1982, dated 1 June 1982, Ku Klux Klan files, Vermont State Archives; Brattleboro Police Department, "Brattleboro Police Department's History," www.brattleboropolice.org/history; Vermont Advisory Committee, "Civil Rights Developments in Vermont," 5.

24. Ted Tedford, "Burlington Man Reports Threats by Ku Klux Klan," *Burlington Free Press,* 11 June 1982, 1B; Vermont Advisory Committee, "Civil Rights Developments in Vermont," 5–6; *Burlington Free Press,* 29 June 1982, 4B; *Town Crier* (Brattleboro), 7 July 1982, 1.

25. Perry Bradley, "Klan Presence Shocks Residents," *Foster's Daily Democrat* (Dover, N.H.), 28 September 1989, 1; Ku Klux Klan recruitment card, Rochester Historical Society, Rochester, N.H.; *Union Leader* (Manchester), 18 May 1999, C1.

26. *Lewiston Daily Sun,* 27 January 1981, 1; Pete Daly, "'Organizer' of KKK Urged More Active Role," *Portland Evening Express,* 27 January 1981, 8.

27. Gail Geraghty, "'Klansman' Surfaces in Gray: Residents Express Outrage over KKK's Home Deliveries," *Portland Evening Express,* 8 May 1987, 1; Dan Allen, "'Klansman' Turns up in Minot, Durham," *Lewiston Daily Sun,* 27 May 1987, 12; Frank Sleeper, "Klan Paper Surfaces in Falmouth," *Portland Press Herald,* 8 August 1987, 19; *Lewiston Journal,* 14 September 1987, 3A; *Portland Evening Express,* 14 September 1987, 3.

28. *Portland Press Herald,* 19 September 1987, 5; Sara Hobson, "Puzzled Rumford Set for Klan Rally," *Maine Sunday Telegram,* 20 September 1987, 14A.

29. Glen Adams, "Town Asks Gawkers to Stay Away," *Lewiston Journal,* 25 September 1987, 3A; *Bangor Daily News,* 22 September 1987, 5; *Lewiston Journal,* 23 September 1987, 3A; Frank Sleeper, "Labor, NOW Oppose Planned Klan Rally," *Portland Press Herald,* 24 September 1987, 18; Sharon Deveau, "Residents Rally against KKK," *Lewiston Journal,* 26 September 1987, 1A; *Lewiston Daily Sun,* 15 September 1987, 1.

30. John Day, "Condemning the Ku Klux Klan: Is There a Moral Copout Here?" *Bangor Daily News,* 26–27 September 1987, 14.

31. Mike Lopez, "Rumford Copes with Klan's Gathering," *Lewiston Journal,* 26 September 1987, 1A, 2A; Glen Adams, "Town Asks Gawkers to Stay Away," *Lewiston Journal,* 25 September 1987, 3A.

32. Dennis Bailey, "Klan Rally Eclipsed by Opponents," *Maine Sunday Telegram,* 27 September 1987, 1A, 16A; *New York Times,* 27 September 1987, sec. 1, 26.

33. *Lewiston Journal,* 28 September 1987, 2A; Marie M. Fortune, "Saying No to the Klan," *Christian Century* 104 (4 November 1987): 958; Bailey, "Klan Rally Eclipsed by Opponents," 16A.

34. Sara Hobson, "Small Ku Klux Klan Rally Dispersed near Mall," *Maine Sunday Telegram,* 12 June 1988, 34A; *Bangor Daily News,* 13 June 1988, 9.

35. *Portland Evening Express,* 9 September 1988, 40; Frank Sleeper, "Two Wearing Klan Hoods Are Arrested at Riverton," *Portland Press Herald,* 9 September 1988, 11–12.

36. *Portland Press Herald,* 14 September 1988, 31, 9 January 1992, 4B; *Bangor Daily News,* 26 January 1990, 7; Joanne Lannin, "Teen-Age Feud Divides Madison," *Maine Sunday Telegram,* 1 December 1991, 1B.

37. On the Americanization of French-Canadian descendants, see Mark Paul Richard, *Loyal but French: The Negotiation of Identity by French-Canadian Descendants in the United States* (East Lansing: Michigan State University Press, 2008), esp. chaps. 10 and 11.

38. Adam Fifield, "'Jews Are the Enemy'—An Interview with Maine's Grand Dragon," *Maine Progressive* (Stillwater), 6:12 (September 1992): 9; Renee Ordway, "Police Official Says Neo-Nazis, KKK Here," *Bangor Daily News,* 25 March 1993, 5.

39. A. Jay Higgins, "2 Mainers Indicted in Racial Attack," *Bangor Daily News,* 8 August 1996, A1, A3; *Bangor Daily News,* 26 June 1996, B4, 12 September 1996, B1, 18 October 1996, B6; John Hale, "Mainers Decry Racism," *Bangor Daily News,* 27 June 1996, A1.

40. John Hale, "Mainers Decry Racism," A1, A10.

41. John Day, "Condemning the Ku Klux Klan," 14.

Conclusion

1. Hiram Wesley Evans, "The Klan: Defender of Americanism," the Imperial Wizard of the Ku Klux Klan in an authorized interview by Stanley Frost, *Forum* 74 (December 1925): 809.

2. See, for example, Robert Alan Goldberg, *Hooded Empire: The Ku Klux Klan in Colorado* (Urbana: University of Illinois Press, 1981); Leonard J. Moore, *Citizen Klansmen: The Ku Klux Klan in Indiana, 1921–1928* (Chapel Hill: University of North Carolina Press, 1991); Kathleen M. Blee, *Women of the Klan: Racism and Gender in the 1920s* (Berkeley: University of California Press, 1991); Shawn Lay, ed., *The Invisible Empire in the West: Toward a New Historical Appraisal of the Ku Klux Klan of the 1920s* (Urbana: University of Illinois Press, 1992); Shawn Lay, *Hooded Knights on the Niagara: The Ku Klux Klan in Buffalo, New York* (New York: New York University Press, 1995).

3. The former King Kleagle of Maine, F. Eugene Farnsworth, and a former KKK member, Edgar Fuller, both commented in the 1920s on the Ku Klux Klan's role as a terrorist society; some contemporary scholars have as well. See *Rochester (N.H.) Courier,* 30 May 1924, 4; Edgar I. Fuller, *The Visible of the Invisible Empire,* revised and edited by Geo. LaDura (Denver: Maelstrom Publishing, 1925), 177; Phil Goodstein, *In the Shadow of the Klan: When the KKK Ruled Denver, 1920–1926* (Denver: New Social Publications, 2006), 4; David M. Chalmers, *Hooded Americanism: The History of the Ku Klux Klan,* 3rd ed. (1981; repr., Durham, N.C.: Duke University Press, 1987), 424.

4. Richard T. Schaefer, "The Ku Klux Klan: Continuity and Change," *Phylon* 32, no. 2 (1971): 157; Mark S. Massa, S.J., *Anti-Catholicism in America: The Last Acceptable Prejudice* (New York: Crossroad Publishing, 2003), 59–99; Philip Jenkins, *The New Anti-Catholicism: The Last Acceptable Prejudice* (New York: Oxford University Press, 2003), 33, 49, 207.

5. Rhea Côté Robbins, "Bill Leads Way to Raise French Awareness," *Bangor Daily News,* 17 March 2009, online, www.bangordailynews.com (emphasis added); U.S. Census Bureau, n.d., table QT-P13, Ancestry: 2000, Maine, www.census.gov. I am grateful to Susan Pinette, director of Franco-American studies at the University of Maine, for calling to my attention this op-ed piece and to the response by Rogier van Bakel.

6. Robbins, "Bill Leads Way to Raise French Awareness."

7. Rogier van Bakel, "Franco-American History? *Mon Cul!*" blog post, 20 March 2009, www.bakelblog.com, no longer available.

8. For a history of discrimination against Franco-Americans, see C. Stewart Doty, "How Many Frenchmen Does It Take to . . . ?" *Thought and Action* 11 (Fall 1995): 85–104; for examples of discrimination against Franco-Americans in Maine over a century and a half of historical time, see Mark Paul Richard, *Loyal but French: The Negotiation of Identity by French-Canadian Descendants in the United States* (East Lansing: Michigan State University Press, 2008).

9. John Hale, "Mainers Decry Racism," *Bangor Daily News,* 27 June 1996, A10.

10. Constance Backhouse, *Colour-Coded: A Legal History of Racism in Canada, 1900–1950* (Toronto: Osgoode Society for Canadian Legal History by University of Toronto Press, 1999), 217.

11. James W. Loewen, *Teaching What Really Happened: How to Avoid the Tyranny of Textbooks and Get Students Excited about Doing History* (New York: Teachers College Press, 2010), 173.

INDEX

MARK PAUL RICHARD is professor of history and Canadian studies at the State University of New York at Plattsburgh, where he coordinated the Canadian Studies program from 2005 to 2011. He has also taught at the University of Maine at Fort Kent, Northwestern State University of Louisiana, and Landmark College. Originally from Lewiston, Maine, the author earned his undergraduate degree from Bowdoin College and his graduate degrees from the University of Maine and Duke University. Richard's scholarly publications examine the acculturation of French Canadians in U.S. society and nativism in the United States. He is the author of *Loyal but French: The Negotiation of Identity by French-Canadian Descendants in the United States.*